Contents

With this guide use:

the Michelin plans
18, 20, 22 and 24
scale 1 : 15000

the Michelin road maps
101 scale 1 : 50000
196 scale 1 : 100000
237 scale 1 : 200000

the current Michelin Red Guide France
(hotels and restaurants)

the current Michelin Camping and Caravaning Guide

the Michelin Green Guide to Paris

PRINCIPAL SIGHTS

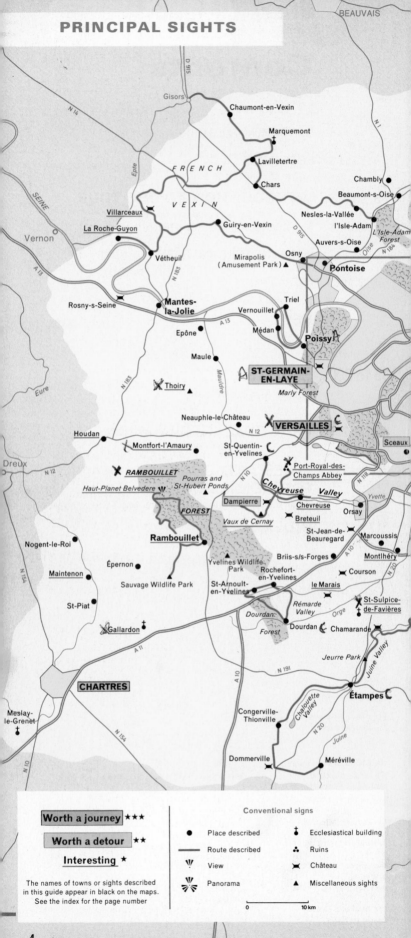

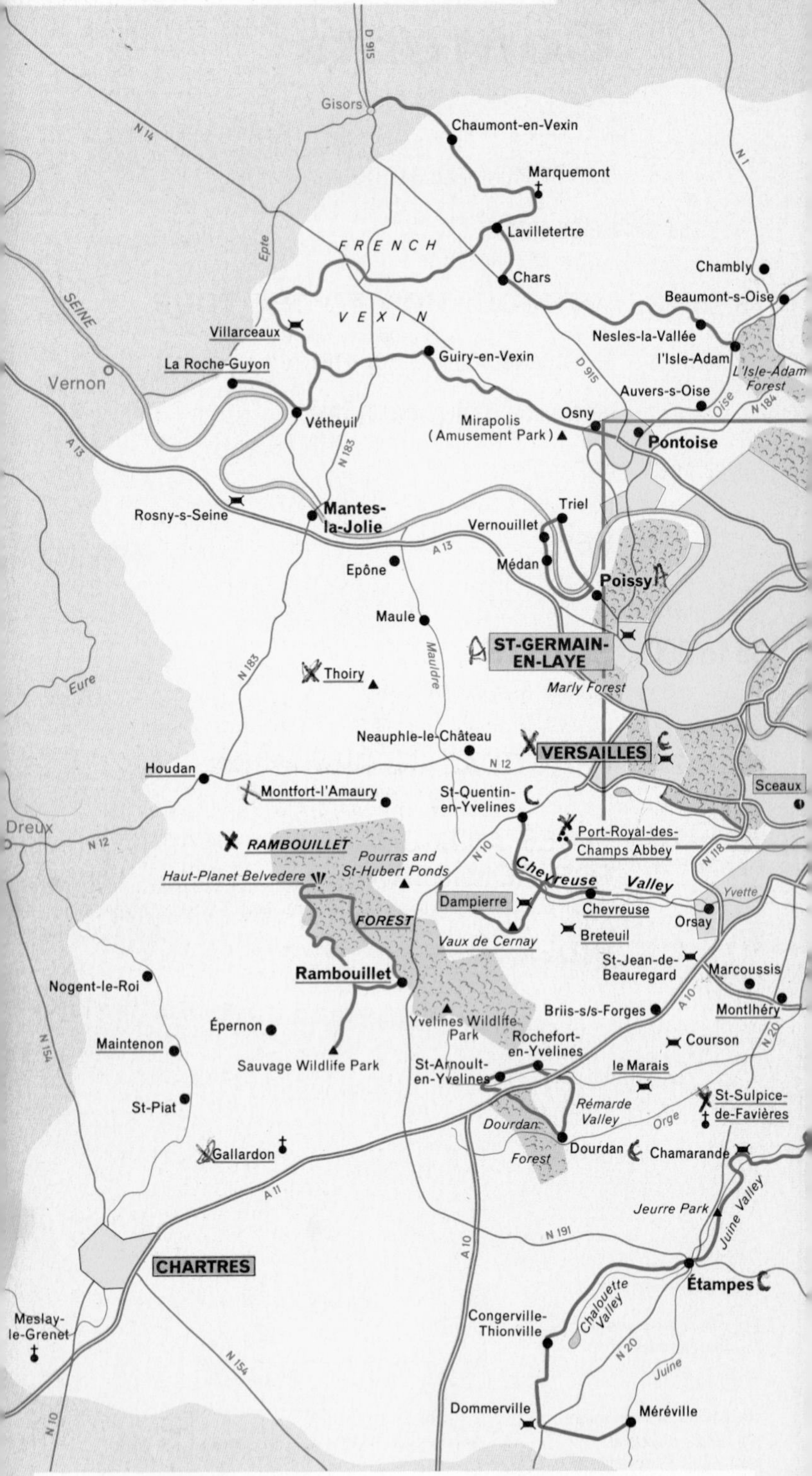

Worth a journey ★★★

Worth a detour ★★

Interesting ★

The names of towns or sights described in this guide appear in black on the maps. See the index for the page number

Conventional signs

- ● Place described
- — Route described
- View
- Panorama
- ✝ Ecclesiastical building
- Ruins
- Château
- ▲ Miscellaneous sights

0 — 10 km

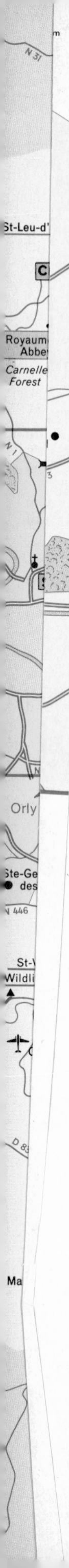

LE-DE-FRANCE

ı area of woodlands and rivers. – The most striking feature Ile-de-France is the wooded belt that surrounds the capital. The outskirts Paris feature several large forested massifs, notably Fontainebleau, ımbouillet and Chantilly, as well as a number of smaller forests like ıusses-Reposes and St-Cucufa, located in delightful settings.
ıis region also presents a great many valleys. Ile-de-France is visited by ree main rivers: the noble Seine, the capricious course of the Marne and e peaceful waters of the Oise, all three characterised by numerous eanders. Like their many tributaries (Grand Morin, Petit Morin, Essonne, ıre...), they weave their way across the meadows planted with poplars and illow trees and between wooded valley sides. These gentle riverside ındscapes afford extremely pleasant walks and drives. The most famous alley is that of the Chevreuse but there are many more to discover: the ıubette, Automne, Grand and Petit Morin, Sausseron, etc.

ı wealth of churches and châteaux. – Art lovers will be surprised by ıe innumerable riches found in Ile-de-France. The Sun King's palace at 'ersailles is famous throughout the world. Many of the prestigious châteaux ıave been made into museums: Chantilly and St-Germain. Other residences ıre noted for their stately façades, their beautiful furniture and the charm of heir landscaped parks: Vaux, Écouen, Champs, Dampierre, Rambouillet, Rueil-Malmaison, etc.
No other French region boasts as many churches as Ile-de-France. In ıddition to the great masterpieces of religious architecture such as Chartres, the "Acropolis of France", St-Denis the mausoleum of French kings and Senlis, a number of other churches are worthy of note: St-Leu-d'Esserent, St-Sulpice-de-Favières, etc.
Former abbeys such as those of Royaumont, Chaâlis and Port-Royal testify to the strong religious faith of the French.

The history of France. – History enthusiasts will be able to cover the ground where so many major events have taken place since prehistoric times.
A trip to Ile-de-France will take them on a tour of French history. They will see the refectory of Royaumont Abbey where St Louis served the monks at table, the fourposter bed where Louis XIV slept at Versailles, the Jeu de Paume, which fostered the French revolutionary spirit, the lawns of Malmaison where Napoleon indulged in outdoor games, the road to Meaux from where Galliéni launched his famous attack during the Battle of the Ourcq...

Town planning in the suburbs. – The replacement of old or insalubrious buildings, the slow migration of town-dwellers to the outskirts of Paris and the arrival of immigrants have prompted the creation of new housing schemes and business districts in the inner suburbs, around La Défense *(see Michelin Green Guide Paris)*, St-Denis, Bobigny, Créteil, Rungis, or even further away from the capital. In some cases the town is partly rebuilt (Mantes), in others a series of new housing developments are added to the locality. Certain architects chose to set up the modern quarters side by side with the old: this was the case of the Sarcelles-Lochères complex – built between 1958 and 1961 – and its oblong-shaped town centre.
Owing to their uniform façades and the poor facilities they offer, some of these schemes have been criticised by the residents, who claim that they create a feeling of isolation, insecurity and boredom. However, with the passing of years, these early problems have gradually been resolved...

The New Towns. – The new town Master Plan of the Paris region was launched by the State in 1965. Its aim is to meet the town-planning requirements of an area which, while still presenting semi-rural characteristics, is threatened by a number of modern evils: overcrowding, urban sprawl, lack of employment, inadequate public transport systems, architectural monotony, etc.
This operation has already enabled architects and town-planners to start work on a number of towns located 10 to 35 km away from Paris. It is estimated that their population – including old towns and villages – will reach 200 000 to 300 000 by the end of the century. The facilities they already offer – employment, public services, sporting venues, social and cultural activities – place them in the same bracket as Paris in the eyes of the local residents.
None of these towns has been conceived as a single locality featuring a ring road and a towering church. Instead they are seen as a constellation of new towns (20 000 to 40 000 inhabitants) separated by green areas reserved for farming or leisure activities. Plans have also been made to equip the surrounding forests with recreational centres (Ferrières Forest).

Cergy-Pontoise *(p 41)*, **Évry** *(p 76)*, **St-Quentin-en-Yvelines** *(p 162)*, **Marne-la-Vallée** *(p 116) and* **Melun-Sénart** *(p 119)* share a number of characteristics: a town centre grouping together public and administrative services, major department stores, offices, several districts or "hamlets" featuring a shopping precinct for pedestrians, and housing or residential estates of homely proportions.
These new towns also offer parks and ponds, areas providing specific equipment and facilities (industry, tertiary sector, arts, sport), one or more leisure parks incorporating a natural or artificial body of water, finally an extensive network of road and rail transport services.

The new town scheme works towards the preservation of the different buildings and monuments situated within its prescribed territory. Numerous village churches and former farm buildings have been restored and converted into libraries, administrative headquarters, reception centres, etc.
Unlike the town-planning policies of the Inner and Outer Ring Plans (Couronnes) which had underestimated the importance of cultural life – at the time the order of priorities was different –, the current campaign has endowed these new towns with considerable resources in terms of art and culture.
The existence of the **Mirapolis** amusement park (Cergy-Pontoise) and the forthcoming inauguration of **Disneyland** at Marne-la-Vallée (1991) lead one to believe that the new towns of the Paris region will not merely become extra *arrondissements* accountable to the French capital, neither will they remain secluded areas cut off from the rest of the country. On the contrary, it is likely they will develop into autonomous localities whose influence will be felt not only in Ile-de-France but throughout the whole country.

In each new town the information centre houses a miniature model of the project and supplies visitors with all the necessary details.

TOURISM – OUTDOOR ACTIVITIES

For full addresses, see the chapter Practical Information at the end of the guide.

Accommodation. – Hotels and restaurants are classified according to the nature and the standard of their facilities *(see the current Michelin Red Guide France).* There exist a number of fine restaurants in the area, located in pleasant or unusual settings.
Most of the camping sites lying within 100km-62 miles of the capital only take in long-term residents. They offer few, if any, facilities for overnight bookings or brief stays. *Read the Michelin Guide Camping Caravaning France.*

Sports and leisure activities. – Ile-de-France offers numerous amenities designed for outdoor activities (riding, rowing, canoeing, sailing, golf, etc). These are sometimes incorporated into local leisure centres or recreational parks.
The picturesque roads that cut across the meadows and forests are a strong incentive to explore the area on a bike. Michelin map no 196 at a scale of 1:100 000 indicates certain lanes which are suitable for cycling.

Rambling. – A total of 4 000km-2 400 miles of long and short-distance footpaths have been marked out in Ile-de-France, in particular GR 1, which forms a loop and which crosses the various forests circling the capital. Topo guides supply detailed itineraries and provide useful advice to ramblers.

Times and charges for admission to sights described in the guide are listed at the end of the guide.

The sights are listed alphabetically in this section either under the place – town, village or area – in which they are situated or under their proper name.

Every sight for which there are times and charges is indicated by the symbol Ⓥ In the margin in the main part of the guide.

Introduction to the tour

The Marble Court at the Palace of Versailles

APPEARANCE OF THE COUNTRY

The vast region known as the Paris Basin borders on Flanders with the great plain of Northern Europe beyond, and is linked by the Burgundy threshold to the Rhône Basin, and beyond the Loire Valley, by the Poitou threshold to the Aquitaine Basin. The altitude is at its lowest in the Seine Valley, downstream from Mantes (14m-46ft at La Roche-Guyon) and at its highest in French Vexin, Pays de Bray, Carnelle Forest, Pays de Goële and Montmirail (200m-656ft or more).

Ermenonville Park

The area presents a fairly homogeneous structure: a lowish limestone plateau cut across by alluvial valleys and dotted with sandy patches. **Ile-de-France** enjoys an Atlantic climate with stormy summers, cool winters and many rainy spells in between. As a result, the area features three types of landscape: arable land on the plateau surfaces, lush valleys and forests. The loess plateau and its fields of wheat and beetroot extending into the far distance, interrupted only by the occasional town, is a somewhat monotonous sight. On the other hand, the picturesque valleys are certainly worth a visit, with their smiling orchards, market gardens and quaint villages. For many centuries, the forested massifs were used as hunting grounds by the court: the finest groves, mainly planted with beeches and oaks, lie on the hillocks dominating the sandy depressions. They have been scrupulously preserved since Colbert's time and offer many interesting excursions for the enthusiastic rambler.

Ile-de-France is also a major industrial centre with many factories and power stations that satisfy the country's growing needs in energy. These are concentrated in four main zones: a belt around Paris, which extends along the banks of the Seine upstream and downstream, the Oise Valley near Creil, the area around Mantes and the region of Melun. Some of the actual plants are not visible, like the underground reservoirs of St-Illiers-la-Ville and Gournay-sur-Aronde, where natural gas is stored in an aquiferous layer of sand covered by a bed of clay at a depth of several hundred metres. Other buildings have become familiar sights, like the Centre d'Études Nucléaires (Nuclear Research Centre) at Saclay.

The formation of the Paris Basin. – The Paris Basin is located in the centre of a huge depression whose outer edges are formed by the ancient massifs of the Vosges, Ardennes and Morvan, the northern Massif Central and Brittany. These ancient massifs – dating from the Primary Era – are separated from the Paris Basin by concentric ridges of hard limestone.

In short, the Paris Basin could be described as a pile of plates stacked one on top of the other. The older and higher outcrops lie on the outer edge of the basin and the ridges get progressively smoother and younger as one approaches the French capital. A detailed study of the topography around Paris shows that the heap of plates is "cracked" towards the northwest: at the end of the Tertiary Era, the Channel separated France from England, where some of the old circular ridges may still be found.

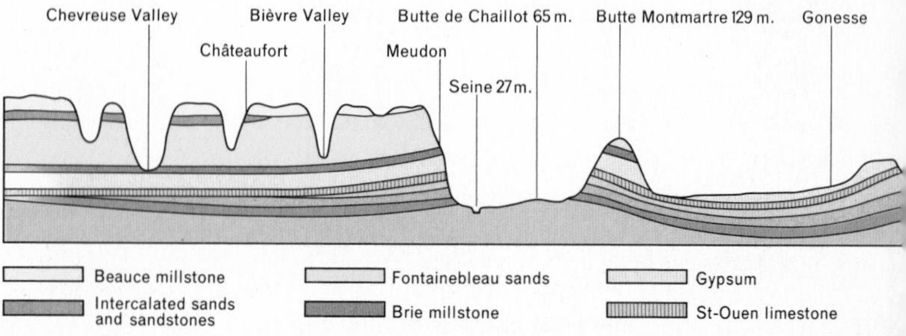

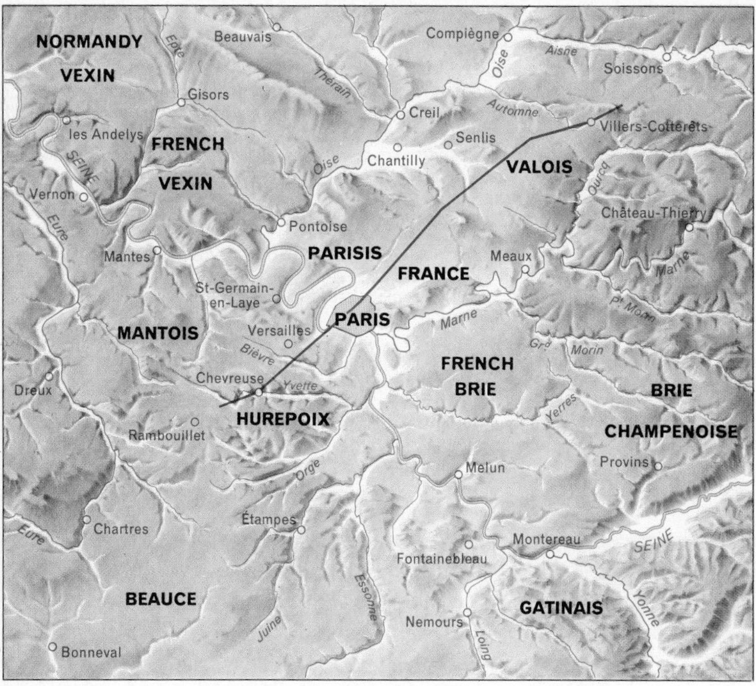

Such a regular arrangement may be explained by the formation of the Paris Basin. At the beginning of the Secondary Era, it formed a huge bay delimited by ancient massifs. The sea gradually accumulated sediments on the bed and around the edges of the bay, causing its whole area to diminish. Simultaneously, the actual bottom of the basin slowly subsided, while the outer ridges of hard limestone were pushed upwards. The area covered in this guide is contained within the inner ranges, i.e. the Ile-de-France cliffs, the Gâtinais hillsides and the heights of Perche.

The Paris Basin features Tertiary sediments deposited by seas, lakes and lagoons. When the sea slowly receded, the deposits formed isolated saltwater lagoons, which were subsequently replaced by lakes. In the case of an important subsidence, the ocean waters would sometimes return to flood certain areas of the basin – the central and southern parts –, leaving a new layer of sediment on top of the former deposits. During the Tertiary Era, the sea deposited conchiferous limestones, then wide banks of sand known as Beauchamp sands, which may be seen outcropping in the Valois, and finally the famous St-Ouen limestone. The subsequent lagoon left behind layers of gypsum and green marl, of which thick strata may be observed in Parisis and the Pays de France. The layer of lake-deposited limestone turned into millstone and eventually became the hard Brie limestone. When the sea returned to flood the basin, the millstone *(see below)* was overlaid by Fontainebleau sands. The surface of these sands then hardened into sandstone. The last lake to occupy the Paris Basin deposited a soft type of limestone called Beauce limestone which frequently develops into millstone. This cavernous rock – a popular building material – occurs when the limestone has been leached away leaving the silica.

The successive subsidences of the Paris Basin caused the terrain to settle and slide towards the centre, forming a series of minor folds. The erosion of the rivers have given the basin its present appearance. To the north and the east, the running waters carved deep valleys in the banks of marl, gypsum and millstone, revealing the coarse limestone where the winds later deposited loess. The layers of millstone and gypsum that had remained intact developed into outcrops and small plateaux. To the south, a constant run-off eroded the soft Beauce limestone and Fontainebleau sandstones: these either disappeared or left banks covered with marl or large boulders.

In the places where the Beauchamp sands (north) and the Fontainebleau sands (south) are exposed, the forest which once covered the whole area has not been cleared. At the end of the Tertiary Era, before the last Glacial Age, the bed of the Seine was 25m-82ft lower than its present level. This depression was subsequently filled in by the river deposits. This phenomenon was brought about by the rising sea levels following the melting of the huge glaciers that covered northern Europe.

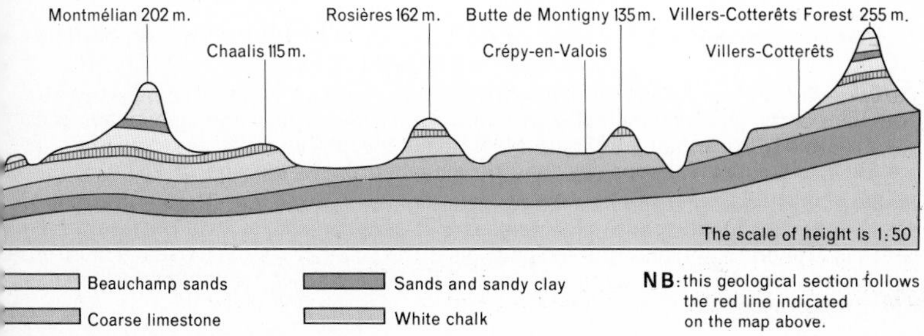

NB: this geological section follows the red line indicated on the map above.

THE FOREST

Ile-de-France is famed for its magnificent forests. Those of Rambouillet and Fontainebleau feature among the finest sights in France.
Most tourists are sensitive to the charm of the woods. Some enjoy the lush greenery of springtime, others prefer the shaded groves of summer, the deep russet tones of autumn or the crisp frosts of winter. Some like to pick flowers and gather fruit and mushrooms, while others content themselves with an improvised picnic. But everyone agrees that they feel more relaxed after a day in the quiet, soothing atmosphere of the forest. Some ramblers are amateur biologists who delight in studying forest fauna and flora in order to understand the many wondrous intricacies of nature.

State forests and private forests. – There exist three types of forest in France: state, private and local authority forests.
The most interesting forests for ramblers are state forests, run by the French Forestry Commission (ONF) since 1966.
They are easily accessible by an extensive network of roads, paths and lanes, and their venerable groves form a picturesque setting indeed. The arborists in charge of state forests apply their expertise to preserving the forest as a natural habitat. The most beautiful French forests used to feature protected forest zones known as "artistic reserves" in which unusually striking trees were left untouched by the axe, even when they died. This practice was given up for the benefit of "biological reserves".
Apart from the footpaths that occasionally cross them, private estates are not open to the public.

Oak

Beech

Trees. – Like all living things, trees need nourishment, breathe and reproduce. The roots of trees draw the mineral nutrients they need from the earth, and the sap running through the trunk and leaves distributes them to all parts of the tree.
All types of terrain do not necessarily suit all types of trees. Chestnut trees, for instance, cannot survive on limestone sites, whereas oaks will flourish on a variety of soils. Like other plants, trees breathe through their leaves and reproduce through their flowers. Flowers will bear fruit providing they are fertilised by pollen of their own species. Very few trees have hermaphrodite flowers – presenting both male and female characteristics – like roses, acacias, etc. Consequently, the pollen is usually carried from the male flower to the female flower by insects, or sometimes the wind.
Trees may also reproduce by their shoots. If a youngish tree trunk is razed to the ground, a number of stool shoots will emerge from the stump. Conifers do not produce offshoots.
The trees of Ile-de-France fall into two categories: deciduous and coniferous.

Deciduous. – These trees lose their leaves every autumn and grow them again in the spring. Beeches, oaks, hornbeams, birches and chestnut trees belong to this category.

Coniferous. – They do not have leaves, but needles, which they lose regularly throughout the year. The needles are renewed every four to five years. Their sap contains resin – they are also known as resinous trees – and the fruit are generally cone-shaped. Pines, cypresses, cedars and fir trees are all conifers. Another resinous species is the larch, which loses its needles every year.

The trees of the Ile-de-France forests. – Most deciduous trees can be found around Paris. The most common species are listed below.

The Oak. – One of the most venerable forest trees. Its hard but beautiful wood is used for both carpentry and ornamental woodwork. In former times, the bark was much sought-after by local tanners. Some of the oaks tower 40m-132ft high and are over 1m-3ft in diameter. This species may be exploited up to the age of 250.

The Beech. – Although it resembles the oak, it is slightly more elegant. The wood is mainly used for modern furniture and railway sleepers. It is also popular as fuel. The trunk of the beech is cylindrical, the bark smooth and shiny. The younger shoots present a crooked, gnarled appearance. Beeches grow as tall as oaks but are no longer commercially viable when they reach 120.

The Hornbeam. – A remarkably tough species. It looks like the beech and although it lives to the same age, it is shorter and its bark features numerous fissures.

The Chestnut Tree. – This tree can grow to very great heights. It can live for up to several hundred years but is generally felled before as the very old trees become hollow and prone to disease. The wood was traditionally used by the cooperage industry for making staves, posts and stakes. Nowadays, it goes towards the production of chip-boards. Chestnut trees will only grow on siliceous soil.

The Birch. – Despite its height (25m-82ft), the birch is a graceful, elegant tree, with its shimmering leaves and its white bark, which peels off so easily. Damp, sandy soil is an excellent terrain for all varieties of birch. The wood is highly suitable as firewood but it is principally used for making wood pulp, paper fibre and other industrial products.

The Scots Pine. – The most commonly-found conifer in Ile-de-France. This species is ideal for reafforestation, particularly in sandy terrain, and since the mid-19C it has been "assigned" to plots of land with meagre or non-existent vegetation. Scots pines have short needles (4 to 6cm – 1.6 to 2.4in) which grow in pairs, smallish cones (3 to 5cm – 1.2 to 2in) and red ochre bark.
Foresters often plant Scots pines alongside other resinous species from exotic or Mediterranean countries (maritime pine). One of the great favourites is the Corsican pine, a tall, noble tree with a perfectly straight trunk. It can grow to a maximum height of 50m-165ft. The old trees develop large grey patches on their bark.

The science of forestry. – If a forest is left on its own, it will invariably deteriorate. In order to fully develop and reach their proper size, trees must be given breathing space and be placed in an environment that meets their specific requirements.
The first step in a reafforestation campaign is to plant fir trees, which have few needs and which produce wood in a very short time. Their roots retain the earth which the runoff usually washes away, and the needles form thick layers of foliage. Then one grows hornbeams, birches and beeches to increase the fertility of the soil. Finally, the ground is planted with oaks. Many of the beech groves are left as this species is considered to be commercially profitable.

Rotations. – The prime concern of foresters is to have trees that will always be ready for commercialisation. Consequently, they make sure that when one area is cleared, another is planted with seedlings. Let us take the example of a 100ha-250 acre forest planted with beeches, divided into 10 units of 10ha-25 acres. If the trees are felled every five years, the youngest generation will reach 50 when the nine older ones will have been cut. Every five years, the unit planted with the oldest trees is cleared. This means that within 50 years the forest is entirely renewed while remaining commercially viable, a technique known as rotation. Forest managers try to avoid exposing a large sector of the forest. Leafy plants such as hazel and mulberry trees set in and risk choking the young shoots. Within each sector, 2, 3 or 4 groups are formed according to the trees' approximate age and a programme of successive fellings is planned. This ensures that only limited areas are deforested at any one time.
Whatever the rotation for a given forest, its appearance is bound to change depending on the thickness of the vegetation and the forestry techniques that have been applied. There are three types of plantation in Ile-de-France.

Groves. – After the land has been sown, natural selection sees to it that the weaker shoots are choked by the stronger ones. The trees – planted fairly close to one another – grow vertically in an upward direction. After some time, the land is cleared around the finer species to encourage them to develop and eventually these are the only ones that remain. This grove, where the widely-spaced trees are all the same age, is called a *futaie pleine*. The rotation is rather long, 50 years, or even 80 if one wants very tall trees. *Futaie jardinée* is another type of grove, in which the trees are planted and cut at different times, so that the sector features a variety of "age groups". Older trees are always felled first.
When these groves reach an honourable age, their noble stems, lush dome of greenery and intricate boughs are truly an impressive sight.

Copses. – The trees are younger. Rotation ranges from 5 to 30 years, depending on whether one wants firewood, logs for heating or pit props. A copse is a sector of forest where a group of mature trees are razed to the ground. The shoots growing around the stump develop into a multitude of young bushy, leafy trees.

Copses with Standards. – If, when cutting a copse, one leaves the finest trees standing, these will dominate the new shoots. If they survive a series of fellings, they will grow to be extremely strong. The utilization of copses with standards produces both fuel wood (copses) and timber for industrial purposes (selected species).

Fauna and flora. – Trees are not the only interesting feature of the Ile-de-France forests. The forests swarm with countless varieties of animals and plants.
Stag hunts are still organised in certain forests: a pack of hounds running to the sound of the horn is always a rousing sight.
Forests are a popular haunt among nature lovers. The rich, damp soil is remarkably fertile and favours the growth of moss, lichen, mushrooms, flowers, shrubs and ferns.

Flowers. – April is the season of broom, hyacinths and daffodils. May brings us hawthorn, lily-of-the-valley, columbine and the delightful catkins of the hazel tree.
In June we can enjoy the dazzling sight of broom, heather, campanula, scabious and Deptford pinks. During the autumn season, the tall, slender ferns and the golden leaves are as pretty as the forest flowers.

Fruit. – In July and August, we can taste wild strawberries and succulent raspberries but the blackberries will not be fully ripened until September.
September is the right month for hazel nuts and October offers us sloes and chestnuts.

Mushrooms. – Some varieties of mushrooms – the Russula viresrens, chanterelle comestible and mousseron – are edible everywhere. Other species are difficult to identify and may be dangerous. If in doubt, mushroom pickers should consult a professional mycologist or the local chemist *(pharmacien)*.

THE PAYS AND PROVINCES OF ILE-DE-FRANCE

For a period of 175 years, the core of the Paris region was the Seine *département* and the French capital, governed since 1800 by special political and administrative authorities. After the territorial division of 1964 and the implementation of the regional reform (1976), this area officially became known as the Ile-de-France Region. As in the case of the twenty other regions, two assemblies were created. The Conseil Régional plays the part of a deliberative committee, while the Comité Économique et Social acts in an advisory capacity. At the head of this hierarchy we find the Préfet, an important local personality who is granted the title of Commissaire de la République de la Région et du Département de Paris.

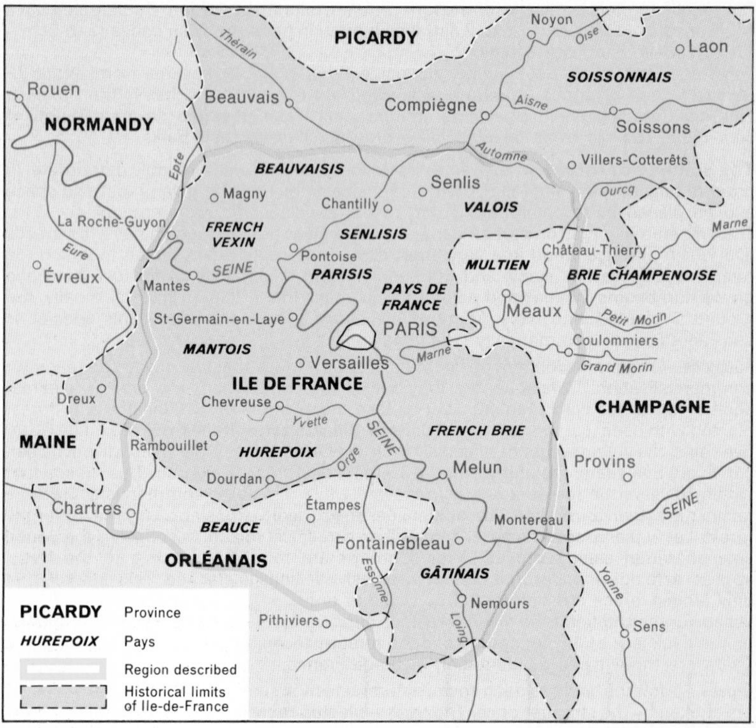

Under the reign of Clovis, Ile-de-France was part of the Franks' kingdom, the first French territory with its two capitals Soissons and Compiègne. Clovis' descendants were neatly removed from the throne in 751 by Pépin the Short, whose son Charlemagne was consecrated King of the Franks by the Pope in Rome in 774. In 843, Charlemagne's kingdom was carved up and France designated the land lying west of the provinces bordering the Meuse, Saône and Rhône rivers. The former territory of the Franks was reduced to the Duchy of France, and the two counties of Orléans and Étampes. It was only four centuries later that this duchy was called Ile-de-France. During the Norman invasion, the duc de France valiantly defended Paris and one of the members of this House – Hugh Capet – was elected King of France at Senlis in 987. For the third time in history, the royal robe was worn by a ruler of Ile-de-France. Hugh Capet's descendants governed France until 1848, except during the Revolution and the First Empire (1793 to 1814).

Pays de France. – This arable plateau extending between St-Denis, Luzarches and the Dammartin-en-Goële ridge lay at the heart of royal territory. The layer of marl covering the subsoil has made the area extremely fertile and the huge fields are planted with wheat and beetroot. Art lovers will appreciate the Gothic churches and the stately silhouette of Écouen Château.

Parisis. – Parisis is wedged in between the Oise, the Seine and the Pays de France. This area was once occupied by the Gauls, who gave it its name and who christened the French capital. An alluvial plain sloping towards the Seine and featuring precious few rivers, Parisis is dominated by limestone buttes covered in sands or millstones.
Beyond the industrial suburbs of Paris, market gardens and orchards spread along the limestone slopes of the plain, while the sandy stretches have been planted with forests: tourists may explore the butte of Cormeilles, and Montmorency and Carnelle Forests, or wander through the smiling orchards of the Groslay area, a dazzling sight during the spring season.
The stately abbey ruins, the numerous churches and the historical connections of Parisis – related to heroic acts or local anecdotes – make it one of the most pleasant areas around Paris.

Senlisis. – This region has often been associated with the Valois by geographers and historians but in fact it was part of the king's dominion, the central core of Ile-de-France. Delimited by the Oise, the Dammartin-en-Goële ridge and the actual Valois, Senlisis is

believed to be one of the most picturesque *pays* surrounding the capital. While the arable land is to be found on the silty soils, the sandy areas have favoured the development of forestry.
Senlisis is famed for its highly decorative sights and residences, notably the abbeys of Royaumont and Chaâlis, the keep at Montépilloy, Ermenonville Park, the Commelles Lakes, Chantilly Château, Senlis Cathedral, and the forests of Chantilly, Halatte and Ermenonville.

Valois. – It is limited by Senlisis and the rivers Oise, Automne and Ourcq. The Valois acquired strategic importance as early as Roman times and has remained one of the most important *pays* in French history. First a county, then a duchy, it was twice given to one of the king's brothers. Twice the descendants of this royal line, known as the Princes de Valois, acceded to the throne.

Multien. – An area of ploughed fields demarcated by the Marne, the Valois and the Croële ridge. Multien with its rolling landscapes was the scene of the fighting which took place in September 1914.

French Vexin. – Three rivers circumscribe this limestone platform, the Oise, the Epte and the Seine. The loess covering is an extremely fertile topsoil which favours the growing of wheat and other cereals. Cattle rearing is concentrated in the sylvan valleys planted with poplar trees. The Rosne Buttes, a series of outliers stretching from Monneville to Vallangoujard, are covered in woods. They incorporate the strip of land running north of the Seine.

Mantois. – Situated between the rivers Eure and Oise, the Mantois is a huge plateau presenting forests (east) and arable land (west). Its many brooks and streams have given it a pleasantly fresh, undulating appearance. It is a popular area among tourists, the main centres being Mantes, Poissy, Maintenon and Rambouillet.

Hurepoix. – It is delimited by the Mantois, Beauce, Fontainebleau Forest and the Seine. Like the other areas in Ile-de-France, Hurepoix features a number of buttes capped with limestone which lie between the valleys. In some places, rain and wind have eroded the limestone and revealed the sandstone and its underlying stratum of sand. Such a geological diversity – sand, sandstone and limestone in the hills, marl in the vales – has produced a great variety of landscapes and vegetation, which is one of Hurepoix' main attractions: market gardens spread along the valleys of the rivers Bièvre, Yvette and Essonne, the hillsides are covered in woodland and the plains below offer lush green pastures.

Gâtinais. – Limited by the Seine, Hurepoix, Beauce and Champagne, only the northern part of Gâtinais is covered by this guide. The French Gâtinais, a clay plateau, lies to the east of the river Loing while the Orléanais Gâtinais to the west, is an area of sands and sandstones. This second area is covered by Fontainebleau Forest, a popular sight on account of its splendid groves and sandstone boulders. The lush valley of the Loing is dotted with charming small towns: Château-Landon, perched on the edge of the plateau, Nemours, Montigny-sur-Loing and Moret.

French Brie. – French Brie is located between the Seine and the Grand Morin and features Brie Champenoise as its northern border. These two *pays* differ for historical reasons: the former belonged to the King of France, while the latter was the property of the comte de Champagne. This area is only visited by four meandering rivers: the Seine, Marne, Petit Morin and Grand Morin. A layer of non-porous marl that retains moisture is topped by a covering of millstone and siliceous limestone. This is the famous Brie limestone, which is itself covered with a fine blanket of fertile loess. The area has many large farms (250-400ha – 620-1 000 acres) specialising in the large-scale cultivation of wheat and sugar beet. The vast expanse of arable land is dotted with small groves and spinneys. The less fertile pockets of land have been planted with forests, like around Sénart and Ferrières.
The Brie valleys are generally attractive and Vaux-le-Vicomte Château as well as the towns of Champs and Blandy are certainly worth a visit.

GARDENS

Three successive trends were to define the official canons of ornamental gardening in Ile-de-France.

16C. – Gardens were not considered an essential part of an estate, they fell into the same category as the outbuildings. Generally speaking, they were shaped as geometrical figures and resembled a chessboard. On each of these squares, carefully-trimmed spindle and boxwood formed arabesques and other elaborate patterns. These motifs were called *broderies*. Gardens were enclosed by a sort of cloister made of greenery or stonework, from which visitors could enjoy a good view of the garden. The actual grounds were cut across by paths whose crazy paving featured fragments of marble, pottery and brick. Water did not play any role in the decoration. Many gardens included fountains and basins but they were circled by balustrades and tall plants. They were there to be observed in their own right and for people to admire their ornamental statues and water displays.

17C. The Formal Garden. – André Le Nôtre (1613-1700) invented the formal garden. Its purpose was two-fold: to enhance the beauty of the site and to provide residents with a superb view from the château. Its main features were fountains, stately trees, flowers, statues, terraces and a sweeping perspective.
The château was fronted by a "Turkish carpet", parterres with flowers and evergreen shrubs forming arabesques and intricate patterns. These were symmetrically flanked by basins with fountains and low copings, usually decorated with statues. The fountains were set up on the terrace that bore the château and the upper lawns. This was the starting-point of the central perspective – a green carpet of lawn *(tapis vert)* or a canal – which was lined with groves of tall trees.
The groups of trees planted along the perspective were designed to be perfectly symmetrical. They were crossed by a network of lanes: the clearings at these in-

Aerial view of Vaux-le-Vicomte Château and Gardens

tersections afforded splendid vistas extending into the far distance. The lanes were lined with hedges that concealed the massive tree trunks and were used as a backdrop to marble statues. Hedges were fragile and expensive to grow and most of them have been removed. On some estates, their initial height – 6 to 6m (20 to 27ft) – has been greatly diminished. Each bosquet of trees featured a "curiosity". This could be a fountain with elaborate waterworks, a colonnade or a group of sculpted figures. Thanks to the extreme diversity of architects' plans and the many ornamental styles of the parterres, these formal gardens were never monotonous. They were conceived as an intellectual pursuit. The pleasure they gave visitors derived from their stately proportions and perspective, the skilful design and the sheer beauty of each separate detail.

18C. The Landscape Garden. – It was no longer fashionable to tame nature and subject her to a network of geometric patterns. The tendency in the 18C was to imitate nature. The landscape garden – also called Anglo-Chinese garden – consisted of lush, rolling grounds dotted with rocks and tall trees, pleasantly refreshed by swirling streams and tiny cascades. The river would pass under a rustic bridge and flow into a charming pond covered in water-lilies and circled by willow trees. Sometimes, a mill or the occasional dairy would give the garden a rural touch. Let us not forget that the 18C was the Age of Enlightenment and this thirst for philosophy was also reflected in contemporary gardening with the invention of **fabricks** *(fabriques)*. This technical term – which designates an architectural work of art in a painting – referred to the symbolic or exotic monuments dotted across landscape gardens. Antique temples and medieval ruins were very much in vogue. Tombs and mausoleums were popular before the French Revolution and there was a marked preference for Chinese and Turkish sculptures. In some gardens, an Oriental pagoda would be seen standing alongside a crumbling tower, symbolising the fragility of human achievements. In others, an unfinished temple would remind visitors of the limits of science.
Sentimentality, romance and melodrama were popular features of many art forms in the 18C. The trend also affected the layout of landscape gardens and a number of new sights made their appearance: the secret lovers' grotto, the bench of the grieving mother, the grave of the rejected suitor, etc.
Most of these parks were badly wrecked during the Revolution and very few of their monuments survived. The most outstanding example of an 18C fabrick is the Cassan Pagoda at L'Isle-Adam *(illustration p 102)*.

HISTORICAL TABLE AND NOTES

BC	**Celts and Romans**
6C	A great many Celtic tribes settle along the valleys of the Paris Basin.
4C	The Celts from beyond the Rhine, known as the Belgae, settle along the banks of the rivers Oise and Aisne.
52 to 51	Caesar conquers the land surrounding the Paris Basin.
AD	
Circa 250	St Denis evangelises the population around Paris. First Bishop of Lutetia, he is martyred in Montmartre *(see the Michelin Green Guide Paris).*
	From the Merovingians to the Valois
486	Clovis defeats the Roman army at Soissons and occupies the territory stretching from the Somme to the Loire. His kingdom is called Francia in Latin.
843	France (Melunois, Parisis, Vexin, Roumois and Pays de Caux) is ceded to Charles the Bald following the Treaty of Verdun.
911	The Treaty of St-Clair-sur-Epte puts an end to the Normans' ambitions in Ile-de-France.
987	Hugh Capet, duke and suzerain of the land extending from the Somme to the Loire, is elected King of France in Senlis *(qv).*
Early 12C	Abbot Suger of St-Denis, the minister of both Louis VI and Louis VII, undertakes the reconstruction of the famous abbey *(qv).*
1108-1137	Louis VI, the Fat, faces acts of rebellion from his vassals.
1180-1223	The counties of Valois, Clermont and Meulan are annexed by Philippe Auguste.
1285	End of the conflict opposing the Capetian kings to the comtes de Champagne *(p 128).*
1307	At Maubuisson Abbey Philip the Fair and his advisers decide to arrest the Templars.
1337-1453	Hundred Years' War. Ile-de-France is badly ravaged by the fighting.
1360	The Treaty of Brétigny, near Chartres, cedes Aquitaine to the King of England.
1419	The Duke of Burgundy is assassinated at Montereau *(qv).*
1441	The liberation of Pontoise *(qv)* ends the English supremacy over Ile-de-France.
1465	The Battle of Montlhéry opposes Louis XI and Charles the Bold.
1547	François I dies in Rambouillet *(qv).* He is succeeded by Henri II.
1561	The Poissy Symposium *(qv).*
1589	Henri III is murdered at St-Cloud *(qv).*
	From the Bourbons to the Revolution
1593	Henri IV is converted to Catholicism *(p 111)* after convincing most of his subjects. He is crowned King of France.
1640	Death of Cornelius Jansen. His treaty *Augustinus* spreads a wave of controversy, with dire consequences for the theologians of Port-Royal *(qv).*
1661	Fouquet arrested *(p 173).* Louis XIV commissions the construction of a huge palace at Versailles.
1671	The town of Versailles is born *(qv).*
1682	Bossuet is appointed Bishop of Meaux *(qv).*
1715	Death of Louis XIV at Versailles. He is succeeded by Louis XV.
1774	Death of Louis XV at Versailles. Louis XVI comes to the throne.
1778	Jean-Jacques Rousseau dies at Ermenonville *(qv).*
1783	The Treaty of Versailles ends the American War of Independence *(p 199).*
5 May 1789	The States General hold their royal opening session at Versailles.
	From the First to the Second Empire
1806-1814	Napoleon takes up residence in Malmaison *(qv).*
1812	Pope Pius VII, held prisoner by Napoleon, is exiled to Fontainebleau.
1814	France is invaded. The Emperor tries to protect the capital from the enemy's assaults. He abdicates at Fontainebleau on 6 April *(qv).*
1837	The Paris-Le Pecq railway line is officially opened.
1870 and 1871	Paris is besieged by the Germans. Fighting breaks out around the capital.
1871	The German Empire is proclaimed in the Hall of Mirrors on 18 January *(p 184).* The Revolutionaries of the Paris Commune are defeated (18 March–28 May). The French government moves to Versailles, where it remains until 1878.
	From the Third to the Fifth Republic
1875	The constitution founding the Third Republic is voted at Versailles.
1890	The Dutch painter Vincent Van Gogh commits suicide at Auvers *(qv).*
1914	France's destiny is at stake on the heights of Multien *(p 134).*
1918	Second Victory of the Marne.
1919	The Treaty of Versailles ends the First World War.
August 1944	Liberation of Paris. General Leclerc's 2nd Division leaves Rambouillet to march on Paris, while the 3rd American Army, led by General Patton, advances towards Reims, Verdun and Metz along the Chartres-Étampes-Fontainebleau axis (known as Liberty Way).
1964	The Seine and the Seine-et-Oise are replaced by six new *départements* located outside the boundaries of Paris: Hauts-de-Seine, Seine-St-Denis, Val-de-Marne, Essonne, Yvelines and Val-d'Oise.
1976	The Ile-de-France Region is created.

ART

ABC OF ARCHITECTURE

To assist readers unfamiliar with the terminology employed in architecture, we describe below the most commonly used terms, which we hope will make their visits to ecclesiastical, military and civil buildings more interesting.

Ecclesiastical architecture

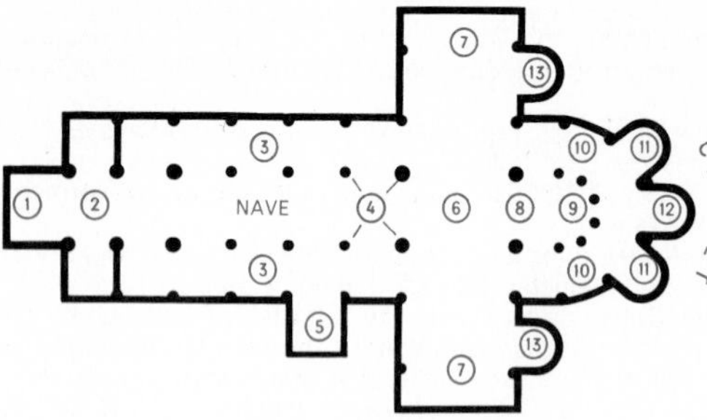

illustration I

Ground plan. – The more usual Catholic form is based on the outline of a cross with the two arms of the cross forming the transept: (1) Porch – (2) Narthex – (3) Side aisles (sometimes double) – (4) Bay (transverse section of the nave between 2 pillars) – (5) Side chapel (often predates the church) – (6) Transept crossing – (7) Arms of the transept, sometimes with a side doorway – (8) Chancel, nearly always facing east towards Jerusalem; the chancel often vast in size was reserved for the monks in abbatial churches – (9) High altar – (10) Ambulatory: in pilgrimage churches the aisles were extended round the chancel, forming the ambulatory, to allow the faithful to file past the relics – (11) Radiating or apsidal chapel – (12) Axial chapel. In churches which are not dedicated to the Virgin this chapel, in the main axis of the building is often consecrated to the Virgin (Lady Chapel) – (13) Transept chapel.

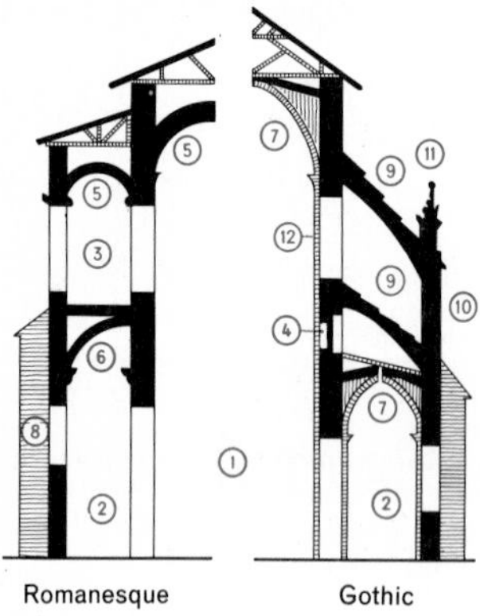

◄ illustration II

Cross-section: (1) Nave – (2) Aisle – (3) Tribune or Gallery – (4) Triforium – (5) Barrel vault – (6) Half-barrel vault – (7) Pointed vault – (8) Buttress – (9) Flying buttress – (10) Pier of a flying buttress – (11) Pinnacle – (12) Clerestory window.

illustration III ►

Gothic cathedral: (1) Porch – (2) Gallery – (3) Rose window – (4) Belfry (sometimes with a spire) – (5) Gargoyle acting as a waterspout for the roof gutter – (6) Buttress – (7) Pier of a flying buttress (abutment) – (8) Flight or span of flying buttress – (9) Double-course flying buttress – (10) Pinnacle – (11) Side chapel – (12) Radiating or apsidal chapel – (13) Clerestory windows – (14) Side doorway – (15) Gable – (16) Pinnacle – (17) Spire over the transept crossing.

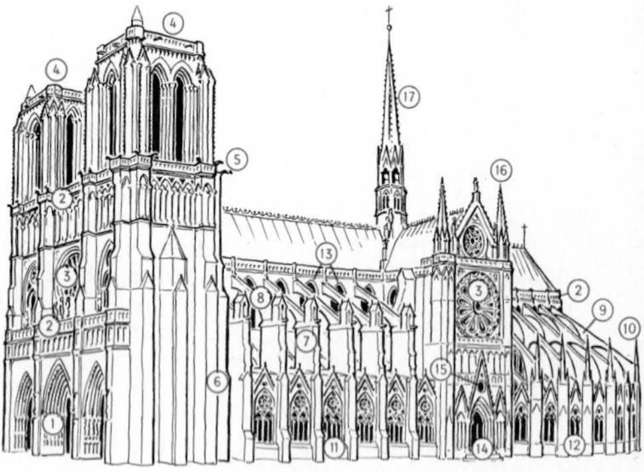

illustration IV

Groined vaulting:
(1) Main arch – (2) Groin
(3) Transverse arch

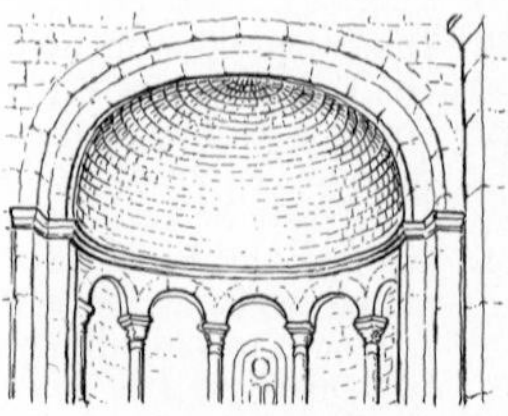

illustration V

Oven vault:
termination of a barrel vaulted nave

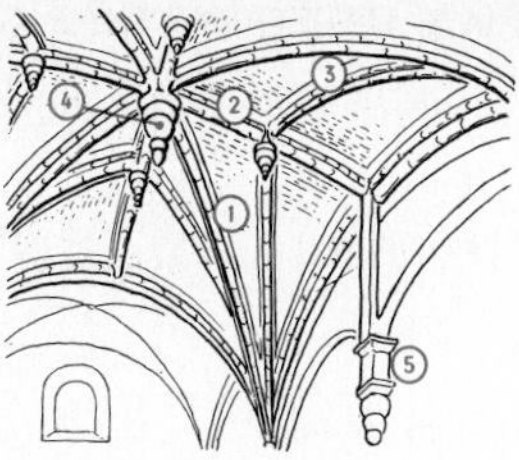

illustration VI

Lierne and tierceron vaulting:
① Diagonal – ② Lierne
③ Tierceron – ④ Pendant
⑤ Corbel

illustration VII

Quadripartite vaulting:
① Diagonal – ② Transverse
③ Stringer – ④ Flying buttress
⑤ Keystone

▼ illustration VIII

Doorway: ① Archivolt. Depending on the architectural style of the building this can be rounded, pointed, basket-handled, ogee or even adorned by a gable – ② Arching, covings (with string courses, mouldings, carvings or adorned with statues). Recessed arches or orders form the archivolt – ③ Tympanum – ④ Lintel – ⑤ Archshafts – ⑥ Embrasures. Arch shafts, splaying sometimes adorned with statues or columns – ⑦ Pier (often adorned by a statue) – ⑧ Hinges and other ironwork.

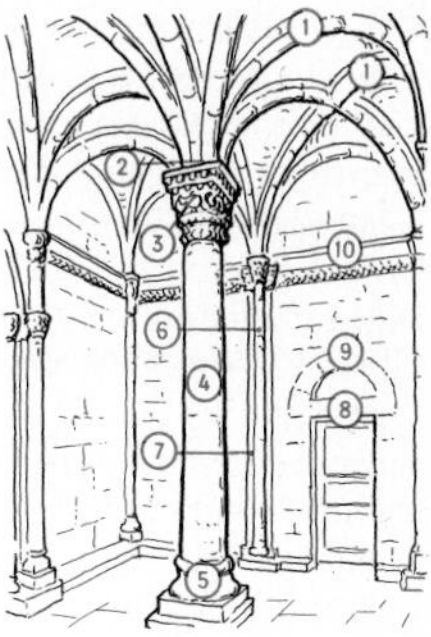

illustration IX ▶

Arches and pillars: ① Ribs or ribbed vaulting – ② Abacus – ③ Capital – ④ Shaft – ⑤ Base – ⑥ Engaged column – ⑦ Pier of arch wall – ⑧ Lintel – ⑨ Discharging or relieving arch – ⑩ Frieze.

Military architecture

illustration X

Fortified enclosure: ① Hoarding (projecting timber gallery) – ② Machicolations (corbelled crenellations) – ③ Barbican – ④ Keep or donjon – ⑤ Covered watchpath – ⑥ Curtain wall – ⑦ Outer curtain wall – ⑧ Postern.

illustration XI

Towers and curtain walls: ① Hoarding – ② Crenellations – ③ Merlon – ④ Loophole or arrow slit – ⑤ Curtain wall – ⑥ Bridge or drawbridge.

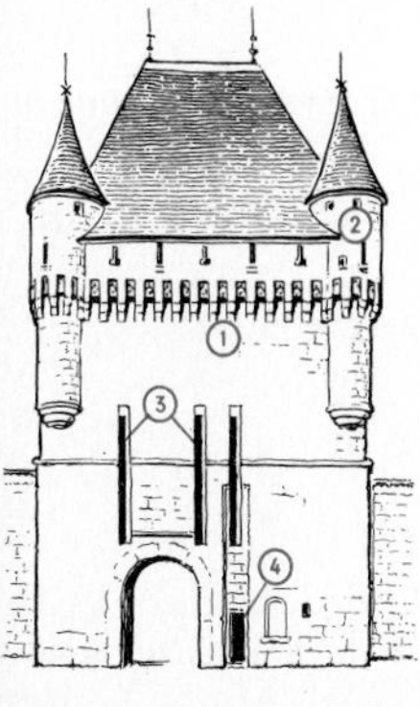

◀ illustration XII

Fortified gatehouse: ① Machicolations – ② Watch turrets or bartizan – ③ Slots for the arms of the drawbridge – ④ Postern.

illustration XIII ▶

Star fortress: ① Entrance – ② Drawbridge – ③ Glacis – ④ Ravelin or half-moon – ⑤ Moat – ⑥ Bastion – ⑦ Watch turret – ⑧ Town – ⑨ Assembly area.

illustration XIV

Organ

① Great organ case – ② Little organ case – ③ Caryatids – ④ Loft

Abacus: illustration IX.
Aisle: illustration I.
Altarpiece or **retable:** illustration XVIII.
Ambo: an elevated lectern or pulpit situated in the chancel; usually occur in pairs.
Ambulatory: illustration I.
Apsidal or **radiating chapel:** illustration I.
Arcade: succession of small arches; when attached to a wall they are known as blind arcades.
Arching: illustration VIII.
Archivolt: illustration VIII.
Arch shaft: illustration VIII.
Arms of the transept: illustration I.
Asymmetrical merlon: oblong-shaped merlon in which length exceeds width.
Atlante: male figure used as a support.
Attic: a low storey over the main cornice.
Axial or **Lady Chapel:** illustration I.
Baluster or **banister:** uprights (posts or pillars) supporting the handrail of a staircase.
Barrel vaulting: illustration II.
Bay: illustration I.
Buttress: illustration III and p 23.
Campanile: a bell tower, usually separate from the main building.
Capital: illustration IX.
Caryatid: female figure used as a support.
Chevet: French term for the east end of a church; illustration I.
Coffered ceiling: vault or ceiling decorated with sunken panels.
Coping: protective covering of stone or brick around the edge of a well.
Corbel: illustration VI.
Corinthian order: Greek architectural order characterised by scroll capitals almost entirely covered in curled acanthus leaves.

◀ illustration XV

Dome on squinches:
① Octagonal dome – ② Squinch – ③ Arches of transept crossing

illustration XVI ▶

Dome on pendentives:
① Circular dome – ② Pendentive – ③ Arches of transept crossing

Crypt: underground chamber or chapel.
Curtain wall: illustration X.
Diagonal arch: illustrations VI and VII.
Dome: illustrations XV and XVI.
Doric order: Greek architectural order with plain capitals.
Embrasures: illustration VIII.
Equilateral arch: pointed arch with its radii equal to the span.
Ex-voto: offering or inscription made in pursuance of a vow.
Flamboyant: latest phase (15C) of French Gothic architecture; name taken from the undulating (flame-like) lines of the window tracery.
Fluted: vertical grooves in column shafts.
Flying buttress: illustration II.
Fresco: mural painting executed on wet plaster.
Gable: triangular part of an end wall carrying a sloping roof; also applied to the steeply pitched ornamental pediments of Gothic architecture; illustration III and p 23.
Gallery: illustration III and p 23.
Gargoyle: illustration III.
Groined vaulting: illustration IV.
Haut-relief: sculpture or carved work projecting more than one half of its true proportions from the background.
High altar: main altar usually placed in the chancel.
High relief: haut-relief.
Historiated: decorated with figures of people or animals.
Ionic order: Greek architectural order with double scroll capitals.
Keep or **donjon:** illustration X.
Keystone: illustration VII.
Lancet arch: narrow arch with a sharply pointed head.
Leaf: one of two or more parts of a door or shutter.
Lintel: illustrations VIII and IX.
Loophole or **arrow slit:** illustration XI.
Low relief: sculpture or carved work projecting very slightly from the background.

Machicolations: illustration X and XII.
Merlon: raised part of an embattled parapet between two embrasures; illustration XI.
Moat: ditch surrounding a fortress, generally filled with water.
Mullion: a vertical post dividing a window.
Narthex: illustration I.
Nave: illustration I.
Oculus: small round window.
Organ case: illustration XIV.
Oven vaulting: illustration V.
Parclose screen: screen separating a chapel or the chancel from the rest of the church.
Pendant: illustration VI.
Pepperpot roof: conical roof.
Peristyle: row of columns surrounding or adorning the façade of a building.
Pilaster: engaged rectangular column.
Pinnacle: illustrations II and III.
Piscina: basin for washing the sacred vessels.
Pointed arch: diagonal arch supporting a vault; illustrations VI and VII.
Porch: covered entrance to a building.
Portico: a space enclosed by colonnades fronting a building or located in an inner court.
Projection: any part of a structure that is cantilevered, jetties out or projects.
Quadripartite vaulting: illustration VII.
Reliquary: casket containing the relics of a saint.
Retable or **altarpiece:** illustration XVIII.
Rose or **wheel window:** illustration III and p 23.
Semicircular arch: roundheaded arch.
Shaft or **column:** illustration VIII.
Shingles: wooden slips used as roofing tiles.
Side aisle: illustration I.
Side chapel: illustrations I and III.
Spire: illustration III.
Stalls: illustration XIX.
Tracery: intersecting stone ribwork in the upper part of a window.
Transept: illustration I.
Tribune: illustration II.
Triforium: small arcaded gallery above the aisles; illustration II.
Twinned or **paired:** applied to columns or pilasters grouped in twos.
Tympanum: illustration VIII and p 23.
Wainscot or **panelling:** timber lining to walls.
Watch turret or **bartizan:** illustration XII.

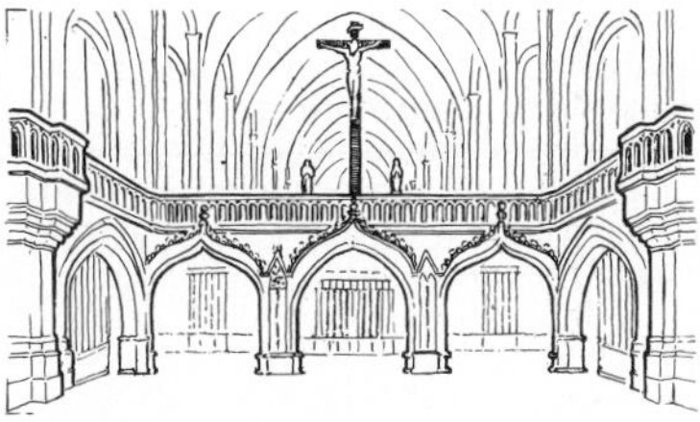

illustration XVII

Rood-screen: this replaces the rood-beam in larger churches, and may be used for preaching and reading of the Epistles and Gospel. Many disappeared from the 17C onwards as they tended to hide the altar.

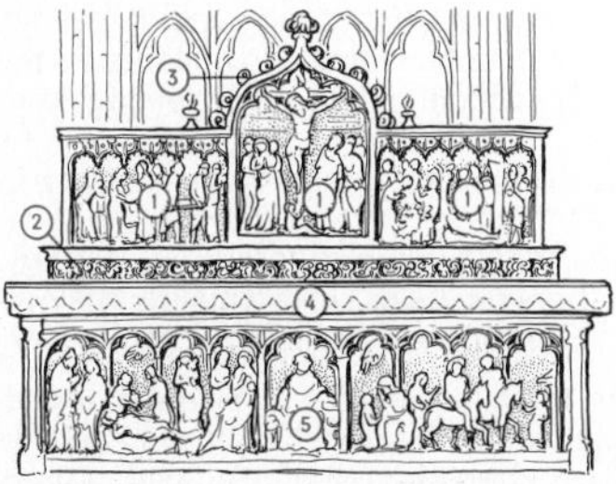

illustration XVIII

Altar with retable or altarpiece
① Retable or altarpiece – ② Predella – ③ Crowning piece – ④ Altar table – ⑤ Altar front

illustration XIX

Stalls
① High back – ② Elbow rest – ③ Cheek-piece – ④ Misericord

RELIGIOUS ARCHITECTURE IN ILE-DE-FRANCE

A church is basically a chancel reserved for members of the clergy, where one finds the high altar and the reliquary, and a nave which accommodates the congregation. This simple layout characterised the early churches that were built on a basilical plan. During the Romanesque period, the plan of the church developed into a cross. The narthex at the entrance would receive those who had not been baptised. The nave was enlarged by aisles. In places of pilgrimage, an ambulatory and side aisles were added onto the chancel to facilitate processions. The architects of Gothic, and later, classical churches respected this layout as it was convenient for celebrating Mass and easy to build.

Romanesque Art 11-12C

Romanesque statue-columns
The Royal Doorway of Chartres Cathedral

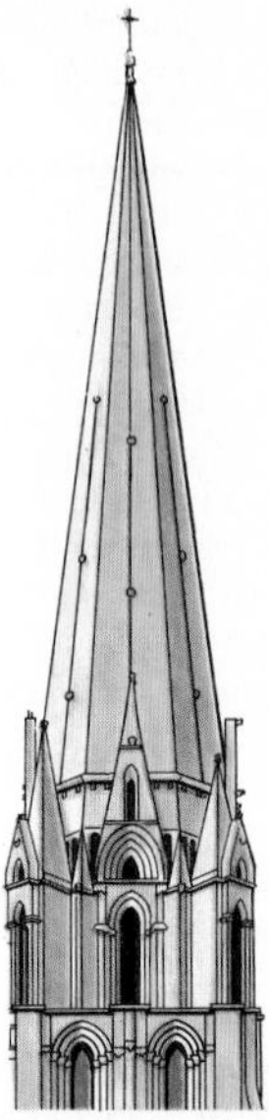

Romanesque Spire
Chartres Cathedral

Architects in Romanesque times knew how to build huge, lofty churches but the heavy stone vaulting would often cause the walls to settle or cave in. They therefore decided to make the windows as small as possible and to build on aisles surmounted by galleries, which served to support and balance the sombre nave.
The church at Rhuis and the Royal Doorway of Chartres Cathedral are two splendid examples of this art in the Ile-de-France region.
One of the main types of covering in Romanesque churches is groined vaulting, in which two identical barrels are perpendicular to one another. The barrel lying in the axis of the nave rests upon the transverse arch, while that set at a right angle is supported by the main arch or by a recess in the wall.

Gothic Art 12-15C

There was no brutal transition between Romanesque and Gothic architecture. It was a slow, natural process. Gothic art – typified by quadripartite vaulting and the use of diagonal arches – was invented in response to the demand for wider, higher and lighter churches. It was decided to have the vaulting rest on a series of arches so that the walls would only have to bear the weight of the vaulting at the springing. As a result, the sections of wall in between these points could be dispensed with and replaced with stained glass windows *(p 27)*. This technique greatly enhanced the luminosity of church interiors. Gothic art originated from Ile-de-France, where it produced many masterpieces, but it later spread to northern France, Champagne and Normandy. It developed over a period of four centuries, ranging from the sombre 12C Romanesque sanctuaries to the light churches of the 13C, and to the extravagantly ornate 15C constructions. Building a church was a costly, lengthy operation because both public taste and building methods would change as the work progressed. It was rare to find a church presenting entirely homogeneous features reflecting a given period in history. In fact many architects would keep a close eye on their colleagues' accomplishments and use them to their advantage.
Towards the late 13C, famous personalities and guilds were granted the privilege to have a chapel built in their honour in one of the side aisles. In exchange, they were expected to make a generous contribution that went towards building or maintenance.

Flying buttresses. – In early Gothic churches, the pillars in the nave were propped up by pieces of masonry concealed up in the galleries. During the 12C, these walls were limited to arches supported by sturdy piers. Soon afterwards, the galleries themselves were replaced with a row of flying buttresses. A number of high openings were thus incorporated into the church interior, producing a far more luminous nave.
From then onwards, high churches could be schematically described as stone cages consisting of columns supporting diagonal arches and resting upon two or three levels of flying buttresses. These came to rest on a series of tall pillars bearing pinnacles.

West fronts. – Most west fronts were given a western exposure. Each nave had its own doorway flanked by buttresses: these were bare in the 12 and 13C, ornate in the 15C. The tympanum featured ornamentation and in the 14C, its gable presented an elaborate display of stone carvings, while the sides were adorned with crockets. In the 13C rose windows were fairly small but in the 14C they were enlarged so as to cover the west front and provide light for the nave. As the windows grew larger, the church façades grew lighter. A gallery was built at the foot of the towers in order to break the rigid vertical perspective created by the buttresses and the bell towers. In the 15C it was reduced to a balustrade and the gables were embellished by further ornamentation.

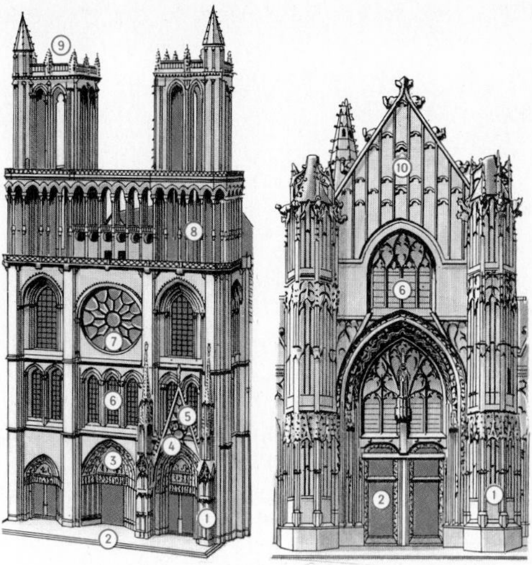

Gothic West Fronts

12 and 13C Collegiate Church, Mantes — 15C St Peter's Church, Senlis

1) Buttresses - 2) Doorways - 3) Tympanum - 4) Gable - 5) Sloping features - 6) Windows - 7) Rose window - 8) Gallery - 9) Tower with platform - 10) Gable

Theoretically speaking, the west front should have been graced with decorative stone carvings. However, in many cases, this part of the building was the last to be completed and architects were often obliged to forego ornamentation, and even the towers, owing to insufficient funds.
In some churches, the transept crossing also featured a pair of remarkable façades *(Chartres, qv)*.

Spires. – After introducing open-work façades, architects decided to alleviate the spires of Gothic churches. During the Flamboyant period, the open-work masonry was markedly ornate. In Ile-de-France, a great many spires were added onto bell towers in the 19C by disciples of Viollet-le-Duc.

Diagonal arches. – Towards the end of the 11C, groined vaulting *(p 18)* was extremely common. As it was difficult to build and liable to crack, a group of architects from England, Milan and Ile-de-France decided to reinforce the groins. They soon realised that by building these diagonal arches first and by consolidating them with a small amount of rubble, one obtained vaulting that was both sturdy and light. The thrust of the vaulting was fully supported by the arches, with the result that the walls only bore the weight of the masonry in the places where the arches came to rest. This meant that the walls in between could be dismantled and replaced with openings. This discovery heralded the age of quadripartite vaulting.

Elevations. – Gothic elevation reflects a continual search for higher, lighter buildings, as evidenced by the plans of its bays and different levels.

Transitional Gothic (A) *(illustration p 24).* – It featured diagonal vaulting. The nave was lit directly by means of tiny clerestory windows. The triforium below – a narrow place of passage – and the gallery were instrumental in supporting the walls as high up as possible. Generally speaking, the church had openings behind the gallery, but never behind the triforium, which was placed under the gallery. Some cases of semicircular arches are still observed.

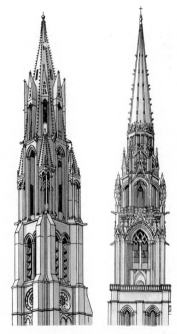

Gothic Spires

13C Former Cathedral, Senlis — 16C New Bell Tower, Chartres

The pillars of the main arches initially consisted of a thick column. This was later replaced by twinned columns supporting the arches and the colonnettes above. This transition took place between 1125 and 1190.

Lancet Gothic (B) *(illustration p 24).* – This was the great period in Gothic architecture. It lasted approximately from 1180 to 1250, and produced some of France's finest masterpieces: Chartres, Amiens and Reims.
The arches and the arching around the windows were pointed and shaped as a lancet. The clerestory windows were surmounted by a round opening. As for the gallery, it was replaced by flying buttresses.

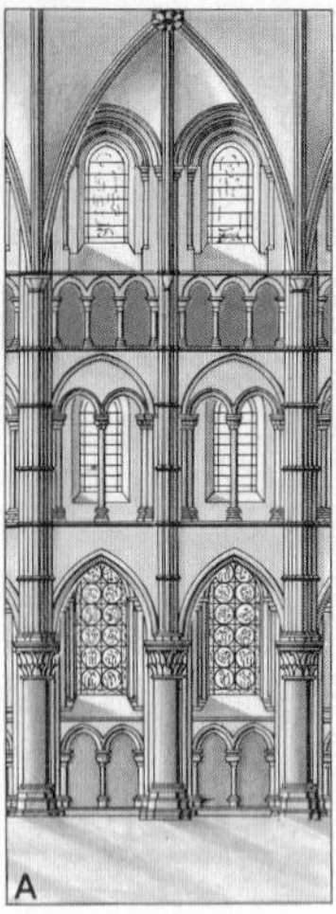

Transitional
(12C)

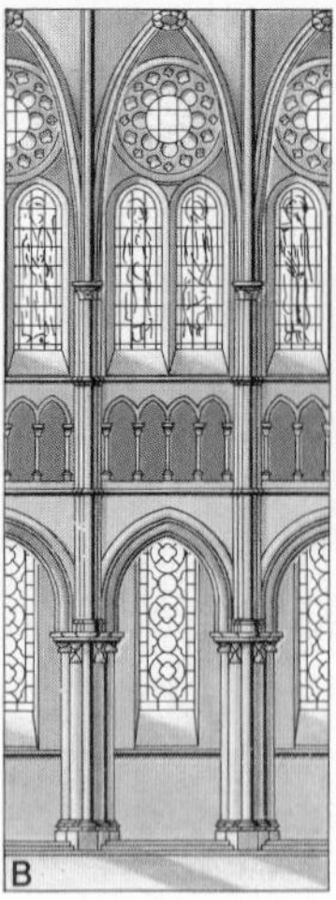

Lancet
(early 13C)

Radiant
(late 13C - early 14C)

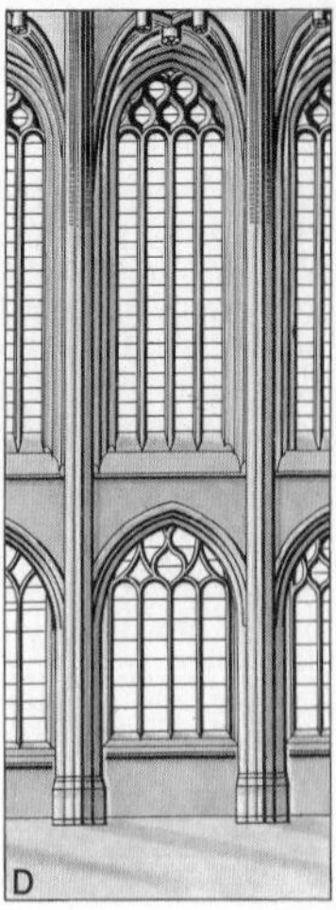

Flamboyant
(15 and 16C)

The numerous colonnettes originating from the vaulting rest upon the shaft that bears the weight of all the main arches. More often than not, this pier is a large round column flanked by four colonnettes.

Radiant Gothic (C) *(illustration above).* – The beginning of this period can be traced back to 1250 and the reign of St Louis. It ended around 1375, during the Hundred Years War which blocked the progress made by medieval architects.

The Gothic style was at the summit of its art. The wall area is reduced to a minimum and the stringers upholding the vaulting are doubled by another series of arches. The wall at the back of the triforium is decorated with stained glass. The vertical perspective of the triforium is continued by that of the clerestory windows.

If the chancel does not feature an ambulatory, the clerestory windows, triforium and ground floor windows form one huge single stained glass window.

In many cases, the colonnettes start from the ground at the point where they surround the pillar of the main arches. Two slight mouldings – level with the main arches and the springers – are the only features that break their vertiginous ascent.

Flamboyant Gothic (D). – This was the last stage in Gothic architecture which could develop no further and which gave in to ornamental excesses.

The vaulting was covered with numerous arches, the tracery of the openings and rose windows took on tormented shapes (e.g. flames). The triforium disappeared, replaced by the clerestory windows. The arches came to rest on columns or were continued by ribbing level with the pillars. The latter were no longer flanked by colonnettes. In some churches, the ribs formed a spiral around the column.

Flamboyant architecture characterised the 15C and part of the 16C, but Renaissance art was soon to make an appearance, introducing curved tracery and classical sculptures.

Vaulting. – *Illustrations p 19.* – Quadripartite vaulting, in which the thrust is supported by the four main arches, is easy to install in a square-shaped bay. In the 12C, bays were enlarged and it was no longer possible to build square bays: the pillars propping up the walls would have been too far apart. The problem was initially resolved by covering the bays two by two thus forming a square again: an extra transverse arch was then added and made to rest on slim pillars alternating with stout piers.

This type of vaulting – upheld by three diagonal arches – is known as sexpartite vaulting on account of the number of its divisions.

When the more sophisticated diagonal arches were able to support the vaulting above rectangular bays, the intermediary resting points were eventually discarded.

Notre-Dame Cathedral, Senlis

After the 15C, the concern that Flamboyant architects showed for decoration prompted them to put in additional ribbing of an extremely complex design: it formed liernes and tiercerons, and subsequently stars and intricate networks. The main supporting arches were flanked by ornamental arches of no practical use. The keystones – usually pendant – grew thinner and longer.

Renaissance Art 16C

With the influence of Italian culture, which favoured the return of antique themes, Gothic art was dropped. In religious architecture, quadripartite vaulting was replaced by coffered ceilings and barrel vaulting. Columns were given capitals copied from the antique, imitating the Ionic and the Corinthian orders. Architects introduced basket-handled arches and semicircular or rectangular openings. Inverted brackets replaced flying buttresses. Church fronts, and sometimes the north and south façades too, kept their heavy ornamentation. Spires were replaced by small cupolas and open-work pinnacles.

Renaissance Bell Tower
St-Maclou Cathedral, Pontoise

Classical West Front
St-Louis Cathedral, Versailles

Classical Art 17 and 18C

Grandeur and stateliness were the chief characteristics of religious architecture in France during the classical period: superimposed rows of Greek columns (Doric, Ionic and Corinthian), doors surmounted with carved pediments, imposing cupolas and scrolled architraves above the transept crossing. In many buildings, the nave was fronted by a peristyle featuring a row of columns. St-Louis Cathedral in Versailles is a perfect example of this style.

THE MONASTERIES OF ILE-DE-FRANCE

Tourists may be surprised by the vast number of priory, convent and abbey ruins that are found in Ile-de-France. Numerous localities and street names still testify to the many religious communities that did not survive.

Abbeys in the history of Ile-de-France. – There would be no abbeys if people did not feel a strong calling to take up ecclesiastical duties. But there would also be no abbeys if the clergy were not given land. After the 5C, when the victorious Franks carved up the Gallo-Roman territory, it would have been impossible for any community to survive without the help of donations. There were a great many aspiring monks in France up to the 19C, and all these different communities were almost entirely dependent on their benefactors' generosity. As the suzerain of Ile-de-France was none other than the supreme ruler of France, the king, this region was graced with an abundance of local monasteries.

In the early days of Christianity, towards the late 4C, Ile-de-France was covered with forests and therefore quite fertile: it attracted monks who wanted to live in peace and escape the terrible famine plaguing the country. Soon afterwards, the Merovingian monarchs, who had been strongly backed by the clergy, encouraged the creation of religious foundations, to which they contributed quite considerably (Château-Landon). The wealthy Carolingians continued to enrich these abbeys and the practice was kept up by the Capetians and their vassals for over 800 years (Chaâlis, Dammarie-lès-Lys and Royaumont).

One of the reasons why French kings favoured monasteries was that the monks used to reclaim uncultivated land, and the monasteries were constantly praying for their patrons. Religious faith was strong in those days – 10 to 17C – and a king would donate an abbey for a variety of motives: to thank God for a victory, to seek expiation for an offence committed against the Church, to express his own personal belief or to offer a dowry to dowager queens or royal princesses about to take the veil.

Religious Orders. – Most people mistakenly believe that the term abbey is applied to any Christian community, male or female, whose members lead a frugal, secluded life. In actual fact, an abbey designates a group of men or women placed under the authority of an abbot or an abbess, who live according to a rule approved by the Pope. The monks' day is usually divided into chores related to community life, and spiritual and liturgical duties, which are the main purpose of the association.
The abbot or abbess generally enjoys the same rank as a bishop. All abbeys have an abbot: he is elected by his fellow companions and incarnates the spiritual and temporal master of the abbey. After the 16C, the Pope gave the king of France the right to personally appoint abbots and abbesses. These prelates were called commendatory abbots and they usually lived in the king's entourage.
Sometimes, to administer new domains or to fulfil the wish of a patron who wished to receive monks on his land, the abbots would build a priory. This small community was supervised by a prior who was answerable to the abbey. The Cistercians set up numerous *granges,* farming colonies run by lay brothers.

Monastic Rules. – The Benedictine Order – created by St Benedict in the 6C – was undoubtedly the most flourishing order in France. Its members founded over one thousand abbeys throughout the country. The Benedictine rule was subsequently reformed and this led to the creation of two separate orders. The first originated from Cluny, in Burgundy, in the 10C but unfortunately all the Cluniac houses died out during the Revolution. The second – the Cistercian Order – was, and still is, extremely powerful. It was St Bernard of Cîteaux, also a native of Burgundy, who founded the order in the 11C. He was a firm believer in ascetism and introduced a number of new rules: he proscribed elaborate ceremonial and the decoration of churches, monks could no longer be paid tithes, neither could they receive or acquire land; strict rules were laid down on diet, rest was limited to seven hours and the friars had to sleep in their clothes in a common dormitory. The monks shared their time between liturgical worship – 6 to 7 hours a day –, manual labour, study and contemplation. In the 17C, the abbot Rancé added further austerities to the Cistercian rule (silence, diet). This new rule was named after La Trappe, the monastery near Perseigne where it saw the light of day. It is presently enforced in abbeys of strict observance.
The two other main orders who founded abbeys in France were the Augustinian friars and the Premonstratensian canons, both dating from the 12C.
Other communities include the Carmelite Order, the Order of St Francis (Franciscans and Capuchins), the Order of Preachers and the Society of Jesus (Jesuits). These however do not follow monastic rules and they do not found abbeys. Their activities (missionary work, caring for the sick) bring them into contact with the lay world. They live in convents under the authority of the Mother Superior, the prior, etc.
A collegiate church is occupied by a community of canons accountable to their bishop.

Monastic buildings. – The cloister is the centre of an abbey. Thanks to its four galleries, the nuns and monks may take their walks under cover. One of the cloister walls adjoins the abbey church, while another gives onto the chapter house, where friars meet to discuss community problems under the presidency of the abbot. The third gallery opens onto the refectory, and the fourth onto the calefactory. This is the only room with heating and the monks come here to study or do manual labour. The dormitory is generally placed above the chapter house. It communicates with the church by means of a direct staircase so that the monks may readily attend early morning and night mass.
Lay brothers – believers who cannot or will not take the holy orders – are granted a separate status. They spend most of their time in the fields and the workshops, and have their own dormitory and refectory. They may not enter the chapter house or visit the chancel of the church. Since the Vatican II Council, lay brothers have become more and more involved in the life of the community.
Visitors are not allowed to enter the monastic buildings and are lodged in the guest house. The poor are housed in the almshouse. The monastery also features an infirmary, a novitiate, sometimes schools, and the buildings needed to run the abbey: barns, cellars, wine press, stables and cowsheds.

The cloisters at Royaumont Abbey

STAINED GLASS

Since the early Middle Ages, church windows have been adorned with coloured glass. Unfortunately, few of these early productions have survived.
During the Gothic period, master glaziers played an important role in the completion and the ornamentation of churches: thanks to them, both the clergy and the congregation could appreciate the shimmering light that came streaming through the roundels. But stained glass is not purely decorative. To the Church it is an invaluable teaching aid, permanently communicating catechism, sacred history and the lives of the saints.

The art of making stained glass. – Stained glass is a juxtaposition of coloured pieces of glass held together by strips of lead. The glass is divided into panels to ensure perfect solidity. When the various coloured pieces have been selected and cut to shape, the glazier completes the shading and finer points of the figures with touches of grisaille: this is a brownish pigment containing silica, which blends with the glass in the melt. The glass panels are then reassembled and fixed in place in the window.
Patches of lichen may develop on stained glass windows. It starts to attack the lead after 100 years and has been known to break through the glass after 300 to 400 years. But it is man not erosion that must be blamed for the disappearance of so many early stained glass windows: in the 18C many were dismantled and replaced by plain glass, which afforded a better view of the nave.

Notre-Dame de la Belle-Verrière
Detail of 12-13C stained glass, Chartres Cathedral

The development of stained glass. – Technical developments in glass making were prompted by artistic trends but also by the search for greater economy and the wish to produce lighter tones.

12C. – Stained glass windows are small, with fairly heavy borders. The ornamentation around the main figures is limited in the extreme.

13C. – Thanks to the generosity of wealthy patrons, the churches of Ile-de-France feature exceptionally beautiful stained glass windows. To ensure perfect cohesion between the panels and the leading, the iron armatures are fastened to the walls.
The clerestory windows represent tall, isolated figures. In the lower windows, that can be observed more closely, the medallions depict scenes telling legends, i.e. the lives of the saints. This genre is known as **historiated stained glass.** The panels offer many architectural furnishings and embellishments. The borders are heavy and the rendering of the scenes shows a marked attempt at realism. Historiated roundels are set in a grisaille framework enhanced by brightly-painted rose windows. The daily lives of craftsmen are evoked by lively anecdotal scenes. The lower windows are generally divided into panels composing geometrical motifs (stars, diamonds and clover leaves).

14C. – Churches have lost part of their wealth and the area occupied by stained glass windows has considerably increased. For reasons of economy, more and more grisaille is produced, its starkness softened by delicate shading and graceful foliage motifs. Angels and rosy cherubs adorn the barer parts of the windows. Borders become smaller and lettering makes an appearance. In the second half of the 14C, glaziers discover that silver staining can be used to accentuate a variety of bright colours: yellow on a white background, light green on blue, amber on red, etc.

15C. – The leading is no longer produced by means of a plane, it is stretched on a wire drawing bench. The lead strips are thinner, therefore more supple and are able to hold together larger and flatter panes of glass than previously. Glaziers work with a lighter type of glass and the colours used in the decoration are less vivid. In some churches, two thirds of the window is taken up by grisaille: these panels feature Gothic canopies with high gables and open-work pinnacles. The quality of the craftsmanship is remarkable. For the first time, master glaziers sign their own work and introduce original themes.

16C. – Stained glass draws inspiration from the works of the great painters and from contemporary engravings. Glaziers have become masters at cutting the glass from the main sheets – using a diamond and no longer a red hot iron – and they also excel at painting with enamels. Stained glass windows develop into large, transparent paintings in which minute attention is given to detail, perspective and design. In some buildings, religious themes are replaced by classical scenes taken from antiquity.

17 and 18C. – The use of coloured glass is gradually dropped. Stained glass is painted and decorated with enamels.

Three great periods in architecture – widely admired and imitated throughout Europe – originated from Ile-de-France: the Louis XIV, Louis XV and Louis XVI styles.

Écouen

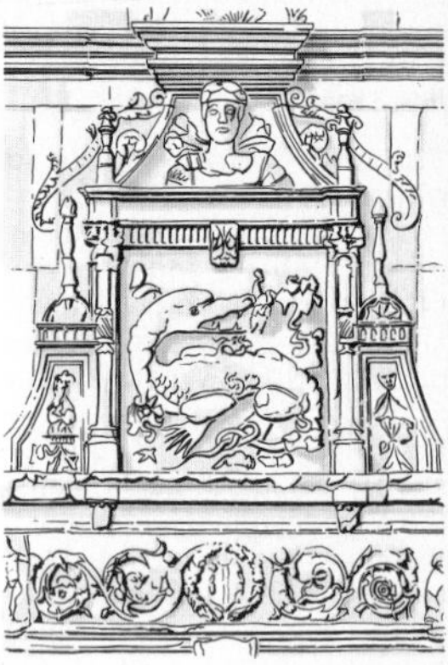

François I's House at Moret-sur-Loing

Renaissance style (16C). – After the 15C, medieval castles were converted into residential châteaux. Windows were enlarged, doors and openings were richly adorned. The towers were only there for decorative purposes and by the second half of the 16C they were considered superfluous. Façades were embellished with statues and rows of superimposed columns. Roofs were high and presented a single slope.

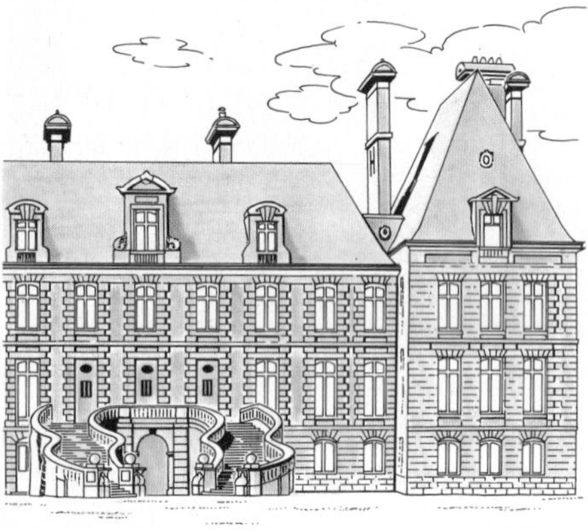

Courances

Louis XIII style (1580-1640). – Its main characteristics were the exact symmetry of the main building and the use of brick panels set into white stonework. Sculpted ornamentation was either limited in the extreme or non-existent. The proportions of these châteaux were of the utmost simplicity. They usually consisted of a central block flanked by two end pavilions.

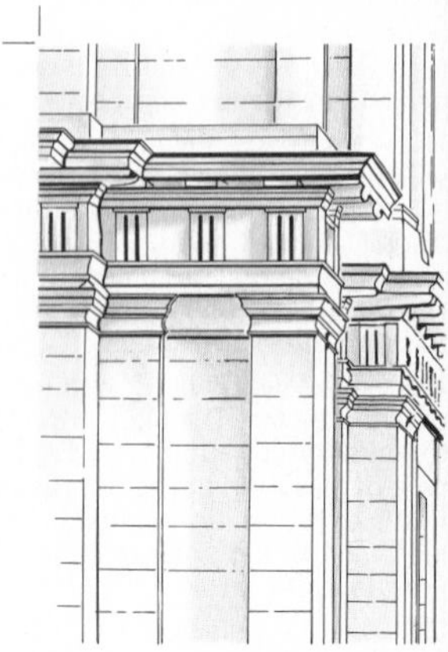

Maisons-Laffitte

Louis XIV style, first period (1640-1660). – Under the skilful hand of François Mansart, civil architecture gave up the amiable character it still showed under the Louis XIII period and acquired a far more noble appearance. Columns and pilasters never ran higher than a single floor of the château. Triangular and arched pediments were growing popular. Roofs were still fairly high and featured numerous chimneys.

Versailles

Louis XIV style, **second period (1662-1710).** – The ground floor was taller, the first floor fairly high, while the second floor remained low. The flat roof was concealed by a balustrade. The horizontal lines of the building were broken by the rows of sturdy columns and tall windows. Ornamental sculpture was limited to the rooftop and the summit of the front pavilions. The statues were inspired by antique models.

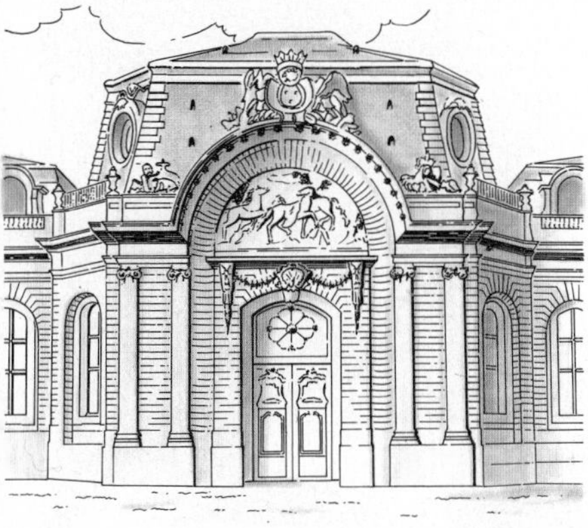

The Great Stables at Chantilly

Louis XV style **(1700-1750).** – After 1700, the Louis XIV style and its harsh angles were mellowed by soft, rounded contours. Under Louis XV, curves were definitely in. Windows and pediments featured intricate ornamentation, while the decoration of the façades remained somewhat austere. Generally speaking, the châteaux resumed modest proportions. Columns disappeared and roofs consisted of two sloping planes.

Petit Trianon, Versailles

Louis XVI style **(1750-1793).** – The Louis XV elegance was still felt but the excessive use of curves brought back right angles. Columns made a remarked comeback. The ornamentation of the façades was severe in the extreme. Many of the motifs were taken from antiquity, a trend that introduced the Pompeian (1790-1804) and the Empire style, characterised by simple design and tall, imposing columns.

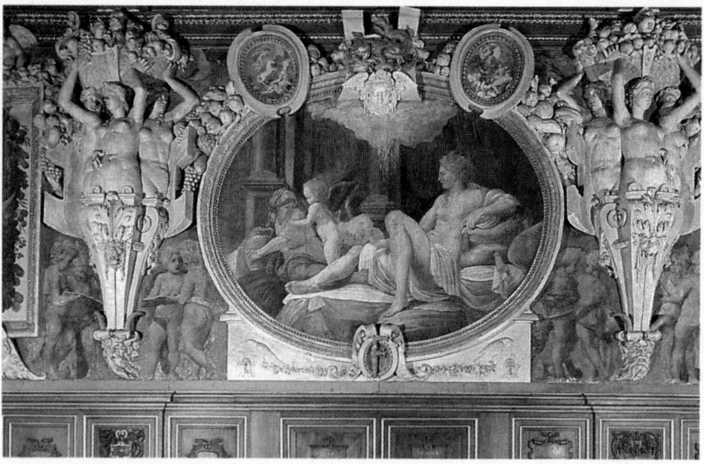

Fresco by Primaticcio in François I Gallery, Fontainebleau

Renaissance: First School of Fontainebleau. – The decoration was loosely inspired by the great Italian masters. The wainscoting was surmounted by frescoes edged by fine stucco work. The coffered ceilings featured dark timbering.

The Dining Room at Gros Bois

Louis XIII Style. – The decoration was decidedly less ornate. The walls were hung with huge tapestries or mural paintings. The base of the walls was adorned with wood panelling. Decorative beams were still very much in vogue.

The Venus Salon in Versailles

Louis XIV Style. – The sober, austere lines contrasted sharply with the rich, sumptuous materials used for ornamentation. The walls were lined with marble. The ceiling was divided into decorated panels, separated by motifs in gilded stucco.

Madame de Pompadour's Bedroom, Champs

Louis XV Style. – Corners and right angles were banished. Straight lines were broken by a profusion of curves, arabesques and foliage motifs. Marble was replaced by wooden panels of remarkably light tones.

Louis XVI's Gaming Room at Versailles

Louis XVI Style. – Lightness and elegance were the two major characteristics of this style. Although most of the interior decoration was governed by straight lines, the rectangular panels were mellowed by series of arabesques and floral motifs.

Napoleon I's Bedroom at Compiègne Château (Flandres-Artois-Picardie Guide)

Empire Style. – The wainscoting was replaced by crimson or emerald wall hangings. The interior architecture – relying on straight perspectives and Roman arches – was austere in the extreme.

PAINTING

Although a considerable number of painters were employed in the interior decoration of the many châteaux and abbeys around Paris, it was not until the 19C that painters began to show an interest in the landscapes of Ile-de-France.
Between the 13 and the 18C, the great masters would use landscapes as a background to their work. For some, this would be purely decorative, while for others the composition and colour scheme would serve to convey the atmosphere. The two main French 17C representatives were Claude Lorrain and Nicolas Poussin.

Camille Corot (1796-1875). – He was the pioneer of contemporary landscape painting in France. Corot lived in Barbizon from 1830 to 1835. He worked in Fontainebleau Forest and all over Ile-de-France. He studied the contrasts and soft hues of light in the undergrowth, along the shaded paths and on the edge of the plain. He later took up painting lakes in an attempt to produce more delicate tones. The ponds at Ville-d'Avray were his favourite on account of their subtle reflections. He also enjoyed painting the lakes of Mortefontaine, and the Seine river in the Mantes region.

The Painters of the Oise. – The group was founded in 1845 by two of Corot's disciples, Charles-François Daubigny (1817-1878) and Jules Dupré. Daubigny liked to capture the rippling waters of the Oise, the bright patches of greenery and the blossoms in the orchards and groves. He led a quiet life: his work paid well and received universal acclaim. He could often be found working on the Ile de Vaux off Auvers, or in a small rowing boat he had converted into a studio. Jules Dupré (1811-1889), a close friend of Théodore Rousseau, used darker colours and belonged to the Barbizon School. He seldom left his house in L'Isle-Adam.
Honoré Daumier (1808-1879) – who established his reputation as a lithographer and a satirical cartoonist – met with serious financial difficulties. Pressed by Dupré, he left the French capital and moved to Valmondois in 1865.
In 1866, **Camille Pissarro** (1830-1903) settled in Pontoise for a first two-year stay. The nearby streams and rivers did not catch his attention. Instead he concentrated on meadows, grassy slopes, country villages and street scenes featuring peasant women, deliberately portrayed in a poetical manner. His gift for expressing the vibrations of light, his pedagogic qualities and his kindliness made him the father figure of the Impressionist movement.

The Barbizon School. – Its representatives drew inspiration from the forest landscapes around Fontainebleau and the nearby plain of Bière. The founder of the movement was **Théodore Rousseau** (1812-1867). He settled in a modest country cottage in 1847 and stayed there until his death in 1867. Diaz and Charles Jacque were among his close friends. They were merry, good-hearted companions in spite of their financial misfortunes: their work brought in precious little money. It was only towards the end of the Second Empire that their talent was acknowledged. **Troyon** (1810-1865) specialised in rural scenes representing cattle. The highly-respected sculptor of animals **Barye** also took up landscape painting because of his love of nature. As for **Jean-François Millet** – who moved to Barbizon in 1849 and resided there until he died – his work evokes simple country life.
Generally speaking, these artists favoured dark colours reminiscent of the bark of trees and the undergrowth. The type of subjects they chose included stormy skies, filtered sunlight and the dusky shades of crepuscule. These sombre tones were criticised by their detractors, who claimed they painted with "prune juice".
Around 1865, a r[illegible] group of artists fell under the spell of these magic woodlands. Frédéric Bazille, Pierre-Auguste Renoir, Alfred Sisley and Claude Monet settled in Chailly, but did not associate themselves with the Barbizon community. They did however accept advice from their elders: Diaz encouraged the young Pierre-Auguste Renoir to work with lighter tones. This generation, too, contributed towards sowing the seeds of Impressionism.

Impressionism. – The second-generation artists wanted their work to create an impression of light and to convey the different vibrations of colour. The term "Impressionist" was in fact coined by a sarcastic journalist in 1874, but the group decided to adopt the word as they felt it reflected the double revolution they had brought about in the field of painting.

The Impressionist Revolution. – The Impressionist movement revolutionalised artistic conventions on two counts: it paid little attention to form and invented a new technique. Up to then, the representation of reality was fundamentally important and no artist would have dared to neglect the lines and shapes of his subject, whether it be a portrait, still life or landscape. Painters showed little concern for light and its effects, considered a minor component. Priority was given to subject matter. With the Impressionists, light and the analysis of its effects became the principal subject. All the rest – contours, scenes and people – was simply an excuse to paint light. Religious and historical works as well as family portraits and everyday scenes were no longer interesting in themselves. The Impressionists' favourite subjects were those which enabled them to play with light: water, snow, material, flesh, flowers, leaves, fruit, mist and smoke.
They wish to capture the infinite depths of the skies, the shimmering of light on water, a dress or a human face. When depicting the undergrowth, they want to show how the russet tones glitter in sunlight, how bright colours sparkle when the light changes and how colours are perceived in misty and smoky atmospheres.
Artists could no longer resort to traditional techniques to render such fleeting and indefinite concepts. Priority was given to the vibrations of light around the edges of objects and therefore the process that applied paint along contours was banished. Traditionally, the layers of paint were applied slowly, and they acquired their definitive colour after the oil had solidified. They were then coated with varnish to produce a transparent effect and give depth to the colours. Naturally, this technique was far too lengthy to capture the ephemeral quality of light. Consequently, the Impressionists developed a technique that suited their purpose, i.e. which involved very little oil and

which dispensed with varnish. Their art consisted of applying quick, small dabs of colour. The exact shade was conveyed by the juxtaposition of touches of pure colour, the final effect being assessed by the eye of the viewer.
The Impressionists were harshly criticised, even insulted at times, and it was only after a twenty-year struggle that their work was truly acknowledged. A great many Impressionists derived inspiration from Ile-de-France.

The painters. – The Impressionist School was founded in Honfleur. It was there that a painter from Le Havre named Claude Monet (1840-1926) was given advice by Eugène Boudin, a seascape specialist also known as the "lord of the skies". Following his example, Monet and later the Dutch artist Jongkind worked on the luminosity of the landscapes around the estuary of the Seine. They were soon joined by Bazille and Sisley, with whom they had made friends at the Gleyre studio. Although the group remained separate from the Barbizon School, it often sought inspiration from Fontainebleau Forest. As for Pissarro, Cézanne and Guillaumin, who met at the Swiss Academy, they were called "The Famous Three" *(le Groupe des Trois)*.
All these painters were strongly supported by one of their elders, a certain Édouard Manet (1832-1883). This rebellious character upset artistic conventions and scandalised the public by the boldness of his colours and compositions. It was he who encouraged the Impressionists to pursue their efforts at light painting.
In 1863, after many failed attempts to be represented at official showings, the Impressionists were invited to an "Exhibition of the Rejected" organised at the instigation of Napoleon III. The Impressionist School was finally born.
In 1871, Pissarro at Pontoise and Docteur Gachet in Auvers attracted a small group of pupils, amateur painters and friends, namely Paul Cézanne. Another group, based in Argenteuil and Louveciennes, included Renoir, Monet, Sisley and Degas, who had first studied under Jean-Auguste-Dominique Ingres. Claude Monet developed an original technique and became the leader of the movement. His style was to inspire Manet, and later Berthe Morisot. After 1880, the group broke up but its members remained faithful to light painting. Sisley moved to Moret, seduced by the river Loing, while Monet settled in Giverny, on the banks of the Epte *(Michelin Green Guide Normandy Seine Valley)*. For practical reasons, Pissarro left the valley of the Oise and chose to live in Eragny, near Gisors. Armand Guillaumin withdrew to Crozant in the Creuse valley.
Georges Seurat (1859-1891) remained in Paris but concentrated on the landscapes around the capital and along the coasts of the Channel. His technique consisted of breaking down the subject matter into small dabs of colour, each consisting of a series of dots *(points)*. Maximilien Luce (1858-1941) also experimented with this method – known as Pointillism or Divisionism – in the vicinity of Mantes.
Paul Cézanne moved to Aix-en-Provence, where he perfected a new technique. With large patches of bright colour, he produced stylised volumes while accentuating the outlines and the depth of his subject.
Renoir travelled to Africa and returned via Venice, a trip which inspired him to paint some of his finest works. Edgar Degas and Toulouse-Lautrec (1846-1901) resided in the capital. They were fascinated by circuses and theatres where the swirling dancers and performers were showered with complex illuminations created by artificial lighting.

The Dawn of the Twentieth Century. – Preceding the advent of Cubism and the new art forms that emerged in the wake of WWI, the Nabi and the Fauvist movements also set up their easel, sometimes even their studio, in the picturesque outskirts of Paris. Returning from his stay in Pont-Aven, where Paul Gauguin taught him the magic of representing shapes by composing in flat, bold colours, Paul Sérusier converted his friends of the Académie Jullian and created the Nabi movement (a Hebrew word meaning a prophet). Maurice Denis (1870-1943) became the founder of the group, which featured names such as Bonnard, Roussel, Vuillard, Maillol, Vallotton, etc.
The early Fauvist School was represented by extremely diverse artists, namely Dufy, Braque, Derain and Vlaminck (together in Chatou), as well as Marquet... They owe a lot to Vincent Van Gogh, who died in Auvers in 1890, leaving behind a collection of brilliant paintings, consisting of strong, vigorous touches of pure colour *(p 36)*.
Even today, Ile-de-France and its charming landscapes attract a great many figurative artists. Dunoyer de Segonzac (1884-1974) is famed for his work – mainly engravings – which represents rural scenes with touching sincerity.

Mantes Bridge by the landscape painter Camille Corot

Key

Sights

★★★ **Worth a journey**
★★ **Worth a detour**
★ **Interesting**

Sightseeing route with departure point indicated

Ecclesiastical building: Catholic - Protestant

Building (with main entrance)

Ramparts - Tower

Gateway

Gardens, parks, woods

Statue - Viewing table

Miscellaneous sights

Castle, Château - Ruins

Wayside cross or calvary - Fountain

Panorama - View

Lighthouse - Windmill

Dam - Factory or power station

Fort - Cave

Megalithic monument

Other symbols

Motorway (unclassified)

Interchange complete, limited, number

Major through road

Dual carriageway

Stepped street - Footpath

Pedestrian street

Unsuitable for traffic

1429 Pass - Altitude

Station - Coach station

Metro station - Cable-car

B Ferry (river and lake crossings)

Swing bridge

Ferry services:
Passengers and cars
Passengers only

Airport

Hospital - Covered market

Main post office (with poste restante)

Tourist information centre

Car park

Police station (Gendarmerie)

Barracks

Cemetery - Synagogue

Stadium

Racecourse - Golf course

Outdoor or indoor swimming pool

Skating rink - Mountain refuge hut

Pleasure boat harbour

Telecommunications tower or mast

Water tower - Quarry

③ Reference number common to town plans and MICHELIN maps

MICHELIN maps and town plans are north orientated.

Main shopping streets are printed in a different colour in the list of streets.

Town plans: roads most used by traffic and those on which guide listed sights stand are fully drawn; the beginning only of lesser roads is indicated.

Local maps: only the primary and sightseeing routes are indicated.

Abbreviations

A	Local agricultural office (Chambre d'Agriculture)
C	Chamber of Commerce (Chambre de Commerce)
H	Town Hall (Hôtel de ville)
J	Law Courts (Palais de Justice)
M	Museum
P	Préfecture Sous-préfecture
POL.	Police station
T	Theatre
U	University

Ⓥ Times and charges for admission are listed at the end of the guide

Additional sign

Deciduous, coniferous trees

Ile-de-France

The Apollo Basin in Versailles Park

ARGENTEUIL

Pop 96 045

Michelin map 101 fold 14 – Michelin plan 18

Located northwest of Paris, on the west bank of one of the Seine's loops, this industrial suburb is also noted for its market garden produce (asparagus). Its quiet, charm inspired Claude Monet to paint his *Views of Argenteuil.*

Argenteuil History Museum (Musée du Vieil Argenteuil). – *Rue P. Guienne.* The archaeological room on the ground floor houses a miniature model of the town as it stood in 1789. Relics of the former priory (columns, capitals), ruled by the Abbess Héloise in the 12C, are on exhibition, together with a Merovingian dugout (7.5m – 25ft long) recently discovered on the island of Argenteuil.
On the first floor, the "wine growers' room" reminds visitors that the area was once an important wine-growing region. A second room is devoted to recent history and boasts an impressive reproduction of the Baltard food market in miniature, whose metal framework was manufactured in the Joly factory in Argenteuil. The other collections on the first floor consist of paintings and engravings depicting the town.

ASNIÈRES

Pop 71 220

Michelin map 101 fold 15 – Michelin plan 18

At no 89 Rue du Château one can see the **former château** that belonged to the Count Voyer d'Argenson, governor of Vincennes and son of Louis XV's adviser.

Dogs' Cemetery (Cimetière des Chiens). – *Pont de Clichy.*
It lies on the former Ile des Ravageurs and over 100 000 pets have been buried there since 1899, including a lioness, a gazelle, a monkey and even a lemur. Note the unusual monuments and curious epitaphs.

AUVERS-SUR-OISE

Pop 5 722

Michelin map 196 fold 6

This hamlet stretches over 7km – 4.5 miles from the Oise River to the escarpment ending the Vexin plateau. The old path, now a series of narrow streets winding their way from Valhermeil to Cordeville, still carries the memory of the artists who covered it with fame. Here and there, panels indicate the scenes portrayed by painters, ranging from Daubigny to Vlaminck. However it is the district around the church that constitutes the favourite "place of pilgrimage" of art lovers.
Doctor **Paul Gachet** (1828-1909) moved to Auvers in 1872, although he had kept his surgery in Paris. An enthusiastic painter and engraver, with an unquenchable thirst for novelty and an extremely wide and varied medical experience – whether in epidemics, war wounds or mental disorders – he was the centre of attraction for a new generation of painters, known as the "Impressionists".
The seventies were an exciting period for a great many artists of that time, further stimulated by Pissarro's presence at Pontoise. Cézanne's talent blossomed during his three visits to Auvers and Pontoise (1873, 1877 and 1881), when he executed no less than one hundred paintings, working both outdoors and in the doctor's studio.
In May 1890, it was **Van Gogh's** turn to be invited by Paul Gachet. The Dutch painter managed to find spiritual relief by throwing himself into work but this state of well-being was only a brief interlude: overcome by another bout of madness and especially the guilty feelings he felt for his brother Theo, on whom he was totally dependent, Van Gogh committed suicide in an open field and died in his room at the Ravoux café on 29 July 1890.

SIGHTS

Church (Église). – The best view is from the back of the terrace, near the east end. The well-proportioned chevet and 12C bell tower were rendered by Van Gogh in one of his expressive paintings, presently exhibited at Orsay Museum in Paris. A bust portraying the painter Charles-François Daubigny stands at the foot of the church.

Van Gogh's Monument (Monument de Van Gogh). – In the Van Gogh Park (Tourist Information Centre), located in Rue du Général-de-Gaulle. Van Gogh's statue is the work of the sculptor Ossip Zadkine.

Auvers Church by Van Gogh

Van Gogh's Grave (Tombe de Van Gogh). – The famous Dutch painter is buried in the cemetery that lies on the plateau *(directions show how to get there from the church)*. His tomb stands against the left-hand wall. His brother Theo, who lent him moral support all his life and who died soon after him, rests by his side. **View** of Auvers' bell tower.

★ BARBIZON — Pop 1 273

Michelin map 196 fold 45 – 6 miles northwest of Fontainebleau – Local map p 89

The village of Barbizon, which was part of Chailly until 1903, was a popular spot with landscape painters *(see p 32)*. The hamlet still carries memories of the artists who made it famous. The Bas-Bréau coppices are a telling reminder of the Impressionist period, greatly cherished by the Goncourt brothers.

The Barbizon Group. – Breaking the rules of studio work and official art, the Barbizon artists were landscape painters who perfected the technique of working directly from nature after two great masters: Théodore Rousseau (1812-1867) and Jean-François Millet (1814-1875). The local people were happy to welcome these nature-loving artists who rose at dawn and whose genius and mischievous nature enlivened local feasts and banquets. Next came the writers, seduced by the beauty of the forest and the congenial atmosphere of this small, international community: George Sand, Henri Murger, the Goncourt brothers, Taine, etc.
Millet, now a patriarch on account of his nine children, died after a life of hard work, his eyes forever riveted on the landscapes of the Bière plain. Like Rousseau, he was buried at **Chailly Cemetery** (Cimetière de Chailly) *(plan of graveyard at entrance)*.

HIGH STREET (GRANDE RUE) *time: 1 hour*

From the Chailly road (D 64) to the forest.

Barbizon is a long street lined with hotels, restaurants and villas. Every one of these buildings bears commemorative plaques of the artists who stayed there.

Father Ganne's Old Inn (Ancienne Auberge du Père Ganne). – This former grocery run by "Father Ganne" offered lodgings to artists and soon became an important meeting place for contemporary painters: it was already shown to tourists in 1850. The communal living room still evokes the carefree, but nonetheless laborious, existence of Father Ganne's guests, their mischievous sense of humour and their inclination to paint every inch of surface available, like the wooden dresser. The second room is devoted to contemporary landscape painters.

Barbizon School Museum (Musée de l'école de Barbizon). – Located behind the war memorial, in the old barn that Théodore Rousseau used as a studio. The small adjoining church was built at a later date.
The museum presents documents relative to the old part of the town and a number of original works by Rousseau, along with engravings by Diaz, Troyon and Charles Jacque.

Monument to Millet and Rousseau (Monument de Millet et Rousseau). – A bronze medal embedded in the rock is the work of Chapu *(see p 119)*.
Behind this monument, a plaque set into another rock commemorates the 100th anniversary of the proposal to create protected forest zones, an early step towards nature conservancy: the first one was created in 1853 at the instigation of Rousseau *(see p 12)*.

BEAUMONT-SUR-OISE — Pop 8 312

Michelin map 196 fold 7

Beaumont-sur-Oise is an extremely old city which developed around the year 1000 and became royal property in the 13C. Its strategic location above the Oise River prompted the construction of a sturdy citadel in the 10C. More recently, it was discovered by Émile Zola, who made it the setting of his novel *The Dream*.

Castle (Château). – The relics of this ancient castle are quite impressive and feature several towers and a Romanesque donjon.

St Lawrence's Church (Église Saint-Laurent). – The nave, built in the early 13C, is flanked by double side aisles; the round pillars with foliage capitals support the ribbed vaulting and the transverse arches. The chancel dates from the late 12C.

BIÈVRE Valley

Michelin map 101 folds 23 and 24 – Michelin plan 22

The river, which bears the old Gallic name Castor (beaver), takes its source at St-Quentin pond *(p 162)*. Downstream from Antony, it goes underground and flows into the Seine at the bridge, Pont National near Porte de Bercy. Its former Parisian course has been turned into a sewer. The remarkably clean water was used by the Gobelins craftsmen for dyeing purposes and by the manufacturers of printed calico (Oberkampf in Jouy, Dollfus and Koechlin in Bièvres).
Upstream from Bièvres, the valley is unspoilt and has retained its rural charm.

Bièvre Springs Lakes (Étangs des Sources de la Bièvre). – A row of three artificial lakes (**Étangs du Val** and **Étang du Moulin-à-Renard**) has been designed to accommodate fishing and sailing activities in a wooded recess of the valley. A series of footpaths offers easy access. Swimming and canoeing are forbidden.
Between La Minière and Buc, the **Étang de la Geneste** is for fishing only.

FROM BUC AQUEDUCT TO BIÈVRES

9km – 6 miles – about 2 hours

Buc Aqueduct (Arcades de Buc). – This aqueduct was built in 1684 to channel the waters coming from Sarclay plateau towards the fountains of Versailles. The best view is from downstream, alongside the Jouy road.

Jouy-en-Josas. – *Description p 104.*

Ⓥ**Vauboyen Mill** (Moulin de Vauboyen). – The 16 and 17C mill lying at the edge of the water was converted into a gallery for contemporary art and a cultural centre. One of the barns was turned into a chapel decorated by the guests. Jacques Villon produced the study for the stained glass window on the left. A bronze Christ by the sculptor Volti stands behind the glass pane of the high altar; up above in the timberwork, a *Nativity Scene* by Commère. Each stage of the *Way of the Cross* was painted by a different artist.
The exhibition rooms display works belonging to the French School of Figurative Art, and drawings published by Pierre de Tartas, executed by outstanding contemporary artists.

Ⓥ**Bièvres.** – Pop 3 950. The **French Museum of Photography★** (Musée Français de la Photographie) stands at no 78 Rue de Paris, in the direction of Le Petit Clamart. This museum presents visitors with a history of photography from a technical and artistic viewpoint. It boasts many interesting exhibits, ranging from Da Vinci's studies to the very latest apparatus, relying on sophisticated technology. We learn about the crucial discoveries of Nicéphore Niepce, who took the first photograph on 5 May 1816, Daguerre and his photographic process, the advent of amateur photography in 1888 (George Eastman-registered trademark Kodak), the invention of miniature cameras (Leica) in 1925, etc.
The museum brings to the visitor's attention the relentless, if sometimes naive, quest for technical advancement, which also involves a high degreee of workmanship: to wit, the large-size cameras, all masterpieces of cabinet-making and leatherwork. The collections on the first floor are devoted to the bygone industry of amateur photography: note the plate cameras prevalent during the golden years (1910-1945). 15 000 apparatuses altogether, including 300 Kodak cameras, are exhibited, along with a million photographs.

BLANDY

Pop 609

Michelin map 196 folds 34 and 46 – 11km – 7 miles east of Melun

This Brie village developed around an imposing fortress of pentagonal dimensions built in the plain.

Ⓥ**Castle (Château).** – The castle was fortified in the 14C on the orders of King Charles V, redesigned in the 16 and 17C, then partly demolished and converted into a farmhouse in the 18C. The outer walls are flanked by five towers, of which the highest (35m – 115ft) was used as a donjon.
A limestone funeral sarcophagus was recently unearthed and it is thought that the castle stands on an old Merovingian burial ground. The rocky shelf offers a **panorama** of the Brie countryside.

BOULOGNE-BILLANCOURT

Pop 102 595

Michelin map 101 folds 14 and 24 – Michelin plan 22

Owing to the presence of the **Renault factories,** Boulogne-Billancourt is an important centre for the automobile industry. The compagny's modest beginnings are to be traced back to the Billancourt district: in 1898, with the help of his brother Marcel, 21-year old engineer Louis Renault produced his first car, working in his parents' garden. Admittedly, it wasn't very powerful – three quarters horsepower – but in those days, "direct drive" was quite a discovery. Today, the Boulogne plant is the most important in the group and houses, not only the company headquarters, but also a factory for mechanical engineering, an assembly plant for bodywork and a machine tool division.

★**Albert Kahn Garden (Jardin Albert-Kahn).** – *1 Rue des Abondances.*
Ⓥ Created in the early 20C by a banker called Albert Kahn, this garden is now the property of the Hauts-de-Seine *département* and offers several aspects of landscaping and ornamental gardening: stately cedar trees surrounding a small lake, the picturesque wilderness of the rocky Vosges forest, the exhuberant foliage of a true Japanese garden. The park is at its best in late spring.
Alongside the garden, at nos 9 and 10 Quai du 4-Septembre, the Nature Centre (Maison de la Nature) and the state-owned Albert Kahn Photography and Film Museum (Photothèque-Cinémathèque Albert-Kahn) arrange for films to be shown. The Nature Centre houses a library and a reference department, and organises group activities for children on the subject of environment.

★**Paul Landowski Museum (Musée Paul-Landowski).** – *14 Rue Max-Blondat.*
Ⓥ Under a garden dotted with monumental works, lies a crypt containing a precious collection of documents, studies and drawings by Paul Landowski (1875-1961), a sculptor belonging to the interwar period. His works adorn several squares and monuments in Paris (*Ste Geneviève* on Tournelle Bridge) and abroad (*The Reformation* in Geneva, *The Corcovado Christ* in Rio de Janeiro, the Sun-Yat-sen Mausoleum in Nanking).

ⓥ **Municipal Museum (Musée Municipal).** – *Town Hall annexe, 26 Avenue André-Mouzet.*
The museum was originally founded as a local history one but in recent years it has concentrated on artistic creation between the two World Wars, a prosperous period for the Boulogne-Billancourt area.
In the hall of paintings one can admire Quinsac-Monvoisin's famous *Meeting of 9 Thermidor,* together with works by Huet, Latouche, Jaulmes and many other artists seduced by the romantic landscapes of Séguin island. The hall of sculpture testifies to the importance that this art had acquired in the area: more than twenty artists took up residence in Boulogne-Billancourt during the thirties, following in the footsteps of the great Bartholdi, Lipchitz, Despiau, Janniot, Poisson and Landowski were among them. A third room presents various artistic trends that prevailed between WWI and WWII: the Paris School with Volovick, Naiditch and Pikelny, Cubism with Juan Gris, Souverbie and Martel, Expressionism with Waroquier.
The reference room contains documents on activities that played a key role in the town's development: laundering, aviation, the automobile industry and films.

Le BOURGET Airport

Michelin map 101 folds 7 and 17 – Michelin plan 20

Le Bourget airfield was created in 1914 and rapidly became an important airport and military air base. It was from here that Nungesser and Coli set off on their *White Bird* on 8 May 1927, in a doomed attempt to reach the American coast. Thirteen days later, in the early hours of 22 May, Lindbergh successfully landed his *Spirit of St Louis* in Paris, after achieving the first Atlantic crossing in the history of aviation. Costes and Bellonte were the first to accomplish this feat in the opposite direction when *Question Mark* touched European ground on 1 September 1930.
Since the Charles-de-Gaulle airport at Roissy has become operational, Le Bourget caters mainly for private aircraft and business flights.
Every two years, Le Bourget hosts the International Aeronautics and Space Fair *(see chapter on Principal Festivals at the end of the guide).*

★★ **Aeronautics and Space Museum (Musée de l'Air et de l'Espace).** – The former air ⓥ terminal, now called the Great Gallery, covers the early years of aviation. 45 items are exhibited; among the oldest are the nacelle belonging to the balloon *La France* (1884), and the first glider *Le Biot* which flew for the first time in 1879. Many aircraft belonged to early 20C pioneers: Vuia's I-bis (1906), Henri Fabre's hydroplane (1910), the great Guynemer's Spad 13 and the Breguet 14 evoke WWI, the first war to be fought in the airs. Six exhibition galleries house an outstanding collection of civil and military aeronautical equipment from France and abroad: over 100 rare aircraft, miniature models, engines, coloured slides and documents presenting space discoveries since 1919. We learn about the pioneering flights between the continents in interwar years. After the fighters of WWII, modern history is represented by the first jet planes and by the space capsules *Apollo 13* (USA) and *Soyouz T6* (USSR). The heavier aircraft, like Concorde and the Ariane rocket, are exhibited on the esplanade.

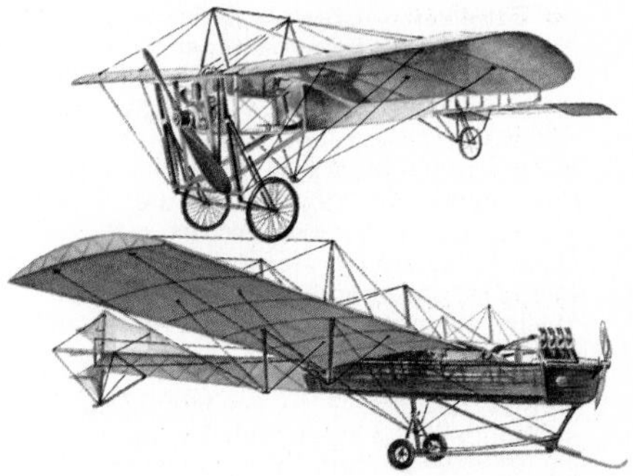

Aeronautics and Space Museum, Le Bourget

BOUSSY-ST-ANTOINE — Pop 5 984

Michelin map 101 fold 38

This former estate, protected in part, is a welcome break in the surrounding network of towns. Alongside the old family mansion, now the Town Hall, we find a small, unpretentious church amidst shaded paths and on the site of the former cemetery, a converted farmhouse.

Old Bridge. – One of the many old stone bridges that still span the Yerres, it dates back to the 15C and runs parallel to a ford, which remains visible. Thanks to the peaceful waters and the pleasant, shaded setting, it may be considered one of the most evocative haunts of this ancient valley.

Town Hall (Mairie). – The estate on which it stands belonged to the Dunoyer de Segonzac family in the 19C. In his youth, the painter André Dunoyer de Segonzac (1884-1974) used to come here to spend the summer months.

ⓥ **Dunoyer de Segonzac Museum** (Musée Dunoyer de Segonzac). – One of the estate buildings houses the collections donated by the artist himself, according to an original formula: a "library-museum" catering for both bookworms and art lovers. A number of works tell of the drawing and engraving talents of this great illustrator: war scenes from WWI, landscapes of Ile-de-France and the Saint-Tropez area, which he and Colette were among the first to discover (bequeathed by the artist).

Jarcy Mill (Moulin de Jarcy). – *4km – 2.5 miles to the southeast.* When you reach the old bridge, take Rue du Moulin-Neuf and proceed upstream. When in Perigny, turn right into Rue de Varennes-Jarcy. When crossing this locality, you can get to the mill by turning right into Rue Boïeldieu.
Site of the Yerres Valley, a popular spot for weekend outings. The dark, quiet waters serve a former mill, converted into an inn.

★ BRETEUIL Château

Michelin map 101 fold 31 – 6km – 4 miles to the south of Chevreuse

Built of brick and stone in the Louis XIII style, this château, formerly called Brévilliers, consists of one central building flanked by two lowish wings. The rooms on the first floor display numerous family souvenirs, contemporary furniture and present historic scenes featuring wax figures.
Special lighting effects enhance the beauty of the **Teschen Table★**, a pedestal table inlaid with hard stones, gems and fragments of petrified wood. It was a present from the Empress Maria Theresa to Louis-Auguste de Breteuil (1730-1807), the successful arbitrator of the Teschen Treaty (1779), which ended a serious territorial dispute between the Empire and Prussia.
Other items of interest include Queen Marie-Antoinette's souvenirs: a spinning-wheel belonging to the Dauphiness and a portrait of the Dauphin Louis XVII by Koucharsky. We may also see Louis XVIII's wheelchair, attributed to Jacob Desmalter. A group of twenty waxworks occupy the kitchens and sculleries, re-enacting King Edward VII's visit to the château on 3 May 1905.
The **park** slopes steeply down towards two ponds. Admire the vistas of the surrounding landscapes. The park has several recreational areas.

BRIE-COMTE-ROBERT

Pop 10 565

Michelin map 101 fold 39

This former capital of Brie Française has remained a market town. The best way to approach it is from the south or the west, as one can get a good view of the church, silhouetted against a backdrop of cornfields and picturesque roofs.
Robert I, comte de Dreux and brother of Louis VII, gave his name to the town in the 12C and ordered the construction of the castle. The work was completed by his son Robert II, who contributed to the city's development in the 13C.

SIGHTS

St Stephen's Church (Église St-Étienne). – Note the open-work spire of this imposing Gothic monument and the harmonious lines of the flying buttresses. The flat east end was built first, in the 13C. It features a large rose window and a clerestory gallery. There is less unity of style at the west end, where the plain main doorway (13C) is surmounted by a gallery and a Renaissance rose window.
In the interior, the triforium adds a touch of Gothic elegance to the nave. The first four bays were redesigned in the 15 and 16C.
The 13C **stained glass rose window★** at the east end is truly a work of art. It consists of 12 divisions: around the central pane, representing Christ in Majesty, are arranged the 12 Apostles and, on the outer edge, the 12 Labours of the Months.
The martyrdom of St Stephen is represented by a 17C gilt wood carving on the altar front and by the painting (1723) on the main altarpiece.

Castle (Château). – In the late 12 to early 13C, this square construction was surrounded by a moat, with 4 round fortified towers, one at each corner, and two square towers erected above two opposite doorways; today, only the Brie entrance still stands. In the interior, excavations have revealed the layout of the ground floor. The ruins are now part of a public garden.

Former Hôtel-Dieu. – The superb 13C Gothic façade of this former hospice features quintuple arcades.

EXCURSION

Soignolles-en-Brie. – *Round tour of 25km – 16 miles. Leave by the N 19 and proceed east; after 4.5km – 3 miles take the left turning to Grisy.*

Grisy-Suisnes. – Pop 1 407. Since 1966, this rose growers' village boasts a church built in the modern style. The tortured lines of the roof end in a long, elegant spire (42m – 132ft). The wooden figure of Christ by Louis Leygue is a contemporary version of the one in the Sacré-Cœur.

Return to the N 19 and turn right when you get to the main Coubert crossroads.

Soignolles-en-Brie. – Pop 1 113. A pleasant spot on the banks of the Yerres river. The road to Melun crosses the river and the hamlet. Leaving the village, start driving up the hill, then turn left for Barneau. Drive through it and stay at the same altitude until you reach a large oak and a cross. Drive past and turn left to ford the Yerres.

You arrive at a hairpin bend on a steep, winding road and turn right.

Just before you get to a railway bridge, you can glimpse the locality of Soignolles, set back in the valley (benches and statue of the Virgin).

Cross the railway and return to Coubert.

BRIIS-SOUS-FORGES Pop 1 850

Michelin map 101 fold 33

Situated south of the Chevreuse valley, this old fortified village owes its name to a Celtic term meaning "greasy soil" or "silt of the earth".

Ⓥ **Church (Église).** – The square-shaped tower (39m – 128ft) dates from the 12C and ends in four gables showing the cardinal points. Under the bell tower, we discover a beautiful Romanesque chapel: the chancel has oven vaulting, and groined vaulting on the ceiling.

Keep (Donjon). – This is all that remains of the Briis stronghold. The sturdy keep – the base of the walls is 3 m – 9 ft thick is surmounted by four bartizans, covered with pepperpot roofs in the early 20C.

BRUNOY Pop 23 899

Michelin map 101 folds 37 and 38

Brunoy was inhabited as far back as prehistoric times – observe the menhirs along the banks of the Yerres – and it became a seigniory in the 11C. Until the 17C, the estate belonged to the Brunoy and the Lamoy families. After the Revolution, this lush, peaceful locality attracted a number of Parisian celebrities, namely the actor Talma and the silversmith Christofle at the end of the 19C.

Ⓥ **Municipal Museum (Musée Municipal).** – Five rooms explain the history of Brunoy and its vicinity from prehistoric times up to the present day. The archaeological room displays silex tools, polished axes and arrow heads ranging from the Lower Palaeolithic to the Neolithic era, as well as relics from the Bronze Age to the Gallo-Roman period. The 18C hall pays tribute to the golden age of Brunoy Château – destroyed during the Revolution – which was noted for its impressive fountains.

St Medard's Church (Église Saint-Médard). – The interior has fine wooden panelling highlighted with gilding and 18C furniture. Two paintings by Restout adorn the church: *Virgin and Child* and *Saint Joseph with Jesus.*

CARNELLE Forest

Michelin map 196 fold 7

Carnelle Forest (975ha – 2 408 acres), which stretches from the Oise to the Presles Valley, is one of the highest landmarks around Paris (209m – 686ft). It used to belong to the Conti, who owned l'Isle-Adam, and three-quarters of the land is planted with oaks and beeches. Copses of chestnut trees line the northern and western slopes. Footpaths are clearly marked for those wishing to explore the forest.

Turquaise Stone (Pierre Turquaise). – This covered passage is an important Megalithic monument made of huge sandstone blocks.

Blue Pond and Small Pond (Étang Bleu et Petit Étang). – Former blue-tinged marl quarries provide the setting for these two artificial lakes in the middle of the forest. There is easy access to the edge of the water and to nearby paths which encircle the lakes. Swimming is forbidden.

CERGY-PONTOISE

Michelin map 101 fold 2 – Plan and description of Pontoise p 139

A vast town-planning operation known as the New Town of Cergy-Pontoise was launched in 1966.
When the project reaches completion, the locality should form a horseshoe extending along the inner banks of the Oise's last loop with a population estimated at 200000. The central area has been designed as a green belt and includes several bodies of water totalling 297 acres, forming the **Cergy-Neuville** lakes: it is devoted exclusively to nature and water sports.
The new town itself is divided into quarters, located mainly on the north bank: "Cergy-Préfecture", "Cergy-St-Christophe", "Cergy-le-Haut", "Versants de l'Hautil". These are interesting places to visit on account of their location – both on plateaux and on slopes –, the diversity of their schemes (Jouy-le-Moutier Hamlet) and the boldness of certain architectural projects, especially in the public sector.

Cergy-Préfecture. – *Information Bureau on the square in front of the préfecture.* The town centre of Cergy-Pontoise has always been a striking landmark: the préfecture building is the shape of an upturned pyramid and the Arts and Community Centres stand out on account of their bright green and blue ceramic façade.
Skirt the préfecture to take in the sweeping perspective of the **Town Park** (Parc Urbain): the bell tower of the old church is silhouetted against the sloping banks of the Oise and, further back, the Hautil hills.

EXCURSIONS

The Loop of the Oise. – *Round tour of 13km – 8 miles – about 1/2 hour.* Leave Cergy-Préfecture via Boulevard de Cergy, a southwest route which ends at Cergy-Village.

Cergy-Village. – A small rural islet preserved at the geographical centre of Cergy-Pontoise. A square extends in front of **St-Christophe Church,** on a site where an uncompleted 16C nave once stood. Access to the church is through a Renaissance portico built in the shape of a triumphal arch. The surviving chancel and aisles were built on the foundations of a Romanesque sanctuary, of which only the two lower levels of the tower remain. The upper level and the spire, featuring Gothic embellishments, are both Renaissance.

Follow the main street (Rue Nationale), which takes you to Rue de Puiseux and continue towards Cergy-St-Christophe.

Cergy-St-Christophe. – The Great Axis of Cergy-Pontoise is the material representation of the symbolic line dividing the loop of the Oise. It starts at the **belvedere tower** (tour belvédère) conceived by Dani Karavan, located in the middle of an arena-shaped complex designed by Ricardo Bofill. At the top of the 190 steps, admire the plunging view of the Cergy-Neuville lakes, Pontoise and Mirapolis amusement park: on a clear day one can see Paris. The Great Axis also embraces the Orchard, the Paris Esplanade and the Terrace: developments will complete the main axis.

Through Vauréal, proceed to Jouy-le-Moutier.

Jouy-le-Moutier. – Pop 6 560. A stately church whose Romanesque tower and stone spire (12C) dominate the area.

Cross the Oise river and follow directions to the Cergy-Neuville lakes.

Cergy-Neuville Lakes (Étangs de Cergy-Neuville). A total of 618 acres of artificial lakes has been created in the sand quarries, involving a large-scale reafforestation and landscaping operation. A guarded swimming area of 19 200yd^2, riding and cycling paths, tennis courts and facilities for many other outdoor games and sports are available to the public *(see chapter on Practical Information at the end of the guide).*

Return to Cergy-Pontoise town centre via Boulevard de l'Hautil.

Mirapolis. – *Use the free shuttle service from the RER station at Cergy-St-Christophe or take the N 14 or the A 15 motorway.*
Mirapolis is a huge amusement park covering 135 acres and offering numerous leisure activities related to tales, legends and epics. In addition to Gargantua – a giant 35m – 115ft hollow statue – visitors of all ages may feast their eyes on the Palace of Wonders, the History of the Earth, the Descent of the Great Rapids, the City of Ys, the Forest of Broceliande, the Impressionists' Garden and the Enchanted Castle, where a 20C Leonardo da Vinci robot presents his own discoveries. Not to mention the cinema and its hemispherical screen, the biggest roller coaster in Europe and the exciting adventure playgrounds. Thanks to the many refreshment bars and restaurants, a trip to Mirapolis can easily become a whole day's outing.

Gargantua at Mirapolis Amusement Park

Osny. – *Along the A 15 motorway, then the N 14 and branch off at Osny-Beaux-Soleils.*

Fire Brigade Museum (Musée Départemental des Sapeurs-Pompiers). – *1 Rue des Beaux Soleils.* This small museum houses an extremely wide selection of curios: a collection of old-fashioned manual pumps (1824-1900), numerous helmets from France and abroad, including a 1780 model, a 1937 Renault ambulance and a remarkable Delahaye first-aid vehicle from 1925. Note the underwater diving suit and the 19 and early 20C uniforms.

Other suggestions for a children's outing

Mer de Sable Amusement Park near Ermenonville
Sauvage Wildlife Park in Rambouillet Forest
St Vrain Wildlife Park
Thoiry Wildlife Park

CERNY Aerodrome

Michelin map 196 fold 43 – 1.5km – 1 mile north of Ferté-Alais

Alongside the airfield, where first flights are celebrated during summer weekends, a "flying" museum of aviation has seen the light of day.

ⓥ **Jean-Baptiste Salis Museum (Musée Jean-Baptiste Salis).** – *In the new hangar.* The first item exhibited – the 1919 Blériot XI, rebuilt in 1954 – evokes the heroic days of flying.
One may also admire a splendid collection of Morane (fighters, trainers, aerobatics), a reconnaissance Bréguet 14 bomber of the type used as mail planes in 1919 for the opening ot the Toulouse-Rabat link, an Albatros, an unusual Fokker triplane, one of the many Piper Cubs (reconnaissance) that droned above the battleground of WWII, De Havilland's twin-engined Swift Dragon DH 89, serving the Paris-London link (1937), restored for the 1981 Paris-New York cross-Atlantic race under the name of *Blue Way,* presently sporting the colours of the R.A.F.

★ CHAÂLIS Abbey

Michelin map 196 fold 9

The estate lies on the edge of Ermenonville Forest, facing the Mer de Sable amusement park *(qv).* Until the 19C, it evoked the gentle, romantic charm suggested by religious contemplation. Later, and up to 1912, Chaâlis inspired its last owners to collect works of art and to entertain some of the most notable personalities of their time.

A prosperous abbey. – Chaâlis is a Cistercian abbey *(see Monasteries in Ile-de-France p 25),* built on the site of a former priory in 1136 by Louis the Fat. The monks led a modest country life, husbanding the land, cultivating vines, keeping bees and fishing in the lakes. Saint Louis paid frequent visits to the abbey: he took part in the monks' prayers and duties, even waited on them, cared for the sick and watched over the dying.

Decadence. – During the 16C, the abbey was held in commendam and the abbots were appointed by the king. The first was the Cardinal Ippolito d'Este, son of Alfonso d'Este and Lucrezia Borgia, a distant cousin of François I (the Cardinal's brother, Ercole II d'Este, married Renée de France, the second daughter of Louis XII). Better known as Cardinal of Ferrara, this enthusiastic art lover had his private chapel decorated with murals and commissioned fine gardens. However he preferred his Tivoli residence, the Villa d'Este, where he died in 1572.
In the 18C the ninth abbot, one of the Great Condé's grandsons, attempted a costly operation to restore the abbey, to plans by Jean Aubert, the architect who designed the Hôtel Biron in Paris and the Great Stables at Chantilly. It was a disaster: after only one side of the building had been completed (1739, presently the Château-Museum) work was interrupted. This financial crisis prompted Louis XVI to close down the abbey in 1785.
During the upheaval of the French Revolution, Chaâlis was badly pillaged and the greater part of the building destroyed.

Restoration. – The estate frequently changed hands. Romantic painters and poets appreciated the melancholy charm of the old walls and their lush, verdant setting. In 1850 the highly distinguished Mme de Vatry bought the abbey ruins. She converted the 18C building into a château, had the park refurbished and entertained lavishly. These efforts were pursued by Mme de Vatry's heirs and by the very last owner, Mme Jacquemart-André, who founded the Paris museum that bears her name. She died in 1912 and bequeathed the estate to the Institut de France. Its first curator was the art critic Louis Gillet (1876-1943).

Chaâlis Abbey

★ FORMER ABBEY *time: 1 hour*

★ **Church Ruins.** – Ready for consecration in 1219, Chaâlis Abbey was the first Cistercian church built in the Gothic style. Of the original walls there remain a staircase turret, the northern arm of the transept, surrounded by radiating chapels – an unusual feature –, a section of wall from the north aisle with blind arcades.

Abbot's Chapel (Chapelle de l'abbé). – Built around 1250, it is a fine example of Gothic splendour at the time of the Sainte-Chapelle of Paris. On the right, a bronze bust portraying Mme Jacquemart-André marks the site of her grave.

⊙ **Rose Garden (Roseraie).** – Beyond the chapel a strange 16C crenellated wall with asymmetrical merlons *(see p 20)* sets the boundaries of the rose garden. Above the heavy archway is displayed the coat of arms of Cardinal Louis d'Este, nephew of Cardinal of Ferrara.
Before visiting the museum, go to the north of the château and admire the perspective of the park with its flower beds and dazzling lake, restored in the 19C.

⊙ **Château-Museum (Château-Musée).** – The highly typical **Monks' Room** (Salle des Moines) houses miscellaneous furniture from the 15C with Gothic embellishments, miniature paintings, carved panels, works of art, mainly of Italian origin, numerous religious figures (French 14 to 16C), ceramics, stained glass windows, etc. The metal fireback in the fireplace bears the letter K, symbolising the coat of arms of the abbey. The first floor gallery opens onto a reference room (detailed plans of the abbey) and **Jean-Jacques Rousseau 's Hall of Memories** (galerie du souvenir de Jean-Jacques Rousseau): in 1923 this collection was donated to the Institut de France by the last Marquis de Girardin.
On the way out, you may admire two panels painted by Giotto, believed to have come from an altarpiece in the Santa Croce Church in Florence *(St John the Evangelist* and *St Lawrence).*

CHAMBLY

Pop 6 218

Michelin map 196 folds 6 and 7

It is believed that the superb parish church of Chambly was founded by Saint Louis.

⊙ **Church (Église).** – Built in the 13C and completed in the 14C by the addition of a huge belfry and three doorways, this church offers a unified façade of remarkably well-balanced proportions. The chancel, flooded with light coming in through the clerestory windows with their radiant tracery, is characteristic of the Gothic style that prevailed in Ile-de-France in the late 13C *(see p 24).*
In the centre of the chancel, four painted panels, formerly belonging to an **altarpiece**★ by the Flemish school, tell the story of Gregory the Great (the Miraculous Mass of Saint Gregory is represented on the two central panels). The other scenes are relative to the Ascension, the Ressurection, the Passion and Pentecost.
The organs – of unknown origin – date from the 17C. They have recently been restored and feature 26 ranks of pipes. Certain parts of the instruments are considered historic monuments: the cases, mechanism and balcony rail.

★ CHAMPEAUX Church

Michelin map 196 south of fold 34

In the 12C a collegiate church was founded here by the theologian Guillaume de Champeaux, the teacher and subsequently the adversary of Abelard. The canons acquired an honourable reputation on account of their religious and musical accomplishments. In addition to Guillaume, who became the bishop of Châlons-sur-Marne and later the abbot of Clairvaux, Champeaux blessed the Church with three bishops, a cardinal and a pope.

The Horseman Misericord (detail), Champeaux Church

⊙ **Church (Église).** – Construction began with the transept in 1160, then the nave, finished in 1220, and eventually the chancel, started in 1270 and completed only in 1315. A large square tower with no spire was erected next to the first bay of the nave.

Interior. – The main part of the church is elegant and radiant with light. The nave is surmounted by sexpartite vaulting *(see p 24).* The arches extending to the end of each double bay are supported by a thick column, and the intermediate arches by a slim pier, consisting of two colonnettes joined together. These alternating structures, pleasing to the eye, are a rare occurrence in Gothic architecture.

The chancel, flat at the east end, is extremely light (fragments of a Renaissance stained glass window) and houses several quite remarkable headstones from the 13 and the 14C, with detailed engravings : in the apse Rose des Marets, next to her husband in his knight's costume, a canon wearing a chalice, in the right aisle a deacon carrying the Gospel. The **Canons' Stalls** (Stalles) were made in 1522 and represent a series of sculpted misericords treated with great verve. In the 18C they were nearly removed from the church on account of their flippant, humorous rendering.

CHAMPIGNY-SUR-MARNE

Pop 76 260

Michelin map 101 folds 27 and 28 – Michelin plan 24

This locality occupies almost the entire loop on the south bank of the Marne. A pleasant walk can be taken upstream from Champigny Bridge.
On the heights, a monument surrounded by four cannon commemorates the sanguinary days of 30 November and 2 December 1870 when the Parisians, besieged by the Prussians, tried to break through the enemy's lines. Their unfortunate leader, General Ducrot, who had solemnly vowed to either "do or die", had to withdraw to Paris the following day, alive but beaten.

Tremblay Park (Parc du Tremblay). – This former 75 ha – 185 acre racecourse has been turned into a vast recreational area, offering many leisure activities.

Ⓥ **St-Saturnin Church (Église St-Saturnin).** – Its pleasing architecture and peaceful setting still evoke the charm of an old Champigny village. The oldest part of the building is the 12C bell tower. The 13C nave has remarkably pure lines and exudes a serene, gentle atmosphere; it is lit by means of the small round windows placed above the triforium. There are several interesting examples of foliate capitals carved with foliage typical of the Paris area. In the north side chapel, a ravishing Gothic sculpture *(Christ standing before Pilate, St Peter cutting the ear of Malchus)* serves as an altar front.

Ⓥ **National Resistance Museum (Musée de la Résistance Nationale).** – *88 Avenue Marx-Dormoy.* The role of the Resistance and the daily lives of the French are presented in chronological order, from the first Fascist incursions into France up to the Revolution.

★ CHAMPS Château

Michelin map 101 south of fold 19 – Michelin plan 20

Champs, built with the funds of two unfortunate financiers at the end of Louis XVI's reign, is characteristic of 18C architecture and decoration. In 1935, the last owner Mr Cahen d'Anvers offered his residence to the State.

TOUR *about 1 1/2 hours*

★★ **Park.** – A masterpiece of French gardening. Originally created by Claude Ⓥ Desgots, one of Le Nôtre's nephews, it was redesigned by Duchêne in the early 20C according to a plan drawn up in the early 18C, featuring a sweeping perspective of the formal French gardens with elaborate boxwood patterns, fountains and groves.

★ **Château.** – When the construction of Champs was completed by J.-B. Bullet Ⓥ in 1716, his contemporaries were struck by the many changes made in the name of comfort. The rooms no longer communicated, the corridors were improved, each bedroom had its own closet and boudoir and a proper dining room was designed (until then the tables were laid in an antechamber). Mezzanines connecting with the ground floor by means of hidden staircases were built at the end of each wing: they provided accommodation for the guests' domestics.
On the first floor, the Music Room offers a superb view of the park. One may visit Mme de Pompadour's Bedroom *(illustration p 31)* – the marquise rented the château in 1757 – and the corner drawing room, embellished by superb rococo **wainscoting★**, and the portrait by Drouais of Mme de Pompadour.
On the ground floor, visitors are shown round the grand salon, the dining room and the smoking room, where we see a portrait of Louis XV by a representative of the Van Loo school. The **Chinese Salon★★** (Salon Chinois) is decorated with ornamental panels painted by Huet. The armchairs are upholstered with Beauvais tapestry depicting scenes from the *Fables* of La Fontaine: one of the collections executed after the cartoons of Oudry, director of the Beauvais manufacture.
The visit ends with the Boudoir, tastefully decorated with attractive scenes in monochrome blue.

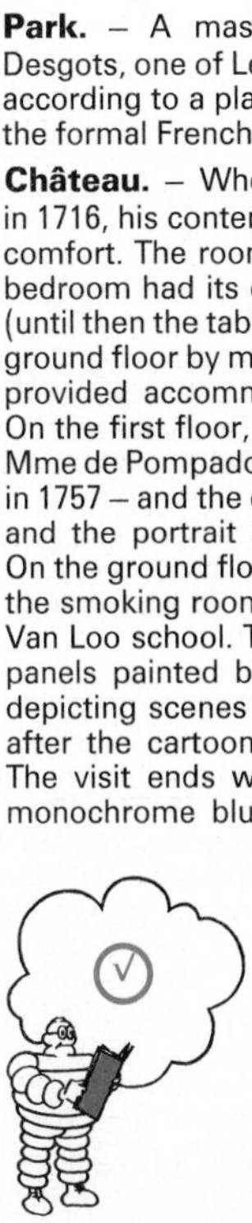

In order to give our readers the most up to date information the times and charges for admission to sights described in the guide are listed at the end of the guide.

The sights are listed alphabetically in this section either under the place – town, village or area – in which they are situated or under their proper name.

Every sight for which there are times and charges is indicated by the symbol Ⓥ in the margin in the main part of the guide.

★★★ CHANTILLY Château

Michelin map 196 fold 8

The name Chantilly brings to mind a château, a forest, a racecourse and, generally speaking, the world of horse racing. In view of its remarkable setting, its park and its museum with its treasures, the Château of Chantilly definitely deserves to feature among the major sights of France.
Chantilly is rapidly becoming an important cultural centre thanks to the activities of the *Centre des Fontaines,* whose library boasts 600000 titles (philosophy, religion, art, etc.).

HISTORICAL NOTES

From Cantilius to the Montmorency. – Over the past 2000 years, five castles have occupied this part of the Nonette Valley.
Above the ponds and marshes of this area rose a rocky island where Cantilius, a native of Roman Gaul, built the first fortified dwelling. His name and achievement gave birth to Chantilly. In the Middle Ages the building became a fortress belonging to the Bouteiller, named after the hereditary duties they carried out at the court of the Capetians. Originally in charge of the royal cellars, this Bouteiller de France was one of the king's close advisers.
In 1386 the land was bought by the chancellor of Orgemont, who had the castle rebuilt. The feudal foundations bore the three subsequent constructions. In 1450 the last descendant of the Orgemont married one of the Barons of Montmorency and Chantilly became the property of this illustrious family. It remained in their possession for 200 years.

Constable Anne, duc de Montmorency. – Anne de Montmorency (1492-1567) was a devoted servant to a succession of six French kings from Louis XII to Charles IX. This formidable personality gained a reputation as warrior, statesman, diplomat and art enthusiast. He remained the leading notability of the land after the king for forty years, excepting for a few brief periods. Childhood friend and companion-in-arms to François I, close adviser to Henri II, he even had some influence over Catherine de' Medici, who looked favourably upon the man who had cured her of sterility.
Constable Anne owned 600 fiefs, over 130 castles and estates, 4 mansions in Paris and a great many duties and offices. He was immensely wealthy. When he went to court he was escorted by 300 guards on horseback. Through his five sons and the husbands of his seven daughters he controlled most of the country's highest duties and had connections with Henri II, as well as with a number of other distinguished French families.
In 1528 the feudal castle of the Orgemont was demolished and Pierre Chambiges replaced it by a palace built in the French Renaissance style. On a nearby island Jean Bullant erected the charming château which still stands today: the Little Castle (Petit Château). It was separated from the Great Castle (Grand Château) by a moat – now filled in – which was spanned by two superimposed bridges. An aviary was set up in the tiny garden on the island. Constable Anne ordered great loads of earth and built the terrace that bears his statue. Plans were made for new gardens and the best artists in town were hired to decorate the two palaces. Chantilly had become one of the most celebrated sights of France and even Charles V expressed his admiration when he was shown round the estate.
In 1567 Montmorency, aged 75, engaged in hostilities against the Protestants and perished in the Battle of St-Denis. It was no easy task to kill this energetic soldier: five strokes of the sword cut his face to ribbons, two blows of the bludgeon smashed his head and an arquebus caused his spine to snap. Before collapsing, Constable Anne broke his opponent's jaw with the pommel of his sword.

The last love of Henri IV. – Henri IV would often take up residence at Chantilly, together with his companion-in-arms Henri I de Montmorency, the son of Constable Anne. At the age of 54 the king fell in love with his host's ravishing daughter Charlotte, aged only 15. He arranged for her to marry Henri II de Bourbon-Condé, a shy and gauche young man, whom he hoped would prove a complaisant husband. However the day after the wedding, Condé left the capital with his wife. Henri IV ordered them to return to Paris.
The young couple fled to Brussels, where they stayed under the protection of the king of Spain. Henri IV raged, implored, threatened and even went as far as to ask the Pope to intervene but he was murdered by Ravaillac. Only then did the two fugitives return to France.

Sylvie and her poets. – Henri II de Montmorency, the godson of Henri IV and the most brilliant and extravagant knight at court, married Marie-Félicie Orsini, goddaughter to Marie de' Medici. A charming, generous and highly-educated young woman, she was a close friend of the poets Mairet and Théophile de Viau. The latter – to whom she extended her protection when he was pursued by the Parlement de Paris – addressed her as Sylvie. The name remained associated with the pavilion built for Henri IV in 1604, a retreat where Marie-Félicie spent many enjoyable hours. Encouraged by Louis XIII's brother, the scheming Gaston d'Orléans, Henri de Montmorency plotted against Richelieu. He was defeated at Castelnaudary near Toulouse and made a prisoner after receiving eighteen wounds, including five by bullets. The last of the Montmorency was beheaded in Toulouse in 1632.
By way of an apology, Henri II de Montmorency bequeathed to Cardinal Richelieu the two *Slave* statues by Michelangelo, presently exhibited at the Louvre. The ones at Chantilly and Écouen are replicas. Beside herself with grief, Marie-Félicie withdrew to the Visitation convent in Moulins and remained there until her dying day.

View of Chantilly by the 17C French School (*c* 1680)

The Great Condé. – Charlotte de Montmorency and her husband the Prince of Condé – the couple persecuted by Henri IV – inherited Chantilly in 1643 and the château remained family property until 1830. Descendants of Charles de Bourbon, like Henri IV, the Princes of Condé are of royal blood and the heir apparent to the throne was called the Duke of Enghien.

The Great Condé was the son of Charlotte and Henri II. He applied himself to renovating Chantilly Château with the same energy and efficiency he had shown in military operations. In 1662 he commissioned Le Nôtre to redesign the park and the forest. The fountains at Chantilly were considered the most elegant in France and Louis XIV made a point of outclassing them in Versailles, however difficult this proved to be. The work lasted twenty years and the result was a splendid achievement, part of which still stands today.

All the great writers of the 17C stayed at Chantilly, including Bossuet, Fénelon, Bourdaloue, Boileau, Racine, La Fontaine, Mme de la Fayette, Mme de Sévigné, La Bruyère, who was tutor to the prince's grandson, and Molière, to whom Condé granted permission to perform *Tartuffe.*

The last of the Condé. – The Prince of Condé died in Fontainebleau in 1686, to the king's great dismay. During the religious ceremony preceding the burial, Bossuet delivered a funeral oration which became famous.

The great-grandson of the Great Condé, Louis-Henri de Bourbon, alias "Monsieur le Duc", was an artist with a taste for splendour. He gave Chantilly a new lease of life. He asked Jean Aubert to build the Great Stables (Grandes Écuries), a masterpiece of the 18C, and set up a porcelain factory which closed down in 1870.

The château at Enghien was built by Louis-Joseph de Condé in 1769. His grandson the Duke of Enghien, who had just been born, was its first occupant. The father of the newly-born baby was 16, his grandfather 36. The young prince died tragically in 1804: he was seized by the French police in the Duchy of Baden and shot outside the fortress of Vincennes on the orders of Bonaparte.

During the French Revolution the main building was razed to the ground while the smaller château was spared. Louis-Joseph was 78 when he returned from exile. His son accompanied him back to Chantilly and the two of them were dismayed: their beloved château was in ruins and the park was in a shambles. They decided to renovate the estate. They bought back the plots of their former land, restored the Little Château, redesigned and refurbished the grounds. The prince died in 1818 but the duke went through with the work. He was an enthusiastic hunter and used to go hunting every day at the age of 70. Thanks to his efforts, Chantilly became the lively, fashionable place it had been in the years preceding the Revolution. As in former times, the receptions and hunting parties attracted crowds of elegant visitors. The renovation and restoration work was a source of income for the local population. The duke was worried about the Revolution of 1830, which raised his cousin Louis-Philippe to the throne, and considered returning to England. A few days later, he was found hanging from a window at his castle in St-Leu. He was the last descendant of the Condé.

The Duke of Aumale. – The Duke of Bourbon had left Chantilly to his great-nephew and godson the Duke of Aumale, the fifth son of Louis-Philippe. This prince gained recognition in Africa when he captured Abd el-Kader and his numerous relations. The Revolution of 1848 forced him to go into exile and he returned only in 1870, and in 1873 he presided over the court martial that sentenced Marshal Bazaine.

From 1875 to 1881 the duke commissioned Daumet to build the Grand Château in the Renaissance style. This castle, the fifth, still stands today. Back in exile between 1883 and 1889, he died in 1897 and the Institut de France inherited his estate at Chantilly, together with the superb collections that constitute the Condé Museum.

The first races. – The first official race meeting was held in Chantilly on 15 May 1834 at the instigation of the members of the Société d'Encouragement, an association founded in 1833. The patronage of both the Duke of Orléans and the Duke of Nemours, and the fashionable trends introduced by the Jockey Club dandies, appreciative of the soft lawns, combined to make these races a major social event (*Prix du Jockey-Club* in 1836, *Prix de Diane* in 1843). One should remember that before the opening of Longchamp in 1857, Parisian races used to be run on the hard ground of the Champ-de-Mars. The hunting parties, concerts, firework displays and aquatic entertainments at Chantilly delighted racegoers and socialites.
By the end of the 19C the races had attracted huge crowds of visitors and the Railways for Northern France set up a transport system whose efficiency has never been matched. In 1908 it became necessary to introduce 40 to 50 special trains composed of 16 carriages. The regulations were seriously infringed when a group of trains taking passengers back to Paris (leaving every three minutes) were running on the wrong side of the track between Chantilly and St-Denis.

The riding capital. – With a total of over 3000 horses trained on the tracks in and around Chantilly, the city of the Condé may be considered the capital of French thoroughbreds. Jobs for 1 000 stable-lads and a number of similar occupations take up 10 % of the farming population of the Oise *département*. Each stable-lad rides three horses every morning.

The racecourses. – *Private.* 100 trainers attend to their respective charges from sunrise to noon, either on the sandy or grassy tracks of the four courses, or along the sand-covered paths of the forest (in particular the constable's road, also known as Lions' Way or Piste des Lions). A great many race meetings take place during the racing season in the month of June.

TOUR

Several roads lead to the château. If you are coming from Chapelle-en-Serval and crossing the Forest of Chantilly, you suddenly discover the château when you reach the Lions' crossroads. It appears to be floating on the water, in a superb setting of stones, ponds, lawns and stately trees. If you are coming from Paris along the N 16, do not drive through the town but turn left after the lower road and into the shady Route de l'Aigle which skirts the racecourse. Finally, if you are coming from Senlis, you get a good view of the château and its park when crossing Vineuil. From then on, turn left at each crossroads.
Go up the ramp. The 18C Enghien Château (Château d'Enghien) is set back on the right; access to it is limited to the curators whom the Institut chooses from among its own members.
One should try to picture Chantilly Château at the time of the Condé *(illustration p 47)* when the two main buildings were still divided by an arm of water: the 16C Petit Château (also called Châtelet) and the Grand Château, for which Daumet used the foundations of the former stronghold.
Cross the constable's terrace, which bears the equestrian statue of Anne de Montmorency, and enter the court of honour through the main gate, flanked by the two copies of Michelangelo's *Slaves.*

★★MUSEUM (MUSÉE)

Ⓥ To quote Raoul de Broglie, former curator of the Chantilly collections, any hope of achieving such a superb display of exhibits today would be vain, even if one enjoyed unlimited purchasing power. The layout of the museum may surprise visitors. Unlike contemporary collections, the works of art are not classified according to their period or their author. Italian and Flemish Primitive paintings are found next to 19C works and illuminations of manuscripts side by side with oil paintings.

Chantilly Château

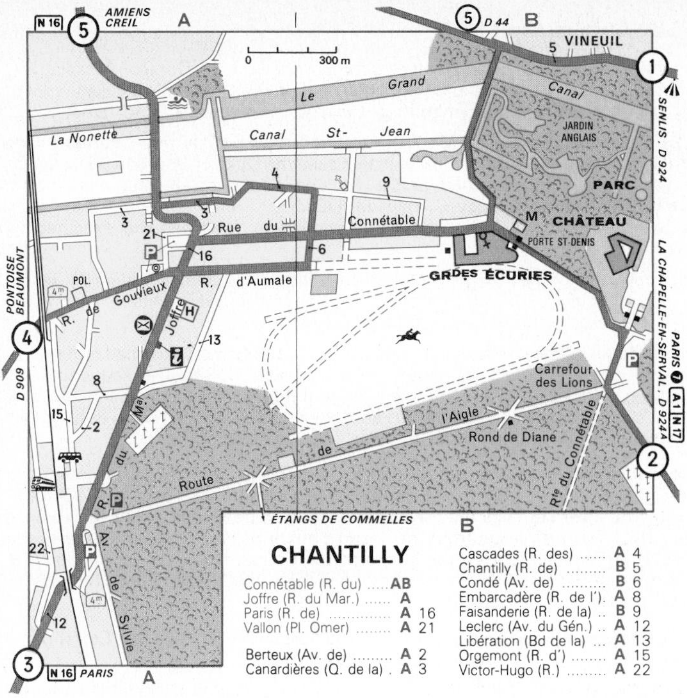

From 1852 onwards the Duke of Aumale, then in exile, turned collector and amassed his collection (the Standish library, paintings from the Dukes of Sutherland and Northwick) with a view to embellishing his future residence emptied at the Revolution. More interested in compiling an impressive collection than in founding an educational museum, the Duke of Aumale would add to his selection whenever he made a new acquisition or would devote a separate room to his favourite works. The curators have respected this layout.

According to the terms of the duke's legacy, the Institut must agree "to make no changes to the interior and exterior architecture of the château". Moreover, it is not allowed to lend any of the exhibits.

The reception hall is the starting point for guided tours of the Chapel and the various apartments – if a group has already formed, it is best to join it – as well as for unaccompanied tours of the collections. If you have started with the collections, it is advisable to interrupt your visit when the guards announce that a guided tour of the apartments is about to begin.

★ **Princes' Suite (Appartements des Princes).** – Situated in the Little Castle, this suite, occupied by the Great Condé and his descendants, was embellished with Regency and rococo **wainscoting★★**, especially in the 18C thanks to the Duke of Bourbon. It was not occupied by the Duke of Aumale who had taken up residence on the ground floor.

The antechamber and part of the library, which we owe to the Duke of Aumale, are located on the site of the old moat.

Library (Cabinet des Livres) (**1**). – Contains a splendid collection of manuscripts, including that of **The Rich Hours of the Duke of Berry** *(Les Très Riches Heures du duc de Berry)* with 15C illuminations by the Limbourg brothers. This extremely fragile document is not permanently exhibited but visitors may see a facsimile by Verlag of Lucerne. Another interesting reproduction is Gutenberg's Bible, formerly the property of Cardinal Mazarin.

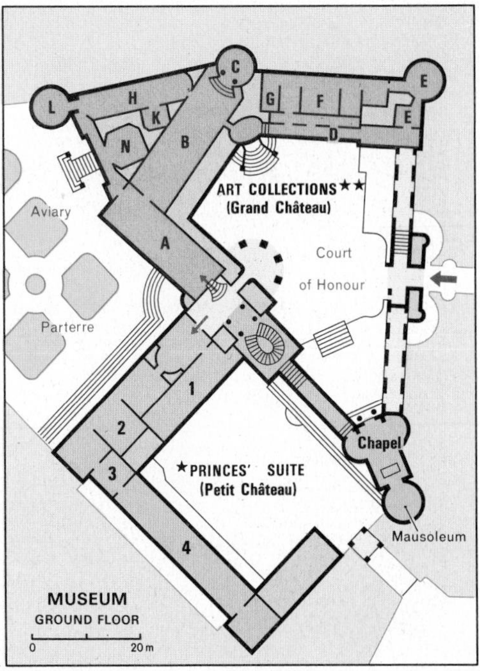

Among the ornamental motifs feature the monogram of the Duke of Aumale (H O standing for Henri d'Orléans) and the Condé coat of arms (France's "broken" coat of arms with a diagonal line symbolising the younger branch of the family).

Prince's Chamber (Chambre de Monsieur le Prince) (**2**). – This title referred to the Condé Prince who was on the throne, in this case the Duke of Bourbon (1692-1740), who had wainscoting installed at the far end of the room, into which were embedded panels painted by C. Huet in 1735.
Note the famous Louis XVI commode, designed by Riesener and executed by Hervieu.

Monkey Room (Salon des Singes) (**3**). – A collection of Monkey Scenes *(Singeries)* dating from the early 18C: a masterpiece by an anonymous draughtsman, complete with a fire screen: the Monkeys reading lesson.

Prince's Gallery (Galerie de Monsieur le Prince) (**4**). – The Great Condé had ordered his own battle gallery, which he never saw completed (1692). The sequence was interrupted from 1652 to 1659 during his years of rebellion. A painting conceived by the hero's son portrays him stopping a Fame from publishing a list of his treacherous deeds and asking another Fame to issue a formal apology.

Chapel (Chapelle). – An **altar★** attributed to Jean Goujon and 16C wainscoting and stained glass windows from the Chapel at Écouen were brought here by the Duke of Aumale. The apse contains the **mausoleum** of Henri II de Condé *(see p 47)* (bronze statues by J. Sarrazin taken from the Jesuit Church St-Paul-St-Louis in Paris) and the stone urn which received the hearts of the Condé. Up to the Revolution, the Condé necropolis was at Vallery in Burgundy, where another sepulchral monument celebrating Henri II still stands.

★★ **Art Collections (Grand Château).** – Cross the **Deer Gallery** (Galerie des Cerfs) (**A**), a reception area furnished for the Duke of Aumale.

Painting Gallery (Galerie de Peinture) (**B**). – It offers a medley characteristic of 19C work: Poussin *(The Massacre of the Innocents),* Corot *(A Pastoral Concert),* Fromentin *(Hawking),* along with De Troy's *Oyster Lunch* and Lancret's *Ham Lunch,* formerly at Versailles, in the dining room of Louis XV's private apartments,... In addition note the portraits of Mazarin and Richelieu by Philippe de Champaigne.

Rotunda (Rotonde) (**C**). – The *Loreto Madonna* by **Raphael, Piero di Cosimo's** portrait of the ravishing Simonetta Vespucci, who is believed to have been Botticelli's model for his *Birth of Venus,* and Chapu's kneeling statue of Joan of Arc listening to voices.

Logis Gallery (Galerie du Logis) (**D**). – Minor portraits painted in the French style of the 16 and 17C (Biencourt donation), including ones of Constable Anne, Henri II and Charles IX.

Smalah Hall and Minerva Rotunda (Salle de la Smalah et Rotonde de la Minerve) (**E**). – Family portraits of the Orléans (17, 18 and 19C) and of Louis-Philippe's relations in particular: Bonnat's picture of the Duke of Aumale at the age of 68.

Orléans Chamber (Salle d'Orléans) (**F**). – The glass cabinets contain **soft-paste Chantilly porcelain** manufactured in the workshops founded in 1725 (armorial service bearing the Condé coat of arms or the Duke of Orléans' monogram).

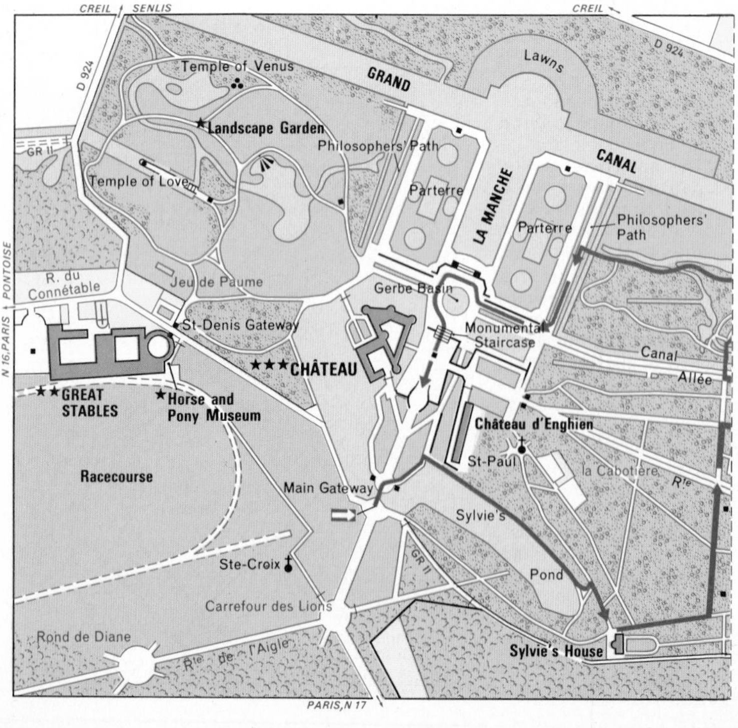

Clouet Collection (Cabinet des Clouet) (**G**). – A precious collection of small and extremely rare paintings executed by the Clouets, Corneille de Lyon, etc. portraying François I, Marguerite de Navarre (stroking a little dog), Henri II as a child, etc.

Psyche Gallery (Galerie de Psyché) (**H**). – The 44 **stained glass windows** (16C) that tell the story of the loves of Psyche and Cupid came from Constable Anne's other family home, Écouen Château. Opposite, we can admire the **Clouet drawings**★★ which are exhibited alternately as the museum possesses a total of 363 portraits.

★★★ **Sanctuary** (Sanctuaire) (**K**). – It houses the museum's most precious exhibits: Raphael's *Orléans Madonna,* named after the noble family, *The Three Ages of Womanhood,* also known as *The Three Graces,* by the same artist; *Esther and Ahasuerus,* the panel of a wedding chest painted by Filippino Lippi and last but not least forty miniature works by Jean Fouquet, cut out of Estienne Chevalier's book of hours, a splendid example of French 15C art.

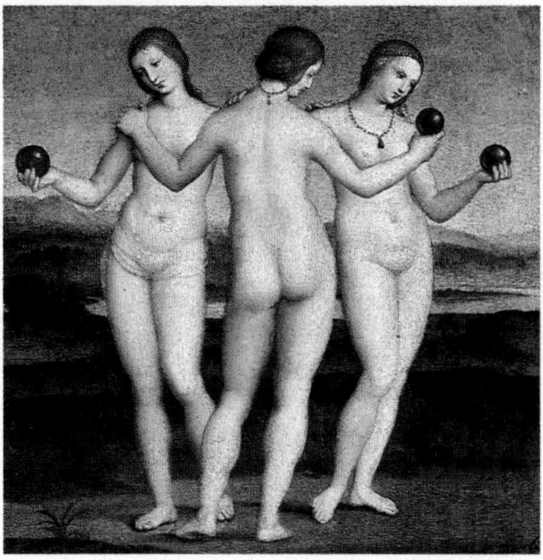

The Three Graces by Raphael, Chantilly

Jewel Room (Cabinet des Gemmes) (**L**). – It contains jewels of stunning beauty. The Pink Diamond (Diamant Rose), alias the Great Condé (of which a copy is permanently on show) was stolen in 1926 and subsequently found in an apple where the thieves had hidden it. The room also boasts an outstanding collection of enamels and miniatures.

Gallery (Tribune) (**N**). – Above the cornice of this many-sided room are painted panels representing family homes and other buildings (Aumale, Palais-Royal, Écouen, Guise, Villers-Cotterêts and Twickenham) connected with the Duke of Aumale and the house of Orléans.
The paintings include *Autumn* by **Botticelli,** *Love Disarmed* and *Pastoral Pleasures* by **Watteau,** a portrait of Molière by **Mignard,** and on the "Ecouen Wall", three superb works by **Ingres:** a self-portrait, *Madame Devaucay* and *Venus.* Amidst the portraits note Philippe de Champaigne's *Angelique Arnauld,* Abbess of Port-Royal.

★★ PARK *round tour about 1 hour*

Follow the route indicated on the plan and walk past Sylvie's Pond.

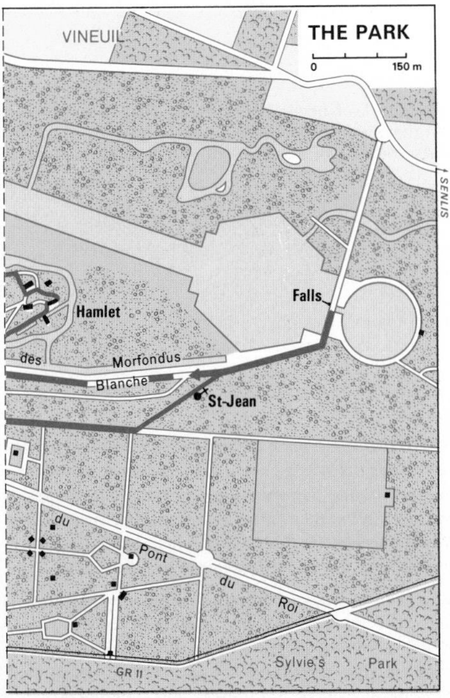

Sylvie's House (**Maison de Sylvie**). – A small garden pavilion where Marie-Félicie enjoyed meeting her close friends, surrounded by pleasant grounds. The Duke of Aumale added on a rotunda and decorated it with Louis XV panelling – depicting hunting scenes – he had brought back from his retreat in Dreux Forest, which also belonged to the Orléans family.

St-Jean Chapel (**Chapelle St-Jean**). – It was erected by Constable Anne in 1538, together with six other chapels, in memory of the seven churches of Rome he had visited in order to gain the favours accorded by this pilgrimage. He obtained from the Pope the same privileges for the chapels at Chantilly.
In addition to St-Jean, two of the other chapels still stand on the estate: St-Paul, located behind the Château of Enghien, and Ste-Croix, on the lawns of the racecourse.

Take the Allée Blanche lined with chestnut trees and follow the Canal des Morfondus going towards the falls.

Falls (La Chute). – These tiered waterfalls mark the start of the Grand Canal.

Turn around and cross the Canal des Morfondus by means of a footbridge.

Hamlet (Hameau). – Dating from 1775, it was built before the more famous Trianon. Under the influence of Jean-Jacques Rousseau, French princes used to seek new horizons by creating miniature villages.
One can visit the mill and a few half-timbered buildings. These used to accommodate the kitchen, the dining room and a billiards room. The barn provided a living room that was restored by the Duke of Aumale. All the big parties included supper in this charming spot in the park.
Skirt the brook of this small village.

Parterres. – They are framed by two avenues of stately lime trees, called "The Philosophers' Path" because the great writers who visited Chantilly used to pace up and down the shaded avenue, exchanging their views and ideas.
Le Nôtre diverted the course of the Nonette to make the Grand Canal and the Manche.
Lying in the axis of the Manche, we discover the circular Vertugadin lawns, flanked on either side by delightful stretches of water. Between the Manche and the round Gerbe basin, stands Coysevox's statue of the Great Condé, framed by the effigies of La Bruyère and Bossuet (the statues of Molière and Le Nôtre, both seated, may be seen in the near distance). An imposing flight of steps (Grand Degré) leads from the parterres up to the terrace: on either side of the staircase are grottoes with statues of the rivers.

★★ GREAT STABLES (GRANDES ÉCURIES)

Jean Aubert's masterpiece constitutes the most stunning piece of 18C architecture in Chantilly *(illustration p 29)*. The St-Denis Gateway – built astride the road leading to town – marks the site of an uncompleted pavilion. The most attractive façade of the stables faces the racecourse.
At the time of the Condé, this architectural complex housed a total of 240 horses, 500 dogs and around 100 employees (grooms, drivers, whips, etc.).

★ **Horse and Pony Museum (Musée Vivant du Cheval et du Poney).** – This museum is Ⓥ brought to life by the presentation of the stalls and boxes: built under the Duke of Aumale, they are occupied by 25 saddle and draught animals – 20 horses and 5 ponies – bred in France or in the Iberian peninsula.
In the central rotunda, 28 m – 92 ft high, admire the water playing in the **fountain,** the basin of which was once used as a trough.
The east gallery stages a demonstration of thirty international equestrian events – in hunting and sport – by means of paintings and figures made of papier mâché. The exhibition focuses on three aspects of riding: the harness, the rider's costume and the general atmosphere of the competition.
Twenty-five rooms set up in the former sheds present the art of horse riding, and a number of related professions: the blacksmith's trade, a veterinary's operating theatre, etc.
The tour ends with a demonstration of **dressage riding** *(about 1/2 hour)*. The excellent acoustics, the enchanting costume of the riding master and the comments regarding the various exercices are a strong incentive to take up riding. Equestrian entertainments on the theme "Riding and the Arts" take place in the kennels' quarry at night.

★ LANDSCAPE GARDEN

Ⓥ It was laid out on the surviving relics of Le Nôtre's park in 1820. Its charm derives from the pleasant groves (plane trees, swamp cypresses, weeping willows) rather than from the symbolic monuments: remains of a Temple of Venus and a Temple of Love.

André Le Nôtre, *a gardener of genius*

During the lifetime of Le Nôtre (1613-1700) the French formal garden acquired its definitive form. Le Nôtre's perfection of this art was a conscious intellectual pursuit, to achieve a grandeur of composition combining parterres, basins, fountains, statuary, terraces and sweeping perspectives. Describing Le Nôtre's gardens ***La Fontaine*** *said* ***"Intelligence is the very soul of these marvels".*** *In this he was a man of his time ruled by the same guiding principles as* ***Molière, Corneille, Descartes*** *and* ***Bossuet.***

Le Nôtre's masterpieces can still be seen at many of the royal residences and stately homes in Ile-de-France: ***Versailles*** *(the gardens are his undoubted masterpiece)* ***Vaux-le-Vicomte*** *(the gardens are one of his earlier works);* ***St Cloud*** *(park designed for Louis XIV's brother);* ***St Germain-en-Laye*** *(the Grand Terrace);* ***Fontainebleau*** *(the parterre);* ***Sceaux; Chantilly*** *(for the Great Condé);* ***Courances*** *and* ***Dampierre.***

CHANTILLY Forest

Michelin map 196 folds 7 and 8

This vast wooded area covers approximately 6300ha – 15500 acres of land, painstakingly regrouped by hunting enthusiasts over a period of 500 years. The present vegetation, patchy and mediocre in places owing to the poor soil and the trampling of the game, features oaks, hornbeams, lime trees and Scots pines, in copses and groves *(p 13)*. Since 1973, efforts have been made to regenerate the forest by planting copses of oak and beech seedlings. Chantilly Forest, which belongs to the Institut de France, presents an intricate network of forest roads suitable for country walks. The light, porous soil of the woodlands favour riding activities and training sessions take place at the Petit Couvert crossroads every morning. The forests of Coye, Orry and Pontarmé are for rambling only.

COMMELLES PONDS (ÉTANGS DE COMMELLES)

Round tour 7.5km – 5 miles – about 1/2 hour – avoid at weekends

Leave Coye-la-Forêt by Route des Étangs, a northbound road which follows the banks of the Thève.

The road reaches the first of the ponds, Étang de la Loge, when it draws level with Queen Blanche's Castle.

Queen Blanche's Castle (Château de la Reine Blanche). – In 1825, this old mill was restored in the troubadour style by the last of the Condé, the Duke of Bourbon, who used it as a hunting pavilion. It stands on the site of a legendary château, believed to have been built by Queen Blanche de Navarre, wife of Philippe VI of Valois, after her husband's death around 1350.
An avenue of noble beeches lining the banks completes this delightful **site★**.

Commelles Ponds (Étangs de Commelles). – They were used as fishponds by the monks from Chaâlis Abbey. The road to the north does not actually skirt the ponds but it provides access to the car parks located on the banks and to the causeways that crisscross the body of water. This makes it possible to explore the ponds on foot.

Turn right, cross the third causeway and follow the forest road – called Rocade Sud – from la Fosse to Rohan.

A clearing located half a mile away on the right is now a recreational area.

Downstream from Queen Blanche's Castle, the road skirts the Thève Valley. Return to Coye.

CHARENTON — Pop 20 689

Michelin map 101 fold 26 – Michelin plan 24

Since Roman times, 19 bridges have stood on this site, playing a key role in the defence of Paris up to Henri IV's reign.
The Archbishops of Paris owned a summer residence here, **Conflans Château**, which was once the property of the Dukes of Burgundy.The 18C wainscoting is displayed in the Carnavalet Museum *(see Green Guide to Paris)*.
The locality of Charenton, extending between the Seine and the Bois de Vincennes, was built on the Gravelle plateau which overlooks the confluence of the rivers Seine and Marne. Several underground cellars with an average temperature of 12°C – 53.6°F have been blasted out of the rough limestone quarries: they are used by the famous wine merchants Nicolas to store 6 million bottles, including some of the top quality wines from Bordeaux, Burgundy and other wine-growing regions.

★ **French Bread Museum (Musée Français du Pain)**. – *Métro: Charenton-Écoles.*
Ⓥ *25 bis, Rue Victor-Hugo. At the far end of the courtyard, to the right.*
A host of exhibits related to the history of breadmaking are gathered in a picturesque attic with a fine timberwork roof: irons for making waffles and hosts (14-19C), cake tins and bread marks. One display is devoted to the Bakers' Guild. The art of making bread is an extremely ancient profession, as demonstrated by the Egyptian loaves (2400 BC) and the corn loft (2000 BC) discovered in the graves of Egyptian dignitaries.
Note the funeral bust (600 BC) portraying a Pharaoh seated in front of 3 loaves, symbolising his daily ration, a Roman cake tin representing the goddess Victoria and bearing the abbreviated name of the first confectioner known in Rome, Dulcarius (400 BC), beautifully-sculpted dough troughs, miscellaneous engravings and documents, including household accounts giving the gastronomic expenses of Louis XIV and Catherine de' Medici.

CHARS — Pop 1 329

Michelin map 196 fold 4

Most of the villages dotted along the Viosne Valley have interesting churches. The one at Chars deserves a special mention.

Church (Église). – Built in the 12C, it was redesigned in the 13 and the 16C. The Renaissance tower dates back to 1562. The interior is on the sombre side, owing to the russet tones of the stained glass windows. The 12C and early 13C **chancel★** and its five radiating chapels are truly impressive, as is the transept, rebuilt in the 16C after the bell tower had collapsed. The arches are embellished with chevron motifs; the galleries open behind round headed arches. The upper level presents a series of rose windows, an unusual ornamental feature typical of Ile-de-France.

★★★ CHARTRES

Pop 39 243

Michelin map 196 folds 37 and 38

Chartres is the capital of Beauce, France's famous corn belt. But for tourists, the town is known mainly for its cathedral. This magnificent building reigns supreme over a picturesque setting of monuments and old streets.

★ **A bird's eye view.** – To get a good view of the cathedral dominating the Eure Valley, walk round the aviation memorial (YZ) which rises above the east bank of the Eure: the **vista**★ is truly impressive.

HISTORICAL NOTES

A town with a destiny. – Since ancient times Chartres has always had a strong influence over religious matters.

It is believed that a Gallo-Roman well located on the Chartres plateau was the object of a pagan cult. It is thought that in the 4C this was transformed into a Christian cult by the first evangelists. Adventius, the first known bishop, lived during the middle of the 4C. A document from the 7C mentions a bishop Béthaire kneeling in front of Notre-Dame, which points to the existence of a Marian cult.

In 876 the chemise belonging to the Virgin Mary was offered to the cathedral by Charles the Bald, confirming that Chartres was already a place of pilgrimage. Up to the 14C, the town of Chartres continued to flourish. Three representations of the Virgin are the subject of a special cult which has survived through the ages: Notre-Dame de Sous-Terre, Notre-Dame du Pilier, Notre-Dame de la Belle-Verrière, but the cathedral features altogether 175 different illustrations portraying Mary.

It should be noted that neither the cathedral nor the crypt contains any tombs: Chartres is a temple devoted exclusively to the Virgin, who remains protected from corruption.

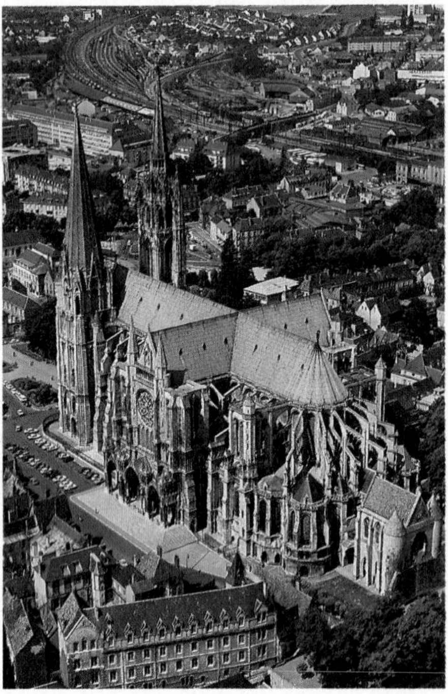

Aerial view of Chartres Cathedral

The Pilgrimage. – Consecrated to the Assumption of the Virgin in 1260, Chartres attracted huge crowds of pilgrims in the Middle Ages. The sick were housed in the northern gallery of the crypt. When the cathedral was thronged with visitors, the nave served as a shelter and provided night-time accommodation. A second statue – Notre-Dame du Pilier – was placed in the high church to pay tribute to the adoration of the faithful.

Charles Péguy made the pilgrimage to Chartres on two occasions, in 1912 and 1913. After WWI his attachment to Notre-Dame and the strong influence it had on his work, inspired a small group of enthusiasts and, after 1935, the members of the "Students' Pilgrimage" *(p 203)*.

★★★ CATHEDRAL *time: 1 1/2 hours*

The 4 000 carved figures and the 5 000 characters portrayed by the stained glass windows demanded a lifelong commitment from the specialists who studied them. The most famous expert is probably Étienne Houvet, a custodian who died in 1949: he photographed the building in minute detail.

A neat, swift construction. – The building rests upon the Romanesque cathedral erected by Bishop Fulbert in the 11 and 12C: there remain the crypt, the towers and the foundations of the west front, featuring the Royal Doorway and fragments of the Notre-Dame de la Belle-Verrière stained glass window. The remaining sections of the cathedral as it now stands were built in the wake of the Great Fire of 1194: princes and dignitaries contributed generously to the work, while the poor offered their labour. These efforts made it possible to complete the cathedral in 25 years, and to add on the north and south porches 20 years later. With the result that the architecture and decoration of Notre-Dame form a harmonious composition, almost unparalleled in the history of Gothic art. By some miracle, the Wars of Religion, the French Revolution and the two World Wars spared the famous basilica, which Rodin referred to as "The Acropolis of France" on account of its aesthetic and spiritual value. Only the cathedral's "forest" – the superb roof timbers – were destroyed by flames in 1836, and subsequently replaced by a metal framework.

EXTERIOR

West front. – The two tall spires and the Royal Doorway form one of the most perfect compositions encountered in French religious art. The New Bell Tower on the left was in fact built first. The lower part dates back to 1134. Its present name dates from the 16C, when Jehan de Beauce erected a stone spire to a height of 115m-377ft, to replace the wooden steeple which had burned down in 1506. On the right, the 106m – 348ft Old Bell Tower (*c* 1145 to 1164) is a masterpiece of Romanesque art, severe in the extreme, in sharp contrast to the florid Gothic spire *(illustrations p 22 and 23)*. The Royal Doorway and the three large windows above date from the 12C. All that surmounts this ensemble was built at a later date: the rose window (13C), the 14C gable and the king's gallery featuring the Kings of Judah, the ancestors of the Virgin. On the gable, the line of descendants ends with the Virgin offering her son to the flat expanses of the Beauce.
The **Royal Doorway**★★★ (Portail Royal), a splendid example of late Romanesque architecture (1145-1170), represents the life and triumph of the Saviour. The Christ in Majesty on the central tympanum and the statue-columns are famous throughout the world. The elongated features of the biblical kings and queens, prophets, priests and patriarchs study the visitors from the embrasures. While the faces are animated, the bodies remain terse and rigid, in deliberate contrast to the figures adorning the arches and the capitals. Statues were primarily designed to be columns, not human beings *(illustration p 22)*.

North porch and doorway. – Walk round the west front to the left then go back a few steps to get a good view. The main part of the cathedral is extremely high and unusually wide. The problem of how to support it was brilliantly resolved with the construction of three-tiered flying buttresses: the lower two arcs were joined together by colonnettes. The elegant Clock Pavilion (Pavillon de l'Horloge) near the New Bell Tower is the work of Jehan de Beauce (1520).
The ornamentation of the north porch is similar to that of the doorway, executed at an earlier date. The characters – treated more freely than those on the Royal Doorway – are elegant and extremely lively, illustrating a new, more realistic approach to religious art. The statue of St Modesta, a local martyr who is pictured gazing up at the New Bell Tower, is extremely graceful.
Once again, the decoration of the three doors refers to the Old Testament. The right door pays tribute to the biblical heroes who exercised the virtues recommended in the teachings of Christ. The central panel shows the Virgin and the Prophets announcing the coming of the Messiah. The door on the left presents the Annunciation, Visitation and Nativity, together with the Vices and Virtues.
Go through to the bishopric's garden, whose raised terrace commands a view of the town below standing on the banks of the Lower Eure. Before reaching the garden gate, look left and note the archway straddling a narrow street and communicating with the walls of the Notre-Dame cloister.

East end. – The complexity of the double-course flying buttresses – reinforced here as they cross over the chapels – and the sweeping disposition of the radiating chapels, chancel and arms of the transept are breathtakingly beautiful. The originally detached 14C St-Piat Chapel was joined to Notre-Dame by a stately staircase.

South porch and doorway. – Here, the high stonework is concealed by a constellation of colonnettes. The perspective of these planes, stretching from the arches of the porch to the gables, confers to this arm of the transept a sense of unity that is lacking in the north transept.
The theme is the Church of Christ and the Last Judgment. In the Middle Ages, these scenes would usually be reserved for the west portal but in this case the Royal Doorway already featured ornamentation. Consequently, the scenes portraying the Coming of a New World, prepared by the martyrs, were destined for the left door embrasures, while those of the Confessors (witnesses of Christ who have not yet been made martyrs) adorn the right-hand door.
Christ reigns supreme on the central tympanum. He is also present on the pier, framed by the double row of the 12 Apostles with their lean, ascetic faces, draped in long, gently folded robes.
Among the martyrs, note the statues standing in the foreground: St George and St Theodore, both admirable 13C representations of knights in armour.

South transept doorway, Chartres Cathedral

These figures are quite separate from the columns – the feet are flat and no longer slanted – and are there for purely decorative purposes.
The most delightful feature of the sculpted porch is the display of medallions, grouped in sets of six and placed on the recessed arches of the three doorways: the lives of the martyrs, the Vices and Virtues, etc.
Returning to the west front, note the the Old Bell Tower and its ironical statue of a donkey playing the fiddle, symbolising man's desire to share in celestial music. At the corner of the building, stop to admire the tall figure of the sundial Angel.

★ **Access to New Bell Tower.** – The tour (195 steps) takes you round the north side and leads up to the lower platform of the New Bell Tower. Seen from a height of 70m – 230 ft, the buttresses, flying buttresses, statues, gargoyles and Old Bell Tower are truly impressive. It is still possible to recognise the former Notre-Dame Cloister thanks to the old pointed roofs. Enclosed by a wall right up to the 19C, this quarter was frequented by clerics and especially canons.

INTERIOR

Enter the cathedral by the Royal Doorway. The main nave (16m – 52ft) is wider than any other in France (Notre-Dame in Paris 40ft, Notre-Dame in Amiens 46ft). However, it has single aisles. The vaulting reaches a height of 37m – 121ft and the interior is 130m – 427ft long. This nave is 13C built in the style known as early or lancet Gothic: the gallery has disappeared but has been replaced by a blind triforium *(illustration p 24)*.
Seeing that Notre-Dame was a noted place of pilgrimage, the chancel and the transept had to accommodate large-scale ceremonies; they were therefore wider than the nave. In Chartres, the chancel, its double ambulatory and the transept form an ensemble 64m – 210ft wide, stretching from north to south.
A vigilant eye will immediately notice the gentle slope of the floor, rising slightly towards the chancel. This made it easier to wash down the church when the pilgrims had stayed overnight.
As soon as one enters, one is struck by the state of semi-darkness prevailing in the nave. This creates an element of mystery which was by no means intentional: it can be ascribed to the gradual dimming of the stained glass windows over the centuries.

★★★ **Stained glass windows.** – The 12 and 13C stained glass windows of Notre-Dame constitute, together with those of Bourges, the most important collection in France.
The Virgin and Child and the Annunciation and Visitation scenes adorning the tall windows at the far end of the chancel produce a striking impression.

The Three Kings (detail),
Central Window of West Front,
Chartres Cathedral

West front. – These three 12C windows used to throw light on Fulbert's Romanesque cathedral and the dark, low nave that stood behind, which explains why they are placed so high. The scenes – read from bottom to top – illustrate the fulfilment of the prophecies: on the right the Tree of Jesse, in the centre the childhood and life of Our Lord (Incarnation cycle) and on the left Passion and Resurrection (Redemption cycle). Visitors may feast their eyes on the famous 12C "Chartres blue", whose clear, deep tones are enhanced by reddish tinges, especially radiant in the rays of the setting sun. For many years, people believed that this particular shade of blue was a trade secret. Modern laboratories have now established that the sodium compounds and silica in the glass made it more resistant to dirt and corrosion than the panes made with other materials and in other times.
The large 13C rose window on the west front depicts the Last Judgment.

Transept. – This ensemble consists of two 13C rose windows, to which were added a number of lancet windows featuring tall figures. The themes are the same as those on the corresponding sculpted doorway: Old Testament (north), the End of the World (south).
The north rose (rose de France) was a present from Blanche of Castile, mother of St Louis and Regent of France, and portrays a Virgin and Child. It is characterised by the fleur-de-lis motif on the shield under the central lancet and by the alternating Castile towers and fleurs-de-lis pictured on the small corner lancets. The larger lancets depict St Anne holding the infant Virgin Mary, framed by four kings or high priests: Melchisidek and David stand on the left, Solomon and Aaron on the right.
The centre roundel of the south rose shows the risen Christ, surrounded by the Old Men of the Apocalypse, forming two rings of medallions. The yellow and blue chequered quatrefoils represent the coat of arms of the benefactors, the comte de Dreux Pierre Mauclerc and his wife, who are also featured at the bottom of the lancets.

The lancets on either side of the Virgin and Child picture four striking figures – the Great Prophets Isaiah, Jeremiah, Ezekiel and Daniel – with the four Evangelists seated on their shoulders. The morality of the scene is simple: although they are weak and lacking dignity, the Evangelists can see further than the giants of the Old Testament thanks to the Holy Spirit.

★ **Notre-Dame de la Belle-Verrière** (1). – An extremely famous stained glass window. The Virgin and Child, a fragment of the original 12C window, has been mounted in 13C stained glass *(illustration p 27)*. Admire the superb range of blues.

Other stained glass windows. – The aisles of the nave and the chapels around the ambulatory are lit by a number of celebrated stained glass windows from the 13C *(see p 27)* verging on the sombre side. On the east side, the arms of the transept have received two works of recent making, in perfect harmony with the early fenestration: St Fulbert's window (south crossing 2), donated by the American Association of Architects from the François Lorin workshop – 1954), and the window of Peace (north crossing 3), a present from a group of German admirers (1971). In the Vendôme Chapel (4), one is struck by the radiance of a 15C stained glass window. It illustrates the development of this art, which eventually led to the lighter panes of the 17 and 18C.

★★ **Parclose screen.** – Started by Jehan de Beauce in 1514, it was finished in the 18C. An admirable piece of work, consisting of 41 sculpted compositions depicting the lives of Christ and the Virgin. These Renaissance medallions, evoking Biblical history, local history and mythology, contrast sharply with the Gothic statues of the doorways.

Choir. – The marble facing, the Assumption group above the high altar and the low reliefs separating the columns were added in the 18C.

Organ (5). – The case dates from the 16C.

Virgin of the Pillar (Vierge du Pilier) (6). – This wooden statue (*c* 1510) used to lean against the rood screen, now sadly disappeared. The richly clothed Virgin is the object of a procession celebrated annually *(see chapter on Principal Festivals at the end of the guide)*.

ⓥ **The Treasure.** – St-Piat Chapel was designed to receive the treasure of the cathedral. The reliquary – presented in the form of a glass cabinet – displays the Virgin's Robes, which the faithful pilgrims of the past saw as a "Sacred Chemise". One may also admire some beautiful liturgical objects, engraved belts from the 17C, threaded with sea shells by converted Indians, and remains of the 13C rood screen, destroyed in the 18C.

★ **Crypt.** – *The entrance is outside the cathedral, on the south side (see plan below).*
ⓥ This is France's longest crypt (220m – 722ft long). Generally speaking, it dates from the 11C and features Romanesque groined vaulting. It has a curious shape: the two long galleries joined by the ambulatory pass under the choir and the nave and give onto seven chapels. The central area, which has been filled in, remains unexplored. Of the seven radiating chapels, only three are Romanesque. The other four were added by the master architect of the Gothic cathedral to serve as foundations for the chancel and the apse of the future building.

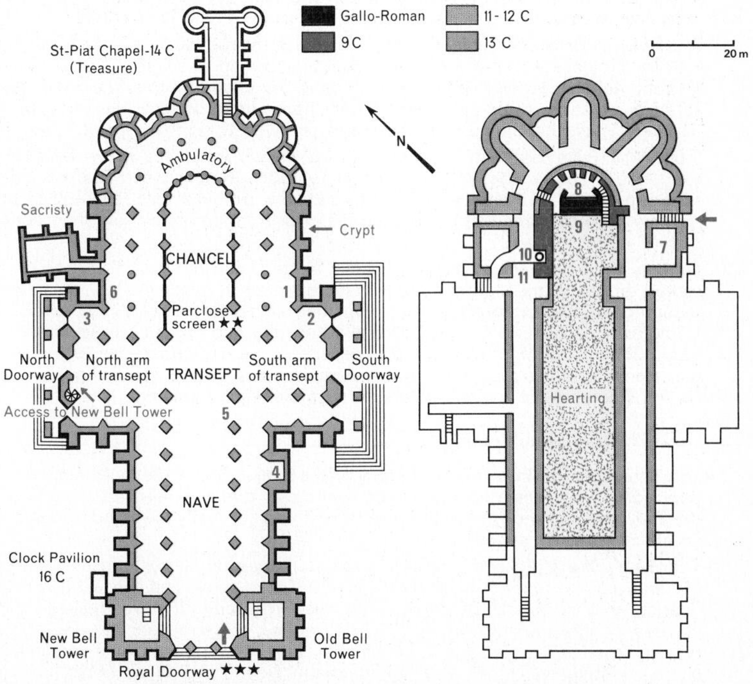

CATHEDRAL ★★★ CRYPT ★

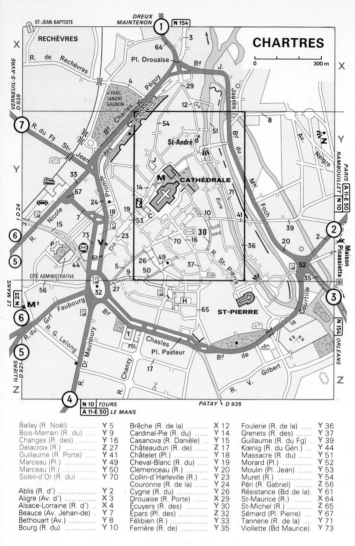

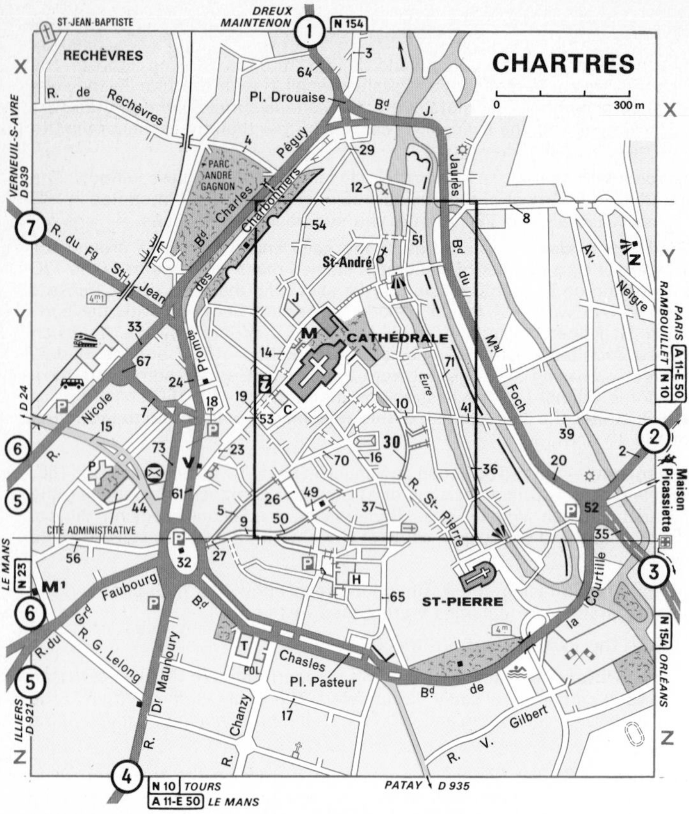

Ballay (R. Noël)	Y 5	Brêche (R. de la)	X 12	Foulerie (R. de la)	Y 36
Bois-Merrain (R. du)	Y 9	Cardinal-Pie (R. du)	Y 14	Grenets (R. des)	Y 37
Changes (R. des)	Y 16	Casanova (R. Danièle)	Y 15	Guillaume (R. du Fg)	Y 39
Delacroix (R.)	Z 27	Châteaudun (R. de)	Z 17	Kœnig (R. du Gén.)	Y 44
Guillaume (R. Porte)	Y 41	Châtelet (Pl.)	Y 18	Massacre (R. du)	Y 51
Marceau (Pl.)	Y 49	Cheval-Blanc (R. du)	Y 19	Morard (Pl.)	Y 52
Marceau (R.)	Y 50	Clemenceau (R.)	Y 20	Moulin (Pl. Jean)	Y 53
Soleil-d'Or (R. du)	Y 70	Collin-d'Harleville (R.)	Y 23	Muret (R.)	Y 54
		Couronne (R. de la)	Y 24	Péri (R. Gabriel)	Z 56
Ablis (R. d')	Y 2	Cygne (R. du)	Y 26	Résistance (Bd de la)	Y 61
Aligre (Av. d')	X 3	Drouaise (R. Porte)	X 29	St-Maurice (R.)	X 64
Alsace-Lorraine (R. d')	X 4	Écuyers (R. des)	Y 30	St-Michel (R.)	Z 65
Beauce (Av. Jehan-de)	Y 7	Épars (Pl. des)	Z 32	Sémard (Pl. Pierre)	Y 67
Bethouart (Av.)	Y 8	Félibien (R.)	Y 33	Tannerie (R. de la)	Y 71
Bourg (R. du)	Y 10	Ferrière (R. de)	Y 35	Viollette (Bd Maurice)	Y 73

Descending towards the south gallery, one can see the originals of the statues on the Royal Doorway, gathered in St Martin's Chapel (7): the sundial Angel, etc. A staircase, starting from the ambulatory, leads down to a lower crypt.

St Lubin Crypt (Crypte St-Lubin) (8). – This served as the foundations of the 9C church. A thick, circular column with a visible base is supported by a Gallo-Roman wall (9), its bond easily recognisable by the alternating bricks and mortar. The crypt was a safe place that protected the cathedral treasures in times of social unrest or natural disaster. Thus, the Chemise of the Virgin survived the Great Fire of 1194.

Saints' Well (Puits des Saints-Forts) (10). – The lower part of this 33m – 108ft-deep shaft has a square section characteristic of Gallo-Roman wells. The coping is contemporary. The name dates back to 858: it is believed that several Christian martyrs from Chartres were murdered during a Norman attack, and their bodies thrown down the well.

Our Lady of the Underground Chapel (Chapelle Notre-Dame de Sous-Terre) (11). – A sacred retreat where pilgrims indulge in fervent praying. Since the 17C, the chapel, together with the north gallery of the crypt, has played the part of miniature church. It originally consisted of a small alcove where the faithful came to venerate the Virgin. The interior of the chapel and its decoration were refurbished in 1976. On this occasion, the 19C statue of the Virgin was replaced by a more hieratic figure, based on the Romanesque model, enhanced by a Gobelins tapestry.

ADDITIONAL SIGHTS

★ **Old Chartres (St-André Quarter and banks of the Eure).** – *Follow the route indicated on plan p 59.* This pleasant walk takes you past the picturesque hilly site, the banks of the Eure River, an ancient quarter recently restored and lastly the cathedral which is visible from every street corner.

St Andrew's Church (Église St-André). – This Romanesque church, presently desecularised, was the place of worship of one of the most active and densely-populated districts in town. Most of the trades were closely related to the river: millers, dyers, curriers, cobblers tanners, drapers, fullers, tawers, serge makers, etc. The church was enlarged in the 13C, and in the 16 and 17C it received a chancel and an axial chapel, resting on arches that straddled the Eure and Rue du Massacre. Unfortunately, both these structures disappeared in 1827.

Cross the Eure by a footbridge (**B**): enjoy the nice **view★** of the old hump backed bridges. At the foot of the dilapidated nave of St Andrew's lie the remains of the arch that once supported the chancel. Wander upstream: the wash houses and races of former mills have been prettily restored. Rue aux Juifs leads you through an ancient quarter which has recently been renovated, featuring paved streets bordered by gable-ended houses and old-fashioned street lamps.

Rue des Écuyers (**30**). – One of the most successful restoration schemes of the old town. At nos 17 and 19 the houses have 17C doorways with rusticated surrounds, surmounted by a bull's eye window. Stroll down the street until you reach Rue aux Cois. The corner building is a delightful half-timbered villa (**E**), with an overhang in the shape of a prow. Opposite stands the turret of Reine Berthe's staircase (**F**), a 16C structure, also half-timbered.

ⓥ **Loëns Loft (Grenier de Loëns)** (**S**). – From the 12C onwards, this half-timbered barn with treble gables – located in the courtyard of the old chapter house – was used to store the wine and cereals offered to the clergy as a tithe. Recently renovated for the International Stained Glass Centre, which organises stained glass exhibitions, the building now features a large hall with beautifully-restored roof timbering on the ground floor and a magnificent 12C cellar with three naves.

ⓥ **Museum of Fine Arts (Musée des Beaux Arts)** (**M**). – It occupies the former Episcopal Palace, built in several stages between 1620 and 1780. The reception rooms (now the painting gallery featuring Zurbaran's *St Lucy*) flanking the main entrance and especially the suite belonging to the bishops, ornamented with rich tapestries, provide a choice setting for the museum's exhibits. A group of glass cabinets display miscellaneous souvenirs left by General Marceau.
The 12 large **enamels★** by Léonard Limosin, representing the 12 Apostles, were commissioned by François I in 1545. They were a present from Henri II to Diane de Poitiers, intended for her Anet residence.
A collection of contemporary glasswork includes the molten glass bust of the philosopher Émile-Auguste Chartier better known as Alain (1868-1951), executed by Navarre.
The Italian Parlour, which acts as anteroom to the chapel, houses a late 14C wayside cross: the four-lobed openwork medallion depicts the peaceful death of St Francis. The new exhibition rooms of the museum host temporary shows of modern art. They also contain a collection of works by Vlaminck, bequeathed to the museum. These illustrate the painter's penchant for the Perche area, where he settled in 1925 (note in particular the picture named *The Haystacks*).

Ballay (R. Noël)	5	Herbes (R. aux)	42
Bourg (R. du)	10	Petite Cordonnerie (R. de la)	57
Brêche (R. de la)	12	Pied Plat (Tertre du)	59
Cardinal-Pie (R. du)	14	Poissonnerie (Pl. de la)	60
Cheval-Blanc (R. du)	19	St-Éman (R.)	63
Çois (R. aux)	22		
Écuyers (R. des)	30		

Rue du Cygne. – The street has been widened into a little square planted with trees and shrubs (flower market on Tuesdays, Thursdays and Saturdays) and is at present an oasis of calm in this lively shopping district in the town centre.
At the end of Rue du Cygne, on Place Marceau, a monument celebrates the memory of the young local general who died at Altenkirchen (1796) at the age of 27. His ashes have been shared among Chartres (funeral urn under the statue on Place des Epars), the Panthéon and the Dome Church of the Invalides in Paris.

Jean Moulin's Memorial (Monument de Jean Moulin) (**Y V** *on plan p 58*). – The *préfet* of Chartres during the German invasion, Jean Moulin braved the enemy on 17 June 1940 when, despite having been tortured, he refused to sign a document claiming that the French troops had committed a series of atrocities. Afraid of dishonouring his country, he attempted to commit suicide. Jean Moulin was dismissed by the Vichy government in November 1940 and, from then on, he planned and coordinated underground resistance, working in close collaboration with General de Gaulle. Arrested in Lyons on 21 June 1943, he did not survive the harsh treatment he received from the Gestapo. He was buried with great pomp in the Panthéon in December 1964.

★ **St Peter's Church (Église St-Pierre)** (Z). – This 12 and 13C Gothic church used to belong to the Benedictine abbey of St-Père-en-Vallée. The porch-bell tower dates from pre-Romanesque times. The Gothic **stained glass windows★** can be traced back to a period that is not represented in Chartres Cathedral: the late 13C and early 14C, before the widespread introduction of yellow staining *(p 27)*.
The oldest glass windows are those adorning the south bays of the chancel, portraying tall, hieratic figures from the Old Testament. The stained glass panes of the semicircular chancel, offering the most vivid tones, were mounted around 1300. Here the characters have been treated more freely.
The last windows to be painted were those of the nave (*c* 1305-1315). They feature an alternation of medaillions and religious figures (apostles, bishops, abbots).

⊙ **School Museum (Musée de l'École)** (Z M[1]). – A classroom belonging to the old École Normale (teachers' training college) houses educational material and furniture evoking the schools of yesteryear: abacuses, magic lanterns using paraffin, books advocating humanist ethics, a collective money-bank with a separate compartment for each pupil, etc.

⊙ **Picassiette House (Maison Picassiette)** (Y). – Built and decorated by Raymond Isidore (1900-1964), this house offers an amazing medley of naive art. A number of monuments and a great many religious scenes are suggested by mosaic compositions made with extremely diverse materials: pieces of crockery, fragments of tinted glass, dollops of cement, etc. Visitors are given a complete tour of the house, including the "chapel", the Black Courtyard (tomb crowned by a replica of Chartres Cathedral), the summer house (frescoes): the garden is dotted with statues and features a large-scale mosaic depicting the town of Jerusalem.

CHÂTEAU-LANDON Pop 3 011

Michelin map 61 fold 12 – 15km – 9 1/2 miles south of Nemours

This small Gâtinais town is believed to be the cradle of the Plantagenet dynasty: Henry II, King of England in 1154, was a descendant of Foulques le Réchin, who was born at Château-Landon in 1043.
The excellent, tough limestone rock one finds around Souppes and Château-Landon served to build Notre-Dame Church; it was also used for the construction of many 19C monuments in Paris: the main staircases at the Sorbonne and the Bibliothèque Nationale, stone flooring of the Panthéon, etc.

SIGHTS

★ **The site.** – The best way to approach Château-Landon is from Dordives, along the D 43, or from Ferrières, along the D 32.
When you have crossed the bridge spanning the first arm of the river, park the car and take a walk round to appreciate this fortified site, rendered even more impressive by the stonework of **St-Séverin Abbey,** supported by massive buttresses. The towers and the buttresses of this abbey date back to the 13C. There are 11C frescoes in the chapel.
Go back to the car. Cross the bridge over the second arm of the Fusain and turn right into Rue du Bas-Larry, which follows the retaining wall of the abbey. Take the steep streets that skirt the abbey (14 and 16C) and then proceed along Rue de la Ville Forte, which leads you to the old curtain wall.

Place du Larry. – This shaded terrace gives onto Place du Marché and offers a superb panorama of the southern quarter of the town and its distinctive landmarks: the round "Solicitor's Tower", St-Thugal Tower – the remains of a Romanesque church incorporated into the outer wall – lastly the old St-Séverin Abbey, occupying the point of the fortified spur.

Notre-Dame Church (Église Notre-Dame). – An easy sight to spot on account of its open-work, ethereal 15C tower and its arches opening onto the skies. Stand at the far end of Place du Marché to enjoy the view of the bell tower soaring above the Romanesque east end.

EXCURSION

Gâtinais porches circuit, via Puiseaux. – *47km – 30 miles – allow 3 hours. Leave Château-Landon to the west, by the road to Beaumont and Boësse.*

In the triangle formed by Puiseaux, Château-Landon and Nemours, a number of Gâtinais villages possess simple country churches, built along identical lines: a single nave, a semicircular apse and a bell tower with a saddle-back roof. *Most of these churches are closed.*
Several of the churches are fronted by stone porches accommodating a gallery of arcades and covered by a single sloped roof. These porches were probably all built around the same time during the 12C. They remind one of the strong sense of community that prevailed among villagers in past times.

Mondreville. – Pop 280. Beautiful Romanesque **porch★**, with lateral openings.

Boësse. – Pop 287. In the 17C, the village set on a slight mound with its winding streets was qualified as "a sort of walled hamlet". The church is surrounded by flower beds and fronted by a huge porch reminiscent of a cloister gallery.

Proceed towards Puiseaux, via Echilleuses.

Along one of the ridges of this plateau, to the right, stands the village of Bromeilles, where a few tiny vineyards are still cultivated by local growers.

Puiseaux. – Pop 2 610. This busy cereal market of the Gâtinais area used to have a priory, an offshoot of St-Victor Abbey in Paris, a famous centre for medieval theology, of which it still bears the emblem. The 13C church presents a strangely twisted spire (65m – 213ft) which dominates the countryside. The Town Hall gardens afford a view of the bell tower and the southern façade, restored and fitted with a new aisle in the 15C.
The main part of the church, with pointed vaulting, features an elegant transept, a rose window and the remains of a triforium. The keystone above the transept crossing presents two twin representations of the Puiseaux coat of arms: the official blazon of St-Victor Abbey and a more popular version depicting a well and a bucket. In the north aisle, a chapel used as an oratory contains a 16C **Holy Sepulchre★**

CHÂTENAY-MALABRY — Pop 28 582

Michelin map 101 folds 24 and 25 – Michelin plan 22

It is believed that Voltaire was born in Châtenay in 1694. There remain several houses dating from the 17 and 18C. Part of the wooded valley (many tree nurseries) is now occupied by the park of the **Vallée-aux-Loups** an estate where Chateaubriand lived from 1807 to 1817.

★ **St-Germain-l'Auxerrois Church (Église St-Germain-l'Auxerrois).** – *2 Rue du Lavoir.* The parish church and its splendid Romanesque bell tower have survived on the old village square. The 11C building – redesigned in the 13C – has undergone serious restoration work, which has given it a new lease of life. Under pointed vaulting of the utmost simplicity, we find the chancel, consisting of a single square-shaped bay and lit by the rays of sun filtering through a modern stained glass window. The central nave, with a fine timber roof resting on joists, has remarkably pure lines. The nave and the choir present a superb collection of crocket capitals, while the small bay to the left of the chancel features historiated capitals depicting unusual or unsophisticated scenes. The elegant spiral staircase leading up to the bell tower is made of chestnut *(châtaignier)*, a tree which gave its name to the commune.

★ **Chateaubriand's House: Vallée-aux-Loups (Maison de Chateaubriand).** – ⓥ *87 Rue Chateaubriand.* Owing to the article published by *Mercure de France* in 1807, in which he spoke out against Napoléon's tyrannical reign, **François-René de Chateaubriand** (1768-1848) was forced to leave the French capital. The author of *The Genius of Christianity* and *Atala* acquired Wolves' Valley estate, a modest cottage located in a clearing surrounded by fallow land, within a stone's throw of the Paris gateway, Porte d'Orléans.
In the company of his wife, Chateaubriand spent ten happy, peaceful years at Châtenay. All his efforts were aimed at embellishing the estate and perfecting his writer's talents. Thanks to his friends' generosity, he abolished the copses – which had yielded only one beautiful tree, an acacia – and created a "literary park" which evoked his travels round the world: cedars of Lebanon, swamp cypresses from Virginia, magnolia trees, reeds from the Nile, etc. In *Memories from beyond the Grave,* Chateaubriand reveals that he cherished these trees, even wrote odes to them, and thought of them as his family.
This author was also a proficient architect: onto the brick façade, he added an antique portico supported by two caryatids and two columns made of grey marble. It soon became a popular meeting-place: Chateaubriand entertained his friends and delivered readings of his recent works. This tradition was to continue at Mme Récamier's salons at Abbaye-aux-Bois. Chateaubriand had always served the Bourbons loyally, and they in turn had showered him with praise. However, when he spoke up against Decazes, Louis XVIII's favourite, they cut off his allowance, plunging him into dire financial straits. Broken-hearted, he had no alternative but to sell to Mathieu de Montmorency. The new owner was a friend of Mme Récamier, who paid frequent visits to the estate between 1818 and 1826.

Chateaubriand's house at Châtenay-Malabry

The interior has been refurbished to look just like it did at the time of Chateaubriand and Mme Récamier, complete with souvenirs, engravings, manuscripts and some fine pieces of furniture. Note the **récamier** or couch where Mme Récamier posed for David and the staircase with double flights of steps designed by Chateaubriand. A 25 min videotape presents a biography of the artist, revolving around his work and the houses he occupied.
The façade is fronted by a vast lawn, surrounded by tall, stately trees, some of which were planted by the author himself. One can glimpse Velleda Tower, which Chateaubriand used as a library.

CHAUMONT-EN-VEXIN — Pop 2 697

Michelin map 55 south of fold 9

Chaumont-en-Vexin developed around the site of a former stronghold and played a key role in the country's defence against the Duke of Normandy and, later, the Anglo-Norman dynasty, up to the end of the Hundred Years War. Today, Chaumont is just a large county town, dominated by its church.

★ **St John the Baptist's Church (Église St-Jean-Baptiste).** – The church on the hillside rises well above the tree tops. The only means of access is a 14C flight of stone steps starting from the town centre. While the actual church (16C) was built in Flamboyant Gothic, the only tower – added on later – is characteristic of Renaissance architecture. The north portal offers a felicitous combination of Flamboyant gables and recessed arches with a Renaissance tympanum.
The interior is remarkable for its radiance and the delicacy of both the arches and the vaulting.

★ CHEVREUSE — Pop 4 823

Michelin map 101 fold 31 – Local map p 53

Dominated by the remains of the old castle, this hamlet lies in an attractive **site★** in a protected part of the countryside called Chevreuse Valley, also known as Yvette Valley. Chevreuse has kept its provincial charm, especially around the small market square (Place des Halles).
In the 16C, the fief of Chevreuse became the property of the Guise family. The last of the Guise to hold the title, duc de Chevreuse was Claude de Lorraine, who was also lord of Dampierre.
He married Marie de Rohan, who had become the widow of Constable de Luynes, Louis XIII's favourite, at the age of 21. The new Duchess of Chevreuse, a close friend of Anne of Austria, played a key role at court, both as politician and courtisane. Richelieu and Mazarin went to great pains to uncover her many intrigues and she was exiled on three separate occasions. After the death of her second husband, who had given her no child, the duchess ceded Chevreuse to the duc de Luynes, the son from her first marriage. This enterprising woman died at the age of 79, in a state of humility and penance. In 1692 the Duchy was bought by Louis XIV, who generously financed the St-Cyr School for the daughters of poor but noble families founded by Mme de Maintenon. Dampierre then replaced Chevreuse as the ducal seat and the castle slipped into a state of neglect.

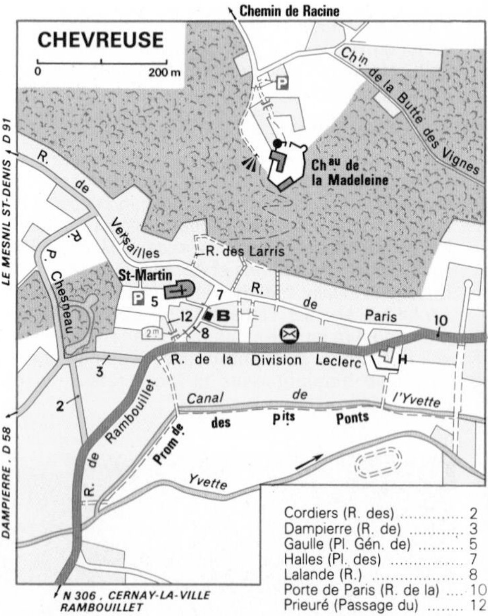

Racine's Lane (Chemin de Racine). – Racine's uncle, a certain M. Vitart, was the intendant of Chevreuse. In 1661 he summoned his nephew to the estate to supervise the restoration work under way at the castle. Racine was intensely bored during this period of "captivity" and he headed all his correspondance Babylonia. He consoled himself by frequenting the Cabaret du Lys (**B**), which still stands at no 3 Rue Lalande (plaque).
The young poet enjoyed walking through the woods to Port-Royal. In 1939 – the tercentenary of Racine's birth – this route was marked with commemorative plaques, each bearing two verses of poetry. The lane runs from the castle to St-Lambert-des-Bois on the D 46 (half a mile).

SIGHTS

St Martin's Church (Église St-Martin). – *When you reach the main crossroads in town, take Passage du Prieuré, a narrow, covered street which leads directly to the car park. Enter on the right side.*
The church was built with honey-coloured millstone and although its construction was spread over 5 centuries (12 to 17C), the architecture has not suffered. The noble 12C bell tower ends in a slate steeple. The carved panels on the west doorway were taken from Port-Royal Abbey. The interior presents a splendid chancel with an ambulatory, an extremely rare feature among country churches. The remains of some late 16C stained glass windows, set in modern borders, are to be found in the central part of the apse *(Crucifixion, Annunciation)*. There are two wooden figures of Christ: one on the high altar, and a 16C one near the entrance to the sacristy. The organ, by L.A. Cliquot in 1732, features a typically French-style case and a loft decorated with 18C panelling. The impressive open-work staircase is 15C.

Madeleine Castle (Château de la Madeleine). – One can get there by car if one follows the steep road signposted from no 30 Rue Porte-de-Paris. Of the eight perimeter towers – 5 were round and 3 were square – only four remain. The oblong-shaped 11C keep lost its parapet but was subsequently crowned with a saddle-back roof: it is misleading when seen from a distance as it strongly resembles a chapel. The Guards' Tower (Tour des Gardes) on the right has kept its machicolations and its three superimposed chambers supported by a central column. The castle stands in a very pleasant setting. A public footpath will lead you back to the village.

Promenade des Petits-Ponts. – A picturesque walk runs along the banks of the Yvette Canal, where there were once 22 tanneries. The municipal wash house, recently restored, has retained its old-fashioned charm.

★ CHEVREUSE Valley

Michelin map 196 folds 28 and 29

The Upper Yvette Valley – also known as Chevreuse Valley – was urbanised at an extremely rapid pace. The better-preserved sites are located upstream from the village of Chevreuse. Founded in 1984, the **Upper Chevreuse Valley Regional Nature Park★** (Parc Naturel Régional de la Haute Vallée de Chevreuse) with its headquarters in Dampierre-en-Yvelines, covers a total of 25600ha – 63260 acres, representing 19 communes of the Yvelines *département*. This vast stretch of land on the outskirts of Paris is one of the best protected rural sites against the evils of urban sprawl. The plateau – a combination of forests and arable land – is cut by steep gorges overgrown with lush greenery. The park aims to preserve and improve France's rural landscape and architectural heritage, to promote agriculture and commerce without spoiling the countryside and to encourage people to learn about their own history and natural surroundings. The Chevreuse Valley offers a number of châteaux (Dampierre, Breteuil), Port-Royal-des-Champs Abbey, the Yvelines Wildlife Park and a network of footpaths for rambling enthusiasts.

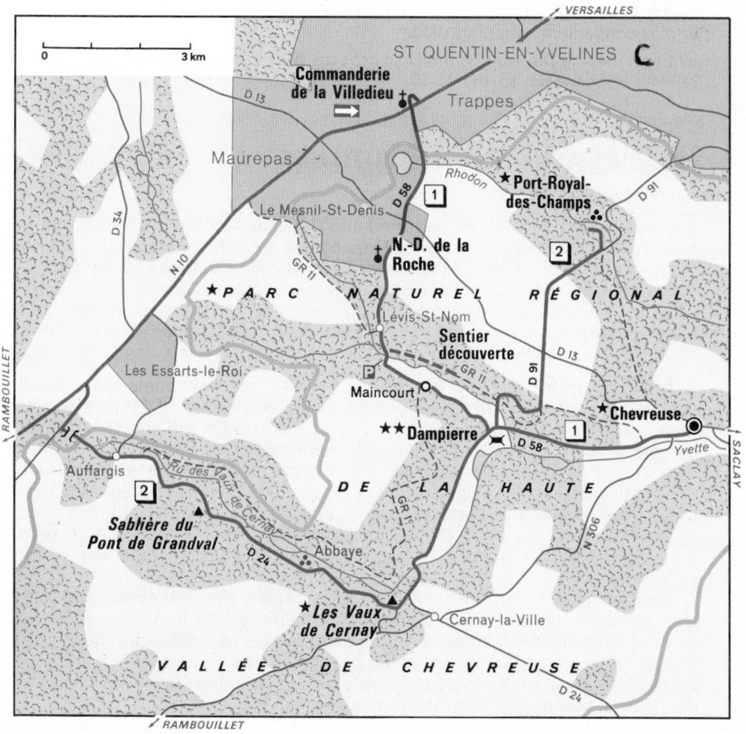

1 FROM THE N 10 TO CHEVREUSE

via the Yvette Valley

12km –7.5 miles – about 1 1/2 hours.

If you are coming from Versailles, leave the N 10 and proceed towards the commandery at Villedieu (link road on the right).

Villedieu Commandery. – *Description p 162.*

Turn left; take the bridge spanning the N 10 and follow directions to Le Mesnil-St-Denis.

⊙**Notre-Dame de la Roche.** – The 13C church of this former priory has been enlarged, and the priory itself made into a horticultural school. The north transept houses the funeral vault of the Lévis-Mirepoix family, installed in the 19C. The three statues portraying the ancestors of the dynasty – presently exhibited in the choir – constitute a fine example of 13C sepulchral art: Guy de Lévis I, companion-in-arms to Simon de Montfort during the crusade against the Albigensians, where he was proclaimed Marshal of the Faith, his son and Guy de Lévis III.

Follow the D 58 and cross the Yvette; you may park the car on the right after the first crossroads.

Discovering Maincourt. – *Explanations are provided by the board at entrance; leaflet from the visitor centre in Dampierre and at the Tourist Information Centre at St-Rémy-lès-Chevreuse.*
The path stretches over 1 300m – just under 1 mile – and features 14 observation points which afford a good view of the beautifully-preserved natural site of Maincourt. We also see how the land has adapted to the changes in human society since the Middle Ages (it is advisable to bring boots in wet weather).

★★**Dampierre Château.** – *Description p 69.*

Continue to drive down the Yvette Valley until you reach Chevreuse.

★**Chevreuse.** – *Description p 62.*

2 FROM PORT-ROYAL-DES-CHAMPS TO THE N 10

via Les Vaux de Cernay and Auffargis

22km – 14 miles – about 1 1/2 hours

★**Port-Royal.** – *Description p 141.*

This road crosses the plateau linking Port-Royal to the Yvette Valley. It follows a steep incline towards Dampierre, well-known among cyclists on account of its 17 hairpin bends.

★★**Dampierre Château.** – *Description p 69.*

★**Les Vaux de Cernay.** – *Description p 172.*

The D 24 follows the uper valley of the rivulet Les Vaux de Cernay and skirts the huge estate belonging to the former Vaux de Cernay Abbey, concealed behind high stone walls. An ornamental gate in wrought iron, executed in the style of Louis XV, marks the end of the domain.

Pont de Grandval Sand Quarry (Sablière du Pont de Grandval). – Small sandy area, made into a convenient stopping-place.

Without leaving the woods, the D 24 crosses Auffargis and, after dipping under the railway, leads back to the N 10.

CONFLANS-STE-HONORINE

Pop 29 003

Michelin map 101 fold 2

Situated at the confluence – distorted into Conflans – of the rivers Oise and Seine, this important maritime centre receives barges from Rouen, northern France and Belgium. The second part of the town's name dates back to the 9C. Up to then, the mortal remains of St Honorine, a 3C martyr, had rested in Graville, near Le Havre. In 875, the villagers were besieged by the Vikings and fled the area, taking with them the precious relics of their patron saint. Every town they stopped at took on the name of the saint and their exodus ended at Conflans.

A meeting place for mariners. – In the 18C, very few boats sailed the Seine between Rouen and Paris, and Conflans was a small town of farmers and quarry men, perched on a hillside, at the foot of the church and the Montjoie Tower donjon. After 1850, the development of steam navigation and the intensification of river traffic with the coal and industrial areas of the North via the Oise and St-Quentin canal, made Conflans one of the major ports of call for European barges. In Conflans, Andrésy and Maurecourt, several hundred barges – grouped into rows of ten – are moored along the quays: some await their cargo, others have been detained for longer periods because they need servicing, repairing, or simply victualling.
A great many concerns, including shops and cafés, derive their income from the river transport: in former times most of the mariners' business was conducted in cafés. A considerable number of retired bargees take up residence in Conflans, their children receiving state education are housed at a boarding school and the 70m – 230ft barge made of reinforced concrete – moored along Quai de la République – contains a chapel and the mariners' social centre.

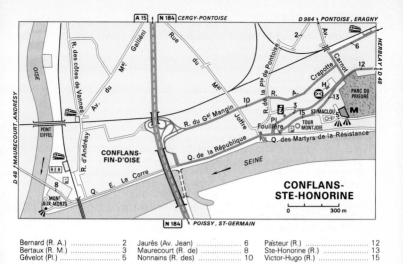

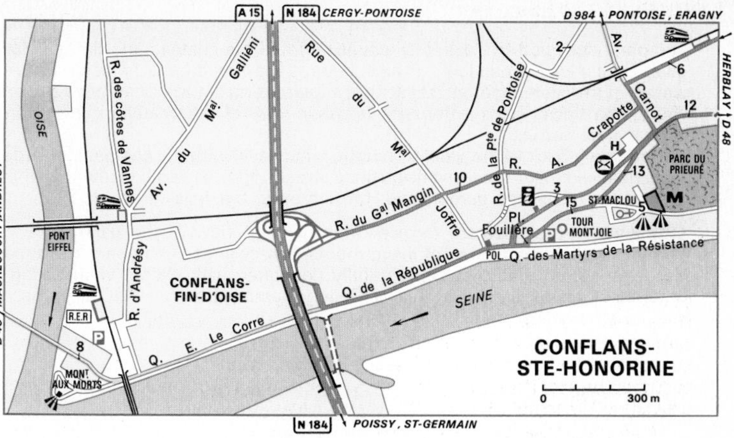

Bernard (R. A.)	2	Jaurès (Av. Jean)	6	Pasteur (R.)	12
Bertaux (R. M.)	3	Maurecourt (R. de)	8	Ste-Honorine (R.)	13
Gévelot (Pl.)	5	Nonnains (R. des)	10	Victor-Hugo (R.)	15

SIGHTS

The confluence of the Oise. – *1.5km – 1 mile to the west, following Quai de la République and Quai E. Le Corre.*
After the railway viaduct, bear left until you reach "Pointil", the headland dominated by the Mariners' Memorial.
Interesting **view** of the river traffic and as well as the road and metalwork railway bridge known as Pont Eiffel (built in 1890, rebuilt later) spanning the Oise. If you follow the Seine downstream from Pointil, you will discover the imposing structure of the Andrésy dam and lock, built in 1957, without doubt one of the most sophisticated of the 7 dams installed between the Lower Seine and the port of Gennevilliers.

Views from the Château. – Behind the church, the former Gévelot Château occupies the site of the priory that contained the relics of St Honorine. The former priory park is now open to the public.
You can get a lovely **view★** of the river, the port and the church either from Place Jules-Gévelot – a terrace fronted by railings – or from the balcony of the Municipal Health Centre (Centre de Santé Municipal), located in the priory park.

Ⓥ **Inland Water Transport Museum (Musée de la Batellerie) (M).** – *Set up in the château.*
Start your visit on the first floor. In room 5 an illustrated map of France presents 53 types of old-fashioned riverboats, long before the barge – a boat from northern Europe – introduced the seeds of standardisation. In an adjoining room, a number of old engravings and recorded commentaries explain the difficulties involved in sailing through Paris.
The large exhibition hall on the ground floor provides a history of the various forms of propulsion and contains many miniature models. Note the fascinating retrospective of "mechanical" navigation along the Seine: first warping (hauling the boat by means of a winch and a hawser), then conventional towing, and after 1955 pushing, a technique borrowed from the Americans. The years that followed saw the development of self-propelled barges. A collection of documents are concerned with passenger traffic and pleasure boats.
Navigational instruments and other sailing aids are on display in the courtyard of the museum.

Information in this guide is based on tourist data provided at the time of going to press. Improved facilities and changes in the cost of living make alterations inevitable: we hope our readers will bear with us.

★★ COURANCES Château

Michelin map 196 fold 44 – 5km – 3 miles north of Milly

The luxuriant vegetation and rippling waters surrounding Courances Château make this setting one of the most attractive sights in Ile-de-France.
Built around 1550 by Gilles le Breton for Cosme Clausse, Secretary of Finance to Henri II, the château acquired its present appearance in the 17C. It is a good example of the Louis XIII style: a brick building with sandstone quoins and window trims, pointed roofs and a sparsely-decorated exterior. In the 19C the entrance front was embellished with a replica of the horseshoe staircase at Fontainebleau *(illustration p 28)*.
The château is still surrounded by a moat and a splendid avenue on the opposite side of the road completes this sweeping perspective.

★★ **Park.** – The approach to the château is very grand. Walk through the gate and cross the forecourt, a vast stretch of lawn divided by a central path and flanked by two canals reflecting the noble plane trees.

The park, designed by Le Nôtre, extends behind the château and the rear façade gives onto a lush, green lawn. A path leads to the Grand Canal, which receives the waters of the École. Another, set at right angles, skirts the small cascades and brings you to the flower beds, offering a fantastic view of the château mirrored in the crystal-clear water.
Before going back to the gate, turn right, when level with the château, towards the ruins of an old fuller's mill and its gushing stream. From the embankment on the left, admire the Japanese garden and, further back, the falls of an old mill.

Château. – The southern terrace offers a good view of the park.
The tour includes a number of living rooms, low-ceilinged chambers and annexes. Note the corner dining room, tastefully decorated with walnut wainscoting and ornamental plates, and the Monkeys' Gallery, named after three 16C tapestries with scenes of monkeys mimicking man.

COURBEVOIE

Pop 59 931

Michelin map 101 fold 14 – Michelin plan 18

Courbevoie (winding path) owes its name to the sinuous route which led to the Gallo-Roman settlement situated on the edge of the plateau. In 1840 the Emperor's Remains were brought to Courbevoie, where they rested for one night, "on the banks of the Seine", in accordance with Bonaparte's wishes. The commemorative stele erected on Place du Port in 1940 has been moved to Place Napoléon Ier, in the modern Paris suburb of La Défense.

Roybet-C-Fould Museum (Musée Roybet-C-Fould). – *178 Boulevard St-Denis. In Bécon park.*
Installed in the Swedish and Norwegian pavilion built for the 1878 World Exhibition, this museum displays works by Carpeaux – who died in Courbevoie in 1875 – documents on the history of the town and the return of the Emperor's Remains, together with an impressive collection of dolls from the 18C to the present day. The terrace in the **park** offers a pleasant view of the Seine and the stately façade of the former Charras barracks, built for the Swiss Guards under Louis XV and reassembled in Courbevoie in 1962.

COURSON Château

Michelin map 196 fold 30 – 9km – 5.5 miles west of Arpajon

The former residence of Guillaume de Lamoignon, the first president of the Parlement de Paris (1676), Courson Château is surrounded by a park boasting some superb species of European and exotic trees, along with an extravagant display of colourful flowerbeds.

Château. – The living rooms on the ground floor, in particular the Italian-style lounge, bear the mark of two of Bonaparte's faithful followers, the Arrighi cousins, natives of Corte in Corsica and subsequently Dukes of Padua. Their mother's portrait is an arresting example of pure, uncompromising realism. One wing of the château houses a large collection of religious paintings by 17C Spanish artists.

★ **Park.** – *Follow the route marked with arrows; it changes according to the flowering season.*
In 1820 the park was redesigned in the English style by the first Duke of Padua, under the guidance of the landscape architect Berthault. It was further embellished in 1860 by the Bühler brothers and, after 1920, by the comte Ernest de Caraman, friend and imitator of Albert Kahn *(see p 38)*. Several rare tree species can be admired – cedar, sequoia and tulip trees – while the fragrant Corsican pines evoke the homeland of the Arrighi family.
The shrubs of lilac, azalea and rhododendrons in full bloom are a dazzling feast for the eyes.

CREIL

Pop 36 128

Michelin map 56 folds 1 and 11
Town plan in the current Michelin Red Guide France

The industrialisation of the last century contributed to the development of Creil, as did its role of railway junction and fluvial port. The town originated from a royal castle built on a small island in the Oise. This historic site is now occupied by the Town Hall, dating from the 20C.

Gallé-Juillet Museum (Musée Gallé-Juillet). – Built on top of the low, vaulted chambers of the castle belonging to Charles V, this museum has retained the furnishings and the charm of a wealthy 19C mansion house. Visitors are presented with the life of a provincial family, running from pre-WWI days to the heroic death of the only heir: Maurice Gallé.
The collections include the lead-glazed earthenware and black stoneware produced in the 19C by the local Creil factory and its twin manufacture in Montereau, both sadly disappeared. All these exhibits – in particular the familiar plates illustrating rebuses, hunting, topical and humourous scenes – are characterised by painted decoration.

CRÉPY-EN-VALOIS Pop 12 277

Michelin map 56 folds 12 and 13

A visit to Crépy-en-Valois is a good opportunity to discover one of the oldest regions in France, Valois, a heavily forested area *(p 15)*. The upper part of the town is strategically placed on a plateau, stretching between the gullies of two streams.

The Valois dynasty. – For over two and a half centuries, from 1328 to 1589, the French throne was occupied by the descendants of Charles I, comte de Valois and brother of Philip IV the Fair.
The last representatives of this dynasty, Charles VIII, François I, Henri II and III, contributed to the development of Italian – therefore Renaissance – art in France, while giving kingship a new, authoritarian stamp.

Capital of Valois. – The Counts, and subsequently, the Dukes of Valois made Crépy their new capital. A 10C castle, as well as several monasteries and churches, testify to the importance Crépy had acquired between the 11C and the 14C. It was only after Henri II's reign that the princes showed a preference for Villers-Cotterêts. In 1790 the reorganisation of the French *départements* split the old Valois territory between the Oise and the Aisne. Crépy's age of splendour was over.

CRÉPY-EN-VALOIS

Bergeron (R.) 2
Cardin (R. A.) 3
Chopinet (R. G.) 4
Damainville (Crs) 6
Fossés (R. des)
Gambetta (Pl.) 8
Gaulle (R. Ch. de)
Jeanne-d'Arc (R.) 9
Jeu-de-Paume (Crs) .. 10
Levallois-Perret (Av. de) 12
Lion (R. du) 13
Nationale (R.)
Nerval (Av. G. de)
République (Pl. de la). 14
Rousseau (R. J.-J.) ... 16
St-Lazare (R.)
Senlis (Av. de) 18
Soissons (R. de) 19
Tournelles (R. des) 20
Ursulines (R. des) 21
Victor-Hugo (Bd)

All symbols on the town plans are explained in the key p 34.

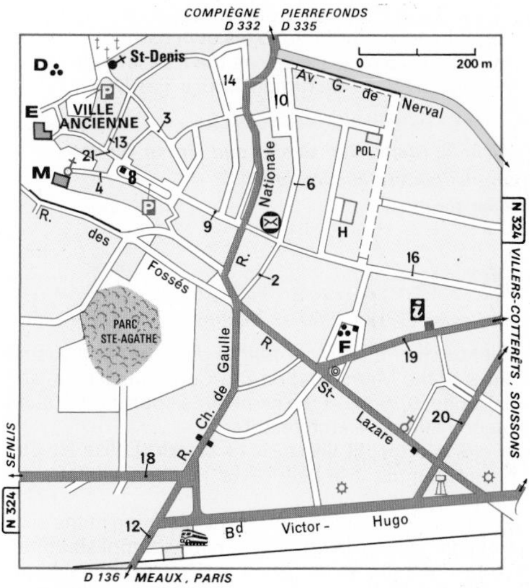

★OLD TOWN *time: 1 1/2 hours*

Place Gambetta (8). – This square has retained its quaint medieval charm. Among the 18C buildings, the house at no 15, **Maison des Quatre Saisons,** features four rococo grotesque masks representing the four seasons.

Follow Rue des Ursulines, then turn right and proceed along Rue du Lion.

At no 5, note the 14C mansion **Hôtel du Lion** with its crow-stepped gables typical of the area around Soissons.

St Denis' Church (Église St-Denis). – The majestic 16C transept consists of two bays. The nave was built in the 12C, the aisles in the 15C. The south aisle presents several small stone slabs celebrating the memory of the Ursuline nuns *(see below)*: Sister Marguerite Sconin de St-Xavier (1616-1645), one of Jean Racine's aunts, features among them.

Ⓥ **St-Arnould Abbey (Abbaye St-Arnould)** (D). – The ruins of this abbey – the necropolis of the counts of Valois – are at their most impressive when seen from the edge of the walls they dominate. On the opposite side stand the remains of a Gothic church. Excavations have uncovered a series of 11C colonnettes with their capitals, belonging to a former crypt.
Take the opposite direction to St-Denis and return to the town centre along a paved street; after a bend it leads you to the **House of the Ursulines' Intendant** (Maison de l'Intendant des Ursulines) (E), a superb 18C building and further along, to the entrance of the Ursuline convent, occupied by an order of nuns who taught in Crépy from 1623 to 1791.

Return to Place Gambetta and proceed along Rue Gustave-Chopinet, the first street on the right.

Old Castle (Vieux Château). – This building houses some charming collections from the Museum of Archery and Valois.

Ⓥ **Museum of Archery and Valois** (Musée de l'Archerie et du Valois) (M). – Archery is a traditional sport in the Valois area and there are still many clubs today. These groups originated from part-civil, part-military associations set up in the Middle Ages to train the militia in peace time.
Wary of the strong religious and loyalist views of the archers, the members of the 1789 Constituent Assembly incorporated them into the National Guard. But tradition survived and archers' confederations reappeared in the 19C, with a view to fostering social and sporting activities.

The main exhibition room of the museum presents the history and traditions of archery in a lively manner: documents depicting St Sebastian, the patron saint of archers, the internal hierarchy of the Guild, the "provincial bouquet" ritual, in which a formal procession is conducted around a bouquet of honour arranged in a commemorative vase. The glass cabinets display a great variety of bows and crossbows, ranging from the very first primitive weapons to the sophisticated models of today, used for international competitions and consisting of metal, fibreglass and exotic wood...
The high-ceilinged rooms in the castle and the chapel contain a **collection of religious works★**. The majority of these are restored and preserved statues from country churches in the Valois area: an early 16C Virgin and Child from Le Luat, a 15C nursing Virgin from Nanteuil-le-Haudouin, and several other figures representing St Martin, St Sebastian, the Virgin and a St John from Gilocourt.

ADDITIONAL SIGHT

St Thomas Church (Église St-Thomas) (F). – *It is approached through Rue St-Lazare.*
These distinguished ruins are the remains of a Gothic church built outside the ramparts in 1182 in memory of Thomas Becket, Archbishop of Canterbury, twelve years after he was murdered in his own cathedral. The ruins include the west front, the first bay of the nave as well as the truncated tower and its 15C spire. The rest of the grounds have been turned into a garden.

*The **Michelin Maps, Red Guides** and **Green Guides** are complementary publications. Use them together.*

★ CRÉTEIL

Pop 71 705

Michelin map 101 fold 27 – Michelin plan 24

The chief town of the Val-de-Marne *département* resembles an old town built along the banks of the Marne and on Ste-Catherine Island, and once noted for its market garden produce, while at the same time sporting the characteristics of a modern city with unconventional architecture.
In the old quarter, **St Christopher's Church** (Église St-Christophe) has kept its 12C porch, surmounted by a bell-tower, its chancel, flat at the east end, and its elegant triforium.
The new town is an example of town-planning in the sixties, such as the Montmesly development, as well as more recent accomplishments. The head architect Pierre Dufau designed the general plan and entrusted each quarter to a different building contractor. With the result that each district bears its own distinctive stamp: the Échat office buildings near Henri-Mondor Hospital, the administrative quarters surrounded by fountains and greenery, Croix des Mèches where traffic and pedestrians have been separated, Montaigut landscaped garden nestling in the centre of an arena-shaped complex, lastly, the Palais quarter, noted for its high towers and the bustling commercial and leisure centre.

★**Town Hall (Hôtel de Ville)**. – *1 Place Salvador Allende.*
An audacious piece of architecture, consisting of two imperfect cylinders. The lower of the two houses public services on the ground level, while the upstairs is used for weddings and local authority meetings. The second cylinder revolves around a central axis and hangs from concrete arms acting as outer brackets. The serpentine motifs on the **square★** in front of the Town Hall are the work of Vasarely.

The new town centre in Créteil

Quai de la Croisette. – Take a pleasant walk along the artificial lakes that are part of the **Leisure Centre** (Base de Loisirs), offering facilities for sailing, swimming and fishing *(see chapter on Practical Information at the end of the guide).*

Préfecture. – *Avenue du Général de Gaulle.*
The bronze façades of the préfecture building dominate the landscaped mound on which it stands. The ground floor entrance hall is quite splendid.

Deportation Memorial (Monument de la Déportation). – It stands on the open area, facing the préfecture. The monument is the work of J. Cardot (1975).

Regional Archives (Archives Départementales). – *Rue des Archives.*
A set of sombre buildings, supported by high metal framework.

★★ DAMPIERRE Château

Michelin map 101 fold 31 – Local map p 63

Dampierre, situated in the narrow upper part of the Chevreuse Valley, is closely associated with two distinguished families, the Luynes and the Chevreuse.

★★ **Château.** – From 1675 to 1683 Jules Hardouin-Mansart rebuilt Dampierre Château for Colbert's son-in-law the duc de Chevreuse, a former student at Port-Royal and the mentor of the duc de Bourgogne. The château – restored by Félix Duban during the reign of Louis-Philippe – remains the property of the Luynes family.

Dampierre Château

TOUR *time: 40 min*

The main body of the château opens onto a courtyard which is overlooked by two arched buildings. The pinkish tones of the brick harmonise with the sober stonework trims and columns, contrasting sharply with the darker hues of the park.
On the ground floor, visitors may admire Cavelier's Statue of Penelope in the hall leading to the living rooms embellished with Louis XV wainscoting, the suite occupied by Marie Leczinska, and an imposing dining room decorated with Louis XIV panelling. The first floor houses the Royal Suite, which welcomed Louis XIV, Louis XV and Louis XVI. The splendid 17 and 18C furnishings are beautifully preserved and remind one of the King's Suite at Versailles: the furniture, portraits, wainscoting, medallions and overdoor panels.
The most amazing achievement stands at the top of the great staircase. The Minerva Room (Salle de la Minerve) is a formal reception room by Duban during the Restoration period. The great Ingres was commissioned to paint a fresco representing the Golden Age: it was never completed. The duc Honoré de Luynes, who conceived the whole project, ordered a colourful 3m – 10ft statue of Minerva, a miniature replica of the legendary gold and ivory Parthenon Minerva executed by Phidias in the 5C BC.

Park. – The estate walls surrounding the grounds – where wild deer may be seen running freely – circle a 30ha – 74 acre garden featuring hundreds of flowers and plant species. Depending on the season, one may enjoy the attractive sight of numerous shrubberies in full bloom: tulips, hyacinths, irises, poppies, roses, azaleas and rhododendrons. The river and ponds are edged with aquatic plants.

The layout diagram on page 3 shows the* Michelin Maps *covering the region. In the text, reference is made to the map which is the most suitable from a point of view of scale and practicality.

DEUIL-LA-BARRE

Pop 16 388

Michelin map 101 fold 5 – Michelin plan 18

Deuil-la-Barre is situated between the Seine River and the hills of Montmorency. In spite of its proximity to the French capital, it has retained its rural charm.

Notre-Dame Church (Église Notre-Dame). – *Place des Victimes du V2.* Consecrated in the 12C, the church suffered serious damage in October 1944 following the crash of a German V-2 missile.
The remarkable **historiated capitals★** (12C) which adorn the transept crossing are the most interesting feature of the church. The one situated to the right of the last bay of the nave tells the story of Cain and Abel: it represents Abel's death and the sacrifice preceding this first murder. Opposite is a 20C replica of the capital illustrating the Original Sin: the left-hand side shows Adam and Eve fleeing from the Garden of Eden, while on the front the couple are separated by the snake, coiled round a tree. The capital surmounting the northeast pillar of the crossing portrays Daniel in the Lions' Den. The Prophet stands in the centre, holding the tails of the two lions with human heads. The capital facing it is decorated with masks and foliage motifs. The 11C capitals in the nave are based on the Corinthian order and present foliage embellishments: they are surmounted by square abacuses.
Note the two superb keystones on the transept crossing: the first bears the coat of arms of Deuil Priory, the second that of the famous royal abbey of St-Florent in Saumur, under whose jurisdiction the priory was placed. Admire the fine Gothic ambulatory.

ⓥ **Municipal Museum of Chevrette (Musée Municipal de la Chevrette).** – *Rue Jean Bouin.* The first room explains the origins of Deuil-la-Barre and Notre-Dame Church. Observe the shrine containing the reliquary of St Eugenius who, according to legend, was martyred in this very building. The second room presents the history of Chevrette Château: in the 18C, many philosophers and writers of the *Encyclopédie* – namely Grimm, d'Holbach, and Diderot – paid frequent visits to Chevrette and even Jean-Jacques Rousseau took up residence there.

DOURDAN

Pop 8 057

Michelin map 196 fold 41

Nestling among the remains of the venerable Yveline Forest *(p 145)*, the former capital of Hurepoix became a place of residence for royalty as early as Capetian times. At the sight of such delightful woods, one understands why these kings were so passionately fond of hunting.
The main square – an important trading place for cereals – was designed to protect the "corn route" running from Beauce to Paris, and to ward off the feudal lords from Montlhéry, Rochefort and Chevreuse. Louis XI and his successors gave the enjoyment of their estate either to their favourites or to their more faithful followers. After 1661 Dourdan remained the property of the Orléans family.

★ **Place du Marché-aux-Grains.** – This charming square, officially renamed Place du Général-de-Gaulle, is built on a slight slope and accommodates the major sights of Dourdan: the stronghold *(see below)*, the medieval covered market (rebuilt in 1836), of which the attics have been converted into rooms and offices, and the 12-13C church with its pointed 17C steeple adorned with tiny lantern turrets.

ⓥ **Castle (Château).** – Dourdan Castle was built by Philippe-Auguste in 1222. The entrance gatehouse is flanked by two sturdy towers. The square curtain wall, surrounded by a moat, has a fortified tower at each corner and one half-way along each side. Although it has lost its third level and its crenellated balcony, the keep is by far the most remarkable feature of the castle. It was used to defend the most exposed part of the stronghold and was separated from the bailey by a moat which Sully, one of the owners, had filled in. St Louis came to stay at Dourdan and Philip the Fair used it for his hunting parties. In the 19C, the castle was restored in the style of Viollet-le-Duc.
Walk round the outside of the castle, starting from the moat and go towards the right as this way one can get a good view of both the fortress and the church.

Virgin and Child with a Parrot
by Pieter Coecke Van Aelst, Dourdan Museum

Ⓥ**Keep and museum** (Donjon et musée). – The museum, located in an old salt loft which was converted into a dwelling place in the 19C, houses several collections: note the archaeological exhibits dating from Gallo-Roman and medieval times (funeral urns, cups, jugs, etc.), and the wonderful **Virgin and Child with a Parrot★**, a 16C painting by Pieter Coecke Van Aelst.
Return to the bailey then proceed towards the keep. The second floor platform (71 laborious steps) commands a pleasant view of the town, the church towers and the wooded hillsides of Hurepoix.

EXCURSION

Rémarde Valley and Dourdan Forest. – *Round tour of 24 km – 15 miles – allow 2 1/2 hours. Leave Dourdan to the north.*

St-Cyr-sous-Dourdan. – Pop 774. From the embankment one can look down on the Jubilee Farmhouse, also called Turret Farmhouse, flanked by two conical towers, and on the gracious silhouette of the church.

Turn round and when you reach the D 27 crossroads, turn right to go to Rochefort-en-Yvelines.

You suddenly discover, perched on a hill, the remains of a huge fortified castle built in the Louis XVI style by a financier in the years preceding WWI. On the left, the bell tower of Rochefort Church nestles among the pines.

Rochefort-en-Yvelines. – Pop 610. The village is built on a series of terraces stepped up the hillside. The Town Hall (18C) has been set up in the former bailiwick. The 18C façade giving onto the high street shows a prison wall, complete with its narrow doorway, arch and massive voussoirs. It bears the following inscription in Latin: "Woe to the Evil, Felicity to the Good".
Leave the car on the square, behind the town hall (the road is on the right, beyond the old prison). Climb the steps leading to the church and cross the cemetery at the top. Note the Romanesque doorway at the foot of the bell tower and the charming display of tiered roofs crowning the east end. The chancel is 12C. Pleasant **view★** of the village and Hurepoix Forest in the far distance.

Ⓥ**St-Arnoult-en-Yvelines.** – Pop 4 448. Originally, the **church** developed from a sanctuary built for the tomb of St Arnoult, a Merovingian prince who later became a missionary bishop. The nave acquired its present appearance as early as the 12C. The west front, however, lost its symmetry in the 16C, when the left aisle and the bell tower were added.
The general impression of the **interior★** is one of Romanesque simplicity. The restoration of the walls revealed fragments of several mural paintings. The 15C nave with panelled vaulting boasts some superb beams, adorned at each end by monstrous heads carved in the wood *(p 96)*. The right aisle features two ancient statues: St Fiacre, the patron saint of gardeners, and St Scariberge, the wife of St Arnoult, then comte de Reims.

When leaving St-Arnoult, turn left and take the D 836 to Dourdan.

Dourdan Forest. – The road takes you across the massif of St-Arnoult. The plateau – planted with oak copses and groves – drops steeply when it reaches Orge Valley.

Take a right turning 1 500 m – 1 mile after the motorway underpass.

The road follows the Orge Valley, passing through the hamlet of Petit-Ste-Mesme.

A left turning will bring you back to Dourdan.

★★ ÉCOUEN Château

Michelin map 101 fold 6

Access is through the forest, on foot; cars must be parked at the entrance to the forest.

Nestling in a 17ha – 42 acre park on a small hillock, this château was originally intended for Constable Anne de Montmorency *(qv)* and his wife Madeleine of Savoy, who lived there from 1538 to 1555.
When Constable Anne's grandson Henri II de Montmorency was beheaded in 1632, the château reverted to the Condé family but was later confiscated during the Revolution. Napoleon I salvaged the estate in 1806 by founding the first school for the daughters of members of the Légion d'Honneur. In 1962 the château and its grounds were ceded to the Ministry of Culture, who undertook to turn it into a state museum devoted to Renaissance art.

TOUR *time: 1 hour*

Exterior. – Écouen Château reflects the transition of French art from the Early Renaissance period (Châteaux of the Loire) to the High Renaissance during Henri II's reign *(illustration p 28)*.

Courtyard. – The buildings feature square pavilions at each corner and are surmounted by elaborate dormer windows. The beautiful east range was destroyed in the 18C and replaced by a low entrance wing.
The porticos bearing replicas of ancient columns on the south wing that housed the constable's suite feature a frontispiece by Jean Bullant, designed to receive Michelangelo's famous *Slaves* (originals in Louvre) in the lateral niches at ground floor level. They were a present from Henri II to Anne de Montmorency.

North Terrace. – Sweeping **view** of the surrounding cereal-growing countryside.

★★ **Renaissance Museum (Musée de la Renaissance).** – The exhibits on display belonged to the Renaissance collections of the Cluny Museum in Paris. Écouen Museum presents a wide range of works dating from the 16C and early 17C, which introduce visitors to the various branches of the decorative arts: furniture, wainscoting, tapestries and embroideries, ceramics, enamels, etc. Most of the exhibits were made in France, Italy or the Netherlands. They represent a small selection but the ambience they create is in keeping with the life of the rich during the Renaissance. The original interior decoration consists mainly of grotesques, painted on the friezes below the ceiling and the embrasures of the windows. But it is for its **painted fireplaces** that Écouen is famed. Created during the reign of Henri II, these chimneypieces are representative of the first Fontainebleau School *(see p 79)*: the central biblical scene is painted on an oval or rectangular shaped medallion; the hazy landscapes depicting antique ruins, fortresses and humble cottages are in imitation of Niccolo dell'Abbate.

Ground Floor. – The monograms A and M (Anne de Montmorency and Madeleine of Savoy) have been included in the decoration of the chapel, built in 1544 and covered by painted vaulting resting on diagonal arches. Unfortunately the stained glass and the altar sculpted by Jean Goujon were taken to Chantilly. The first room in the south wing boasts a superb collection of arms with interesting models of swords and rapiers.

The small rooms in the west wing are each devoted to a particular trade or technique: do not miss the reconstruction of a 16C goldsmith's workshop, complete with a drawing frame set in an inlaid chest.

The northwest pavilion was formerly occupied by Catherine de' Medici.

Musicians' scene in the Tapestry of David and Bathsheba, Écouen

First Floor. – In the south wing, visitors are shown round the constable's bedroom and Madeleine of Savoy's suite, both interesting on account of the period furniture. The west wing is almost exclusively taken up by the **Tapestry of David and Bathsheba**★★★ (*c* 1515), a 75m – 246ft hanging divided into ten sections which tells of the romance between King David and Bathsheba. The outstanding quality of the tapestry – woven with wool and silk threads, as well as silver braid – is equalled only by that of *The Hunts of Maximilian* in the Louvre, without doubt the two most precious examples of 16C Brussels tapestry work existing in France.

The hanging starts in Abigail's Chamber, follows Psyche's Gallery and ends in the King's Apartment, situated in the northwest pavilion. For explanations of the numerous emblems and monograms read the paragraph entitled "Henri II's Château" *(p 80)*.

The king's suite occupied the northern wing: the floor tiles were made specially for the château in 1542 by the Rouen potter Masséot Abaquesne. The room also houses the reconstruction of a section of paving, consisting of 75 heraldic earthenware tiles. A winged victory, sculpted in the central panel of the monumental fireplace, turns to face a raised sword, symbolising the constable's charge.

Second Floor. – In the northeast pavilion, many pieces of Isnik pottery (mid-16C to early 17C) are exhibited in glass cabinets, illustrating the exotic tastes of 16C collectors. The first room in the north wing presents religious stained glass painted according to the grisaille technique (graded tones of black and white): admire the *Virgin and Child*, dated 1544. The second hall deals entirely with French ceramics and covers the work of Masséot Abaquesne *(The Flood)*.

The fifteen marriage chests *(cassoni)* on show in the northwest pavilion form a remarkable ensemble: these painted panels are taken from wooden chests that were presented to newlyweds in sets of two.

The cabinets in the west gallery contain enamels (pieces by Léonard Limosin), tin-glazed pottery or maiolica from Deruta in Italy and glasses (goblets belonging to Anne de Bretagne and Catherine de' Medici).
The southwest pavilion concentrates on silverware (cutlery, jewellery), mainly of German origin. On your way out, note the towering cabinet bearing Cardinal Farnese's blazon. Above the chapel, the former library of Constable Anne – admire the beautifully restored wainscoting – features a collection of miniature waxworks from France and Italy (Leda).

ADDITIONAL SIGHT

St-Acceul Church (Église St-Acceul). – The chancel by Jean Bullant is the most interesting part of the building. The complex rib patterns of the vaulting date it back to the 16C *(at present these are concealed by the temporary supporting timber).* St-Acceul features several Renaissance **stained glass windows★**; those in the left side aisle are dated 1544: *Dormition* and *Assumption of the Virgin, Annunciation* and *Visitation Nativity* and *Adoration of the Magi.*

★ ENGHIEN-LES-BAINS

Pop 9 739

Michelin map 101 south of fold 5 – Michelin plan 18

This is the nearest spa to the capital and a great many Parisians are attracted by the races and canoeing, not to mention the parties and gambling rooms of the casino. The properties of the sulphurous waters of Enghien – used for treating cases of rhumatism, throat complaints and skin diseases – were discovered in 1773. However the beginnings of the resort can be traced back to 1821, with the construction of the Spa Centre (rebuilt in 1935 and restored in 1986).
The locality became a French commune in 1851, when it received its present name. The name Enghien came from a seigniory in the Hainaut (Belgium) to the estate of the Montmorency, which the Condé family inherited after the execution of Henri II de Montmorency in 1632.

★ **Lake (Lac).** – It covers approximately 40ha – 100 acres and is 3 to 17ft deep. A pleasant lakeside road, Rue du Général-de-Gaulle, offers a charming view of the water and surrounding greenery. One may also walk round the lake along Avenue de Ceinture but unfortunately it is screened by the villas and their gardens, except on Pont du Nord and Pont de la Muse.

ÉPERNON

Pop 4 850

Michelin map 196 fold 27 – 13km – 8 miles west of Rambouillet

This small ancient town lies at the confluence of the Rivers Drouette and Guesle: its location on the edge of the Beauce plain and Rambouillet Forest has always made it a privileged sight. The old city has narrow, winding streets built on the slope of a hill: it features old porches with pointed arches and half-timbered houses from the 15C.

Ⓥ **Church (Église).** – A remarkable sight indeed, owing to its location and great unity of style. The interior typifies both 16C architecture and the rustic charm of Chartres country churches *(see Gallardon)*. The nave – supported by octagonal pillars without capitals – is 16C, the chancel arch 13C.
Following a bomb explosion in 1940, which caused the modern plaster vault to cave in, it was decided to restore the 16C barrel vaulting of the main vault, complete with its panelling and painting, and to reconstruct the barrel vaulting of the aisles (note the sculpted heads that terminate the beams in the south nave, their features twisted into expressions of wrath).

ERMENONVILLE

Pop 778

Michelin map 196 fold 9

Ermenonville, famed for its park and its connections with Jean-Jacques Rousseau, lies on the edge of the forest that bears its name.
On 28 May 1778, Jean-Jacques Rousseau arrived at Ermenonville Château, responding to an invitation from the Marquis de Girardin, one of his admirers, who had acquired the estate in 1763.
In a frenzy of joy, the French philosopher rediscovered nature and the "fresh greenery". He went for walks, daydreamed in the park and taught music to his host's children. On 2 July his nomadic existence ended: he suffered a stroke and died at the age of 66. On 4 July, at midnight, he was buried on Poplar Island (Ile des Peupliers), which immediately became a place of pilgrimage. In 1794 his body was exhumed and laid to rest in the Panthéon in Paris.

★ **Park.** – Jean-Jacques Rousseau's park was bought over by a regional association of Picardy in 1983. The 18C Ermenonville Château stands on the opposite side of the road *(not open to the public).*
It was here that the Marquis de Girardin put into practice his theories on the embellishment of the countryside. Initially, Ermenonville was surrounded by sandy, swampy land. The marquis produced a superb landscaped garden in the French style, featuring shaded paths, elegant contours, rockeries and charming brooklets. The most picturesque sites were occupied by a number of monuments, now in a tumbledown condition.

Walks. – *There are no official footpaths directly linking Ermenonville to Chaâlis and the Mer de Sable, via the lakes and the forest. It is necessary to take the N 330 (heavy traffic with many long-distance lorries).*

Jean-Richard Zoo (Zoo Jean-Richard). – *1.5km – 1 mile to the north.* The animals are presented in pleasant, shady surroundings.

★ **Mer de Sable.** – *1.5km – 1 mile to the north.* It is surprising to find sand dunes in this wooded area of Ile-de-France. The sand deposits, dating from the Tertiary Era, form thick layers on the ground. At the end of the Ice Age, this region was probably one vast sandy moor covered with wild heather. The warmer climate prevailing in the Neolithic period produced numerous clearings in the vegetation, accentuated by the eroding influence of the winds.
In the Jean Richard Amusement Park (Centres Attractifs Jean Richard) an amusing road train takes visitors on a tour of the various attractions. The tour ends with a trip round the sand dunes, in a genuine railway carriage, including a stop at Babagattau Village, peopled with legendary figures.

★ **Chaâlis Abbey.** – *3km – 2 miles to the north. Description p 43.*

★ ERMENONVILLE Forest

Michelin map 196 fold 9

Together with the nearby woods of Chantilly and Halatte, the state forest of Ermenonville constitutes one of the more enchanting spots of Paris' green belt. Generally speaking, the soil is sandy, and of poor quality *(see Mer de Sable above)*. 150 years ago, the land was a vast moor covered in heather. After 1840, the clearings in the vegetation were planted with maritime and Scots pines (1 700ha – 4 200 acres): at sunset their reddish trunks glow like those in the Landes forest. As in Fontainebleau Forest, rambling activities continue all through winter.

Roads and paths. – The French Forestry Commission has marked out a number of country lanes suitable for walks, especially around Baraque de Chaâlis crossroads, which is by far the best place in the forest for rambling. Cars are not allowed on the forest roads, except along the Long Road leading to the crossroads. However, road traffic is permitted on the section linking Baraque de Chaâlis to the commemorative monument marking the crash of the Turkish Airlines DC 10 on 3 March 1974, in which 346 people died.

Mortefontaine. – The southwest part of the forest is the continuation of the woods and ponds belonging to Mortefontaine estate. These sites – which delighted Corot and Gérard de Nerval – are unfortunately inaccessible but one can follow the **road running from Mortefontaine to Thiers:** it commands a good view of Vallières Pond seen against a backdrop of rocky hills, moors and spinneys.

ÉTAMPES

Pop 19 491

Michelin map 196 fold 42

Étampes developed as a string of small parishes lining the old road to Orléans, which has now been diverted. The town has preserved a homely character and its humble brook (Louette and Chalouette) adds a touch of freshness to the wash house and the old stone walls.

The Kings and the Gentlewomen. – In the early years of its existence, when France was given to strong religious beliefs, Étampes was patronised by many a ruler: Robert the Pious and Queen Constance, Louis the Fat, Louis VII and Philippe Auguste. During the Renaissance, royalty was more conerned with romance and splendour than with religion and the Duchy of Étampes was offered to the kings' favourite ladies. Queen Anne of Britany was thus succeeded as duchess by Anne de Pisseleu, Diane de Poitiers and Gabrielle d'Estrées.

A market town. – When royal patronage ceased, the town was busy on account of its commercial activities, which continued to thrive despite repeated attacks on the part of the English, the Burgundians, the Huguenots, the League, the Fronde and even bands of mercenaries.
Up to the end of the 17C; i.e. over a period of 150 years, a dozen boats loaded with cargoes of wheat, flour or wine would leave Étampes harbour every morning and head towards Corbeil along the Juine river. It usually took them two or three days to reach Paris.

SIGHTS

Place de l'Hôtel-de-Ville (A 21). – In the 16C the Town Hall was moved to this former town house and several wings were added in the 19C to accommodate the museum.

Place Notre-Dame (A 27). – The shopping centre of the Notre-Dame quarter (market on Saturdays). This narrow square commands a good view of the collegiate church.
Go straight on along Rue du Pont-Doré; enjoy the panorama of Étampes' "river", its bridges and old wash houses.

Turn around; proceed to Notre-Dame via Place de l'Ancienne-Comédie, then Place Notre-Dame.

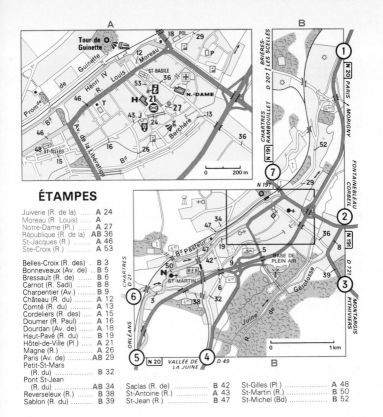

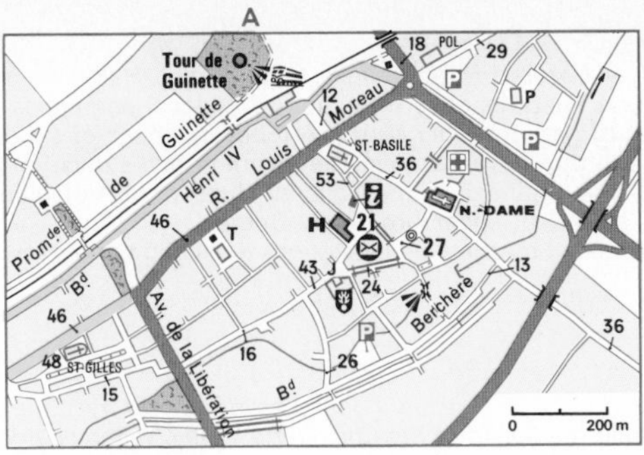

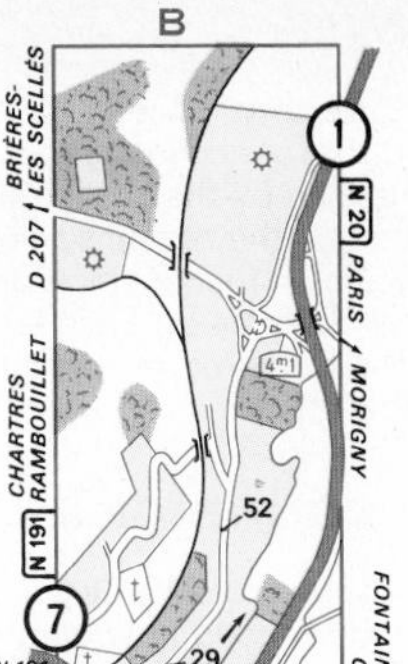
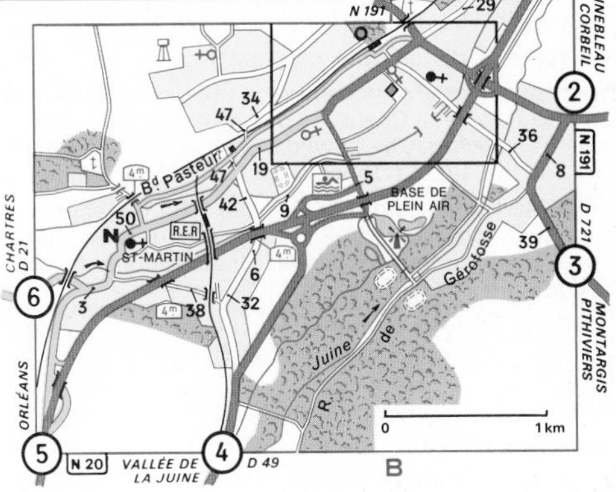

ÉTAMPES

Juiverie (R. de la) ..... A 24
Moreau (R. Louis) ..... A
Notre-Dame (Pl.) ...... A 27
République (R. de la) . AB 36
St-Jacques (R.) .... A 46
Ste-Croix (R.) .... A 53

Belles-Croix (R. des) . B 3
Bonneveaux (Av. de) .. B 5
Bressault (R. de) ...... B 6
Carnot (R. Sadi) .... B 8
Charpentier (Av.) .... B 9
Château (R. du) .... A 12
Comté (R. du) .... A 13
Cordeliers (R. des) .... A 15
Doumer (R. Paul) ...... A 16
Dourdan (Av. de) ...... A 18
Haut-Pavé (R. du) ..... B 19
Hôtel-de-Ville (Pl.) ..... A 21
Magne (R.) .... A 26
Paris (Av. de) ....AB 29
Petit-St-Mars (R. du) .... B 32
Pont St-Jean (R. du) ....AB 34
Reverseleux (R.) .... B 38
Sablon (R. du) .... B 39
Saclas (R. de) .... B 42
St-Antoine (R.) .... A 43
St-Jean (R.) .... B 47
St-Gilles (Pl.) .... A 48
St-Martin (R.) .... B 50
St-Michel (Bd) .... B 52

★ **Notre-Dame Collegiate Church (Collégiale Notre-Dame)** (A). – Squeezed in between the narrow houses of this former military and royal city, the church was fortified in the 13C (east end) and rechristened Notre-Dame-du-Fort. The admirable Romanesque bell tower and its stone spire quartered by open-work pinnacles. On the market side, the south doorway (1130) resembles the Royal Doorway at Chartres on account of its style and the scenes depicted. The doorway was badly damaged during the Wars of Religion (1562), which proved fatal to the statue-columns: kings, queens and prophets of the Old Testament were all beheaded.

★ **Interior.** – The complex, multilateral plan of the church and the irregular disposition of the arches reflect the various stages of construction of the 12C, and the problems encountered in building a church with such limited space. Owing to the variety of angles and the lower level of the floor in the south side aisle, the church offers several varied perspectives. The first two bays of the nave were built in the Romanesque style before 1150.
The double aisles of the chancel open off the transept. The north aisles, built on a sloping plane, end in narrow but lofty axial chapels and constitute a perfect Gothic ensemble. The four keystones form a central core surrounded by figures of kings and angels. The south chapel displays two of the unfortunate statue-columns taken from the south doorway, namely St Peter and St Paul. The heads are recent replacements.
The Sibyls' stained glass window (16C) portrays 12 prophetesses of ancient pagan times: each holds a tablet containing an oracle on the coming of Christ. On either side of the chancel, a staircase leads to the 11C crypt *(bring a small torch)*, decorated in the neo-Byzantine style during the last century.

St Martin's Church (Église St-Martin) (12-16C) (B N). – The strange-looking bell tower built separately from the church in the 16C has slightly curved lines: it had lost its base owing to subsidence and the architect had to redesign the upper parts several times. The foundations of the tower were eventually joined onto the church in 1873. In the interior, the alternating cylindrical pillars and twin colonnettes add a touch of elegance to the triforium of the chancel.

Guinette Tower (Tour de Guinette) (A). – *You can drive there along Rue St-Jean, which straddles the railway and Promenade de la Guinette. We advise against going to the top.*
It stands half-way up a hill, in the midst of a small wood which serves as a public garden and which offers a good view of Étampes. Guinette Tower was once the castle's keep, an observation point where Philippe Auguste kept a close watch on his vassals. He also used it as a prison for his enemies and even for his second wife, Ingeborg of Denmark. Having repudiated her in 1193 almost immediately after their marriage, he kept her in semicaptivity between 1201 and 1213 following the Pope's interdict of 1200. The name Guinette comes from the verb *guigner,* meaning to survey. The plan of the tower, shaped as a four-leaf clover, is an extremely rare occurrence.
In 1589 the donjon was besieged by Henri IV and dismantled, together with the curtain wall, at the request of the local population, who resented being the object of continual warfare. The deep cracks left by the gunpowder explosion are impressive.

Ⓥ **Museum (Musée)** (A H). – *Located in an annexe of the Town Hall.*
The ground floor presents a miscellaneous collection of regional antiquities, enhanced by the admirable 12C gate from old Morigny Abbey, the head of a King of Judah, the remains of one of the Notre-Dame statue-columns, and a dwarf god of Gallo-Roman inspiration – the original is in the National Museum of Antiquities at St-Germain-en-Laye – executed in sheet bronze by Bouray.
The three rooms upstairs present a variety of illustrations depicting the old town of Étampes.

EXCURSIONS

Chalouette Valley. – *15km – 9 miles – allow 1 hour. Leave Étampes by ⑥, the D 21 and proceed upstream along the banks of the Chalouette Valley. When you get to Chalou-St-Mars, turn left and take the D 160.*

The route is dotted with pleasantly-converted country cottages.

Moulineux. – Part of joint commune Chalou-Moulineux. At the bottom of the hill, turn left into Rue de la Chaussée de l'Étang and follow the embankment planted with trees. The **site★** may be viewed from the east end, offering a lovely view of the stately ruins of the 12C St-Thomas de Cantorbery Church *(private property).*

Chalou-Moulineux. – Pop 303. In the 12C this village was the headquarters of a Templars' commandery. From Place St-Aignan, turn left and go down Rue des Templiers; then follow Voie des Hospitaliers to the old wash house (source of the Chalouette).

Congerville-Thionville. – Pop 159. The hamlet is circled by high stone walls and resembles a desert island, lost in an ocean of wheat in the midst of the Beauce countryside.

Drive to Angerville along the D 838 via Pussay (Michelin map 237 fold 28).

Ⓥ **Dommerville Château.** – On the outskirts of Angerville. Built in the late 18C by the marquis de Hallot, Lieutenant General in the king's army, the château consists of the main building and two wings at right angles. The south wing houses the former dining room (rare earthenware stove crowned by a pipe shaped as a palm tree), and a rather grand staircase with a wrought iron and chiselled bronze baluster.

Proceed towards Méréville along the D 145.

Méréville. – *Description p 119.*

Leave the roundabout at Trajan's Column via Rue Laborde.

Bear right and drive under the railway to get back onto the Orléans road the D 49, which leads to Étampes.

Ⓥ **Jeurre Park (Parc de Jeurre).** – *3km – 2 miles to the north along the N 20. Allow 2 hours for the visit.*
At the end of the 19C, a number of monuments taken from the famous Méréville Park *(qv)* have been reassembled here in Jeurre Park.
The most symbolic monuments are Captain Cook's Cenotaph and the Rostral Column. The Cenotaph was executed by Pajou and stands under a sturdy portico featuring Doric pillars. As for the Column, decorated with a bronze sphere and four prows *(rostra)* – an emblem from ancient Rome commemorating a naval victory –, it was commissioned by Laborde to commemorate Lapérouse's voyage and to celebrate the memory of his two sons, who perished off the Californian coast during the expedition. The Temple of Love is an 18C replica of one of the Tivoli temples. Supported by 18 Corinthian columns, it is characteristic of the rotundas that proliferated in France during the neo-classical period.

ÉVRY

Pop 29 578

Michelin map 101 folds 36 and 37

The development of Évry – one of the five new towns of the Paris region *(see introduction p 7)* – now the capital of the Essonne *département,* is characterised by the importance and the originality of its town centre, started in 1970.
The selected site – the centre of the plateau limited by the Orge, Seine and Essonne rivers – was already designated by the 1965 Master Plan known as the outer belt or *grande couronne* town planning operation. The first of the fire new towns and the smallest territorially, Evry opted for the creation of a town centre as cornerstone of the operation from the very beginning. Today Evry now boasts a broad range of urban facilities (business, administration, service – especially transport – leisure, cultural and education). The overall urban area including the communes of Évry, Courcouronnes, Bondoufle and Lisses covers a population of 300 000.
Évry is situated close to Corbeil – a traditional centre for industry and scientific research to the south of Paris – and tends to specialise in the more sophisticated fields of electronics, information and robot technologies, aeronautics and space research.

The Open-Air Factor. – One of the most pleasant green spaces is the park surrounding the Lake. Visitors will doubtless be intrigued by the Lady of the Lake: an imposing concrete sculpture often used as a mountaineering exercise.
To the west of the racecourse and the Kiosque Wood, **St-Eutrope Park** offers several recreational areas. Note the little steam engine which follows narrow gauge tracks over a distance of two miles.

TOWN CENTRE

From the A6 Motorway branch off at "Évry – Ville Nouvelle".

The Évry town centre project is two-thirds completed. When it is finished, it should cover an area roughly equal to that of the Latin Quarter between the Seine and the Luxembourg quarter. In the early stages, priority was given to administrative, commercial and cultural activities. One of the most positive accomplishments of this scheme is the Agora complex.

In the new town, follow signposts to "Centre-Ville", then "Agora" and finally "Agora-Sud". Leave the car at the covered Terrasses parking (upper level). From there, walk to Place des Terrasses.

★ **Agora.** – *Rotunda-shaped information bureau in the middle.*
This covered square is an interesting forum for communication and contacts. Agora – inaugurated in 1975 – marks the link between the shopping centre on the left and the social, cultural and sporting centre on the right and straight ahead. The different levels open onto the Hexagone (plays, exhibitions), the multi-purpose sports hall shaped as a horse's saddle, called the Arena (shows, concerts, indoor sports) and the Studio (conferences, chamber music). The other sporting and leisure facilities (cinema, swimming pool, skating rink) are located at the far end of the passage, facing the entrance.
Go back up to Place des Terrasses. Bear left. Skirt Place Mendès-France and cross Cours Blaise-Pascal, a pleasant route lined with trees, boutiques and cafés. The new district – gradually spreading to the main station – offers offices, flats and shops. From the far end of the terrace, one can see the administrative quarters surrounding the Préfecture: the various offices built around the lake appear to be floating on the water. To the right of the terrace we find a cluster of buildings known as Quartier des Passages (apartments, small shop, and higher education colleges). On the upper level, it is approached by a series of footbridges and gangways.

★ FERRIÈRES Pop 1 340

Michelin map 101 east of fold 30

The shooting parties on Ferrières estate, the luxurious furnishings of the château and the precious collections gathered by the members of the Rothschild dynasty were the talk of the town for over 100 years. The landscape park – created at the same time as the Bois de Boulogne – especially in the vicinity of the lake, is extremely attractive.

A challenge to tradition. – In 1829 James de Rothschild, founder of the French line of the family, acquired 7 500 acres of hunting grounds formerly belonging to Fouché with a view to building a villa which would accommodate his invaluable collections and satisfy his taste for splendour. The baron did not choose a professional architect: he broke with tradition and hired **Joseph Paxton**, an English glass-house and garden designer with a penchant for modern materials such as iron and glass. Already famed for his London Crystal Palace (destroyed in 1936), Paxton erected a rectangular building flanked by square towers, with a central hall equipped with zenithal lighting. Construction work was completed in 1859. The decoration, left in the hands of the baroness, was entrusted to the French specialist Eugène Lami. On 16 December 1862 Napoleon III paid an official visit to the Rothschilds in their new residence. Delighted by the splendid apartments and the 800 head of game for his day's shoot the Emperor planted a sequoia tree as a commemorative gesture *(see plan overleaf)*.
Less than 10 years later, Jules Favre – in charge of Foreign Affairs in the new National Defence government, turned up at the gates of the château on 19 September 1870. In his capacity as Minister, Favre came to see Chancellor Bismarck, who was staying at Ferrières with King William I of Prussia, to ask him to agree to an armistice. The chancellor however made this conditional on the surrender of Strasbourg, Toul and Bitche, and further implied that the cession of Alsace and part of Lorraine was inevitable. Jules Favre left the premises on the following morning but it was only on 28 January 1871 that the town of Paris fell to the hands of the enemy. In 1977 the Baron Guy de Rothschild and his wife Marie-Hélène donated their château and part of the estate to the Confederation of Paris Universities.

CHÂTEAU *time: 2 hours*

Ⓥ **Exterior.** – Its architecture reflects the various styles of the Renaissance period, including the odd eccentricity that occurred in those times.
Although balusters, galleries and colonnades reigned supreme, the façades were each different. The most striking and the most typically English is the main front overlooking the lake, with its centrepiece flanked by turrets and its display of superimposed galleries. Step back to take in the tall decorative stone chimneys, reminiscent of Chambord Château.

Interior. – A pavilion sporting a large clock is fronted by the main entrance porch which bears the baron's monogram (J. R.) and the family coat of arms (the five Rothschild arrows). A staircase of honour leads to the central hall – 130ft wide and 40ft high under the glass ceiling – now stripped of its paintings and tapestries. Above the main door, a row of telamons and caryatids in bronze and black marble support a musicians' gallery, a popular decorative feature under the Second Empire. The Blue Salon, overlooking the park, has busts of the Empress Eugénie and Bettina de Rothschild, the first proprietress of the château.

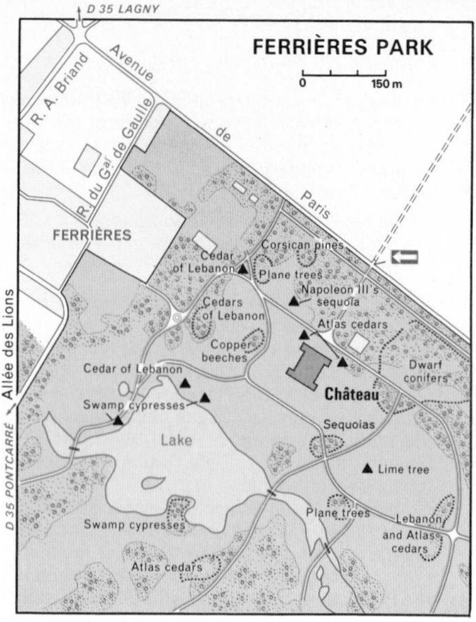

The Louis XVI lounge is the most typical example of Eugène Lami's work: it features off-white wainscoting with pinkish hues, a ceiling mural inspired by Boucher and reproduction Louis XVI furniture. Opposite is the Red Salon, in which the 1870 negotiations took place. It now presents an exhibition on the history of the estate.

★ **Park.** – The park designed by Paxton boasts a number of superb compositions, mainly consisting of ornamental coniferous trees: cedars of Lebanon, numerous Atlas cedars – including the highly decorative blue form – and sequoias, introduced into France around 1850.

Several individual trees also deserve a mention: a cedar of Lebanon with unusually long, spread-eagled branches, swamp cypresses, whose twigs turn deep russet and drop off in winter, copper beeches, groves of plane trees and, on the far side of the lake, feathery weeping species, adding an autumn touch to the tableau.

Outside the park, the Lions' Avenue (Allée des Lions) presents an imposing driveway of stately sequoias.

FERRIÈRES Forest

Michelin map 196 south of folds 21 and 22

Ferrières Forest – acquired by the Ile-de-France region in 1973 – covers 2800ha – 7000 acres and offers picnic and parking areas, numerous footpaths and cycling lanes open all the year round, including a 10-mile trunk road between Beaubourg Wood, Pontcarré and Villeneuve-Saint-Denis. A number of other grassy lanes are practicable in dry weather. One can get to them from the car parks located alongside the N 371, the D 21 and the D 10.

The most attractive sites are Planchette Pond – where fishing permits are issued on the spot by forest wardens –, the lions' or sequoia avenue north of Pontcarré and the plateau planted with elm trees.

South of Pontcarré, the forest is continued by the **Armainvilliers State Forest**, presently undergoing regeneration (mixed groves of oaks and conifers). Picnic areas have been laid out along the N 371, near Étang des Trois-Mares and Étang de la Barrière Noire (D 350).

★ FLEURY-EN-BIÈRE Château

Michelin map 196 folds 44 and 45

Like Courances Château *(see p 65)*, this building dates from the 16C and was designed for Cosme Clausse, Secretary of Finance to Henri II. When the court moved to Fontainebleau, Cardinal Richelieu was Nicolas Clausse's guest on the estate.

From the entrance one can glimpse the stately proportions of the courtyard, sealed off from the street by a stout wall. At the far end, surrounded by a moat, stands the château, built of stone and brick and flanked on its right side by a large stone tower. Several huge outhouses loom on either side of the building. Set back to the right, the gracious Romanesque chapel serves as parish church to the community.

Make up your own itineraries

- ***The map on pages 4 to 6 gives a general view of tourist regions, the main towns, individual sights and recommended routes in the guide.***
- ***The above are described under their own name in alphabetical order (p 36) or are incorporated in the excursions radiating from a nearby town or tourist centre.***
- ***In addition the** Michelin Map **no 196 shows scenic routes, places of interest, viewpoints, rivers, forests...***

★★★ FONTAINEBLEAU Pop 18 753

Michelin map 196 folds 45 and 46

It was not until the 19C that Fontainebleau – which long remained a hamlet of Avon – started to develop, owing to the growing popularity of country residences and the general appreciation of its unspoilt forest.
This residential area has become an important centre for the tertiary industries of southern Seine-et-Marne *département:* the sector includes various workshops and laboratories, a research centre for mining engineers, the European Institute of Business Management and a contemporary archive library a branch of the National Archives.

Military and riding traditions. – Throughout French history, whether under monarchic or republican rule, independent units have been posted to Fontainebleau. Tradition, it seems, favoured the cavalry, present in the 17C with the king's body guard. A number of racecourses and riding schools were created under Napoleon III: the National Centre ef Equestrian Sports perpetuates this tradition *(see the chapter on Principal Festivals at the end of the guide),* while the forest caters for amateur riders.
The history of the town has been marked by several military organisations, notably the Special Military Academy (1803 to 1808, before St-Cyr), the polygon-shaped School of Applied Artillery and Engineering (1871 to 1914) and the SHAPE (Supreme Headquarters, Allied Powers, Europe) headquarters of NATO, which gave the town a cosmopolitan touch from 1947 to 1967.
At present, Fontainebleau houses the Army Sports School, an officers training centre for members of the Gendarmerie Nationale, a Ground Forces Depot, the Service Corps, the Ordnance Corps and a riding centre for the army.

★★★ PALACE

Fontainebleau Palace owes its origins to royalty's passion for hunting; it owes its development and decoration to the kings' weakness for amassing works of art and displaying them in their "family house". This palace has an extremely distinguished past: from the last of the Capetians up to Napoleon III, it was designed for, and occupied by French rulers.

A hunting seat. – A spring in the middle of a forest abounding in game – called Bliaud or Blaut fountain – prompted the kings of France to build a mansion on this spot. The exact date is not known but it was probably before 1137 as a charter exists issued under Louis VII from Fontainebleau, dating from that year. Philippe Auguste celebrated the return of the Third Crusade during the Christmas festivities of 1191; Saint Louis founded a Trinitarian convent, whose members were called Mathurins; Philip the Fair was born there in 1268: unfortunately he also died here following a serious riding accident.

The Renaissance. – Under François I, almost all the medieval buildings were pulled down and replaced by two main edifices, erected under the supervision of Gilles Le Breton. The oval-shaped east pavilion – built on the former foundations – was linked to the west block by a long gallery. To decorate this palace, François I hired many artists: he dreamed of creating a "New Rome", furnished with replicas of antique statues.
The actual building consisted of rubble-work as the sandstone taken from the forest was too difficult to work into regular freestones. The harled façades are enlivened by string-courses of brick or massive sandstone blocks.

The Fontainebleau School – 16C. – The teams of painters and stucco workers were supervised by Rosso, one of Michelangelo's pupils and a native of Florence, also by Primaticcio, a disciple of Giulio Romano who came from Bologna. They developed a decorative technique strongly inspired by allegories with hazy implications. Attention to detail, which typified late Gothic architecture, was no longer in vogue beyond the Loire Valley as it had been during the Early Renaissance.

The Farewell Court at Fontainebleau Palace

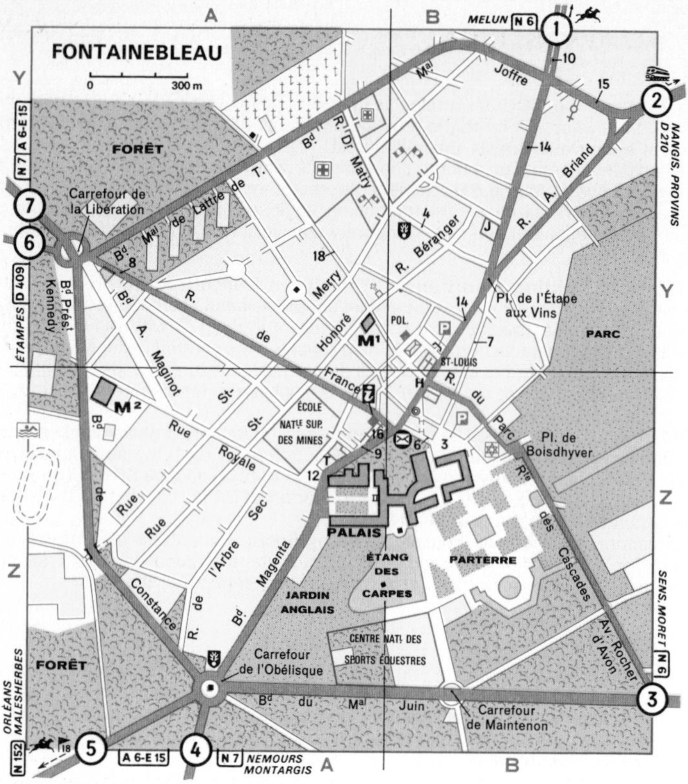

Briand (R. Aristide) ...... BY
Dénecourt (R.) .... AZ 9
Étape-aux-Vins (Pl.) ..... BY
France (R. de) .... AYZ
Grande (R.) .... BY 14
Armes (Pl. d') .... BZ 3
Bois (R. des) .... BY 4
Chancellerie (R. de la) .... BZ 6
Château (R. du) .... BY 7
Churchill (Bd W.) .... AY 8
Foch (Bd du Mar.) .... BY 10
Gaulle (Pl. Gén. de) ..... AZ 12
Leclerc (Bd du Mar.) .... BY 15
Nap.-Bonaparte (Pl.) .... AZ 16
Paroisse (R. de la) .... AY 18

The Fontainebleau artists were more intent on depicting a dreamy form of elegance, characterised by the representation of human bodies arched into arabesque poses.
These painters formed the First Fontainebleau School, which blossomed under the reign of François I. The school created a style of decoration incorporating both stucco and paintings – exemplified by the François I Gallery –, a semi-miniature genre referred to as "French style" by the Italians.
Rosso died in 1540. Primaticcio was sent to Rome to make moulds of famous antique statues – the *Laocoon,* the *Belvedere Apollo* – which were brought back to Fontainebleau and cast in bronze.
In his private suite (Appartement des Bains), the king could feast his eyes on masterpieces by Raphael and Leonardo da Vinci *(The Mona Lisa),* while the tower of the Old Keep housed the silver cutlery, jewellery and other miscellaneous curios that delighted contemporary royalty.

Henri II's château. – Henri II pursued the efforts undertaken by his father. He gave orders to complete and decorate the ballroom, which remains one of the splendours of Fontainebleau Palace. The monograms – consisting of the royal H and the two intertwined C's of Catherine de' Medici – were legion. It has now been accepted that the three superimposed letters from a double D, the monogram of the king's mistress Diane de Poitiers.
When Henri II was killed in a tournament, his widow sent her rival to Chaumont-sur-Loire *(see the Michelin Green Guide Châteaux of the Loire)* and dismissed the foreman Philibert Delorme, who was Diane's protégé. He was replaced by the Italian Primaticcio: those working under him, namely Niccolo dell'Abbate, favoured light, cheerful colours.

Henri IV's palace – 17C. – Henri IV, who adored Fontainebleau, had the palace enlarged quite significantly. The irregular contours of the Oval Court were corrected and he gave orders to build the Kitchen Court and the Real Tennis Court (Jeu de Paume). These he had decorated by a new group of artists, largely of Flemish, and not Italian, inspiration: frescoes were replaced by oil paintings on plaster or canvas. In the same way, the plain wood panelling highlighted with gilding gave way to painted wainscoting. This was the Second Fontainebleau School, whose representatives moved in Parisian circles.

The House of Eternity. – Louis XIV, XV and XVI undertook numerous renovations, aimed at embellishing their apartments. The Revolution spared the château but emptied it of its precious furniture. Napoleon, who became consul, then emperor, thoroughly enjoyed staying at the palace. He preferred Fontainebleau to Versailles, where he felt haunted by a phantom rival. He called the palace "The House of Eternity" and left his mark by commissioning further restoration work. The last rulers of France also took up residence in this historic palace. It was eventually turned into a museum under the Republic.

EXTERIOR *time: 1 hour*

★★ **Farewell Court (Cour des Adieux).** – This former bailey was used only by domestics but its comfortable size soon earmarked it for official parades and tournaments. It was also called the White Horse's Court the day Charles IX set up a plaster cast of the Capitol's equestrian statue of Marcus Aurelius: a small slab in the central alley marks its former location.

The golden eagles hovering above the pillars of the main gate remind visitors that the emperor had made this patio his own court of honour. He gave orders to raze the Renaissance buildings that lay to the west of the court but kept the end pavilions. Walking between the two long wings, one notices that only the one on the left with its brick courses has retained the elegance that characterised the work of Gilles Le Breton, François I's favourite architect. The right wing – which boasted the Ulysses Gallery decorated under the supervision of Primaticcio – was dismantled by Louis XV and rebuilt by Jacques Ange Gabriel.

At the far end of the court the main block, fronted by a balustrade marking the site of the former moat, was completed in several stages ranging from the reign of François I to that of Louis XV. Nonetheless the façades show a certain unity of style. The large horizontal planes of the blue slating are broken by the white façades, the trapezoidal roofs and the tall chimneys of the five pavilions. The celebrated horseshoe staircase executed by Jean Du Cerceau during the reign of Louis XIII, is a harmoniously-curved, extravagant composition clearly reminiscent of royalty's taste for splendour. The staircase served as a majestic backdrop on many occasions. Saint-Simon describes the arrival of the 11 year old Princess Marie Adélaïde of Savoy at Fontainebleau on 5 November 1696 for her betrothal to the duc de Bourgogne. "The entire Court was assembled waiting to receive them on the horseshoe staircase, with the crowd standing below, a magnificent sight. The King led in the princess, so small that she seemed to be emerging from his pocket, walked very slowly along the terrace and then to the Queen-Mother's apartments...".

The Farewell. – On 20 April 1814 the Emperor appeared at the top of the horseshoe staircase. It was one o'clock in the afternoon. The foreign army commissioners in charge of escorting him were waiting in their carriages at the foot of the steps. Napoleon started to walk down the staircase with great dignity, his hand resting on the stone balustrade. His face was white with contained emotion. He faltered a moment while contemplating his guards standing to attention, then moved forward to the group of officers surrounding the Eagle, led by General Petit. His farewell speech, deeply moving, was both an appeal to the spirit of patriotism and a parting tribute to those who had followed him throughout his career. After embracing the general, Bonaparte lowered the flag, threw himself into one of the carriages and was whisked away amid the tearful shouts of his soldiers.

★ **Fountain Courtyard (Cour de la Fontaine).** – The fountain lying on the edge of Carp Lake used to yield remarkably clear water. This was kept exclusively for the king's use and to that end the spring was guarded by two sentinels night and day. The present fountain dates back to 1812 and is crowned by a statue of Ulysses. The surrounding buildings feature stone masonry and the whole ensemble forms a pleasant courtyard. At the far end, the François I Gallery is fronted by a terrace: it rests on a row of arches which once opened onto the king's bathroom suite. The **Pavilion of the Fine Fireplace** on the right is attributed to Primaticcio and was built around 1570. The name originated from the fireplace that adorned the vast first floor hall until the 18C. At that point in history Louis XV – who had arranged the room as a theatre stage rechristening it Aile de l'Ancienne Comédie – dismantled the chimney and the sculpted low reliefs were scattered in all directions. The imposing staircase is in the Italian manner. On the left the Queen Mothers' and Pope's Suite ends in the Grand Pavilion built by Gabriel.

★ **Carp Lake (Étang des Carpes).** – In the centre of the pond – alive with shoals of carp – stands a small pavilion built under Henri IV, renovated under Louis XIV and restored by Napoleon I. It was used for refreshments and light meals.

★ **Golden Gate (Porte Dorée).** – Dated 1528, this doorway is part of an imposing pavilion. It was the official entrance to the palace until Henri IV built the baptistry door. The paintings by Primaticcio have all been restored and the tympa-

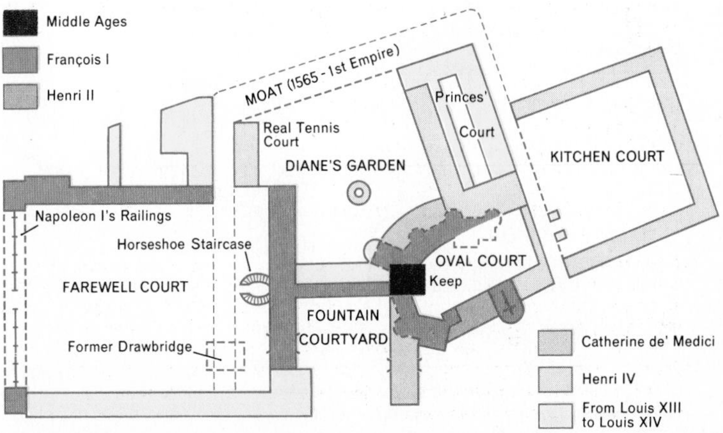

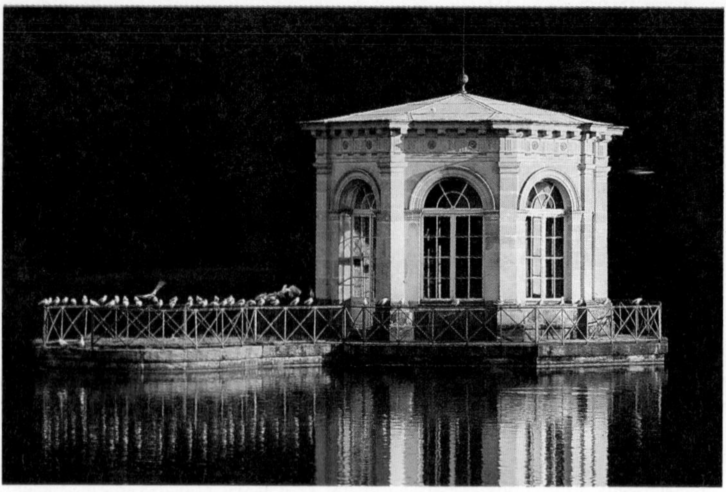

The Pavilion on Carp Lake, Fontainebleau

num sports a stylised salamander, François I's emblem. On the two upper levels are Italian style loggias. The one on the first floor – sealed off by large bay windows – used to house Mme de Maintenon's suite.

The ballroom wing is lined by an avenue of lime trees. The view from the glass front makes one regret that the initial plans to build an open-air loggia were changed on account of the climate. The east end of the two storeyed St-Saturnin Chapel can be seen in the distance.

★ **Baptistry Door (Porte du Baptistère).** – This opens onto the Oval Court. Its foundations were provided by the old drawbridge door – made in *gresserie,* an ornamental type of carved sandstone – in the Farewell Court *(see plan below).* It was the work of Primaticcio. It is crowned by a wide arch surmounted by a dome. The door is named after the christening of Louis XIII and his two sisters Élisabeth and Chrétienne, celebrated with great pomp on a raised platform on 14 September 1606.

★ **Oval Court (Cour Ovale).** – This is by far the most ancient and the most Ⓥ interesting courtyard of Fontainebleau Palace. The site where it stands was the bailey of the original stronghold: of the latter there remains only the keep, baptised St-Louis, although it was probably built prior to his reign. François I incorporated it into the structure he had erected on the foundations of the old castle, shaped like an oval or rather a polygonal figure with rounded corners. Under Henri IV, the courtyard lost its shape, although not its name: the east side was enlarged, the wings were aligned and squared by two new pavilions framing the Baptistry Door. The general layout of the palace was preserved.

Kitchen Court (Cour des Offices). – Its entrance, the Hermes Gate, faces the Baptistry Door and is guarded by two arresting sandstone heads depicting Hermes and sculpted by Gilles Guérin in 1640. The Kitchen Court was built by Henri IV in 1609: it is a huge oblong, sealed off on three sides by austere buildings, alternating

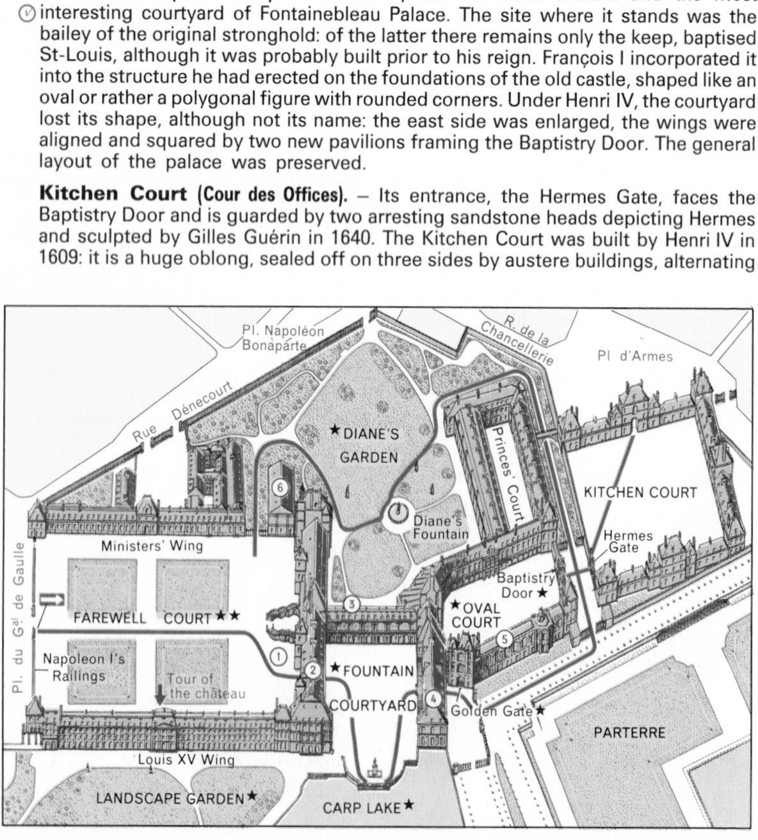

① Horseshoe Staircase ③ François I Gallery ⑤ Ballroom
② Queen Mothers' Wing ④ Fine Fireplace Wing ⑥ Real Tennis Court

with sturdy pavilions. With its imposing porch executed in the style of city gates, it bears a strong resemblance to a square. Walk through the gate and admire its architecture from Place d'Armes: the sandstone front presents rusticated work and has a large niche as centrepiece.
Continue your tour round the palace. You will come to the east and north wings of the Princes' Court, two functional buidings designed or redesigned under Louis XV to provide further accommodation for members of the court.

★ **Diane's Garden** (**Jardin de Diane**). – The formal queen's garden created by Catherine de' Medici was designed by Henri IV and limited by an orangery on its northern side. In the 19C, the orangery was torn down and the park turned into a landscape garden. Diane's fountain, an elegant display of stonework dated 1603, has survived in the middle of the grounds. It has now resumed its original appearance: the four bronze dogs formerly exhibited at the Louvre Museum sit obediently at the feet of their mistress, the hunting goddess.

GRAND APARTMENTS
FIRST FLOOR

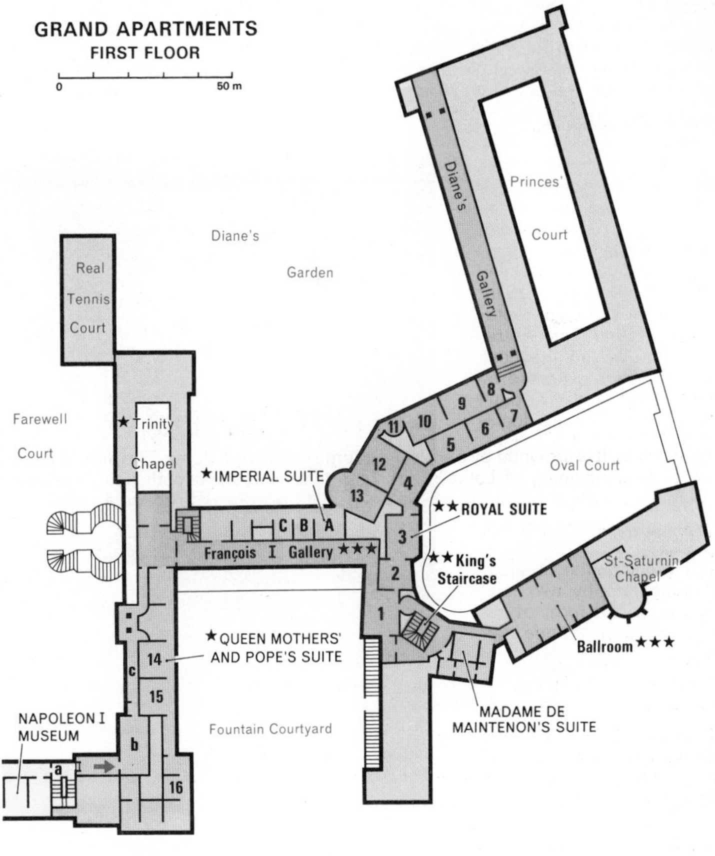

★★★ **GRAND APARTMENTS (GRANDS APPARTEMENTS)**

Ⓥ These are reached by the Stucco Staircase (**a**), the Hall of Splendour (**b**) and the Gallery of Plates (**c**), featuring 128 beautifully decorated pieces of Sèvres porcelain.

★ **Trinity Chapel** (**Chapelle de la Trinité**). – It takes its name from the Trinitarian convent set up on the premises by St Louis. Henri IV had the sanctuary reinforced by vaulting and then decorated. Martin Fréminet (1567-1619), one of the lesser-known followers of Michelangelo, painted the arches with strong, vigorous scenes characterised by daring perspective and foreshortening. These represent the mystery of the Redemption and a number of figures mentioned in the Old Testament.
It was in this very chapel that Louis XV was wedded to Marie Leczinska in 1725 and Louis Napoleon, soon to be Napoleon III, was christened in 1810.

★★★ **François I Gallery** (**Galerie de François Ier**). – Built between 1528 and 1530, it was originally open at both sides, resembling a covered passageway. When Louis XVI enlarged it in 1786, he filled in the windows giving onto Diane's garden. A set of false French windows were fitted for reasons of symmetry. The greater part of the decoration – closely combining fresco and stucco work – was supervised by Rosso, while the wood panelling was entrusted to the Italian master carpenter Scibec from Carpi. François I's monogram and his mascot the salamander were widely represented.
The scenes are difficult to interpret and there are no documents to enlighten us. Basically, they can be split into two groups and lie on either side of the central bay, illustrated by an oval painting depicting two figures: Danaë by Primaticcio and the Nymph of Fontainebleau (1860) after Rosso.

On the east side, near a bust of François I, we find mostly violent scenes, referring to the recent misfortunes of the French king (the defeat of Pavia, the king's captivity in Madrid), the fatality of war and death (the battle between the Centaurs and the Lapiths, Youth and Old Age, the Destruction of the Greek fleet). Beneath the vignette depicting Venus and Love at the edge of a pond, note the miniature picture set in a tablet, representing the château around 1540 with both the François I Gallery and Golden Gate clearly visible.
On the west side, near the entrance, the decor exemplifies the sacred qualities of the royal function – Sacrifice, the Unity of the State – and the concept of filial piety in the old-fashioned sence of the word (Catane's twins Cleobis and Biton): the king, his mother Louise of Savoy and his sister Marguerite d'Angoulême were devoted to one another. The most striking scene is the portrait of an elephant whose caparison bears the royal monogram. The pachyderm was considered the symbol of Science and Wisdom.

★★ **King's Staircase (Escalier du Roi).** – It was built in 1749, under Louis XV, in the bedroom that once welcomed the Duchess of Étampes, François I's favourite. The murals – the history of Alexander the Great – were by Primaticcio (note Alexander taming Bucephalus above the door) and dell'Abbate (Alexander placing Homer's books in a chest on the far wall). The stucco work of the Italian master is highly original: the upper frieze is punctuated by caryatids with elongated bodies.

★★★ **Ballroom (Salle de Bal).** – 30m – 100ft long and 10m – 33ft wide, this room was traditionally reserved for banquets and formal receptions. Its construction was started under François I and completed by Philibert Delorme under Henri II. A thorough restoration programme has revived the dazzling frescoes and paintings executed by Primaticcio and his pupil dell'Abbate. The marquetry of the parquet floor, completed under Louis-Philippe, echoes the splendid coffered ceiling, richly highlighted with silver and gold.
The monumental fireplace is supported by two telamones in the form of satyrs, cast after antique statues in the Capitol Museum in Rome.

The Ballroom Fireplace at Fontainebleau Palace

Mme de Maintenon's Suite (Appartements de Mme de Maintenon). – Note the delicate wainscoting in the Grand Salon, most of which was executed in the 17C.

★★ **Royal Suite (Appartements royaux).** – At the time of François I, Fontainebleau Château featured a single suite of apartments laid out around the Oval Court. Towards 1565, the regent Catherine de' Medici gave orders to double the curved building between the Oval Court and Diane's Garden. Subsequently, French rulers installed their bedrooms, closets and private salons on the side of Diane's Garden. The original suite now houses antechambers, guardrooms and the lounges and salons where the king used to entertain his guests.

Guardroom (Salle des Gardes) (**1**). – The first room of the King's Suite. Louis XIII decorated beam ceiling and frieze.

Keep (Salon du Donjon). – A long triumphal arch leads from the Buffet Hall (Salle du Buffet) (**2**) to a chamber in the oldest tower of the castle. Until the reign of Henri IV, these sombre quarters were occupied by French kings, who used them as a bedroom (**3**) hence its other name, the St Louis' Bedroom. The equestrian low relief portraying Henri IV came from the Fine Fireplace *(p 81)*; it was completed by Mathieu Jacquet towards 1600.

Louis XIII Salon (Salon Louis XIII) (**4**). – It was here that Louis XIII was born on 27 September 1601. His birth is evoked by the coffered ceiling, which depicts cupid riding astride a dolphin. The panel with painted wainscoting is crowned by a set of 11 pictures by Ambroise Dubois: the Romance between Theagenes and Chariclea, executed soon after the king's birth.

François I Salon (Salon François Ier) (**5**). – Of Primaticcio's work there remains only the fireplace.

Tapestry Salon (Salon des Tapisseries) (**6**). – Having been the queen's chamber, the guardroom and the queen's first antechamber, this room became the empress's principal drawing room in 1804, the guardroom once more in 1814 and finally the

Tapestry Salon in 1837. The fireplace dates from 1731 and the Renaissance ceiling in pine wood is the work of Poncet (1835). The furniture was made during the Second Empire. The tapestries telling the story of Psyche were manufactured in Paris in the early 17C.

Empress's Antechamber (Antichambre de l'Impératrice) (**7**). – Formerly the queen's guardroom, this chamber was built on top of the old royal staircase: the ceiling and panelling are both dated 1835. The Gobelins tapestries, executed after cartoons by Le Brun, illustrate the four seasons. The Second Empire furniture features a console, a writing desk in carved oak (Fandinois, 1865) and a set of armchairs of English inspiration. Note the two Indian-style enamel vases produced by the Sèvres manufacture.

Diane's Gallery (Galerie de Diane). – This 80m – 263ft long gilt passageway was decorated during the Restoration and turned into a library under the Second Empire. The painted ceiling portrays Diana and other allegorical figures and eight of the original twenty-four scenes from French history.

White Salon. Queen's Parlour (Salon Blanc. Petit Salon de la Reine) (**8**). – In 1835 it was decorated with furnishings dating from an earlier period: Louis XV wainscoting, Louis XVI fireplace inlaid with bronze, etc. The actual furniture is Empire: chairs in gilt wood by Jacob Frères, settee, armchairs and chairs taken from St-Cloud Château, mahogany console and heads of fantastic animals in bronzed, gilt wood (Jacob Desmalter).

Empress's Grand Salon (Grand Salon de l'Impératrice) (**9**). – Formerly the queen's gaming room, this salon features a ceiling painted by Berthélemy: the scene is Minerva crowning the Muses. The Empire furniture includes chairs and consoles by Jacob Desmalter and a "four seasons" table made in Sèvres porcelain and hand painted by Georget in 1806-1807. The furniture has been upholstered with material woven to the design of the carpet.

Empress's Bedchamber (Chambre de l'Impératrice) (**10**). – This used to be the queen's bedroom. The greater part of the ceiling was designed for Anne of Austria in 1644, the fireplace and the top of the alcove were created for Marie Leczinska in 1747 and the doors with arabesque motifs were installed for Marie-Antoinette in 1787. The brocaded silk was rewoven according to the original pattern in Lyons at the end of Louis XVI's reign.

Among the attractive pieces of furniture, note Marie-Antoinette's bed, designed in 1787 by Hauré, Sené and Laurent, a set of armchairs attributed to Jacob Frères and several comodes by Stöckel and Beneman (1786). The vases are Sèvres porcelain.

Queen's Boudoir (Boudoir de la Reine) (**11**). – A ravishing creation designed for Marie-Antoinette. The wainscoting was painted by Bourgois and Touzé after sketches by the architect Rousseau. The ceiling – representing the tender rays of sunrise – is the work of Berthélemy. The roll-top writing desk and the work table were executed by Riesener in 1786.

Throne Room (Salle du Trône) (**12**). – This was the king's bedroom from Henri IV to Louis XVI. It was Napoleon I who converted it into a throne room. The ornate mural paintings, dating from several periods, were harmonised in the 18C. Above the fireplace is a full-length portrait of Louis XIII, painted in Philippe de Champaigne's studio.

Council Chamber (Salle du Conseil) (**13**). – It already featured in François I's château but was given a semicircular extension in 1773. The ceiling and panelling are splendid examples of Louis XV decoration.

Five pictures by Boucher adorn the ceiling, representing the four seasons and Phoebe, supreme mistress of the starlit skies. The wainscoting presents an alternation of allegorical figures painted in blue or pink monochrome by Van Loo and Jean-Baptiste Pierre.

★ **Imperial Suite (Appartement Intérieur de l'Empereur).** – Napoleon had his suite installed in the wing built by Louis XVI, on the garden side running parallel with the François I Gallery.

Napoleon's Bedchamber (Chambre de Napoléon) (**A**). – Most of the decoration – dating from the Louis XVI period – has survived. The furniture is typically Empire.

Small Bedroom (Petite chambre à coucher) (**B**). – A little private study which Bonaparte furnished with a camp-bed in gilded iron.

Abdication Room (Salle de l'Abdication) (**C**). – According to tradition, the very room in which the famous abdication document was signed on 6 April 1814. The Empire furniture of this red salon dates back to that momentous event.

The François I Gallery leads to the horseshoe vestibule, which lies at the top of the sweeping staircase. This was the official entrance to the palace from the late 17C onwards. Both the gallery of Trinity Chapel and the Queen Mothers' Suite give onto this hall.

★ **Queen Mothers' and Pope's Suite (Appartements des Reines Mères et du Pape).** – Built in the 16C and redesigned under Louis XV following the completion of the end pavilion – now called the Great Pavilion – the suite was named after Catherine de' Medici, Marie de' Medici, Anne of Austria and Pope Pius VII, who stayed there in 1804 and 1812-1814. Napoleon III and Eugénie applied themselves to harmonising, renewing and restoring the decoration and furniture of these apartments.

The ceiling in the Grand Salon (**14**) was taken from the former bedroom of Henri II (1558) and placed here on the orders of Anne of Austria. The decoration – attributed to one of Philibert Delorme's collaborators – represents the Sun and revolving Planets of the Universe.

The state bedchamber (**15**) has a Gobelins tapestry – The Triumph of the Gods – matching the grotesque-style wainscoting executed by the master decorator Jean Cotelle the Elder (1607-1676). The bedroom of the Duchess of Orléans (**16**), previously occupied by the Pope, presents a highly distinguished set of Louis XVI furniture, set off by a superb decor of deep crimson damask.

★ NAPOLEON I MUSEUM (MUSÉE NAPOLÉON Ier)

Ⓥ The museum is dedicated to the emperor and his family: it occupies 15 rooms on the ground level and first floor of the Louis XV wing. Exhibits include portraits (paintings and sculptures), silverware, arms, medals, ceramics (Imperial service), clothing (Coronation robes, uniforms) and personal souvenirs. Thanks to the numerous words of art and furniture adorning their interior, these apartments have kept their princely character.

The rooms on the first floor evoke the Coronation (paintings by François Gérard), the emperor's various military campaigns, his daily life (remarkable folding desk by Jacob Desmalter), the Empress Marie-Louise in formal attire or painting the Emperor's portrait (picture by Alexandre Menjaud) and the birth of the King of Rome (cradles).

The ground floor presents the Emperor's close relations. Each of the seven rooms is devoted to a member of the family: Napoleons's mother, the brothers Joseph, Louis, Jérôme and the sisters Elisa, Pauline and Caroline.

★ SMALL APARTMENTS AND DEER GALLERY (PETITS APPARTEMENTS ET GALERIE DES CERFS)

Ⓥ *These are located on the ground floor below the François I Gallery and the Royal Suite range giving onto Diane's Garden.*

Small Imperial Suite (**Petits Appartements de Napoléon Ier**). – Consists of François I's former bathroom suite (located beneath the gallery), converted into private rooms under Louis XV for the king, Mme de Pompadour and Mme du Barry, and the ground floor of the new Louis XVI wing, situated under the Imperial Suite. The rooms opening onto Diane's Garden have been decorated with Louis XV wainscoting and Empire furniture.

★ **Apartments of the Empress Joséphine** (**Appartements de l'Impératrice Joséphine**). – This suite of rooms adorned with Louis XV panelling was designed for Joséphine in 1808. It lies beneath the grand royal suite.

Under the Council Chamber (1st floor) we find the study, featuring a large rotunda. The Empire furniture here has a feminine touch: Marie-Louise's tambour frame, her easel, etc.

The Yellow Salon constitutes one of the palace's most perfect examples of Empire decoration. The gold coloured silk hangings provide an elegant setting for Jacob Desmalter's choice furniture pieces, set off by a large Aubusson carpet with a white background.

★ **Deer Gallery** (**Galerie des Cerfs**). – Decorated with numerous deer heads (only the antlers are genuine). The mural paintings were renovated under Napoleon III: they represent palatial residences at the time of Henri IV, seen in perspective. It was in this gallery that Queen Christina of Sweden had her favourite Monaldeschi assassinated in 1657. The original casts used to make Primaticcio's 1540 replicas of antique statues are on display in the gallery.

★ GARDENS

These consist of Diane's Garden *(p 83)*, the Landscape Garden, the parterre and the park.

Follow the route indicated on the plan opposite.

★ **Pine Grove Grotto** (**Grotte du Jardin des Pins**). – A rare ornamental composition carved in sandstone, revealing the popular taste for nymphs and bucolic landscapes in vogue towards the end of François I's reign, copied from the Italians. The arches feature rusticated work and are supported by giant telamones giving onto a grotto. Unfortunately the frescoes have disappeared.

★ **Landscape Garden** (**Jardin Anglais**). – It was created in 1812 on the site of former gardens – featuring a pine grove –, redesigned under Louis XIV and abandoned during the Revolution. The Bliaud or Blaut fountain – which gave its name to the palace – plays in a small octagonal basin in the middle of the garden.

Parterre. – This formal garden was started under François I, redesigned under Henri IV and eventually renovated by Le Nôtre. The Tiber and Romulus Basins take their name from a sculpture, based on the antique model, which adorned them in the 16C and then the 17C. The Tiber – melted during the Revolution – was cast after the original (in the Louvre) a second time and is now back in the place Louis XIV had assigned it. Skirt Bréau Canal to get a broad view of the palace.

Until the 18C, a series of cascades marked the end of this first group of tiered fountains. At present there only remains a basin of the same name whose ornate niches are adorned with marble statues.

Park. – It was created by Henri IV, who filled in the canal in 1609 and had the grounds planted with elms, pines and fruit trees. Sixty years before the consecration of the Grand Canal at Versailles, this dazzling sight was a novelty indeed for the *Ancien Régime,* as were the aquatic displays.

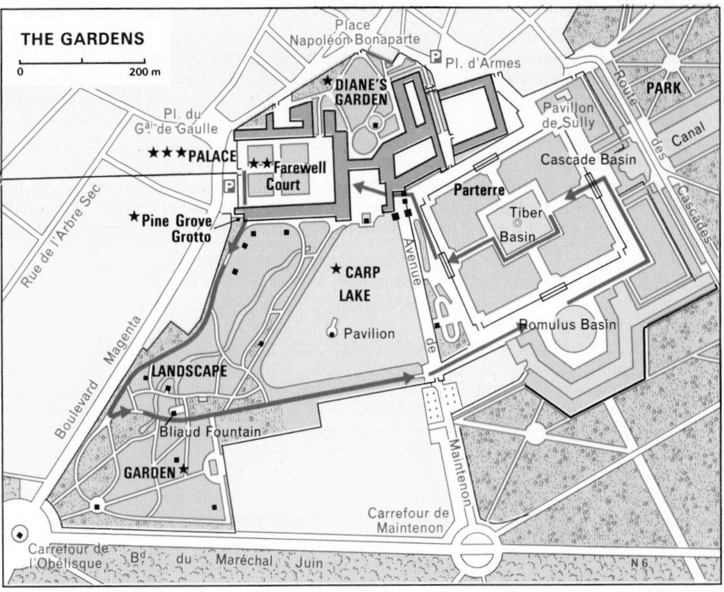

ADDITIONAL SIGHTS

Ⓥ**Napoleonic Museum of Military Art and History (Musée Napoléonien d'Art et d'Histoire Militaire)** (AY M^1). – Contains around one hundred figures, complete with full equipment and arsenal: swordsmen and veterans from the imperial Grand Army, soldiers who fought for the conquest of Algeria and the Second Empire.
The first floor houses a **collection** of statutory **swords and sabres★** dating from the 19C.

Ⓥ**Museum of Figurative Art (Musée d'Art Figuratif)** (AZ M^2). – The second floor of this splendid villa – the headquarters of an international association – has been converted into a painting museum. Over one hundred artists are represented, namely Buffet, Dunoyer de Segonzac, Brayer and Lucien Fontanarosa.

EXCURSIONS

Calvary (Croix du Calvaire). – *5km – 3 miles from the Palace. Leave by Boulevard Maréchal-Leclerc (route ② on the plan). Just before the swimming pool, take the second turning on the left and proceed along Route de la Belle Amélie.*
Almost a mile after the road starts to rise, turn left and you will reach the esplanade and calvary: admire the amazing **view** of the town nestling amidst woodlands.

Avon; By-Thomery. – *Leave Fontainebleau by Boulevard du Maréchal Juin and when you get to the crossroads, Carrefour de Maintenon, turn left into the D 137^E.*

Avon. – Built in the 11C, **St Peter's Church** (Église St-Pierre) features a Romanesque nave surmounted by diagonal arches. While the bell tower was erected in the 12C, the Renaissance door dates from the 15C. The Gothic chancel, the work of architect Jean du Montceau, was completed in 1555. The recently-restored porch was undertaken only in the 18C.

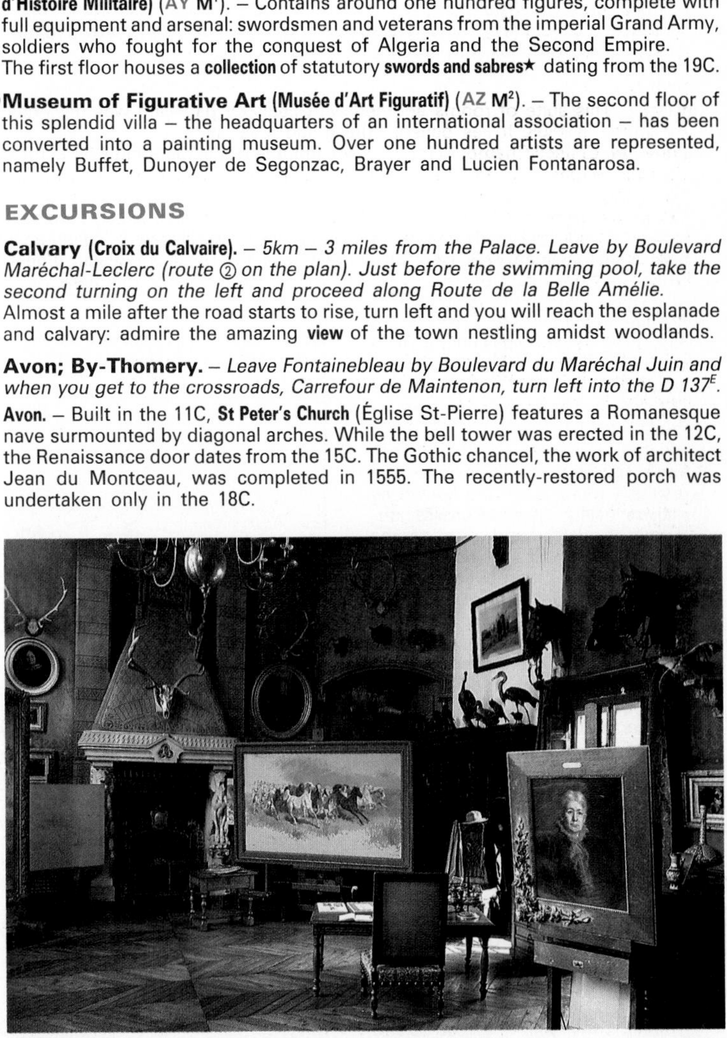

Rosa Bonheur's Studio in By-Thomery

Leave Avon and proceed along the D 137 then turn right on entering the locality of By-Thomery.

Rosa Bonheur's Studio (Atelier de Rosa Bonheur). – In By-Thomery. Rosa Bonheur (1822-1899), a painter of animals widely acclaimed by her contemporaries, bought By Château in 1859 to satisfy her needs for space (she had numerous pets) and tranquillity. The Empress Eugénie paid her a personal visit when she was awarded the French order of merit, the Légion d'Honneur. Another famous visitor, Buffalo Bill, gave her one of his outfits, presently exhibited in the corridor. The tour includes the study (portrait of the artist by Achille Fould, painter and close adviser to Napoleon III), the studio (stuffed animals, deer antlers, her last, uncompleted picture ; *photograph, p 87*) and a small closet furnished with her bed, her wardrobe and a glass cabinet with personal souvenirs.

Bourron Château (Château de Bourron). – *7km – 4.5 miles to the south. Michelin map 237 fold 37. Leave Fontainebleau by ④ the N 7 and turn left when you come to Bourron-Marlotte.*

Built on the remains of a medieval stronghold in the late 16C, the château consists of a large central block flanked by two perpendicular pavilions: these are fronted by two lowish wings (stables). The stone and brick patterns of the façades and the horseshoe staircase evoke the Kitchen Court at Fontainebleau. On the northern side, a swivel bridge spanning the moat leads to another horseshoe staircase. The flower beds to the south afford a good view of the château, its stately and harmonious proportions. Do not miss the charming sight of Ste-Sévère spring, which flows into the Grand Canal to the north of the park. Louis XV came to Bourron Château to meet his father-in-law Stanislas Leczinski, the dethroned King of Poland, who was staying on the estate.

★★★ FONTAINEBLEAU Forest

Michelin map 196 folds 44, 45 and 46

This splendid forest covers a total area of 25 000ha – 62 000 acres: of these, 20 000ha – 50 000 acres – incorporating the Forest of Three Gables (Forêt des Trois Pignons) – belong to the state *(1)*. The venerable Forest of Bière has always provided magnificent hunting grounds, in particular for stag hunting.

The region is especially popular with ramblers and amateur climbers.

GENERAL APPEARANCE OF THE FOREST

Geological formation. – The relief of the forested area comprises a series of parallel sandstone ridges running in an east-west direction.

These ridges are thought bo be the result of a tropical spell that occurred during the Tertiary Era, when strong winds gradually accumulated sand deposits in this part of the Paris Basin. The sand dunes around Fontainebleau subsequently solidified into a hard sandstone matrix and were then buried beneath deposits of Beauce limestone, which had the result of preserving the rolling landscape of this area.

In the places where the upper layer of Beauce limestone was spared from erosion, the valley sides culminate in small **hillocks.** They reach a maximum height of 144m-475ft and bear some of the most charming groves of the forest.

Where the limestone has been eroded to lay bear the sandstone, the resultant rocky areas are known as **platières** locally. These **moorlands** consisting of heather and other shrubs are often cracked and dotted with ponds. When the sandstone layer presents a great many crevices and holes, water seeps through and starts to wash away the underlying sands. The upper sandstone strata is no longer supported. It crumbles as a result, producing picturesque rocky clusters, the famous Fontainebleau **"rochers".**

In the places where the sandstone layer has been eroded away, exposing the sand or the Brie marl and limestone beneath, we find **vales** or **plains** averaging a height of 40 to 80m – 130 to 260ft. The planting of conifers fertilises the soil, making it possible to grow beeches. These produce humus and are eventually replaced by oaks, the ideal tree species for a forest.

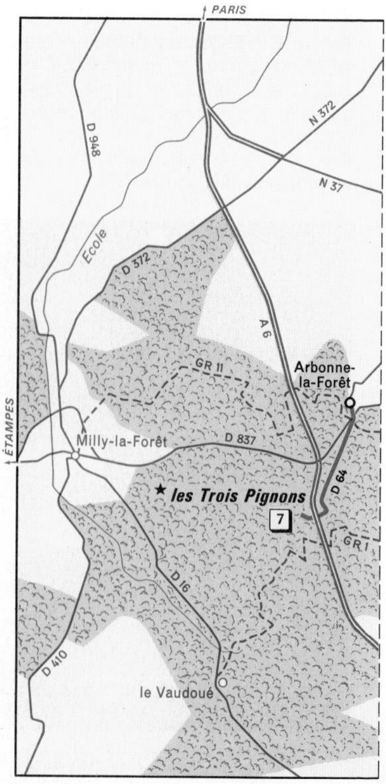

(1) Readers who wish to consult detailed maps should refer to IGN's map at a scale of 1:25 000 (Forest series, no 401).

The forest cover. – The forest was divided into 747 plots in an effort to ensure the best possible plantation. Nine-tenths of the area is under forest, the rest heaths and rocks. Common oaks occupy 8 000ha – 20 000 acres, Scots pines 7 500ha – 18 500 acres and beeches 1 500ha – 3 800 acres. The other species – hornbeams, birches, maritime and Corsican pines, spruce trees, acacias, chestnuts and wild service trees – are the result of former acclimatisation campaigns or remains of the vegetation found on sparsely-wooded moors. Nature reserves cover 416ha – 1 030 acres.

Denecourt-Colinet Paths *(1)*. – These paths lead to the most famous sites of the region. They are the work of two men: Sylvain Denecourt and Sylvain Colinet. The former, who once served in Napoleon's Grand Army, cleared a number of caves, opened up the most attractive sites and laid down 150km – 94 miles of signposted paths.
The routes are discreetly marked in blue on selected rocks or trees, numbered from 1 to 16. The more interesting sights bear a blue star or reference letter (mentioned in the guide published by *Les Amis de la Forêt*). Colinet, a former civil engineer, pursued the efforts undertaken by Denecourt. The signposting was completed after 1975: each major junction was attributed a white, enamel-coated sign with a green border.

Other paths. – In some parts of the forest, the long-distance footpaths marked in red and white coincide with the Denecourt-Colinet routes. The former feature on Michelin maps. *Consult Michelin map 196 Environs de Paris.*
A Grand Tour of Fontainebleau (T.M.F.) 65km – 40 miles long has been marked out in white and green by the French Forestry Commission (O.N.F.: Office National des Forêts).

A haven for climbers. – Around 1910 a few "cragsmen" belonging to the *Club Alpin Français* would go to the Cuvier-Châtillon, Dame-Jeanne and the Eléphant for training climbs. Some even camped overnight next to their favourite rock.
Between the wars, rock climbing schools became extremely popular among French alpine circles and Fontainebleau seemed the ideal place for Parisian climbers, notably the members of the *Groupe de Haute Montagne.*
The dense sandstone rock of Fontainebleau Forest – once described as "good for scouring pans" by a Chamonix guide – presents a wide range of opportunities and difficulties for the proficient climber: overhanging ledges and foliate rocks representing an excellent preparation for advanced expeditions in the Alps, the Himalayas or the Andes. A great many famous mountaineers carried out their training in

(1) The "Guide des Sentiers de promenades dans le Massif forestier de Fontainebleau", published by the Société des Amis de la Forêt de Fontainebleau – based at no 31 Place Napoléon Bonaparte in Fontainebleau – includes a comprehensive list of signposted footpaths (on sale at the Office du Tourisme and in bookshops).
For long-distance footpaths and short-distance routes consult the Topo Guides published by C.N.S.G.R. (see p 202).

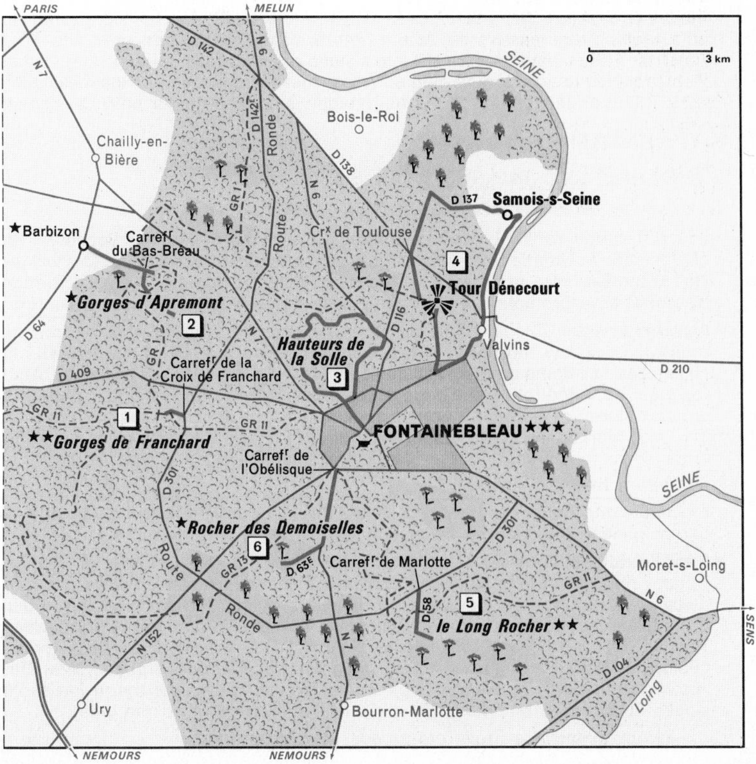

Fontainebleau Forest. Since then, climbing has become quite common in this area. Over a hundred climbing itineraries have been marked out by small arrows painted on the rocks.

Main roads. – *Owing to heavy traffic, try to avoid the N 6, N 7 and Route Ronde, from the Table du Roi crossroads to the Grand Veneur junction. In many cases barriers make it impossible to turn left into the secondary forest lanes.*

★★FRANCHARD GORGES

[1] Round tour starting from Croix de Franchard

1/2 to 2 hours Rtn on foot

From Croix de Franchard crossroads, drive to the huge, shaded grounds of Franchard Hermitage, a popular spot for weekend outings.

Former Franchard Hermitage (Ancien ermitage de Franchard). – This site was occupied by a hermitage which developed in the 12C. In the 13C, a community moved in to look after the pilgrims. By the 19C, celebrations were limited to a country fair on Whit Tuesday. There remain only the walls of the chapel, incorporated into the forest cabin.

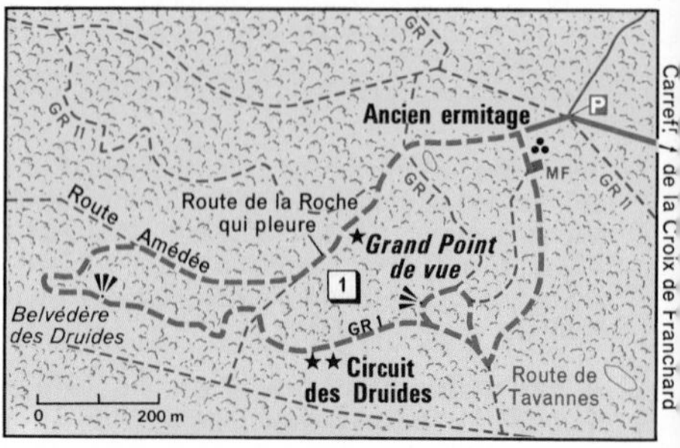

★**Viewpoint** (Grand Point de vue). – *1/2 hour Rtn on foot.* Start from the forest cabin. Once past the fence, skirt the sandy track on the left and start climbing towards the rocks without changing direction. This will lead you to a very sandy road (Route de Tavannes). After 300m – 300 yards, you will spot a mushroom-shaped rock. Turn right onto the plateau and when you reach the rock, bear left towards a bench dominating the ravine. This vista is locally known as Grand Point de Vue. The view of the gorges is breathtaking and in the far distance one can see the Bière countryside and the dark, wooded slopes of Coquibus.

The quickest way to get back to the hermitage is to walk down three steps and bear left. This leads you back to Route de Tavannes.

★★**Druids' Tour** (Circuit des Druides). – *Allow 2 hours.* Proceed to Grand Point de Vue as described above. Upon leaving, turn right after the three steps and follow the blue markings of the Denecourt-Colinet path no 7, which winds its way among laminated rocks, punctuated by the occasional overhang. At the bottom of a first dip in the ravine, cross a sandy track (isolated oak) and start climbing the rocks once more. Follow the climb (↔) signs and go up to the second belvedere, marked with a star. Carry on along the edge of the plateau, facing the view of the gorges, until you reach the **Druids' Belvedere** (Belvédère des Druides) (reference P). Join the signposted lane below which runs eastwards. At the bottom of the gorge, turn right into Route Amédée. At the next fork, turn left into a steep rise known as Route de la Roche qui Pleure (avoid the zigzag route marked in blue that meanders amidst the rocks on the left). This road leads back to the hermitage via a small detour onto the plateau.

★APREMONT GORGES

[2] Round tour leaving from Barbizon

10km – 6 miles – about 3 1/2 hours on foot

Leave Barbizon *(p 37)* by the celebrated Cows' Way (Allée aux Vaches) – the continuation of Grande Rue – which features a splendid forest avenue. This will take you to the **Bas-Bréau crossroads.** The groves bearing the same name were formerly classified as a protected forest zone at the request of the Barbizon painters.

★**Apremont Boulders** (Chaos d'Apremont). – *3/4 hour Rtn on foot starting from the crossroads.* Follow the path marked in blue lying to the left of the refreshment chalet. Start climbing amid an accumulation of rocks of all shapes and sizes. At the top, bear right and follow the edge of the plateau. This affords a good view of the wooded slopes of Apremont gorges and, in the other direction, the plain of Bière. The path marked in blue veers left. A clump of acacia and pine trees marks the entrance to the Robbers' Cave **(Caverne des Brigands)** *(bring a small torch).*

Return to the car.

Proceed along Route de Sully which cuts through the woods and leads onto the barren plateau dominating the distant gorges.

★**Grand Belvedere of Apremont** (Grand Belvédère d'Apremont). – *1/4 hour Rtn on foot.* About 1 mile after the Bas-Bréau crossroads, leave the car at the Cul-de-Chaudron junction. Walk onto the plateau and proceed left along the path marked in blue. When you reach the fork with the Denecourt-Colinet signpost, take a right turning. The lane starts to follow a downward slope, in the midst of a *chaos* (French geological term referring to an accumulation of irregular rocks and boulders). Bear left while remaining at the top of the *chaos.* You soon discover the ravine and its slopes dotted with boulders. The plain of Bière stretches to the west.

Return to the Bas-Bréau crossroads. Park the car.

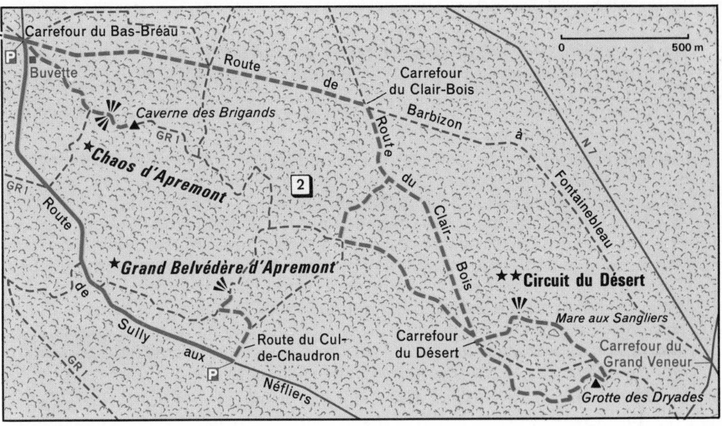

★★ **Desert Tour** (Circuit du Désert). – *3 1/2 hours on foot.* This part of the forest is famed for its dry, barren sites, well-known to painters and film directors in search of a desert location.

Follow the old road from Barbizon to Fontainebleau over a distance of 1 mile and proceed in a southerly direction along Route du Clair Bois. Then take the first lane on the right, Route de la Chouette, which follows a defile and leads back down to Apremont Desert, a valley dotted with numerous boulders, some of which have most unusual shapes. Bear left and walk along path no 6 marked in blue. When you get to the rock resembling an animal with two snouts (reference P), bear right. At the Desert junction, take the path marked in blue. This is difficult to locate and lies between Route du Clair Bois and Route de Milan. This leads you to a ravine flanked by boulders, giving onto a rocky ledge.

Immediately after the Dryads' Cave (Grotte des Dryades), marked with a star, bear left and walk down path "6-6" and up the opposite side of the valley. You will find yourself on a raised platform. To your left lies the Boars' Pond (Mare aux Sangliers). The prominent part of the plateau offers a good **view** of Apremont Desert and the plain of Bière.

Return to the car via the Desert junction and Route du Clair Bois.

★SOLLE HEIGHTS, MONT USSY ROCKS

3 Round tour starting from Fontainebleau

10km – 6 miles – then 1/2 hour Rtn on foot

Leave Fontainebleau by a northwest route, along Rue de la Paroisse, Avenue de Verdun and the cemetery. Proceed along Route Louis-Philippe.

★ **Route Louis-Philippe and Route du Gros-Fouteau.** – These two pleasant roads lead to the heights of Solle. The splendid Gros-Fouteau grove is one of the most ancient plantations of the forest. The name dates back to the 17C, when a superb beech tree (circumference 8m – 27ft) *(fouteau)* was planted near Solle.

The Route des Hauteurs de la Solle gives onto the N 6. Branch off at the first right-hand turning (Croix d'Augas intersection). Proceed towards Fontainebleau along Route de la Butte-aux-Aires.

★ **Mont Ussy Rocks** (Rochers du Mont Ussy). – Leave the car at the first junction of forest lanes you come to after the intersection. Walk a further 100yd until you reach the fork indicating the path marked in blue. Bear right along this path, which overhangs Route de la Butte-aux-Aires and winds its way into the shaded *chaos,* surrounded by pine trees. This brings you to the esplanade called "Point de Vue du Mont Ussy", although in actual fact there is no view. Return to the car via Rue Leclerc, which veers slightly to the right. Drive back to town.

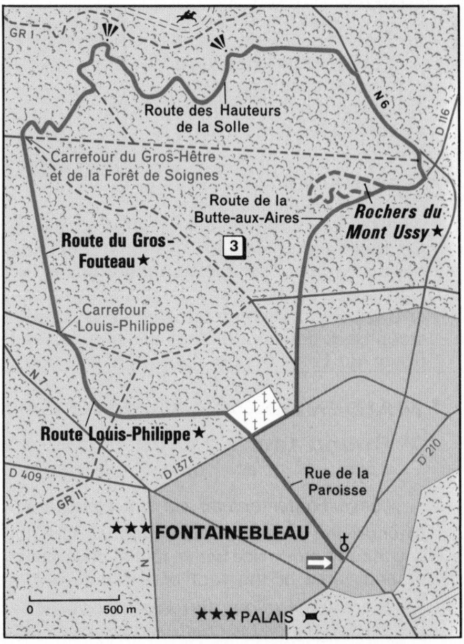

DENECOURT, SAMOIS

4 Round tour starting from Fontainebleau

19km – 12 miles – about 1 1/2 hours – local map p 89

Leave Fontainebleau by ②: just before you get to the railway bridge, turn left into Route de la tour Denecourt.

Denecourt Tower (Tour Denecourt). – Located on the ridge of the Cassepot rock, on top of a heap of boulders, the tower is approached by a narrow, winding lane accessible to cars. It was built by Sylvain Denecourt for the sum of 3500 Francs – a costly investment at the time – and inaugurated by Napoleon III under the name of Fort-l'Empereur. The **panoramic view★** from the summit offers a sweeping landscape of charming woodlands, broken only by a few fields and the modern flats of Avon. Two viewing tables will help you find your bearings. To the north we have the city of Melun, the flare of the Grandpuits refinery, Hérioy village and its church, Ste-Assise station (to its right, one can see with binoculars, two Parisian landmarks, the Eiffel Tower and Montparnasse Tower). To the east we find Fontaineroux, Montereau-Surville, Samoreau and the new blocks of flats in Avon.

At the foot of the mound, take a right turning back into Route Jean-Bart. When you draw level with the Toulouse cross, follow directions to Fontaine-le-Port along the D 116 and 1 mile further on, turn right onto the D 137 towards Samois.

Samois-sur-Seine. – Pop 1 575. This residential district, built on the terraced slopes of the Seine valley, presents a pleasant group of country cottages which line the old paved ramp (Rue du Bas-Samois) leading down to the river.
In the 15C, when Fontainebleau was a tiny hamlet, the population of Samois was estimated at 5000. The presence of islets in the Seine river facilitated the installation of a fortified bridge and the construction of several mills under the wide arches. These disappeared in the 19C and Samois gradually slipped into inactivity.

Drive down to Quai de la Seine to the north, along Boulevard Aristide-Briand. L'Ile du Berceau – a small isle joined to the banks by two footbridges – makes a pleasant walk. It forms an ox-bow lake and accommodates numerous pleasure boats. The whole **setting★** is most engaging.
Proceed upstream along Quai de la Seine and return to Fontainebleau via Valvins.

★★ LONG ROCK (LE LONG ROCHER)

5 Round tour starting from Marlotte Crossroads

1.5km – 1 mile – then 2 hours Rtn on foot

Along Route Ronde branch off towards Marlotte.

After 1/2 mile, before reaching a steep slope, turn left into Route du Long Rocher, a sandy forest lane (O.N.F. board: "Zone de Silence de la Malmontagne").

Park the car at the next crossroads (barrier).
Start walking along Route des Étroitures (first turning on the right).

After 100yd, you will cross path no 11, marked in blue. Turn into it on the right.

Narrow Belvedere (Belvédère des Etroitures). – Reference U. Face south and admire the view of the Loing Valley and the town of Marlotte.

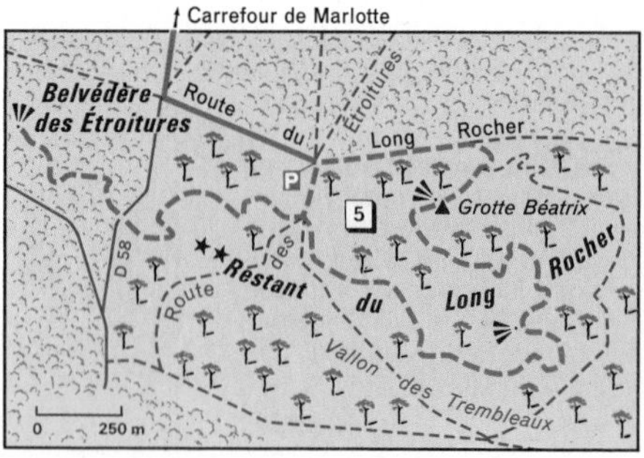

Turn round and follow the signposted path (blue) which weaves its way through the boulders and pine trees. After following a somewhat eccentric route, you reach the top of a plateau called Restant du Long Rocher.

★★ Restant du Long Rocher. – The edge of the plateau, strewn with uneven-sized boulders, affords several nice views of the forest.
Go back to the blue path no 11 and proceed along it in an easterly direction. Leave the plateau via the precipice that houses Béatrix's Cave (Grotte Béatrix). You will walk past a series of boulders used as an exercice by mountaineering schools (red arrows). Further along, the path rises slightly. At that point, branch off and take the steep track downwards that is clearly marked on the left. This will lead you back to Route du Long Rocher. Bear left and you will get back to your starting point.

★ MAIDENS ROCK (ROCHER DES DEMOISELLES)

6 Round tour starting from Fontainebleau

3.5km – 2 miles – then 1 hour Rtn on foot

Leave Fontainebleau via the Obélisque crossroads, ④ and the N 7.

After driving under Vannes Aqueduct, turn right into Route de Recloses. Just before you reach a steep rise with a raised pavement, take a right turning and park the car in a sandy area at the foot of the fern-covered rocks.

Start walking along the forest lane closed by a barrier. At the next fork, bear right and go up towards the crest. You will cross path no 9, marked in blue. Turn left into it.

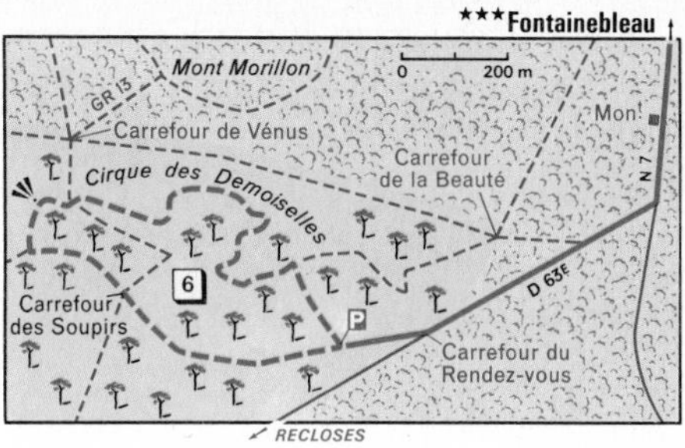

After a series of bends in the Maidens Cirque (Cirque des Demoiselles), the path leads down to a crossroads (Denecourt-Colinet signpost).
Turn right into path no 9. This is also the start of long-distance footpath no 13 (red and white markings). The rocks have smooth surfaces and unusually sharp, pointed crests. A belvedere offers a view of Mont Morillon plain.
Carry on walking along path no 9: it eventually leads to the Sighing Crossroads (Carrefour des Soupirs) which marks the end of the rocky landscape.
Take the road between plots 148 and 156 and then beyond the next crossroads the one between plots 148 and 155 to return to the car.

★ THE THREE GABLES (LES TROIS PIGNONS)

7 Round tour starting from Arbonne

2.5km – 1.5 miles – then 3 hours Rtn on foot

Leave Arbonne to the south.

Take the road to Milly and immediately afterwards bear left towards Achères-la-Forêt (D 64). After 1 mile, the road veers to the left, nearing the motorway. A right turning will lead you off the main road and under the motorway. Park the car.
The Three Gables massif constitutes an unusual extension of Fontainebleau Forest. Mountaineering enthusiasts were the ones to publicise the stony, barren sites of this area, unique in Ile-de-France: dry valleys, eroded peaks and a number of peculiarities common to sandstone landscapes.

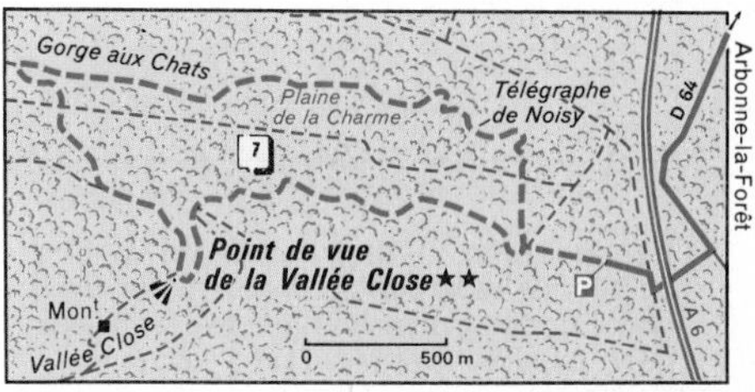

From the car park, go straight ahead and follow the road that skirts the wire fencing of two houses on the right. When you get to the corner of the fencing, bear right and walk to the edge of a slight, sandy depression: you will see the starting point of the Denecourt-Colinet path no 16.
On the opposite side of the depression, in straight alignment with the plaque, is the first blue mark. Having crossed a flat stretch of land dotted with boulders, the path passes the now empty platform of Noisy telegraph transmitter (pulled down) and winds its way onto the plateau. After one hour's walking, you enter a chestnut grove. The path follows the recesses of the impressive Cats' Canyon (Gorge aux Chats), and continues in a southeasterly direction. After a while, it goes south, crossing a sandy, rocky area cleared of trees.

★★ **Viewpoint of Close Valley** (Point de vue de la Vallée Close). – The edge of the plateau offers a pleasant **view**★★ of the massif. In the foreground, a monument crowned by a cross of Lorraine pays homage to the local Publican Resistance network.
The path marked in blue then turns northwards avoiding the wide sandy track previously explored and follows an eastward direction, leading you through oak coppices and clumps of heather, back to the starting point.

FRENCH VEXIN (LE VEXIN FRANÇAIS)

Michelin maps 196 folds 2 to 6 and 237 folds 3 and 4

French Vexin lies between the Oise and the Epte, the river that has been a border to Normandy territory since the Treaty of St-Clair-sur-Epte in 911 *(see the current Michelin Green Guide Normandy Seine Valley)*. This area of Ile-de-France is of great historic and cultural interest.

The Vexin Churches. – The villages of this region are usually grouped together in a most picturesque manner. They present fine examples of rural houses with dry-stone walls.
Religious architecture has greatly benefited from the existence of nearby quarries and by the services of two families of Renaissance architects whose work was fortunately spared by the Wars of Religion. They were the Lemercier brothers and the Grappin, a family from Gisors. While the former had produced St-Eustache (Paris) and St-Maclou (Pontoise) *(p 139)* and had also worked at Épiais-Rhus and Marines, the latter were famed for their accomplishments in Montjavoult, Nucourt, St-Gervais and Vétheuil.
The surrounding villages and hamlets lacked the necessary funds to build new churches and had to be content with extensions or renovations. This is where one can recognise the stamp of a true architect: his work must not only be flawless, but it must also blend in harmoniously with the original stonework.

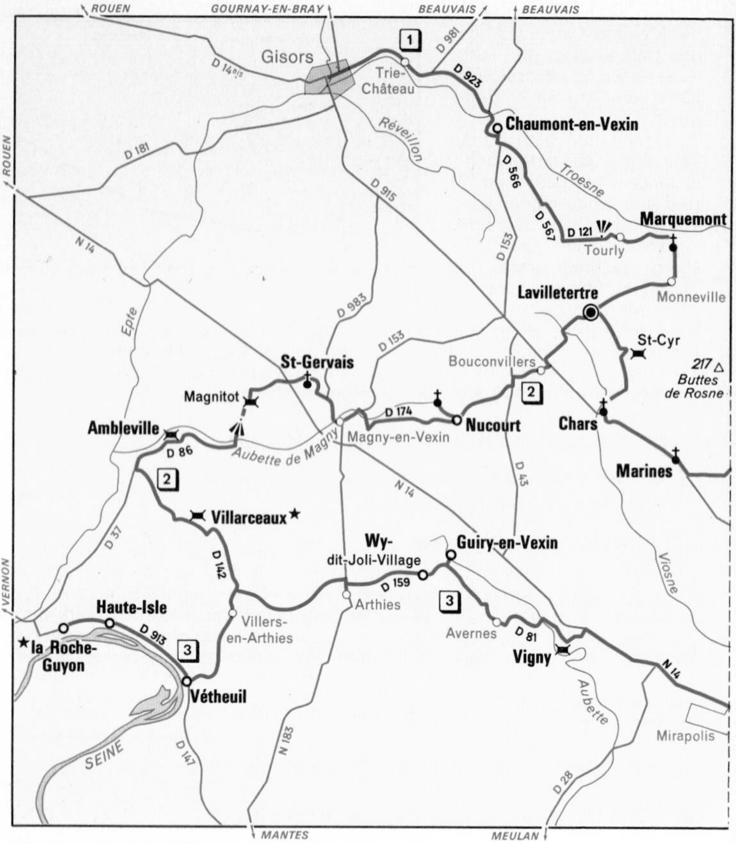

Landscapes. – The French Vexin with its loess covering has been appreciated as a fertile region since Roman times. Today large and highly mechanised farms concentrate on cereals, sugar beet and vegetables. This pleasant rural landscape is interrupted by deeply encased valleys and forested outliers such as the Buttes de Rosne.

THE UPLAND ROUTE

1 From l'Isle-Adam to Gisors *54km – 33 miles – allow 2 1/2 hours*

L'Isle-Adam. – *Description p 101.*

After crossing Parmain, the road reaches a spur of the Vexin plateau and then dips down towards Sausseron Valley.

Nesles-la-Vallée. – *Description p 132.*

Épiais-Rhus. – Pop 452. The village has a splendid Renaissance church characteristic of the area. It was the work of the Lemercier brothers and features an open-work bell tower. The church is perched up on the heights and affords a good view of Cergy-Pontoise in the far distance.

Grisy-les-Plâtres. – Pop 443. Admire the elegant, slender lines of the 13C church. Looking north between Grisy and Bréançon, one can see a stretch of fields and, further away, to the wooded heights known as the Buttes de Rosne.

Marines. – Pop 2 174. A Renaissance chapel with an octagonal base was added on to the 16C church. It is surmounted by a coffered cupola adorned with angels' heads, attributed to Jacques Lemercier.

Chars. – *Description p 53.*

Leave Chars along the road which passes behind the church and climbs up onto the plateau. When you arrive onto the platform, bear left towards Lavilletertre.

On your way you will pass by the **Château of St-Cyr** (17C): nestling in a pleasant setting of greenery, it still presents the image of the lordly manors of the past.

Marquemont Church. – *Description p 116.*

Drive down to the foot of the hill towards Marquemont-Bas.

Turn left into the D 121, which skirts the base of the Vexin escarpment. This is where the Pays de Thelle plateau starts, a flat, lowish stretch of land *(p 116)*. After Tourly, the road takes you back up onto the Vexin plateau, which commands an extensive view of the northern horizons. Turn right and follow directions towards Liancourt-St-Pierre, taking a left turning before you actually reach the locality.

Chaumont-en-Vexin. – *Description p 62.*

Proceed towards Gisors by crossing the Troesne valley and Trie-Château (see current Michelin Green Guide Normandy Seine Valley).

THE PLATEAU

2 From Lavilletertre to Villarceaux

28km – 17 miles – allow 1 1/2 hours – Local map opposite

Lavilletertre. – Leave the town along the road leading to Bouconvillers: a delightful shady avenue running along the valley of the Viosne, which takes its source nearby in a picturesque pond. You will drive past a succession of fields, all under cultivation. Note the clusters of small hamlets in the distance, characterised by their Gothic bell towers.

When entering Bouconvillers, turn left into the main road to Pontoise and follow it for 100m – 100yd. Then turn right towards Nucourt.

Nucourt. – Pop 544. Most of the houses here were rebuilt after the Second World War. The nearby quarries were used by the Germans to assemble their V-1 missiles: as a result the village was consistently bombed by the R.A.F. The quarries have since been made into mushroom beds.

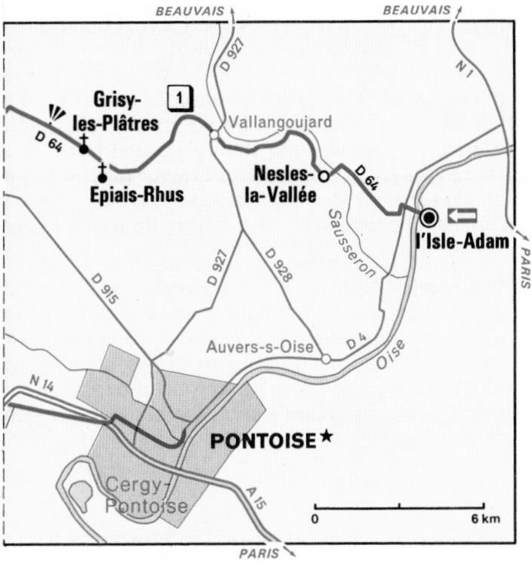

Cross Nucourt bearing right. Drive towards the church standing on its own in the middle of a field.

The church has an unusual silhouette: the tall roof conceals the base of the 12C bell tower while a sturdy but truncated 16C stone tower abuts the west front.

Leave Magny-en-Vexin along the old road to Rouen. Leave the Gisors road on your right and take the first turning on the right towards St-Gervais.

Ⓥ **St-Gervais.** – Pop 688. At the top of a steep incline, the **church** proudly sports a Renaissance façade by Jean Grappin *(p 93)*. The doorway is graced by a triumphal arch. Among the many statues is a 16C one of St Catherine while against the pier is a Virgin and Child and the kneeling figure of St George.

Cross the road to Rouen and turn left after 1 500m – 1 mile.

On the left admire the view of Magnitot estate (late 18C château). The narrow road follows the northern slopes and dips down into the charming valley of the Aubette de Magny. The village of Omerville can be seen nestling on the opposite side.

Ambleville. – Pop 339. The church on the village square adjoins the Renaissance façade of the local château, attributed to a member of the Grappin family *(p 93)*. It was occupied by the Mornay, who owned the neighbouring seigniory of Villarceaux in the 17C.

The road descends into the valley of the Epte. When you reach the St-Louis crossroads, take a left turning, then turn left again toward Chaussy.

★ **Villarceaux.** – *Description p 200.*

VALLEYS, GROVES AND "CLIFFS"

3 From Pontoise to La Roche-Guyon

51km – 62 miles – allow 3 1/2 hours – Local map above

Pontoise. – *Description p 139.*

Leave Pontoise by ⑥, the N 14 the road to Rouen.

Vigny. – Pop 953. Originally built by Cardinal d'Amboise (1460-1510), minister of Ⓥ Louis XII and a dedicated patron of the Italian Renaissance in France, the **château** developed into a pastiche of the Loire châteaux in the 19C.

Guiry-en-Vexin. – *Description p 99.*

Wy-dit-Joli-Village. – Pop 233. Legend has it that while passing through Wy, Henri IV exlaimed *"Le joli village!"* (What a pretty village!) and that the local administration Ⓥ adopted this charming designation. The **Museum of Tools** (Musée de l'Outil) is housed in a recently-discovered steam baths establishment dating from Gallo-Roman times (2C AD). The collection includes wrought-iron objects manufactured after the 14C: anvils, tools used by blacksmiths and farriers, cutting instruments, farming tools, waffle-irons, etc. Note the two signs belonging to a blacksmith and a wheelwright's workshop. The first floor is dedicated to trades of the past, while the ground level presents an exhibition of contemporary creations made on the premises (cocks cut out of metal, works of art).

Proceed west to Arthies, turn right towards Magny-en-Vexin, then take a left turning. Drive to Villarceaux through Maudétour.

★ **Villarceaux.** – *Description p 200.*

Vétheuil. – *Description p 199.*

The road runs parallel with the course of the Seine. The Vexin plateau, incised by a loop of the river, ends in a steep escarpment with a series of chalky spurs.

Haute-Isle. – Pop 233. This former troglodyte village was spread out over five levels of caves *(boves)*. The houses lining the single main street were built in the 18C. Beyond a small graveyard built into a terrace lies the **church**, entirely carved out of the chalk cliff thanks to the generosity of Boileau's nephew. The excavation work started in 1670 and was to last for about ten years. A series of subsequent campaigns were carried out at a higher altitude. The tiny bell tower (23m – 75ft long by 8m – 27ft high)has also been carved out of the cliffs. The retable and parclose around the chancel feature 17C woodwork.

The approch to La Roche-Guyon is impressive as it takes you past the ancient medieval keep.

★ **La Roche-Guyon.** – *Description p 147.*

★ GALLARDON

Pop 2 304

Michelin map 196 fold 39

Nestling in the Voise Valley, on the edge of Beauce and Hurepoix territory, this hamlet has preserved its original, old-fashioned setting. The stepped roofing and tall spire of the church mark the horizon, together with the cylindrical form of a modern water tower and the "Gallardon shoulder", a truncated tower perched at a precarious angle. These three landmarks form a strange **silhouette★**, which may be seen from a distance of several miles and especially from the Rambouillet to Chartres road via Orphin.

Gallardon Shoulder (Épaule de Gallardon). – Best seen from a distance. This fine circular 38m – 125ft tower was partly dismantled in 1443 by Jean Dunois, who resented the constant threat that the tower represented and who feared a new offen sive on the part of the English. The name may have come from the Latin word *specula* (observatory) but the local farmers favour a more colourful explanation: seen from a certain angle, the tower resembles a sheep's shoulder blade stuck into the ground.

SIGHTS

Viewpoint. – If you cross the valley coming from Chartres, park the car when you draw level with the Renault garage and start walking towards the town centre. Just before the first bridge, bear right and follow the banks of the Voise.

You will soon see the church and the leaning tower, which looks as if it is about to collapse at any moment.

Church (Église). – The tiered roofing can be spotted from a distance: it dates from the 13C, when a raised Gothic chancel was added to the building. The steeple is 76m – 250ft high. Take a look at the east end where the tower, its spire and the chancel with double flying buttresses form a light, well-balanced composition.

The **chancel★** is remarkable for its 12C ambulatory – the columns rise from a low parclose wall – and especially for its distinctly Gothic elevation, completed under St Louis. Note the intricate tracery of the clerestory windows in the right-hand bays. Gallardon Church has an unusual nave, featuring a painted wooden barrel vault, consisting of small planks of stave wood cut according to the coopers' requirements. The decoration dates from 1709. The painted motifs – some are very faint – feature a key and a sword, the respective symbols of St Peter and St Paul, the patron saints of the church.

Like in many country churches with timbered ceilings – particularly around - Chartres – the horizontal **tie beams** and vertical **king posts** designed to support the roofing feature carved heads belonging to imaginary beasts. The timbering dates back to the 15C.

GONESSE

Pop 22 923

Michelin map 101 fold 7

It was Hugh Capet who incorporated Gonesse into royal territory. During the 16C, a fancy variety of bread was baked in Gonesse every day and sent to Paris, where it found favour among the wealthy bourgeois. In the 17C Parisian bakers responded by producing a novel speciality – "soft loaves". The inhabitants of Gonesse asked the Parlement to ban these on the grounds that they were harmful to public health. The legal dispute lasted several years but the Parisians eventually won the case.

★ **Church (Église).** – *Rue du Général-Leclerc.*

Built in the 12 and 13C, it stands on a small hillock in the old town centre. Its most interesting feature is the east end. The pier on the main doorway is adorned by a statue of St Peter, the patron saint of the church. Inside, note the timbering of the 13C nave and the 12C chancel, surmounted by diagonal vaulting. Admire the superb organ, embellished by Renaissance paintings. Two pictures are placed above and to the left of the sacristy door: an *Entombment* from the 15C and Fouquet's *Descent from the Cross.*

GRAND MORIN Valley

Michelin map 196 folds 22, 23 and 24

Il you are coming from the south, you will find the Grand Morin Valley a welcome change from the uniform, monotonous Brie countryside. Undulating hillsides crowned with spinneys circle great meadows planted with apple trees. Lined by a double row of poplar trees, the Grand Morin winds its way through this vast, verdant setting: a foretaste of this is provided by the pleasant upland road running from Lagny to Couilly along the N 34.

FROM LAGNY TO COULOMMIERS

59km – 37 miles – about 3 hours

Lagny. – *Description p 105.*

Leave Lagny from the east along the N 34 and make for Chessy.

Ⓥ**Chessy.** – Pop 1 018. The **Brain-Twister's Museum** (Musée du Casse-Tête) *(13 Rue Laguesse)* exhibits 2000 objects from countries all over the world. The oldest is a Chinese puzzle made in the 3C. Among the most striking games feature a superb triacontahedral and a life-size wooden robot consisting of 4508 components. The glass cabinets offer other teasers such as jigsaws and liquid bubble games.

Cross Chessy and turn right when you reach Chalifert Church.

The narrow road soon commands a view of the hillsides that the Marne river skirts between Dampmart and Condé-Ste-Libiaire. Further north, one can glimpse the cereal growing countryside around Multien and the battlefield of September 1914 *(p 134)*. Drive down to Coupvray-Bas, which lies on the floor of the valley.

Coupvray. – Pop 1 416. A well-preserved Brie village nestling in greenery, Coupvray is spread out on two levels. Lower down, near the canal, the quarter of Coupvray-Bas was the birthplace of Louis Braille (1809-1852), inventor of the blind people's Ⓥalphabet. The house has been turned into the **Louis Braille Museum** (Musée Louis Braille). The cottage reflects the lifestyle of a local village family during the last century. The workshop of Louis' father, who was a saddler and a wine-grower, features all the tools of the trade (it was one of these cutting instruments that caused the young boy to lose his sight.)

The room on the first floor presents the basic technique and material relative to the Braille alphabet: slate, guide board, stylus. Visitors may also see an early Braille writing machine and a curious device dating from 1839: it enabled the blind to create letters visible to sighted people by making minute perforations and having them imprinted on tinted paper. On the centenary of his death, in 1952, Louis Braille's relics were transferred to the Panthéon with great pomp. The cemetery – on the road coming from Chalifert – offers only his tombstone and an urn containing the mortal remains of his hands.

Turn around and drive back up onto the plateau to reach the N 34. Cross the river.

Pont-aux-Dames. – The name Pont-aux-Dames (Ladies' Bridge) is believed to have monastic origins. A Cistercian abbey for women was built close to the confluent of the rivers Marne and Grand Morin and destroyed during the Revolution. It used to welcome the "favourite ladies" who had fallen out of favour. In 1774 Mme du Barry took up residence there for a year, banished from court after Louis XV's death. The park occupies the seat of the former abbey. Beyond the great rolling lawns, in a corner of the park, shaded by huge, stately trees, rests the French actor Constant Coquelin, the creator of Cyrano de Bergerac, who died at Pont-aux-Dames in 1909.

Crécy-la-Chapelle. – Pop 2 418. The locality has preserved an old-fashioned appearance owing to its highly distinctive layout of a medieval town: the main streets are arranged concentrically parallel with a series of defensive ditches, fortified by stone walls and towers, many of which still stand today. The Saints' Tower houses a small Ⓥ**Underwater Museum** (Musée Sub-aquatique) which displays objects uncovered from the bed of the Grand Morin (Merovingian sarcophagus). Walk past the Meaux gateway and enjoy the promenade along the outer moat.

The 13C Collegiate Church at La Chapelle-sur-Crécy

★ **La Chapelle-sur-Crécy.** – The **Collegiate Church** *(photograph p 97)* built on the valley floor around 1 250 features unusually sturdy flying buttresses. The bell tower with its four gables is characteristic of Brie architecture. The fragments of a low relief were recovered during renovation work and assigned to the tympanum of the main doorway. Top: Crowning of the Virgin; left: Assumption; right: St Martin; bottom: Offerings of the Magi and Baptism of Christ.
The floor level in the nave was raised by 1.5m – 5ft in the 17C following flooding by the Grand Morin. It has now been lowered to its original level.
The chancel features a three tiered elevation of the utmost simplicity, a fine example of Radiant Gothic. The nave is 13C, the four bays at the west end 15C. Unfortunately there was not sufficient room to harmonise the Flamboyant tracery with the interior architecture.
In the left aisle, next to a St Sebastian, note the statue of St Fiacre, patron saint of Brie and gardeners, clutching a spade.

Turn round and drive back to Crécy. Leave the town via the D 20, the road to Rozay-en-Brie. Branch off 1 mile after Tigeaux, having passed Dammartin Cemetery on your right. Bear left to get to Dammartin Church and pass it on the right.

The road weaves its way along the slope overlooking the south bank of the river and reaches a "modern" village. Turn right at the top of a short rise. At the next junction, take a left turning and follow the route marked "La Celle-d'en Bas – Faremoutiers". Do not cross the river.

Drive up to Faremoutiers. The D 216 follows an upstream route, towards Coulommiers.

Coulommiers. – Pop 12 251. This market town resting on the banks of the Grand Morin is the trading centre for Coulommiers, the famous Brie cheese. The former Capuchin Chapel – presently undergoing restoration work – houses temporary exhibitions.

Make life easier by using ***Michelin Maps*** *with your* ***Michelin Guide.***

★ GROS BOIS Château

Michelin map 101 fold 28 – 2km – 1 mile south of Boissy-St-Léger – Michelin plan 24

The château was built in 1597 for one of Henri IV's financial advisers, the Baron de Sancy. It was subsequently bought by Charles de Valois (1625), the legitimised bastard of Charles IX and Marie Touchet, who had it considerably enlarged. The estate frequently changed hands and its last owner before the Revolution was the comte de Provence, soon-to-be Louis XVIII. The château was sold as state property and acquired by Barras, a member of the Directoire who revelled in leading a life of luxury at Gros Bois. Dismissed by Bonaparte on 18 Brumaire,Barras withdrew to his château. Soon afterwards, he ceded it to Général Moreau. Unfortunately the latter was forced into exile by the First Consul. In 1805 Gros Bois Château became the property of Maréchal Berthier.

Maréchal Berthier, Prince de Wagram. – Born in Versailles in 1753, Louis Alexandre Berthier was the son of the court works surveyor. By the age of 17, he had served in the American War of Independence under the orders of Général Rochambeau. He was promoted Colonel in 1789 and appointed General of the National Guard at Versailles. In 1796, when Napoleon took command of the Italian army, Berthier was chief of staff of the imperial Grand Army. At the time of Bonaparte's abdication (1814), Berthier was made marshal, Prince of Wagram and sovereign Prince of Neuchâtel. He was wedded to the Duchess Marie, niece to the King of Bavaria, and showed sympathy for Louis XVIII. When Napoleon returned from Elba, Berthier refused to follow him and withdrew to Bavaria. A few weeks later, he was found dead under a window of his father-in-law's château in Bamberg. Berthier accomplished wonders at Gros Bois in terms of decoration and furniture. His shooting parties were extremely famous and in 1809 one of these gatherings was attended by all the rulers and princes of the Empire.

Château. – It emerges at the end of a long avenue flanked by lawns lined with chestnut trees. The main block, built by the architect Florent Fournier and completed in the early 17C, is framed by two protruding Louis XIII wings by Jean Thiriot. The whole ensemble – built around the court of honour – is encircled by a dry moat. The tour gives a clear idea of the decoration and furniture that characterises the château at its moments of glory, i.e. during the *Ancien Régime* and under Napoleonic rule. The **furniture**★★ is truly magnificent. The Bailiffs' Room (Salon des Huissiers) features a number of works by Jacob, along with family portraits by Gros (First Empire) and Winterhalter (Second Empire). The Imperial Salon houses several portraits of Napoleon I. The Battle Gallery accommodates a series of 8 paintings executed by Carle Vernet and his pupils, depicting the battles in which the marshal had fought. At the far end of the gallery, the Library has retained its original appearance, except for the ceiling.
The Ballroom lies at the centre of the château and affords a sweeping perspective of the park *(private)*. This room gives onto the Hunting Salon (splendid paintings by Oudry and Desportes) and Berthier's study. All three rooms present typical French ceilings with painted beams.
Only the Dining Room *(illustration p 30)* has preserved its Louis XIII decor where large frescoes (1644) attributed to Abraham Bosse evoke the second wedding of Charles de Valois. Admire the stone fireplace and the painted beams.

GUERMANTES Château

Michelin map 101 south of fold 20

Ⓥ This château has the stately, austere appearance that characterised statesmen's country residences during the *Ancien Régime*.
Charmed by the musical tones of the word Guermantes, Marcel Proust reinstated this title of nobility by introducing it into his literary work.
The central range – built by the Viole family in the 17C – typifies Louis XIII architecture *(illustration p 28)*. After the first sale in 1698, two wings projecting at right angles were built close on the outhouses. Embellished by carved pediments, the gallery pavilion on the left and the chapel are decidedly more ornate: their decoration was entrusted to Robert de Cotte and Charles Perrault.
The tour includes two rooms on the first floor of the main block, in which the Louis XIII decoration has been preserved: the Italian Chamber (1645) with its coved ceiling adorned with cartouches and stucco work attributed to an Italian team who had worked at Fontainebleau; the Viole Bedchamber – note the intertwined Vs – decorated on the occasion of Pierre Viole's wedding to Marie Vallée (*c* 1633). Admire the pristine state of the ceiling. The opposite wing brings you to the main reception room, a gallery measuring 31m – 102ft long and featuring a total of 18 windows: **"La Belle Inutile"**★. The painting of the woodwork was planned by Robert de Cotte and executed by Jean Hanard, who produced the medallions of Roman emperors. The paintings were contemporary reproductions of great masterpieces. The ceiling (1866) we owe to Andrieu, a pupil and collaborator of Delacroix.
A passageway whose walls are hung with charming miniature paintings depicting the four seasons leads to an antechamber: here the decoration – discovered under a thick coat of paint – is believed to be 17C.
A wide, sweeping staircase leads down to the chapel (1705), ornamented by the same artists who did the Belle Inutile, under the supervision of Robert de Cotte.

GUIRY-EN-VEXIN Pop 114

Michelin map 196 fold 4 – Local map p 94

Ⓥ A charming village, offering two highly distinctive landmarks. The former **château** of the marquis de Guiry – built by François Mansart in the 17C – still stands in its pleasant setting of rolling lawns at the heart of the old town.
Ⓥ The **church** – completed in the 16C – features a stately bell tower capped by a stone dome.
Guiry is the research centre for archaeological studies in the French Vexin.

Ⓥ **Museum of Archaeology (Musée Archéologique Départemental).** – A modern building in perfect harmony with the rural landscape houses the exhibits unearthed during the extensive excavations carried out in the area, notably around Épiais-Rhus (Gallic and Gallo-Roman periods) and Genainville (Gallo-Roman sanctuary). Note the splendid sword and its iron sheath stamped with bronze (Tene II), a bronze service (strainer, plates), a man's head made in sheet bronze, several goddesses carved in limestone, a brown and green glass chalice dating from Gallo-Roman times and a Merovingian fibula or buckle in gilded silver.
The museum also features an impressive collection of funeral steles dating back to Merovingian days.

★ HALATTE Forest

Michelin map 56 folds 1, 2, 11 and 12

The state forest of Halatte – 4300ha – 10626 acres interrupted by an area of arable land around Fleurines – stretches over a rolling landscape 100m – 330ft high to the north of Chantilly and Senlis, between the valleys of the Oise and the Aunette. The highest peak is Mont Pagnotte, one of the summits of the Paris region. The familiar beech groves of Ile-de-France surround Mont Pagnotte, a territory fondly cherished by the Capetians. The southern part of the massif presents a miscellaneous composition: oaks, hornbeams, pine trees, etc.

FROM SENLIS TO PONT-STE-MAXENCE OR RHUIS

36 or 40km – 23 or 25 miles – about 2 hours

★★ **Senlis.** – *Description p 167.*

Leave Senlis by the northbound Rue du Moulin Rieul and turn left into Rue des Marronniers.

Aumont-en-Halatte. – A quaint little village, surrounded by flowers and greenery. The activist author Henri Barbusse (1873-1935) took up residence in Aumont (museum). He is best known for his wartime novel *Under Fire* (1917) which recounts the life of the French soldier in the trenches and remains an indictment of war.

★ **Butte d'Aumont.** – *1/2 hour Rtn on foot. Starting from Aumont Church, follow directions to Apremont. Then branch off and turn into the first public lane on the left (chain), a sandy track flanked by wire fences. Climb up the hillock.*

Enjoy the superb **panorama**★ of unlimited wooded horizons: Halatte, Senlis and Chantilly and, after sunset, the twinkling lights of Roissy Airport.

Follow the route that takes you past the **former St-Christophe Priory** (now a medical teaching centre belonging to the *Sécurité Sociale.)*. Nice view of Fleurines and the wood.

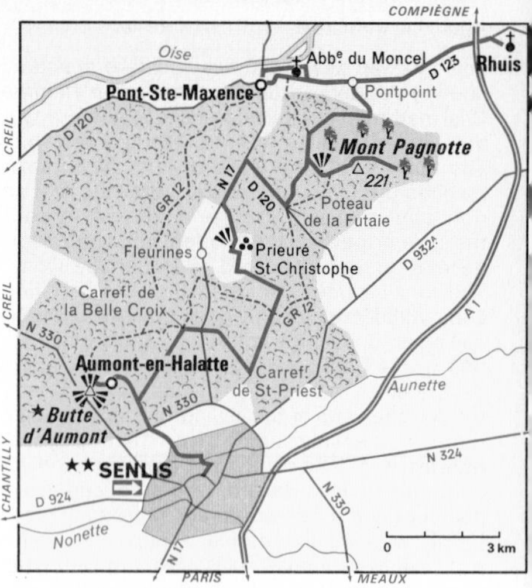

Mont Pagnotte. – Alt 221m – 727ft. The road crosses a felling area and reaches the flat, wooded summit of the hill (television transmitter – signposted footpath along edge of plateau).

The road leaves the forest and brings you back down to Pontpoint.

Follow directions to Pont-Ste-Maxence.

Without actually leaving the locality, the route skirts the imposing walls of **Moncel Abbey** *(p 140)* and arrives at Pont-Ste-Maxence.

Pont-Ste-Maxence. – *Description p 140*

Return to Pontpoint and proceed towards Verberie along the D 123. After driving under the motorway, take the second turning on the right.

Rhuis. – The 11C Romanesque church has an elegant bell tower with a double row of twinned windows. The tower is believed to be one of the oldest in Ile-de-France. The interior features four bays and an apsidal chapel with no vaulting.

L'HAŸ-LES-ROSES

Pop 29 591

Michelin map 101 fold 25 – Michelin plan 22

The town is famed for its spectacular rose garden, located on the edge of a pleasant **park.**

★★ **Rose Garden (Roseraie).** – It was created in 1892 and subsequently embellished by Jules Gravereaux, a man passionately fond of roses who also helped design the famous Parisian department store Le Bon Marché. The flower beds are planted with thousands of wild and grafted roses, coming from countries all over the world. The gardens also feature a display of arches, trellises and colonnades for the climbing varieties which will delight visitors. The selection of roses is enriched every year.

Rose Museum (Musée de la Rose). – It houses a collection of miscellaneous works of art, inspired by this noble flower: engravings by Redouté, embroideries, costumes, curios, ivory ornaments, ceramics, bindings, etc.

HERBLAY

Pop 20 006

Michelin map 101 fold 3

Located on an abruptly ending plateau overlooking a loop of the Seine, the locality of Herblay was once a horticultural centre producing grapes, lilac and various fruit, including figs.

St Martin's Church (Église St-Martin). – *If the gate is closed, enter through the presbytery (door to the left of the church).*
It stands at a height, dominating the banks of the river. Skirt the building to the right and walk to the grassy terrace that edges the small cemetery: enjoy the **view★** of the meander encircling St-Germain Forest in the far distance.
The 16C chancel and north aisle present fragments of Renaissance **stained glass★** which was manufactured in the Beauvais workshops (includes a Tree of Jesse). A group of painted wood statues (17C) including St Martin stands at the far end of the north aisle.

The banks of the River Seine. – *2km – 1 mile to Frette Church.*
Follow the ravine at the foot of the church (Rue du Val) and proceed towards the quay, formerly used for towing purposes: a quiet, pleasant walk can be taken along the stretch of water, which used to be very popular for boating trips (avoid at weekends).

La Frette-sur-Seine was the place of residence of Jacques Chardonne (1884-1968), a moderately well-known French novelist.

★ HOUDAN

Pop 2 973

Michelin map 196 south of fold 14

This old fortified town was built on a promontory delimited by the Vesgre and Opton rivers. Its location is pinpointed by the display of stepped roofing.
Today, Houdan is a busy farming centre. The town once gave its name to a breed of hens, known to be good layers and famed for their succulent flesh. Houdon became France's foremost market for poultry.
A long-standing road post, Houdan has seen a constant stream of cosmopolitan travellers throughout the ages: merchants, pilgrims, mercenaries, etc. The old, crumbling inns along Rue de Paris evoke these early times.

SIGHTS

Keep (Donjon) (**B**). – A huge 12C tower flanked by four turrets. Initially, the ground level admitted no entrance and the keep was reached by a ladder on the first floor. This donjon, now used as a water tower, is all that remains of the Montfort castle. The three sturdy curtain walls – the inner bailey followed the same route as Rue des Fossés – were knocked down, leaving three 16C watch-towers, known as Tour de l'Abreuvoir, Tour Jardet and Tour Guinand.

HOUDAN

Cheval Bardé (R. du) 2
Enclos (R. de l') 3
Fossés (R. des) 5
Mont-Roti (R. du) 6
Pie (R. de la) 8
St-Mathieu (R.) 10
Vieilles-Tanneries (R. des) ... 12

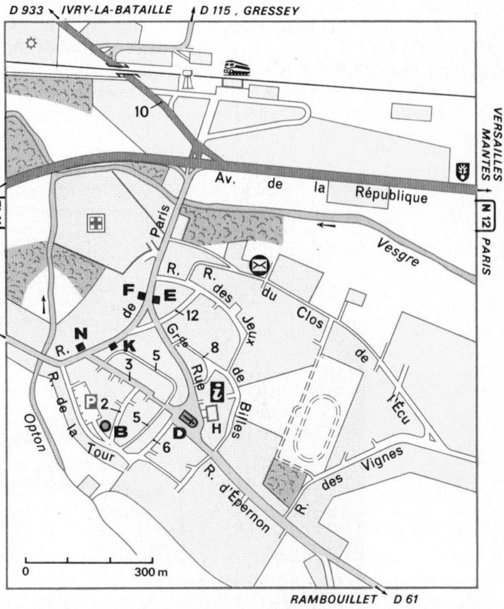

Ⓥ **Church (Église)** (**D**). – The façade and the nave are both Flamboyant. The imposing east end, built in the Renaissance style, dates from the reign of Henri II. Inside, note the large hanging keystones of the intricate ribbed vaulting in the apse and the transept crossing.
The furnishings are unusual in that they provide an example of local craftsmanship from the 17 and 18C: churchwardens' pew, pulpit, lectern, stalls, organ case and altarpiece, depicting the Adoration of the Magi, also decorated by a native of Houdan: Louis Licherie (1629-1679). The organ – the work of Louis-Alexandre Clicquot in 1734 – is one of the few in France which has retained its original aspect.
One of the chapels around the ambulatory celebrates the pilgrimage to the Black Madonna of Montserrat: in 1582 thirty-two inhabitants from Houdan made the journey to Catalonia to pay their respects to the province's patron saint. Observe the small symbolic saw in the hands of Jesus (Montserrat refers to a "sawn-off mountain").

Half-timbered houses. – In Rue de Paris, admire nos 37-39 with their timber structures (**E**) and no 66 (**F**), decorated with a fleur-de-lys motif. Further on, the courtyard of the former town hall (**K**), with a pavilion sporting a large clock, offers all the characteristics of the courtyard of a coaching inn (Auberge du Grand Amiral): stables, bedrooms opening onto galleries.
The Tin Plate Inn (Auberge du Plat d'Étain) (**N**) – observe the beautifully-restored timbering – still provides board and lodging to travellers.

L'ISLE-ADAM

Pop 9 479

Michelin map 196 fold 6

In 1014 a castle built on one of the Oise isles was ceded to Adam de Villiers by Robert II the Pious, Hugh Capet's son. The former erected a priory on the estate. In 1364, the fief was acquired by Pierre de Villiers, whose descendants gained widespread recognition: Jean (1384-1437), Maréchal de Bourgogne, served two Dukes of Burgundy John the Fearless and Philip the Good before becoming one of the king's followers; Philippe (1464-1534), Commander of the Order of St John of Jerusalem, and subsequently Grand Master of the Order of Malta, heroically defended Rhodes against Soliman the Magnificent during five months, and succeeded in obtaining Malta as headquarters for the order. In the 19C Villiers de L'Isle-Adam, the author of *Cruel Tales,* was to become one of the great names of French literature.
In the 16C the land came into the hands of Constable Anne de Montmorency. Louis XIII later offered the estate to Henri II of Bourbon, Prince de Condé. In 1646, Armand de Bourbon, Prince de Conti, moved in with his lavish court.
Honoré de Balzac was a regular visitor at L'Isle-Adam and several of his novels are set in the area. L'Isle-Adam was also home to Henri Prosper Breuil (1877-1961), the renowned archaeologist.

The site. – The château belonging to the Conti was razed during the Revolution The old bridges – in particular Cabouillet Bridge, a 16C stone construction with three arches – command a pleasant view of the Oise, which is still frequented by pleasure boats as in former times *(booking office on the beach).*
L'Isle-Adam has France's largest inland beach now a highly popular water sports centre: it features numerous facilities for yachting, sailing, rowing, canoeing, etc

St Martin's Church (Église St-Martin). – Like St-Martin-de-Montmorency, this church is typical of 16C architecture and presents highly intricate vaulting. The consecration ceremony took place on 1 October 1567, in the presence of Constable Anne. The tower erected in 1869 is a replica of the one adorning the Église de la Trinité in Paris.
The interior offers an important collection well-preserved furnishings. The 1560 **pulpit★** – of German origin – features panels of inlaid woodwork and portrays numerous statues, grouped in sets of four: Great Prophets, Evangelists, Doctors of the Church, Cardinal Virtues (also the three Theological Virtues).
On the northern side stands the funeral chapel of Louis-François de Bourbon (1717-1776), the penultimate descendant of the Conti dynasty, Grand Prior of France of the Order of Malta. The remains of the original monument (1777), including the prince's medallion, have been reassembled.

The Cassan Pagoda at L'Isle-Adam

Cassan Pagoda (Pavillon chinois de Cassan). – *To the northeast, along Rue de Beaumont. Enter through the main gateway of the former park.*
This quaint pavilion rising out of a lake was built to ornament the landscape park of Cassan. The estate used to belong to the financier Bergeret (1715-1785), an enthusiastic art lover and patron of Fragonard. The rest of the estate has been parcelled out into plots.
Brightly decorated in red, green and saffron tones, the pagoda stands on a stone base resting upon arches that house the spillway for the waters of the park (ponds and canals). The pagoda-shaped roof is supported by a peristyle of eight wooden pillars. It conceals the elaborate network of imbricated cupolas which act as a lantern and crown the room, decorated with painted hangings. The mast at the top of the pavilion features several layers of rings adorned with small bronze bells.

L'ISLE-ADAM Forest

Michelin map 106 folds 6 and 7

This state forest covering 1 500ha – 3 800 acres is separated from Carnelle Forest by Ru de Presles Valley. The grounds feature no brooks, ponds or canals and the plantations are coppices with standards. While two-thirds of the forest is oak, the remaining third consists of elms, birches, lime trees...
Up to 1783, the Princes de Conti went to great pains to protect and preserve the forest for hunting purposes (the various plots are often named after gates and doors). Today the estate presents several massifs divided by main roads: the D 64 or Paris road and the N 184 (new route skirting the banks of the Oise).
The altitude varies from 27 to 193m (89 to 634ft). The part of the forest that edges L'Isle-Adam is quite flat. The area close to Maffliers – known as Parc de la Tour under the *Ancien Régime* – offers a higher, hilly landscape. They are cut across by a network of radiating lanes leading to a star-shaped crossroads called **Poteau La Tour.**

★ JOUARRE

Pop 2 704

Michelin map 196 fold 24

Jouarre stands on the upper ridge of a hillside dominating the last loop of the Petit Morin before it flows into the Marne.

The town already featured two abbeys in the 7C. The one for men was short-lived indeed. The one for women adopted the Benedictine rule and survived. It soon acquired a prestigious reputation and the great ladies of France, namely Madeleine d'Orléans, François I's half-sister, were flattered to receive the title of Abbess. Badly damaged during the Hundred Years War, the abbey was rebuilt several times, particularly in the 18C. When the abbey was seized during the Revolution, it was the residence of a fervent, united religious community, close observers of monastic rules and widely praised by Jacques Bossuet. The monastery resumed its activity *c* 1837. The **principle offices** are celebrated according to Benedictine liturgy.

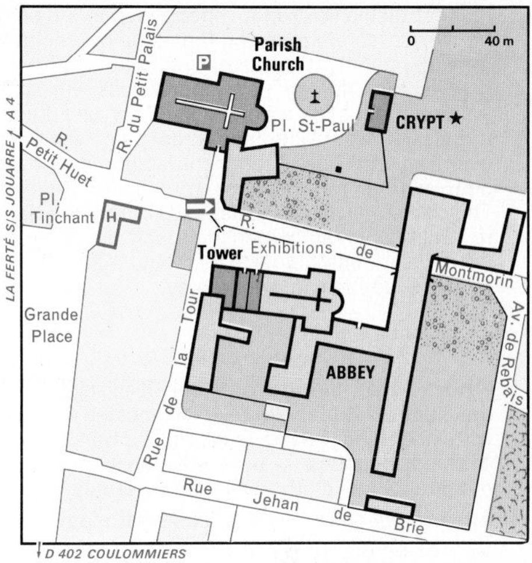

ABBEY : CRYPT

tour: 1 hour

Tower (Tour). – Of the old medieval sanctuary, there remains only this tower which once served as bell tower and porch to the 12C Romanesque church. The interior has been tastefully restored: three vaulted rooms, furnished by Madeleine d'Orléans in the 16C, house souvenirs of the abbey (note the armorial bosses).

★ **Crypt (Crypte).** – It lies behind the parish church, at the far end of Place St-Paul. This square presents an imposing 13C cross resting on a stone base with the Virgin and Child in the centre of a four-lobed medallion. The crypt consists of two formerly underground chapels which were linked up in the 17C.

St Paul's Crypt, the mausoleum of the founding family, is considered to be one of the oldest religious monuments in France. It dates from the 7C.

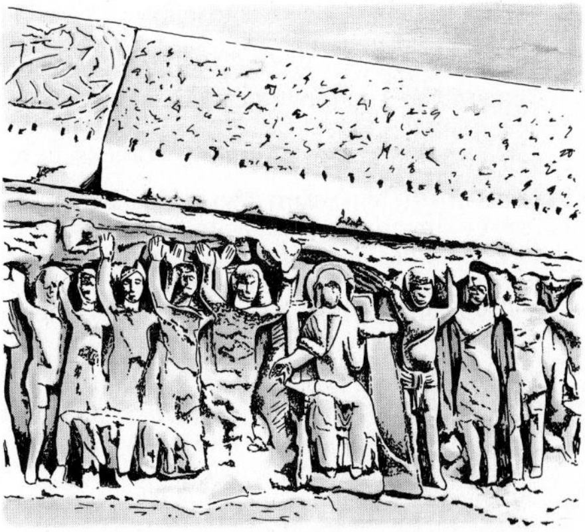

Tomb of St Agilbert in the Crypt of Jouarre Abbey

The crypt is divided into three naves by two rows of columns dating from Gallo-Roman times, made of marble, porphyry and limestone. It is believed that the 7C capitals were made with white marble from the Pyrénées. The famous Merovingian wall near the entrance presents a primitive stone mosaic with geometric motifs (oblongs, squares, diamonds, etc).

The most striking sarcophagus is the Tomb of St Agilbert, Bishop of Dorchester and later of Paris, the brother of Theodechilde: Christ sits enthroned, surrounded by a crowd of praying figures with upraised arms. One of the galleries affords a good view of the low relief at the head: Christ circled by the four Évangelists' symbols (man, lion, bull, eagle). The tomb of Saint Osanne – an Irish princess who allegedly passed away in Jouarre – presents a 13C recumbent figure. The most elaborate decoration is that of the sarcophagus of Theodechilde, the first abbess of Jouarre. A display of large cockleshells adorns a Latin inscription.

St Ébrégésile's Crypt is a small Romanesque church of lesser interest, separate from the first crypt. Recent excavations have revealed the nave of the modest St-Ébrégésile Church, along with several Merovingian sarcophagi.

Above these two crypts, a large room houses the **Brie Museum,** presenting a medley of exhibits relative to regional folklore and history: costumes, tools, paintings, plans,...

ADDITIONAL SIGHT

Parish Church (Église Paroissiale). – *Enter by the transept, at the far end of the blind alley (see plan).* It was rebuilt after the Hundred Years War and completed in the early 16C. The north arm of the transept features an Entombment from the 16C (Michel Colombe's workshop), 15C *Pietà* and two shrines (12 and 13C) covered in silver-gilt, enhanced by enamels, cabochon and filigree work. The south side contains a 16C statue of Our Lady of Jouarre.

JOUY-EN-JOSAS Pop 7 664

Michelin map 101 fold 23 – 6km – 3.7 miles southeast of Versailles – Michelin plan 22

This town has retained a noble aspect owing to the neat, tidy houses and the substantial properties, partly preserved after being ceded to various research and academic centres (HEC). The village was once a secluded spot favoured by frequent visits from Victor Hugo. The former French President Léon Blum and the bacteriologist Professor Albert Calmette are buried in Jouy cemetery.

A textile centre. – In 1760, at the age of 22, **Christophe-Philippe Oberkampf** founded his first textile workshop, specialised in a type of printed calico known as *toile de Jouy*. The factory received the name of Manufacture Royale in 1783 and became a thriving industry. Oberkampf recruited his first skilled workers in Switzerland, and they in turn trained new apprentices. He showed a great interest in scientific advancement and modern technology, and during the Continental System, obtained permission from Napoleon to despatch several envoys to Switzerland, Alsace and even England. This gifted manufacturer employed up to 1 300 workers, a remarkably high number for the time.
The commercial losses sustained during the Napoleonic Wars, the foreign invasion, in which Oberkampf perished, and the advent of competition (over 300 firms in 1815) dealt a deathblow to the Manufacture Royale. In 1843 the company was forced to file a petition in bankruptcy.

SIGHTS

Oberkampf Museum (Musée Oberkampf). – *Montebello Château.* It is housed in the modern Montebello Château, located on the Metz plateau. Five rooms decorated with charming period engravings offer a display of printed calico, material for clothing, hangings – note the two bedspreads. The museum also portrays the patriarchal life of the Oberkampf family and the town of Jouy in former times.

Admirers of Victor Hugo will be able to pay a visit to their favourite author's house. To do so, they should retrace their steps and turn left into Rue Victor-Hugo when they draw level with a large wooden portico.

Victor Hugo's House (Maison de Victor Hugo). – Third building on the right. A commemorative plaque marks the house that Juliette Drouet rented out to the poet and novelist in 1835. His stay here inspired the writing of *Olympio*.

Return to the Town Hall (Mairie) and park the car nearby. Cross the railway tracks on foot and proceed towards the church.

Cartier Foundation (Fondation Cartier). – *Rue du Montcel.* The former estate of Baron Oberkampf houses this prestigious foundation, exclusively devoted to modern art. A 15ha – 38acre landscape park designed by Mme Oberkampf presents an imposing collection of sculptures, notably *Long Term Parking* by Arman (1982), César's *Tribute to Gustave Eiffel*, the *Greenhouse* by J.P. Raynaud (1985) and Bernard Pagès' brightly-painted *Totem* (1983). The Bunker – formerly the Luftwaffe headquarters – has been converted into an exhibition hall. Lastly, the Village constitutes a creative forum for artists from all over the world.

Léon-Blum Museum (Musée Léon-Blum). – *4 Rue Léon-Blum.* The estate which the former French president acquired in 1945 and on which he lived until his death in 1950, provides an interesting vignette of his life and political career. Several of the rooms contain documents relating to his early days, his literary work (essays, reviews) and his role in both the socialist movement and French current affairs. The main room houses his writing desk and his private collection of books.

Church (Église). – *Place de la Division-Leclerc.* The base of the bell tower, dating from the 13C, is the oldest part of the building.
In the interior, at the far end of the single aisle, admire the **Diège★**, a tastefully restored 12C wooden Virgin of colourful tones.

JUINE Valley

Michelin map 196 folds 42 and 43

Travelling upstream the Juine, a tributary of the Essonne, is a most pleasant trip. Unlike so many other rivers in Ile-de-France, it offers visitors two stately homes open to the public, where one can take a walk in the parks on the water's edge.

FROM ST-VRAIN TO ÉTAMPES along the D 17

22km – 14 miles – about 2 1/2 hours

★ **St-Vrain.** – *Description p 163.*

From St-Vrain, drive to Bouray-sur-Juine, then branch off the road to Ferté-Alais and proceed towards Lardy.

Lardy. – Pop 3 028. This residential area features a great many grand mansion houses standing well back in their grounds, often screened by trees and wrought iron railings. One of these houses the local town hall. The grounds are open to the public and offer a charming walk along the banks of the Juine.

The present route follows the north bank of the Juine.

Drive slowly along the wall surrounding Chamarande park and when level with the château turn right into a forest lane that dips under the railway. This will bring you to the car park.

Chamarande Château (Château de Chamarande). – The château was built on the site of a former mansion in 1654: the brick and stone façade is crowned by mansard roofing. Both the main building and the outhouses are circled by a deep, wide moat.

Keep following the avenue and skirt the château.

Standing in the shade of a venerable oak, a stone fountain overgrown with moss is all that remains of the sumptuous water displays that were so popular under Louis XIV. Cut across the former flower beds and walk towards the cluster of pine trees. You will reach the lake, which receives the waters of the Juine.

When you have left the locality of Chamarande, turn off the road to Étréchy and cross the railway tracks on the left. Proceed towards Étampes along the south bank (D 17), via Auvers-St-Georges.

Morigny. – Pop 3 161. Of the former abbey, all that is left is the church, whose nave has been almost entirely destroyed, as evidenced by the shafts of the columns lining the castle walls (former abbatial palace).
The 18C abbatial palace was last occupied by two scientists specialised in prehistoric studies, the comte (1877-1950) and comtesse de St-Périer. It now belongs the University of Paris IV and has become a training centre and a venue for scientific seminars *(private)*.

D 17 will bring you to Étampes.

Étampes. – *Description p 74.*

LAGNY-SUR-MARNE Pop 16 268

Michelin map 101 fold 20

Lagny – situated on the banks of the Marne – used to be a fortified town, the seat of an abbey and is now an international trading centre. The ruling house of Champagne, whose territory spreads east of Lagny, made the town an important road post for itinerant fairs and an outpost against their rivals the Capetians.

The seeds of discord. – In 1544, under François I, a dispute broke out between the monks of St Peter's Abbey and their superior with respect to the price of barley. The inhabitants of Lagny entered into the spirit of the controversy and staunchly defended the friars. As matters grew worse, the town refused to obey a royal injunction and was subsequently assaulted by Captain Jacques de Montgomery, who owned the lordship of Lorges. There followed troubled times, marked by acts of pillage, murder and rape.

SIGHT

Our Lady of Ergotism and St Peter's Church (Église Notre-Dame-des-Ardents-et-St-Pierre). – The present building – the former abbey church – dates from the 13C. Unfortunately, construction work was abandoned and only the chancel was completed. This was probably due to the dying out of the house of Champagne and the subsequent transfer of the county to royal hands *(p 128)*, which put an end to their generous patronage.
The interior of the church is magnificent. The spacious choir is composed of an apse, three radiating chapels, an ambulatory and four bays with double side aisles. The bays were built first.
Note the unusually small clerestory windows, owing to the interruption of building work. They were originally surmounted by timber roofing. This was replaced by plaster vaulting in the 17C but it was not possible to elevate the windows.
Behind the altar lies the chapel of Notre-Dame-des-Ardents: observe the small 14C wooden statue of the Virgin. The name of the chapel dates back to 1127, when an infectious disease called ergotism *(mal des ardents)* raged through the area. It was probably caused by an inferior type of flour, mixed with diseased or ergotised rye, used in times of famine: the victims suffered an extremely high fever and gradually lost their limbs. According to legend, the Virgin Mary answered the prayers of the Lagny inhabitants and put an end to their terrible ordeal.

To see the Gothic east end, leave by the small door to the north of the ambulatory.

★ LARCHANT Pop 538

Michelin map 61 folds 11 and 12

There are two sights to see in Larchant: St-Mathurin Church, a former place of pilgrimage built in the Gothic style, and Dame Jehanne, the highest peak in the Ile-de-France (15m – 50ft), nestling in the centre of a small massif close to Fontainebleau Forest (a popular weekend resort during the summer months).
Up to the 17C, almost all the French kings made the pilgrimage to Larchant: Charles IV the Fair, Louis VI, Charles VIII, François I, Henri III, Henri IV, etc.

The site. – Larchant lies in the dip of a wooded vale forming a great cleft in the southern plateau of Ile-de-France. This site is approached by the A 6 motorway (steep incline following the Villiers parking area).
The village itself – easily recognisable on account of its truncated church tower – may be seen from the D 16, when you come from Chapelle-la-Reine, after the large Chapter farmhouse whose name reminds us that the canons of Notre-Dame in Paris owned the land and built the sanctuary in the 13C.

★ **St-Mathurin Church (Église St-Mathurin).** – *Time: 1/2 hour.* Erected in the late 12C by the chapter of Notre-Dame in Paris with a view to welcoming a pilgrimage to Larchant. The church was burned down during the Wars of Religion (1568): the front and the east end were dismantled, the exterior suffered badly from the flames and the tower collapsed in 1675. The 15C third level has retained its ornate Flamboyant decoration. The imposing bell tower-porch (50 m – 165ft) dominates the village.

Doorway of the Last Judgment (Portail du Jugement Dernier). – 13C. It provides access to the mutilated part of the nave and has been badly damaged by weathering. Its composition has been strongly influenced by Notre-Dame in Paris. Like in the Paris cathedral, Christ is the central character and clearly dominates the other figures. Two angels carrying the Holy Lance and Nails stand by his side. The Virgin and St John are portrayed kneeling to the left and the right of the angels. The tympanum bears a sculpture depicting the Ressurection of the Dead – a replica of the badly defaced original, now inside the church. The arching presents scenes from the Bible: John the Baptist with the Lamb, Moses carrying the stone tablets with the Ten Commandments. The embrasures feature a row of five statue-columns, running from left to right: St James (scrip decorated with cockle-shells), St Andrew (the cross – the X-shaped configuration had not yet made an appearance), St Peter (a book), St Paul (book and sword) and St Stephen (holding a large stone used for stoning).
On the south side, above the sacristy, are three rows of windows latticed with iron. According to tradition, these quarters were occupied by dangerous lunatics in the hope that the pilgrimage would cure them of their ills. It is likely the rooms were also used to store the town's archives and treasure.

Interior. – *Enter the church by the south doorway.* Only the choir, the apse and the Virgin's chapel still feature their original vaulting. The two rows of clerestory windows crowning the apse create an impression of deep harmony, enhanced by the narrow colonnettes protruding from the wall. When it was intact and lit by its 46 windows, the nave must have been a radiant sight indeed.
The **Virgin's Chapel** was added to the north arm of the transept around 1300. Its dainty, narrow proportions typify Radiant Gothic architecture. It opens onto the transept by means of two heavily ornate arches surmounted by two gables.

Dame Jehanne Massif. – *3km – 2 miles to the north along Recloses lane, open to traffic, signposted from Larchant. From there allow 1 hour Rtn on foot.*
The lane lies to the right of Jobert chalet – an important meeting place for climbers and ramblers – and winds its way through the woods and up onto the plateau. After a sharp right bend, park the car at the entrance to a large meadow.
Follow the route marked out in the meadow and enter the wood. At the first junction, carry straight on. When you get to the bottom of the slope, you will discover a barren plateau. Walk straight across it. The lane meets up with the long-distance footpath GR no 13 (red and white markings). Turn right into it. Your route will take you past some of the steep, overhanging cliffs frequented by mountaineering buffs. A number of these rocky ledges command a good **view★** of Larchant.

On the way back, do not miss the junction and the path leading back to your starting point.

LIVERDY-EN-BRIE

Michelin map 196 fold 34 – 6km – 3.8 miles south of Tournan-en-Brie

Retal Farmhouse (15 and 17C), located south of the village, has been specially converted to present visitors with an impressive collection of horse-drawn carriages.

⊙ **Ile-de-France Carriage Museum (Musée de l'Attelage en Ile-de-France).** – The main building houses a selection of coaches used for leisure, sport and travelling purposes, of the type encountered in films, novels and historical books: cabriolet fitted with "braces" (1780), "spring" brougham dating from the First Empire, landau and stagecoach (*c* 1850), coupé models, hunting horsecars, etc. A second outhouse contains a collection of carriages designed for film sets. In the stables twenty horses stand ready to be harnessed.

LUZARCHES

Pop 2 559

Michelin map 196 fold 8

This extremely ancient village of the old Pays de France was the birthplace of Robert de Luzarches (13C), who conceived the plans for Amiens Cathedral.

Church (Église). – The bridge on the diversion of the N 16 affords a good **view** of the local sanctuary: observe the 12C bell tower and east end, and the three apses, each of a distinctive design and elevation.
The church is dedicated to Sts Cosmas and Damian, the two patron saints of surgeons. Made martyrs in 303, these two Arab physicians were in fact brothers and their mortal remains were brought back from Rome by a Crusader who owned the village. Thanks to his generous deed, the local inhabitants were visited and treated free of charge twice a year by four representatives of the Brotherhood of Paris Surgeons, a privilege they enjoyed up to the Revolution.
The celebrations on the Sunday after the saints' feast day (26 September) are reminiscent of old-time pilgrimages.
The restoration of the chancel (1957) has improved the church interior.

★ MAINTENON

Pop 3 390

Michelin map 196 fold 26

This charming town on the banks of the Eure river is renowned for its château, irrevocably linked to the incredible destiny of **Françoise d'Aubigné:** born to a family with Calvinist views in 1635, she became an orphan at the age of 12, the widow of the burlesque poet Paul Scarron at the age of 25, the clandestine governess of Mme de Montespan's children by the age of 34 and the king's wife by the time she reached 48...

The corridors of power. – When her clandestine charge, the duc de Maine, was legitimized, Françoise Scarron made a public appearance at court. Louis XIV, who was extremely fond of his son, used to see her every day. Initially, he found her a trifle pedantic but soon revised his opinion of "the Scarron widow" and succumbed to her charm, intelligence and strong temperament. In 1674 Françoise Scarron bought the Maintenon estate in exchange for 250 000 livres, paid by the king, who then publicly christened her "Madame de Maintenon".

After the queen's death, Louis XIV secretly married Mme de Maintenon in the chapel at Versailles during the winter of 1683-1684. The morganatic queen acceded to the rank of peer and marquise in 1688 – a privilege bestowed on her directly by the king – and from then on she became an extremely powerful figure in the country's political life. When the king died in 1715, she withdrew to St-Cyr School, where she passed away in 1719.

A herculean task. – Between 1685 and 1688, the area around Maintenon was the scene of one of the most ambitious projects of the century: that of diverting the waters of the Eure and bringing them to the fountains of Versailles. François Louvois acted as superviser: he left Sébastien Vauban in charge of the plans and entrusted him with the construction of an 80km – 50 mile long aqueduct linking Pontgouin (Michelin map 60 fold 6) to Tower Pond (L'Étang de la Tour), which already communicated with the Versailles reservoirs by means of the rivulets of the Trappes plateau.

The Maintenon aqueduct was a colossal enterprise, involving a total length of 4 600m – 15 000ft and three superimposed rows of arches, placed 72m – 237ft above the level of the Eure river. In actual fact, it was only possible to fit in one row of arches. The link with the canals installed on the plateaux was to be implemented by means of pressurised pipes acting as a battery of pumps.

The whole operation was carried out like a military campaign: 20 000 soldiers took part in the excavation work, in addition to the 10 000 skilled workers summoned from remote villages and the local peasants who helped cart the materials. The Voise and Drouette were canalised and used to convey the freestones and sandstone rubble taken from Gallardon and Épernon quarries. The shipments of Newcastle coal needed to work the lime and brick kilns, and the pipes and iron bars despatched from Champagne, Belgium and Pays d'Ouche were carried along the Seine and Eure rivers.

In 1689, the wars triggered of by the Augsburg League interrupted the work. The French troops, in poor physical condition, were sent off to the borders to defend their country. The work was never resumed. From then on, Mme de Maintenon ceased her visits to the château: she was offered the unfortunate construction to compensate for the damage to her estate.

SIGHTS

★ **Château.** – The present château occupies the site of a former stronghold circled by the waters of the Eure. The construction work was undertaken by Jean Cottereau, Minister of Finance to Louis XII, François I and Henri II, and completed around 1509. The building is Renaissance.

Maintenon Château

The estate then came into the hands of the d'Angennes family *(p 143)*. In 1674 Louis XIV bought the château from Françoise d'Angennes and offered it to the future marquise de Maintenon. The Marquise left it to her niece, who was married to the duc d'Ayen, son of first Maréchal de Noailles. The château has remained in the hands of this family ever since.

Exterior. – Such decorative details as elaborate dormer windows, stonework tracery and lacelike roof cresting give the entrance front its Renaissance character.
Pass under the archway flanked by two protruding turrets, bearing Jean Cottereau's arms (three lizards) and make for the inner court which is the starting point for tours.
The square 12C keep, now crowned with an elegant roof, is all that remains of the original stronghold. The wing adjoining the keep was built by Mme de Maintenon and the narrow door set in the tower still sports the marquise's blazon, a griffin's head displayed Sable (black).

Interior. – A door depicting St Michael and bearing the lizard emblem gives onto a staircase leading to Mme de Maintenon's suite. It consists of an antechamber, a bedroom – where Charles X spent the night on 3 August 1830 when he fled Rambouillet – and a small cabinet.
After leaving the main block, visitors are shown round the first floor of the Renaissance pavilion, redesigned to accommodate the apartments of Mme de Montespan and her royal charges.
The tour ends with the reception rooms furnished by the Noailles family in the 19C. The Grand Salon bears portraits of the two royal rivals, Mme de Montespan and Mme de Maintenon. In the Portrait Gallery, a collection of paintings represents the illustrious members of the family. The mortal remains of the marquise rest in the chapel of St-Cyr Military Academy. A memorial was erected in her honour in 1980.

Parterre. – It is flanked by charming canals flowing with the waters of the Eure. The bench at the far end of the park commands an extensive view of the Grand Canal and three of the arches of Maintenon aqueduct. Turn round and enjoy the superb **vista**★ of the château, with its elegant towers and grey and pink stone and brickwork.

★ **Aqueduct.** – The fifty odd arches that remain, many of which are crumbling and overgrown with plants and weeds, stretch from Maintenon station – Hôtel de l'Aqueduc marks the start of the bridge – to the D 6, leading to St-Piat. Driving along the road to Gallardon, you will pass under a curious arch of four ribs of archstones hanging suspended in mid-air.

EXCURSION

St-Piat; L'Arche de la Vallée. – *12km – 7.5 miles – to the southwest, then 1 hour Rtn on foot. Leave Maintenon by the D 6, crossing the Eure Valley and leading to Chartres.*

St-Piat. – Pop 836. The village has developed around its 16C church and one of the big mills of the area (now disused).

After leaving St-Piat, take a right turning and drive towards the plateau.

Cross Chartainvilliers, the road running from Maintenon to Chartres, and follow directions to Théléville and Berchères-la-Maingot. On the right, a wooded mound marks the scene of a major excavating operation aimed at diverting the waters of the Eure. The project, called Les Terrasses, was to raise the canal to the upper level of the aqueduct. As we know, it was doomed. After leaving Théléville, the road to Berchères descends into a wooded area. At the foot of the incline, park the car at a large crossroads.

L'Arche de la Vallée. – *1 hour Rtn on foot.* In the dip of the valley, bear right of the bridge and take the cart track that follows the gully of the stream. You will reach the artificial embankment dividing the valley.
This depression was one of the greatest obstacles lying in the way of the canal (save the interruption of the river at Maintenon). A stonework aqueduct had initially been planned but desirous of cutting costs, Vauban installed a closed gallery supported by a ramp, working on the principle of a pump.
Proceed along the foot of the embankment, to the left. This will bring you to l'Arche de la Vallée, a tunnel supported by intricate brick vaulting, remarkably well-designed for such a small watercourse. *Avoid crossing the river as the ground tends to be muddy.* Retrace your steps and turn left into a wide path trodden by horses' hooves leading onto the embankment. You will come to the west funnel: a gallery running to the bottom of the well which was designed to receive the waters from the canal *(bring a torch)*. The passageway used to extend along the upper ridge of the embankment – then much higher – and join up with an east funnel *(private property)*.

★ MAISONS-LAFFITTE Château

Michelin map 101 northwest of fold 13 – Michelin plan 18

The Longueil Supremacy. – The château was built between 1642 and 1651 for René de Longueil, President of the Parlement de Paris, appointed Governor of the royal châteaux at Versailles and St-Germain.
The plans were drawn up by the architect **François Mansart**, a difficult man known to be extremely conscientious: he would not hesitate to knock down one of his own pavilions and rebuild it if he considered it inadequate. The château was designed to receive royalty as it was one of the official places of residence assigned to French rulers. The palace was inaugurated during a brilliant reception celebrated in honour of Anne of Austria and Louis XIV, then aged 13. The Sun King subsequently took up residence at St-Germain and paid frequent visits to Maisons, as did his successors.

From D'Artois to Lannes. – The comte d'Artois, brother of Louis XVI, acquired the estate in 1777 and gave orders to build the famous racecourse. His extravagant parties were attended by everyone at court. In July 1789 he went into exile, accompanied by a staff of 200, and had to wait 25 years before returning to France. Crowned King of France in 1824 under the name of Charles X, he was exiled a second time in 1830 and died in 1836 at the age of 79.
The estate was sequestered during the Revolution and sold to Marshal Jean Lannes, duc de Montebello, in 1804. Napoleon I, who enjoyed the marshal's company, was a regular visitor at the château.

Maisons-Laffitte. – In 1818, the famous banker **Jacques Laffitte** (1767-1844) bought the estate, where he entertained the adversaries of the Restoration: General Foy, the marquis de Lafayette, Casimir Périer, Benjamin Constant, etc. Laffitte did much to secure Louis-Philippe d'Orléans' accession to the throne during the revolution of July 1830 which overthrew Charles X.
This shrewd financier was made Prime Minister to the new king in 1830 but proved unable to calm the disturbances that had broken out in the capital: mistrusted by both the Orleanists and the moderates, Laffitte was forced to resign in March 1831. Ruined, in debt to the tune of 50 million francs, he sold and dismantled the imposing stables and with these funds had the Grand Park parcelled out to accommodate two oblong pavilions. Mansart erected these two beautiful wings along Avenue du Château – presently renamed Avenue du Général-Leclerc – where they formed a very grand entrance to the Longueils' residence. The château frequently changed hands and was bought by the State in 1905.

Maisons-Laffitte Château

TOUR *time: 1 hour*

The château dates from the early part of Louis XIV's reign and has always been considered a model of French architecture. From the main driveway, formerly called the king's entrance – royal visitors would generally arrive from St-Germain Forest, i.e. from the west – admire the splendid display of its tall roofs.
The façade facing the Seine is fronted by a wide moat, a terrace and the staircase of honour. The stone exterior presents classical ornamentation: Doric on the ground floor, Ionic on the first floor and Corinthian on the attic storey level with the dormer windows. The alternating fluted columns and engaged pilasters form a pleasing, well-balanced composition.

Interior. – *Enter through the pavilion on the right.* Although the comte d'Artois made a number of alterations in the 18C, there are no obvious discrepancies between Mansart's austere work, executed around 1650, and the sober stamp of neo-classicism.

Comte d'Artois' Apartments (Appartement du comte d'Artois). – The corner dining room provides a good example of the neo-classical sculpted decoration commissioned by the comte. He hired two experts on Antiquity, Bélanger and Lhuillier, who produced a splendid coffered ceiling, an overdoor representing a group of Fames, a fireplace decorated with bacchantes.

Vestibule of Honour (Vestibule d'honneur). – Lying in the centre of the château, it constitutes a perfect entrance articulated by eight Doric columns. It was originally enclosed by two imposing wrought-iron gates. They were installed in 1650 and later moved to the Apollo Gallery in the Louvre. A group of mythological figures by Jacques Sarrazin incarnate the four Elements: Jupiter (fire), Juno (air), Neptune (water) and Cybele (earth).
The eagles are not those associated with the emperor: their "long eye" *(long œil)* is merely a pun on the proprietors' name.

Grand Staircase (Grand escalier). – One of Mansart's major accomplishments at Maisons, it is characteristic of the period: square plan with straight flights of stairs. Groups of cherubs executed by Philippe de Buyster symbolise Music and Singing Science and Art, War and Peace, Love and Marriage.

Royal Suite (Appartement du roi). – 1st floor. A suite of rooms built in the Italian style, featuring a domed or barrel-vaulted ceiling with no painted decoration. Walk down the Grand Gallery and enter Hercules' Salon (formerly the king's antechamber), which leads through to the **King's Bedroom.** Admire the domed ceiling, the original parquet floor and the handsome bed.

Chamber of Mirrors (Cabinet des Miroirs). – The parquet floor and panelling are masterpieces of marquetry inlaid with wood, bone and tin.

Maréchal Lannes' Bedroom (Chambre Lannes). – The passage leading to the bedroom houses a collection of figurines portraying various corps of the Grand Army. The queen's former bedchamber was redesigned to receive Jean Lannes. The furniture, chandelier and decoration are all Empire. In the centre stands a magnificent Restoration table inlaid with elm wood. The paintings include a scene which shows the emperor's ashes being carried past Sartrouville Bridge in 1804. A display of miniature figures re-enacts in minute detail the Battle of Wagram and Napoleon's farewell at Fontainebleau.

RACECOURSE AND PARK

The racecourse of Maisons-Laffitte, located on the banks of the Seine river, is well known to Paris racegoers.
The training stables and the tracks of this riding centre, second only to Chantilly in importance, lie to the north of the park, on the edge of St-Germain Forest.
A walk in the park around 7am will enable you to witness the morning training of the various "charges": mounted by stable lads, they will be walking or trotting along the sandy lanes. However the most prestigious route for exercising thoroughbreds is a circular ride known as Cercle de la Gloire (Circle of Glory).
The wider tracks used for galloping are not open to the public.

MALESHERBES

Pop 5 014

Michelin map 61 fold 11

This small town located in the upper valley of the Essonne is encircled by a green belt of forests. The nearby outdoor leisure centre of **Buthiers** *(see the Practical Information chapter at the end of the guide)* was created to protect this special landscape of forests which is scattered with sandstone tors some of which have recently been eroded by fluvial action.

Château. – *Leave the town centre by the Puiseaux road. Immediately after Malesherbes Church, a right turning will bring you to the gates of the park. Leave the car opposite the church or in the shade of the trees on Place Mazagran.*
The 14C round towers are all that remains of the castle rebuilt by Grand-Amiral Graville in the 15C.
In the 18C, the estate fell into the hands of Guillaume de Lamoignon, Chancellor of France, who commissioned Vigny, the royal architect, to erect the stone and brick façade. His son – known as Malesherbes – was one of Louis XVI's advisers: a tolerant man, he did much to distribute and popularise the *Encyclopédie* in France. He retired from public affaires in 1788. Four years later, he undertook to defend the king in front of the Convention, assisted by Tronchet and Sèze. Their efforts were of no avail.
Later on, Malesherbes himself was executed, along with his daughter and his son-in-law, Pelletier de Rosambro, one of his granddaughters and her husband (the marquis de Châteaubriand, the writer's elder brother). His two private secretaries were also sent to the guillotine.

Courtyard. – Invisible from the outside, the lush, grassy court still features the original outhouses: large granaries (14C) where the tithes paid in kind were stored on four separate levels, the famous "tower of dues", a pavilion called "Châteaubriand's House" where the 19C French author came to stay and a 14C dovecote with 2000 pigeonholes, able to accommodate 8000 birds. The chapel was completed in the 15C.

Interior. – The ground floor offers a suite of salons which still evoke the happy, carefree lifestyle of the de Lamoignon family on the eve of the French Revolution. The original furniture has been replaced. The tour ends with the bedroom of Henriette d'Entragues and its smal oratory with pointed vaulting.
The chapel houses a recumbent figure of François de Balzac d'Entragues lying ostensibly with his back to his wife. Legend has it that his sullen attitude was directed against his first wife Jacqueline de Rohan, whose conduct had given him cause for displeasure.

Rouville Castle (Château de Rouville). – *2km – 1 mile to the north along the road to Boigneville.* After the building with a weathercock on the right-hand side of the road, turn right into the drive leading to the castle.
Originally built in the 15C, the castle was restored and embellished by one of Viollet-le-Duc's disciples during the last century. The terrace commands a pleasant view of the Essonne Valley and its wooded slopes. The rocks, the noble pine trees, the oratory and the quaint machicolations of the castle make a peaceful, romantic scene.

MANTES-LA-JOLIE Pop 43 585

Michelin map 196 fold 15 – Town plan in the current Michelin Red Guide France

This extremely active town has grown considerably with the industrial development of its suburbs.

Henri IV's Conversion. – Henri IV, who had delivered Mantes from the League in 1590, returned to the town on account of the ravishing Gabrielle d'Estrées. During one of his stays, in May 1593 to be precise, he decided to renounce Protestantism a second time (he had already done so once to escape the Massacre of St Bartholomew). In view of the ceremony, a number of meetings took place between the king, supported by the Protestants Duplessis-Mornay and Sully, and Cardinal Duperron, the Abbot of St-Denis, as well as various other leading ecclesiastic figures. It was during one of these encounters that Henri IV is believed to have pronounced the famous adage "Surely Paris is worth a Mass". The abjuration ceremony took place in the Basilica of St-Denis on 25 July 1593.

★ COLLEGIATE CHURCH OF OUR LADY

(COLLÉGIALE NOTRE-DAME) (AZ) *time: 1/2 hour*

This church – which inspired Jean-Baptiste-Camille Corot to paint one of his most beautiful works – would compare favourably with a great many of France's cathedrals. Il was built by the chapter of a collegiate church which owned a fair amount of land in the area. The funds for this ambitious project were provided by the municipality, William the Conqueror and several Capetian kings.
The construction of the church, started in 1170, ran into the 13C in the case of the nave and the chancel. The chapels were added in the 14C. The church stood within the precincts of the fortified bailey that defended the old royal castle (behind the east end, on the site now occupied by the public gardens).

Exterior. – The west front is the oldest part of the church *(illustration p 23)*. The tower on the left and the narrow gallery linking it to the right tower were renewed in the 19C. Three badly-mutilated doorways adorn the exterior. The one in the centre is dedicated to the Virgin and was executed between 1170 and 1195. Like the north doorway on the left, it features foliated scrolls on the piers and bases of the colonnettes.
A walk round the right side will bring you to the protruding 14C Navarre Chapel. Note the unusual east end, with its gabled apses crowned by a gallery and built onto a high wall circling the ambulatory. This open-work structure admitting large, round bays is surmounted by hefty buttresses. Above the fortified wall, the upper part of the chancel is supported by a series of sturdy flying buttresses.

Interior. – The light, elegant nave (33m – 108ft) is almost as high as that of Notre-Dame in Paris (35m – 114ft). Its elevation – offering an alternation of wide arches, brightly-lit galleries and clerestory windows – marks the transition from Romanesque to early Gothic. The splendid rose window (early 13C) in the west front has been fitted with the original stained glass. As you walk down the nave, note the arrangement of the sexpartite vaulting *(p 24)*. The heavier supporting arches, placed at each end, come to rest on thick pillars, while the lighter ones end in round columns.
The deep, well-lit galleries above the aisles – a feature dating from Romanesque architecture – open onto the nave by a series of bays with triple arcades. Observe the old-fashioned structure of the galleries in the apse and the north part of the choir, surmounted by barrel vaulting.

Navarre Chapel (Chapel of the Blessed Sacrament), built onto the right side of the chancel, forms a separate ensemble. Il resembles a sort of shrine featuring early 14C windows with Radiant Gothic roundels *(p 24)*. It is thought the name comes from the kings of Navarre, who belonged to the ruling house of Évreux (the comtes d'Évreux held the lordship of Mantes from 1328 to 1364).
The entrance to the chapel is graced by four dainty statuettes dating form the 14C. The crowned women carrying a miniature church model are quite likely the founders of Notre-Dame: Jeanne de France, comtesse d'Évreux (1312-1349) and Jeanne d'Évreux, Queen of France by her marriage to Charles IV the Fair in 1324. The other two young women are probably Jeanne de France's daughter: Queen Blanche, who married Philip VI of Valois, and Agnès, wife of the famous Gaston Phoebus, comte de Foix.

ADDITIONAL SIGHTS

Notre-Dame Quarter. – This district has retained its old-fashioned charm. South of the collegiate church, take the narrow Rue du Cloître-Notre-Dame and then turn left into Rue de la Sangle, once a major road linking Paris to Normandy. Soon afterwards, turn left into Rue de l'Abbé-Hua, which runs along the public gardens laid out on the former site of the royal castle (destroyed in the 18C). Enjoy the **view** of Notre-Dame's east end.

Ⓥ **Former Hôtel-Dieu Hospice** (AZ B). – The chapel with its beautifully-restored 18C façade, houses various miscellaneous collections of regional interest, notably the paintings from the Luce Museum, presently exhibited in Mantes Town Hall *(see overleaf)*.

Old Limay Bridge (BY). – This humpback bridge supported by piers with cutwaters used to serve the local mills and fisheries up to 1870. Unfortunately it has since caved in but still features the 1750 Porters' Lodge. It inspired Corot to paint his *Mantes Bridge*, now in the Louvre *(photograph p 33)*. The old stonework still exudes a quiet, gentle charm.

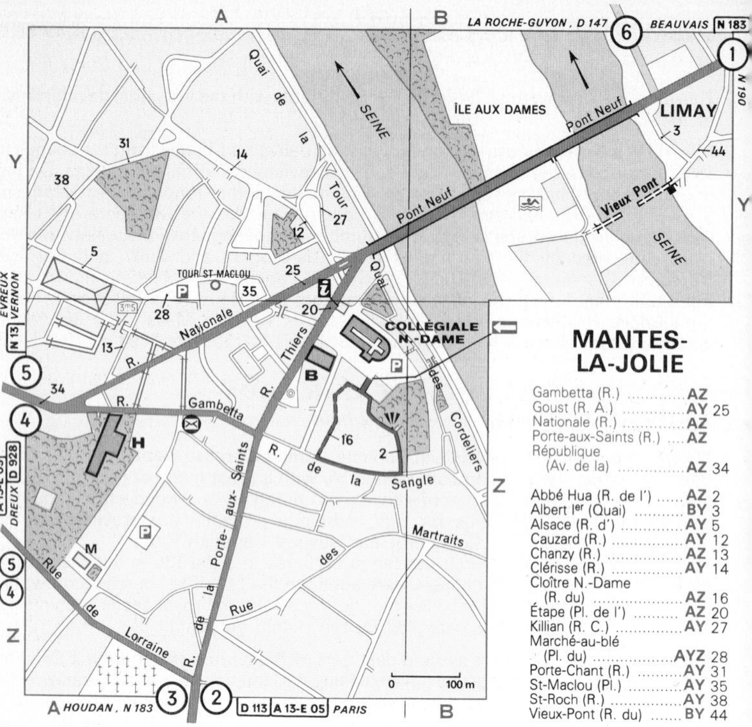

MANTES-LA-JOLIE

Gambetta (R.) .... AZ
Goust (R. A.) .... AY 25
Nationale (R.) .... AZ
Porte-aux-Saints (R.) .... AZ
République (Av. de la) .... AZ 34

Abbé Hua (R. de l') ...... AZ 2
Albert Ier (Quai) .... BY 3
Alsace (R. d') .... AY 5
Cauzard (R.) .... AY 12
Chanzy (R.) .... AZ 13
Clérisse (R.) .... AY 14
Cloître N.-Dame (R. du) .... AZ 16
Étape (Pl. de l') .... AZ 20
Killian (R. C.) .... AY 27
Marché-au-blé (Pl. du) .... AYZ 28
Porte-Chant (R.) .... AY 31
St-Maclou (Pl.) .... AY 35
St-Roch (R.) .... AY 38
Vieux-Pont (R. du) .... BY 44

Luce Museum (Musée Luce) (AZ H). – Exclusively dedicated to **Maximilien Luce** (1858-1941), this museum presents around one hundred works (lithographs, etchings, drawings and paintings) executed during the neo-Impressionist period. Luce was a close friend of Seurat and Pissarro, a sympathetic supporter of the anarchist cause and a contemporary of the Commune. As a result much of his work centres on social issues: the Charleroi smelting works (*The Casting* in 1896), Varlin's execution, his series on the Gare de l'Est during World War I, etc. In the interwar period, Luce concentrated on the landscapes of the Mantes area, in particular Rolleboise, where he spent several months every year.

EXCURSIONS

Rosny-sur-Seine. – Pop 3 934. *6.5km – 4 miles by* ⑤.
Maximilien de Béthune, marquis de Rosny and duc de Sully (1559-1651) was probably born in the old feudal castle of Rosny (now disappeared). In the early 17C he built the present Louis XIII **château**, surrounded it with a dry moat and laid out the very first gardens, dotted with copses and grottoes as was the custom. In 1820 Marie-Caroline de Bourbon-Sicile, carrying the child (the future duc de Bordeaux, later known as the comte de Chambord) of her deceased husband the duc de Berry, withdrew to Rosny, which she had acquired with her dowry. The Duchess was an extravagant but well-meaning and energetic woman: she undertook restoration work at the château, the construction of a hospital whose chapel *(presently undergoing renovation)* received the prince's heart and the creation of a landscape park. She was forced to leave the estate when the 1830 Revolution broke out.

Sully's statue on the road leading out of town towards Mantes used to feature in an imposing composition that stood on Concorde Bridge in Paris. It was executed under the Restoration and moved to Versailles by the City of Paris in 1836.

Épône. – Pop 5 247. *8km – 3.7 miles to the southeast by* ②.
The **Blacksmiths' Museum** (Musée de la Charronnerie) *(leave Épône to the east, just before the N 191)*, founded by the Tour de France Blacksmiths' Guild, presents around sixty draught vehicles, dating from the turn of the century up to the present day, from various French regions. A genuine smithy has been reconstituted to illustrate the type of work carried out by blacksmiths', saddlers, wheelwrights and farriers.

Maule. – Pop 5 422. *14km – 9 miles to the southeast by* ② *the D 113 then the N 191 on the right after Épône.*
The **Bicycle Museum** (Musée du Vélocipède) houses several extremely rare exhibits, ranging from the 1817 *draisienne* to the folding military bike of World War I. The most striking items are a wooden tricycle, a six-seater racing tandem (1898) and a two-speed model featuring a parallelogram.

The times indicated in this guide
when given with the distance allow one to enjoy the scenery
when given for sightseeing are intended to give an idea
of the possible length or brevity of a visit.

★ MARAIS Château

Michelin map 196 southeast of fold 29

From the early 19C to the end of the July Monarchy (1830-48), this charming spot was the delight of a great many prominent writers and political figures, entertained by the excellent Mme de la Briche and her daughter, comtesse Molé.

Château. – It has retained the sober, austere elegance that characterised stately homes towards the end of the *Ancien Regime.* The road bridge spanning the Rémarde affords a good **view** of the château, lying in the perspective of the Grand Canal, crowned by a cupola, and embellished with a central peristyle. The outhouses were built on the site of the original 17C château.
Skirt the château to get a good view of the eastern and western façades. The peristyle and dome of the west front are balanced by a projecting frontispiece with pilasters and capped by an attic featuring three bays. Stepping back towards the gardens, you will enjoy an excellent view of the roofscape: the roof of the central attic storey screens the dome.
The ornamentation of the façades adds a further touch of finesse to the ensemble: the upper cornice featuring carved brackets, the pediments or sculpted panels above the windows, the sculpted friezes indicating the different storeys.

Park. – The public may visit the Grand Canal, the formal gardens and take a stroll in the wooded part of the park.

Museum (Musée). – One of the salons exposes the many intrigues and romances that proliferated at Marais Château at the time of Mme de la Briche. The other exhibits are mainly concerned with Talleyrand : bust of the prince by Bosio, Houdon's sculpture of Mirabeau, portraits of Louis XVIII and Charles X by Gérard, a famous print of the Vienna Congress, numerous caricatures, etc.
One of the rooms is dedicated to **Gaston Palewski** and presents a host of documents relating to his political activities. The early days of his career took him to Morocco in 1923, where he was placed unter the orders of Maréchal Lyautey. Subsequently he served Paul Reynaud and General de Gaulle. The latter appointed him Head of Government in London, Algiers and Paris.

MARLY-LE-ROI — Pop 17 313

Michelin map 101 fold 12 – Michelin plan 18

Although a number of important new housing estates have spread across the Grandes Terres plateau since 1950, stretching towards Le Pecq, the name of Louis XIV remains firmly attached to this town.
Marly was the Sun King's favourite place of residence. Unfortunately, its golden age lasted no longer than twenty years. After the First Empire, only the park remained, an impressive display of greenery bordering the old village, which has welcomed a great many writers and artists: the two Alexandre Dumas, Alfred Sisley, Camille Pissarro, the sculptor Maillol and the tragedienne Mlle Rachel, to name but a few.

The early stages. – We owe the construction of Marly to Louis XIV's desire to retreat from the formal etiquette of Versailles. After the Treaty of Nijmegen in 1678, at the summit of his glory, tired by the continual entertaining at Versailles, the king dreamed of a country residence where he could rest in relative peace, far from the madding crowd. His barony at Marly offered a deep, lush valley which seemed to suit the purpose and he entrusted the Jules Hardouin-Mansart with the plans. Mansart came up with an ingenious idea: instead of designing one huge single pavilion, he conceived a series of 13 separate units. The royal pavilion would stand on the upper terrace, while the other twelve, smaller in size and all identical, would be arranged along a stretch of water. To support his theory, Mansart explained that the decoration of the king's pavilion could symbolise the sun – Louis XIV's emblem – and that the surrounding buildings could represent the twelve signs of the zodiac.

1714 watercolour of the Great Cascade at Marly

To cut down on costs, it was agreed to replace the carved low reliefs by *trompe-l'œil* frescoes. The king, delighted, gave orders to start building in 1679. It took nine years for the whole project to be completed. After working relentlessly all his life, Mansart passed away at the château in 1708.

Further embellishments. – Right until the end of his reign, Louis XIV applied himself to the improvement of his Marly residence. As was his habit, he kept a close watch on the various work under way. He would even show gardeners how to trim the hedges properly.
Behind the royal pavilion rose the steep, wooded slopes of the hillside. The Sun King gave orders to build the River, also called the Great Cascade *(photograph p 113)*, the Wonder of Marly, which was served by the famous "Machine" *(p 115)*: starting from the top of the hill, an impressive series of falls poured down a flight of fifty-two steps of pink marble set into the terraced slope. The whole ensemble – adorned with statues, porticos and rockeries – was completed in 1699..
The same year, the king decided to clear the main perspective and raze the ground that stood in the way, an enterprise that occupied 1 600 soldiers for a period of four years.

Life at Marly. – Apart from his close relations, Louis XIV brought very few guests to Marly: the facilities for accommodation were limited to 24 apartments. It is estimated that 500 lords and 300 ladies altogether were invited to the château over a period of 30 years. The king himself drew up a list of the guests and he personally determined where they should stay: the nearer they were to the royal pavilion, the greater the honour. The "happy few" were not necessarily members of the aristocracy or high dignitaries, but lively, intelligent personalities whose wit and charm would enliven the king's stays.
The formal etiquette in force at Versailles was dropped at Marly. The king shared his meals with his guests, with whom he conversed in a free, casual manner. Hunts, forest walks, outdoor games, card games, games of chance, balls and concerts were a regular feature of life at Marly. The standard of comfort at the palace left something to be desired. In summer, the guests caught fever, in winter they shivered with cold or choked with smoke because it was too damp to start a fire. Louis XIV – who personally undertook to tackle the heating problem – introduced new systems every year but his efforts were all in vain. On 9 August 1715, the king suffered a bout of exhaustion after following the hunt in his carriage. He was taken to Versailles, where he died on 1 September, aged 77.

★ MARLY PARK

You can drive into Marly Park by the Double Gateway (Deux Portes). Then take the first right turning, which cuts through the woods and leads to the car park near the presidential pavilion.

A large esplanade flanked by lime trees in the centre of the park marks the former site of the royal pavilion. A series of slabs define the plans of the building: the large octagonal salon is surrounded by four corner rooms, separated by vestibules. While the decoration in the king's bedroom was red, the colour chosen for the Dauphin was green (although she never occupied it, this room was originally intended for the queen). As for the apartments of Monsieur (Louis XIV's brother) and Madame Elisabeth of Bavaria (his second wife), they were painted in yellow and blue, respectively.
This is where the two perspectives of the park meet. Crosswise, we have the drive leading to the Royal Gates; lengthwise, the route running from St-Germain and the Seine Valley up to the Grand Mirror fountains and the green "carpet" of lawn.

The plans for one of the guests' pavilions are marked out by the slabs lying behind the car park.

The present grounds are suggestive of old Marly, with its terraces, fountains and trimed hornbeam hedges. Further information can be obtained from the museum set up in the new annexe near the Royal Gates.

Royal Gates (Grille Royale). – Louis XIV would use this entrance when he approached the château from Versailles. Admire the charming perspective of the steep road climbing up the hillside and its continuation on the opposite slope, slicing its way through the trees.

⏲ **Marly-le-Roi-Louveciennes Promenade Museum** (Musée-Promenade). – The museum offers extremely precious material now that the 13 pavilions and the garden statues are no longer: the plans drawn up in 1753 and a miniature model of the whole project give one a fair idea of what the king's country residence looked like. Note the interesting approach to 18C ornamental gardening.
The corner of the main pavilion houses the casts of the statues sculpted by Coustou and Lepautre, a painting of the château and its fountains by Martin le Jeune (1723) and numerous line drawings of former copses and spinneys..
The room dedicated to Louveciennes displays a number of items related to Mme du Barry: Pajou's statue of *Loyalty*, a drawing by Moreau le Jeune portraying a banquet held in the Music Pavilion in honour of Louis XV in 1771. It also features the only religious work by Mme Vigée-Lebrun, as well as her two paintings *Summer* and *Autumn*, which were hung at Marly in 1755. Admire one of Desportes' hunting scenes and a Lamentation (1516) taken from St-Vigor Church.
Before leaving the museum, pay a visit to the small chamber presenting the "Marly Machine": it contains drawings and plans, together with a miniature model. The mural painting depicts the waterworks of Versailles park.

Return to the car and leave the park by Avenue des Combattants. Drive down to the horse-pond.

Horse-Pond (Abreuvoir). – After a steep descent – known as Côte du Cœur-Volant – the N 386 leads to the horse-pond, once used as a spillway for the waters of Marly park. From there, the water was conveyed back to the Seine by a system of pipes and drains. The terrace flanked by yew trees above the pond used to bear Coysevox' *Winged Horses* and, at a later date, Guillaume Coustou's *Marly Horses*. Two replicas stand in their place. The original statues once adorned Place Concorde in Paris and have now been moved to the Louvre. Two reproductions have also been installed on the Parisian square.

ADDITIONAL SIGHTS

The Marly Machine. – It was decided to divert the waters of the Seine to supply the fountains of Marly and, subsequently, those of Versailles.
Colbert succeeded in finding a Belgian engineer, Arnold Deville, and a master carpenter, Rennequin Sualem, who agreed to take on the daring project of raising the water 150m – 493ft above the level of the river. The work started in 1681 and ended in 1684. The whole operation involved a considerable amount of equipment: 13 hydraulic wheels with a diameter of 12m – 40ft operated three sets of batteries totalling 225 pumps by means of rods, iron-shod levers and chains. As one can imagine, the noise was deafening. The waters were conveyed from the water tower – set at a height of 163m – 535ft above the Seine – to the Louveciennes reservoirs via an aqueduct with a capacity of 5000 m^3 a day. From there they were channelled to the grounds of Marly or Versailles. Since the 19C, several pumping devices have occupied the site of the famous machine. The last disappeared in 1967.

The site. – The road bridge of Ile de la Loge affords a good view of the 18C buildings *(Quai Rennequin-Sualem at Bougival)* that made up the Marly Machine and the pipes lining the hillside. At the top of the rise stands a white lodge by Ledoux: **Mme du Barry's Music Pavilion.** It was inaugurated on 2 September 1771, during a sumptuous banquet attended by Louis XV. The building was moved to this site and raised a storey in 1934 by the famous perfumer René Coty.

Louveciennes. – Pop 7 338. This small residential town on the edge of Marly Forest still features several substantial properties.
The **church** (12-13C) on the village square was built in the Romanesque style. The polygonal bell tower dates from the 19C. The interior boasts an interesting collection of stone piscinae, resting against the east end.
A walk through the public gardens, along Rue de l'Étang and down Rue du Pont will ⓥ bring you to **Pont Château** (Château du Pont), dating from the 16C. It forms a pleasant sight indeed, with its groves of trees and the rippling waters of its moat. Proceed towards the town hall along Rue du Général-Leclerc. You will discover the arches of the disused aqueduct that used to convey the waters of the Seine to Versailles.

Marshal Joffre's Tomb (Tombeau du Maréchal Joffre). – From the church, follow Rue du Professeur-Tuffier, then Rue du Maréchal Joffre until you reach Chemin des Gressets. The property belonging to the marshal lies at the beginning of the lane. Looking through the gate in Chemin des Gressets, you can see a rotunda-shaped temple containing the relics of this valiant fighter who died in 1931, together with those of his wife. Joffre, who was extremely fond of Louveciennes, insisted on being buried here rather than at the Invalides in Paris.

ⓥ **Monte-Cristo Château (Château de Monte-Cristo).** – To the right of the steep, narrow road descending towards Le Port-Marly, stands the extravagant folly built by **Alexandre Dumas** in 1846, offering a medley of architectural styles (Renaissance, Gothic, Oriental, etc.). It became an object of curiosity among fashionable circles in Paris but Dumas later ran into debt and was forced to sell it. Much of the building has been restored and features medallions depicting Dumas and his favourite authors. Visitors are shown round the ground floor (19C decoration) and the superb Moresque bedroom featuring sculpted panels, stained glass and furniture of Moorish inspiration. The **Alexandre Dumas Museum** (Musée Alexandre Dumas) presents various souvenirs belonging to the writer and his family. Note the small pavilion standing on the hillock opposite the château, known as Yew Castle (Château d'If) the titles of Dumas' works are engraved in the stone masonry.

MARLY-LE-ROI FOREST

This State forest – once royal hunting grounds, jealously guarded by high walls – covers a rough but picturesque plateau planted with oaks, beeches and chestnut trees. The total area is estimated at 2000ha – 5000 acres.
The thicker groves, featuring some very beautiful trees, lie to the west of the road running from St-Germain to St-Nom-la-Bretèche, and in the vicinity of Joyenval crossroads. Consult Michelin map 101 to see which lanes are closed to traffic (barriers). These however may be recommended as cycling paths.

Times and charges for admission to sights described in the guide are listed at the end of the guide.

The sights are listed alphabetically in this section either under the place – town, village or area – in which they are situated or under their proper name.

Every sight for which there are times and charges is indicated by the symbol ⓥ in the margin in the main part of the guide.

MARNE-LA-VALLÉE

Michelin map 101 folds 18 to 20 and 28 to 30

Marne-la-Vallée, one of the five new towns of the Paris region *(p 7)*, was planned as a growth point for the eastern part of the Paris Basin. The initial work started in 1972. The new town is designed as a series of four districts laid out along the main arteries: the A4 motorway, to the north the Val Maubuée section of motorway and the RER (regional express network between Paris and the suburbs).

Noisy-le-Grand is growing into an important regional urban centre with a marked vocation for commerce.

The six communes of the central district – known as **Val Maubuée** – have benefited from their proximity to the Marne river: they are Champs, Noisiel, Torcy, Émerainville, Lognes and Croissy-Beaubourg. They have been the object of several original housing schemes which have attracted a new class of inhabitants.

The **Menier Chocolate Factory** (Usine de Chocolat Menier) – bought out by Rowntree Mackintosh in 1971 – provides an isolated example of 19C industrial architecture (1871-1872), characterised by stone piers, brick panels and iron framing. It is surrounded by a park and its château (**Noisiel Park**, open to the public since 1980), a farming estate (Buisson farmhouse has been converted into a huge public library) and a private railway system. *The old factory buildings are not open to the public.*

The **Arche Guédon** quarter presents a different aspect of town-planning, relying on variety and harmony: pedestrian precints, combination of supermarkets and traditional shops, touch of greenery around Maubuée brook (artificial lakes).

The **leisure centre** (Parc de Loisirs) at **Torcy** *(see the table of Principal Festivals at the end of the guide)* has been laid out around a 23ha – 57 acre stretch of water which offers facilities for swimming, wind-surfing, fishing, hiring water bicycles, riding and rambling.

Walkers, campers, smokers please take care

Fire is the scourge of forests everywhere

MARNES-LA-COQUETTE

Pop 1 634

Michelin map 101 fold 23 – Michelin plan 22

This densely-wooded locality west of Paris developed around the estate of Villeneuve-l'Étang, formerly the property of Napoleon III.

★ **Pasteur Institute – Museum of Applied Research (Institut Pasteur – Musée des Applications de la Recherche).** – *3, Boulevard Raymond-Poincaré.*
Following the fall of the Second Empire, Villeneuve-l'Étang fell into the hands of the State. **Louis Pasteur,** who had already carried out considerable research work, lacked space in Paris: an 1884 decree ruled that he could move to the estate in order to pursue his studies on rabies. In 1885, he successfully invented the first vaccine for human use, a discovery that crowned a lifelong career. His work was continued by a small group of followers who revolutionised contemporary medicine.
The museum lies in the Hundred Guards' Pavilion, occupied by Napoleon III's soldiers in the 19C. It presents the history of the struggle against infectious diseases through the accomplishments of Pasteur and his disciples, namely, Pierre Roux, Yersin, Gaston Ramon, Albert Calmette, Nicolle and Laveran. The exhibition concentrates on three major fields of research: serum therapy, vaccination and chemotherapy. The techniques that made it possible to overcome diseases such as diphtheria, tetanos, typhus, cholera, tuberculosis and poliomyelitis are explained to visitors. Modern research and prospects are also evoked (B-type hepatitis, AIDS, immunology and artificial vaccines).
The room where Pasteur died on 22 September 1895 has remained intact. It features the family measuring rod bearing inscriptions made by Mme Pasteur. The study of Gaston Ramon, who discovered toxoids, has been entirely reconstituted.
The former drawing room houses a collection of instruments reminiscent of 19C medical laboratories: Elie Metchnikoff's microscope, Chamberland's sterilizer and Doctor Roux' optical bench, where scientists could study microbes through a microscope.

MARQUEMONT Church

Michelin map 55 north of fold 19

What once used to be Marquemont village is now a tiny hamlet belonging to Monneville *commune.* There remain only a cemetery and a church on the edge of the Vexin plateau dominating the Thelle countryside.

Access. – Coming from Paris, leave Monneville by a northbound route and turn right into a lane signposted by a yellow board *("Monuments de l'Oise").*
The church was preserved by a group of volunteers, and subsequently restored. The badly damaged nave features only a Romanesque doorway, decorated with a chevron motif. The other parts of the building have remained intact: the chancel and north transept, of Gothic lines, built in the 13C, and the 16C bell tower, crowned by a saddle-back roof as is customary in Ile-de-France.

★ MEAUX Pop 45 873

Michelin map 196 folds 22 and 23 – Locap map p 135
Town plan in the current Michelin Red Guide France

Formerly the property of the house of Champagne *(p 14)*, Meaux was an agricultural centre lying between the rivers Petit Morin and Grand Morin, on the edge of the Multien cereal growing plains and the famous dairy pastures of Brie. It is now an average-sized town, in rapid expansion since the sixties.
In the summer months, a **son-et-lumière performance** featuring a cast of 2 100 re-enacts the moments of glory of Meaux in the charming setting of the Episcopal Quarter *(see the table of Principal Festivals at the end of the guide)*.

Jacques Bossuet, Bishop of Meaux. – Having completed his tutorial commitments towards the Dauphin, **Bossuet** was made Bishop of Meaux in 1682, at the age of 55.
The man later known as the "Eagle of Meaux" exercised his ecclesiastic duties with the utmost assiduity: he kept an attentive eye on catechism, was often seen preaching in his own cathedral and assumed full command of the religious communities in his diocese. For instance, despite his great esteem for Jouarre Abbey *(qv)*, he did not hesitate to have the place besieged because the abbess refused to part with two nuns whose conduct he considered improper.
Bossuet enjoyed working in the huge library of the Episcopal Palace, or in his study at the back of the garden: it was there that he composed five of his most famous sermons, including those dedicated to Louis XIV's wife Marie-Thérèse and the Great Condé. He also wrote a number of books in strong defence of Gallical orthodoxy. He died in Paris in 1704, aged 77, at the height of his intellectual pursuits. As was his wont, his relics rest in his cathedral in Meaux.

MEAUX

Berge (R. du Cdt)
Gaulle (Pl. Ch. de) 16
Grand-Cerf (R. du) 17
Leclerc-et-de-la-2e-D.B. (R. Gén.) 19
St-Nicolas (R. du Fg)
St-Rémy (R.)

Cordeliers (R. des) 7
Cornillon (R.) 8
Henri IV (Pl.) 20
Martimprey (R. de) 23
Notre-Dame (R.) 24
Ursulines (R. des) 31
Vieux-Moulins (R. des) 32

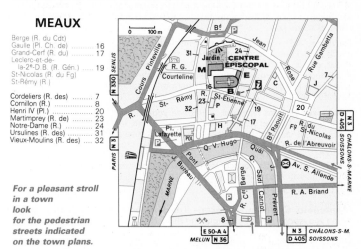

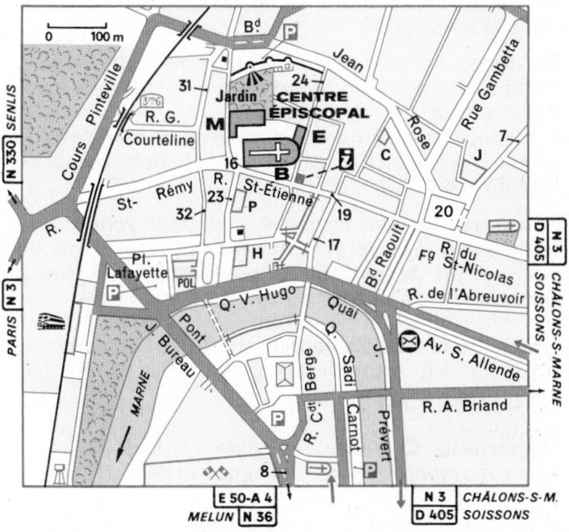

For a pleasant stroll in a town look for the pedestrian streets indicated on the town plans.

★EPISCOPAL QUARTER *time: 1 1/2 hours*

★St Stephen's Cathedral (Cathédrale St-Étienne) (**B**). – The construction of the church continued from the late 12C to the 16C, covering the entire gamut of Gothic architecture. The façade (14-16C) is pure Flamboyant. Only the left tower was completed. The one on the right – a plain bell tower – is called the Black Tower on account of its dark-coloured shingles. The limestone used for the stonework has crumbled in several places and the exterior decoration is badly mutilated. The Wars of Religion contributed to causing further damage.
On the south side, the façade of the transept is an elegant instance of Radiant Gothic. The south doorway – in poor condition – is dedicated to St Stephen.

Enter the cathedral through this doorway.

The interior of the cathedral – restored for the last time in the 18C – contrasts sharply with the badly weathered exterior. The lofty, well-lit nave is an impressive sight. The double side aisles are unusually high owing to the suppression of the upper galleries as in Notre-Dame in Paris. These were removed around the middle of the 13C, which had the effect of heightening the aisles.
The two bays belonging to the nave next to the transept date from the early 13C: their austere appearance typifies early Gothic. The west bays were completed in the 14C and the pillars redesigned in the 15C.
The inner façades of the transepts – in particular that of the south arm – provide a superb example of 14C architecture: the elegant, generous proportions characterise the golden age of Radiant Gothic. Below the huge stained glass window runs an open-work triforium so fine that it allows a full view of the lancets. The chancel – also Radiant Gothic – is a pleasing sight with its double aisles and its five apsidal chapels. Note the pretty 15C Maugarni doorway lying to the left of the choir. A walk round the ambulatory will bring you to Bossuet's tomb, marked by a slab of black marble, visible through the parclose enclosing the chancel.

Old Chapter House (Vieux Chapitre) (**E**). – Believed to have been the chapter's 13C tithe barn. The external staircase is roofed over and dates from the Renaissance period. The ground floor, linked to the cathedral by a wooden gallery, is used as a sacristy and a spare chapel.

ⓥ**Episcopal Palace (Ancien Évêché)** (M). – The old palace houses a **museum** largely dedicated to Bossuet. The building was completed in the 12C and renovated in the 17C. The main front gives onto the garden. The two magnificent Gothic rooms facing the park on the ground floor, the nearby crypt and the upstairs chapel are the oldest parts of the palace. The chapter house contains some of the museum's archaeological collections, dating from prehistoric, protohistoric and especially Gallo-Roman times. The amazing brick ramp was designed by Bishop Briçonnet in the 16C in order that the mules loaded with cereals might reach the attics.
One enters the palace through the Synod's Chamber, which together with the western salons, has been made into a Fine Arts Museum (15 to 19C). Among the many artists feature Floris, Boullogne, De Troy, Bouchardon, Millet and Courbet. The donation made by Annie and Jean Pierre Changeux in 1983 has considerably enriched the collections of 17 and 18C French painting. The exhibition presents an amusing display of medals and counters evoking the 1848 Revolution, the War of 1870 and the Paris Commune. Bossuet's apartment, located in the east wing, has retained its original layout but the decoration was renewed in the Louis XV style. Admire Mignard's portrait of the bishop and a splendid Cressent commode (early 18C). The former library contains an anonymous 17C portrait depicting the wife of Monsieur, Henrietta Maria of England, for whom Bossuet composed his famous sermon. The room also offers a variety of documents and personal souvenirs. The chapel houses the museum's religious works (medieval sculptures, reliquaries and robes), which include several interesting holy-water basins of the type designed for the east end. The head of Ogier the Dane – jack of spades in our modern pack of cards –, the fragment of a 12C recumbent statue, deserves a special mention. The history of the town is also presented to visitors: 1738 plan by Monvoisin, pictures of the old bridge spanning the Marne with its picturesque mills (sadly disappeared), apothecary's shop of the former hospice, Moisan's electric oven (1892) for studying artificial diamonds.

Gardens. – Shaped as a bishop's mitre, they were designed by Le Nôtre in the tradition of French formal gardens. A staircase leads to the terrace, the former watchpath of the old ramparts.
At the top of the steps, one discovers the humble 17C pavilion which Bossuet used as a study. The bishop would retire there to collect his thoughts or to write in the peaceful hours of the night.

Ramparts (Anciens remparts). – *Retrace your steps.*
When you draw level with the first tower (yew tree trimmed into a conical shape), lean over the edge of the terrace. The Gallo-Roman part of the wall (4C) is easily recognisable on account of the fine stonework, crossed by thin layers of brick. The centre of the terrace affords a good **view★** of the gardens, the Episcopal Palace and St Stephen's Cathedral.

EXCURSION

ⓥ**Montceaux Château.** – *10.5km – 9 miles to the east. Leave Meaux by the N 3. When you reach Trilport, turn right into the D 19. The lane leading to the château lies to the left.*
Montceaux Château is closely linked to the names of two Florentine queens and to that of their favourite architect or interior decorator. Catherine de' Medici entrusted the construction work (1547-1567) to Philibert Delorme and the decoration to Primaticcio. As for Marie de' Medici, she chose to hire Salomon de Brosse before he undertook to build the Luxembourg Palace (1617). After 1650, the château became uninhabitable. There remains a superb display of old ruins, overgrown with trees: the entrance pavilion, alas roofless, features a large section of wall with gaping windows. The oblong-shaped moat has remained intact.

MELUN — Pop 36 218

Michelin map 196 fold 4 – Town plans in the current Michelin Red Guide France

Like the ancient city of Lutetia, this town developed around one of the isles of the Seine river.

A town famed for its cheese. – East of Melun, the rich alluvial soils of Brie give way to copses and grazing pastures: this is where the celebrated Brie cheese is made. The traditional Brie from Meaux – measuring 40cm-16ins across – is consumed when it has reached its "peak". The Coulommiers Brie is generally less mature and the Brie from Melun has a firmer consistency and tastes much stronger.

SIGHTS

ⓥ**Museum (Musée).** – *Enter by Quai de la Courtille.*
Set up in the Hôtel de la Viconté – one of Fouquet's residences when he was vicomte de Melun – the museum features two dormer windows dating from Renaissance times. It contains a great many documents and stone exhibits relating to the history of the town. Note the polished axes, the Rubelles earthenware and the fragments of Gallo-Roman pottery.

ⓥ**Vaux-le-Pénil Château (Château de Vaux-le-Pénil).** – *Southeast of town plan (Michelin Red Guide France). Leave Melun and drive upstream along Quai du Maréchal-Foch and then the D 39, leading to Chartrettes. Leave the river bank and bear right along a slight incline. At the top of the ramp, take the first turning on the left.*

This 18C château dominates the river. The rooms on the ground floor and the various basements and underground chambers present a host of objects and documents illustrating Surrealist art: works by Giorgio de Chirico and especially Salvador Dali, who used to stay at the château, numerous photographs of the artists who pioneered the movement and those who represented it.

Le Mée-sur-Seine. – *West of the town plan of Meaux (Michelin Red Guide* ⓥ *France).* The **Chapu Museum** (Musée Chapu) at no 937 Rue Chapu is dedicated to one of the leading names in official sculpture at the beginning of the Third Republic, **Henri Chapu** (1833-1891). The exhibits include miniature models, original plaster casts, bronze statues and a selection of sketches by the artist.

Dammarie-les-Lys. – *3 km – 2 miles along the N 372. Leave Melun by ⑥ (town plan in the current Michelin Red Guide France).* In 1244 Blanche of Castile, Saint Louis' mother, founded **Lys Abbey** (Abbaye du Lys) for a group of nuns belonging to the Cistercian Order *(p 26)*. The pious queen and her son contributed generously to the abbey, which soon became extremely prosperous. When Queen Blanche died, her heart was offered to the nuns and after her son's death, his royal cilice was left to the religious community, who added it to their treasure. All that remains of the 13C sanctuary are the crumbling ruins of the abbey church.

MELUN-SÉNART

Michelin map 196 fold 33

The latest of the five new towns of the Paris region *(p 7)*, Melun-Sénart lies on a plateau bordered with forests – Sénart forest, Rougeau forest, Bréviande wood –, surrounded by densely-populated rural villages. The ten *communes* which make up the new town number 65 000 inhabitants.

A New Town Planning Concept. – Unlike the other new towns of the Paris region, Melun does not feature a modern, ready-made city centre.
Two new localities have seen the light of day: Sénart-Ville Nouvelle and Rougeau-Sénart. The general trend here is towards detached houses, grouped around existing villages. The landscape has been largely preserved, and plans allow for ponds, lakes and canals, giving the area a distinctive "western France" look.
This major town planning operation is still under way in the ten districts and various industrial zones concerned.

Rougeau Forest. – From the N 446 and the D 50, a number of forest lanes lead to recreational areas in the wood. Two paths have been marked out for tourists: one is a fitness trail and the other offers a pleasant tour of the various ponds.

MÉRÉVILLE

Pop 2 674

Michelin map 60 folds 19 and 20

The village was originally built on two adjoining monticles: the first accommodates the church while the second provided the site for the old medieval fortress, now replaced by a covered market.
The town acquired a widespread reputation on account of its park which, at the height of its glory, could be compared to Ermenonville *(the park is closed to the public)*. Jean-Joseph de Laborde, a financier who became court banker under Louis XVI, bought the estate in 1784. Bélanger, the architect who designed Bagatelle, and Hubert Robert conceived the plans for an English landscape garden featuring a number of garden buildings, spread out across both slopes of the Juine Valley. Unfortunately, over the past two centuries, the grounds have been considerably reduced and most of the monuments have disappeared. Several are now in Jeurre Park *(qv)*.

View of Méréville in the 18C

Covered Market (Halles). – Built around 1515, it is still a busy trading place on Friday mornings.
Return to the foot of the hillock and start walking down into the valley. You will spot the top of Trajan's Column on the opposite slope.

Trajan's Column (Colonne Trajane). – Rising to a height of 37m – 122ft this column is an imitation of the famous monument that stands on the Forum in Rome.

MESLAY-LE-GRENET

Pop 197

Michelin map 196 southwest of fold 37

The Dance of Death discovered in 1864 and restored in 1979 is the most interesting feature of the church in Meslay-le-Grenet, a small parish in the Chartres area. It is believed that the work was executed in the last decade of the 15C.

Church: The Dance of Death (Église: La Danse Macabre). – The confrontation between the Living and the Dead starts on the south wall (lower level), where we can see the representations of the Pope, the Emperor, the Cardinal, the King, the Archbishop, the Patriarch, the Constable, etc. It ends on the opposite wall with pictures of the Child, the Usurer and the Hermit. The text accompanying this mural painting – a poem written in 1376 – remains clearly visible.
The upper level tells the story of three young wealthy men driven to repentance by three dead bodies risen from their graves. This moralistic tale – symbolically called The Three Dead and the Three Living – is often associated with dances of death in French folklore.

★ MEUDON

Pop 49 004

Michelin map 101 folds 23 and 24 – Michelin plan 22

The town is located on the slopes of the plateau which bears Meudon Forest. In the mid-18C, Mme de Pompadour acquired **Bellevue** estate and gave orders to build the château. Louis XV paid frequent visits to the estate and in 1757 he bought Bellevue from his favourite. He embellished the house, refurbished the grounds and installed a hot water heating system under the flooring. The last occupants were the two unmarried daughters of Louis XV, the aunts of Louis XVI. They added a botanical garden and a charming hamlet. The estate was pillaged during the Revolution and sold as State property. In the 19C, it was parcelled out into building plots.
All that remains of the former estate is part of the terrace and its balustrade at the junction of Rue Marcel-Allégot and Avenue du 11-Novembre. The wondrous panorama *(belle vue)* of past time has been replaced by a view of modern Paris with, in the foreground, Boulogne-Billancourt, the Seguin islet and the Renault factories *(p 38)*.
On 8 May 1842, the small station on the left was the scene of a train accident in which the explorer **Admiral Dumont d'Urville** died (he had just discovered Adélie Coast in the Antarctic), together with 40 other passengers who had been locked in the compartments according to regulations.

CHÂTEAU AND TOWN

The stately Avenue du Château is lined with four rows of lime trees. Half-way down the street, a plaque on the left marks the little house (no **47**) where **Richard Wagner** composed the score for the *Flying Dutchman* in 1841.

Château of the House of Guise. – A manor house in Meudon dating from the early 15C became the property of the duchesse d'Étampes, former mistress to François I, whose generosity graced the estate with two new wings and a beautiful park. The domain was subsequently sold to Cardinal de Lorraine, who belonged to the House of Guise. He commissioned the sumptuous grotto from Primaticcio, as well as the two superimposed orangeries. During a hundred years, Meudon remained in the hands of the Guise. The family later sold the estate to Abel Servien in 1654 owing to financial difficulties.

Meudon at the time of Servien. – The wealthy Abel Servien, marquis de Sablé and Minister of Finance, commissioned Le Vau to renovate the château at great expense and gave orders to build the terrace, a large-scale project. Servien led a life of luxury but his fortune soon ran out: when he died in 1659, he was in debt to the tune of 1 600 000 livres. Abel's son sold the estate to Louvois, the lord of Chaville.

Meudon at the time of Louvois. – The new owner pursued the efforts of his predecessor, renewing the decoration and embellishing the park. He asked Trivaux to create the perspective and entrusted the plans of the gardens to Le Nôtre, then to Mansart. After Louvois' death, his widow agreed to give Louis XIV her domain in exchange for Choisy Château, which belonged to the king's son, the Grand Dauphin.

Meudon at the time of the Grand Dauphin. – Of the Sun King's six legitimate children, Monseigneur was the only one who did not die in early childhood. He retained little of the worthy principles his tutor Bossuet *(qv)* imparted to him; it was in fact for the Grand Dauphin that the Eagle of Meaux wrote his *Discours sur l'Histoire Universelle.* The king's son delighted in wolf and deer hunting and his favourite reading matter was the obituary page of the *Gazette de France.* He was however an enthusiastic art lover and made considerable changes in the interior decoration of the Old Château. In 1706, he dismantled the grotto and replaced it by a new pavilion that housed his private apartments. This New Château was Mansart's last major accomplishment. In 1711 Monseigneur died of smallpox in Meudon and the following year his son the duc de Bourgogne succombed to the disease. The château came into the hands of a two-year-old boy, who was to become Louis XV. His great-grandfather Louis XIV administered the estate up to 1715.

Meudon abandoned by Royalty. – Until the Revolution, Meudon fell into disrepair. In 1793 the chemist Berthollet and Général Choderlos de Laclos – who wrote *Dangerous Acquaintances* recently adapted for the cinema by Stephen Frears as *Dangerous Liaisons* – set up an artillery research centre in the Old Château. Unfortunately it was so badly damaged by a fire that the whole building had to be razed in 1804. Only the columns of pink marble still adorn the Luxembourg Palace and the Carrousel Triumphal Arch.

The flames spared the New Château, which housed a workshop for military balloons. The famous aerostats which contributed to the victory of Fleurus (1789) were manufactured in Meudon. Napoleon I renewed the furniture in the New Château, which was occupied by Marie-Louise and the King of Rome during the Russian campaign.

In 1870 the terrace was turned into a redoubt for a Prussian battery intent on bombarding Paris. When the Germans withdrew the following year, Meudon was burned down along with St-Cloud. Only two small wings still stand. The central section of the building was restored and made into an observatory.

★**Terrace.** – 450m – 1 480ft long and 136m – 447ft wide, the terrace is planted with handsome trees and sweeping lawns. It lies at an altitude of 153m – 502ft and commands an extensive **view**★ of Meudon, the Seine Valley and the French capital. One of the most impressive trees of the forest stands to the left of the gates. The pedestal like pilasters adorning the breast wall of the upper terrace date from the 16 and 17C.

The far end of the esplanade rests on the former orangeries of the château. From there, visitors may discover Le Nôtre's beautiful perspective with the modern complex of Meudon-la-Forêt in the far distance.

Ⓥ**Observatory (Observatoire).** – On the right stands the observatory, representing the astrophysics section of the Paris Observatory. A large revolving cupola with a diameter of 18.5m – 60ft crowns the central block of the New Château. Note the astronomical telescope dating from 1893.

Founded in 1876 by the astronomer Janssen, this observatory is considered the most important in France. It is also the leading centre in France for aerospace research. A mushroom-shaped tower was added in 1965: its 35m – 115ft shaft attracts the rays of the sun, which are then broken down and analysed under a spectroscope.

Ⓥ**Art and History Museum (Musée d'Art et d'Histoire).** – *11, Rue des Pierres, at the foot of the terrace (one can drive there from the town centre).*

Molière's wife Armande Béjart bought this charming house in 1676, three years after her husband's death.

The museum is partly dedicated to the history of the town, the celebrities who lived there and the châteaux of Bellevue and Meudon (reference library). It also presents the municipal art collections: Dunoyer de Segonzac, Magnelli, Pape, etc.

The formal gardens are dotted with contemporary sculptures by Arp, Bourdelle and Stahly.

Ⓥ**Rodin Museum (Musée Rodin), Villa des Brillants.** – *19, Avenue Auguste-Rodin.*

An indispensable complement to the Rodin Museum in Paris *(see Michelin Green Guide Paris)*. The museum stands next to Villa des Brillants, Rodin's residence and studio from 1895. It contains moulds, sketches and rough sketches by the great sculptor, together with a number of original plaster casts *(The Gates of Hell, Balzac, The Burghers of Calais)*. The façade of the museum was taken from the old château at Issy-les-Moulineaux.

Rodin died in 1917 and his grave was laid out in front of the museum. Sitting pensively on the tombstone is his famous statue *The Thinker.*

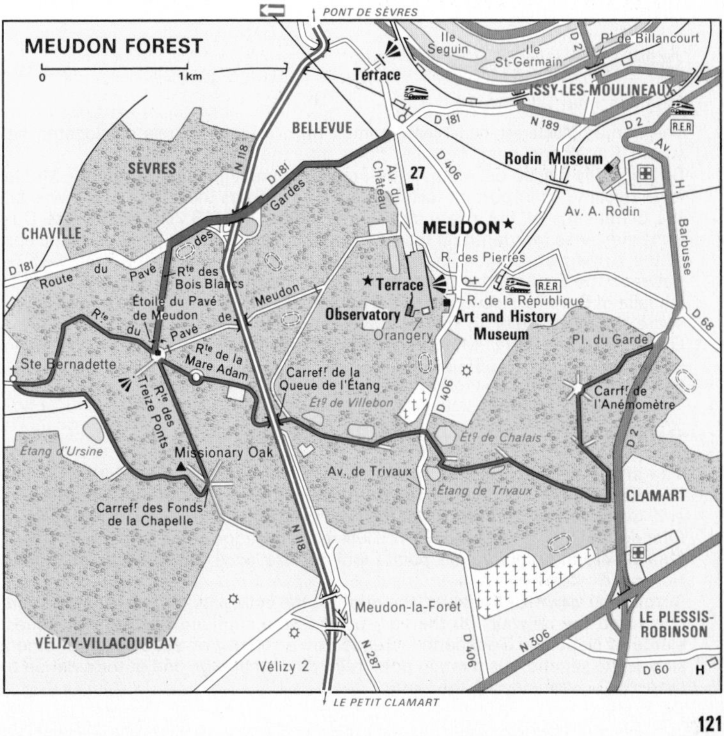

★MEUDON FOREST

This 1 150ha – 285 acre State forest covers a hilly terrain stretching from Sèvres to Villacoublay, planted with oaks, birches and chestnut trees. Although it is cut across by the N118 linking Paris to the Chartres motorway, the forest is popular with Parisian ramblers. Originally designed by the Grand Dauphin to join Meudon to Versailles, the **Pavé de Meudon** is now a charming forest lane. Louvois traced the route for the **Pavé** – also called **Route des Gardes** (D 181) – , a rough path following a steep incline (14 % or 1:7). The suggested itinerary *(see local map p 121)* includes the main points of interest of the wood, all accessible to cars.
The Étoile du Pavé de Meudon, one of the major crossroads of the forest, is the site of a Hertzian transmitter. The nearby promontory offers a sweeping panorama of the woods of Viroflay.
Proceed towards Chaville along Route du Pavé de Meudon. When you draw level with Ste-Bernadette Chapel, a modern building, turn left. The road skirts the town and passes in front of the pond (Étang d'Ursine). From then on it follows a steep incline and winds its way up to the Fonds-de-la-Chapelle crossroads. Turn left into Route des Treize-Ponts. Soon after the junction, at the edge of the road stands the Missionary Oak (Chêne des Missions), a Celtic site carefully reconstituted.
Return to the Étoile du Pavé de Meudon. This time turn right into Route de la Mare Adam. This road will pass the Mare-Adam junction and lead to another crossroads called Queue de l'Étang, where it dips under the N 118.
The forest route skirts the charming lake Étang de Villebon, crosses Avenue de Trivaux, runs between the lakes, Étang de Chalais and Étang de Trivaux, weaves its way through woodland and veers to the left before joining the D 2.

MILLY-LA-FORÊT

Pop 3 795

Michelin map 196 fold 44

The locality of Milly-la-Forêt developed around the old covered market and it is now an important starting point for many of the forest lanes crisscrossing the massifs of Trois Pignons *(p 93)* and Coquibus.
Milly has been a long-standing centre for the growing of medicinal plants, including one variety still considered a local speciality: peppermint. It also grows lily of the valley and a wide range of aromatic herbs for cooking purposes.

Covered Market (Halles). – Located on the town square, the market building – made entirely of oak and chestnut wood – dates back to 1479.

Ⓥ **St-Blaise-des-Simples Chapel (Chapelle St-Blaise-des-Simples).** – *On the way out of the village, along the road to Chapelle-la-Reine.*
In the 12C, the chapel was part of the St-Blaise leper house. More recently, Jean Cocteau decorated the walls in 1859: a huge line drawing above the altar depicts Christ with a crown of thorns and a mural fresco represents the Resurrection of Christ. The walls of the nave are adorned with illustrations of medicinal herbs (mint, belladona, valerian, buttercup and aconite) or *simples* in French.
The chapel houses a bust of the academician Jean Cocteau, executed by the German sculptor Arno Breker, and the poet's grave. The epitaph on the tombstone simply reads: "I remain with you".
The garden surrounding the chapel is planted with common medicinal herbs.

MONTEREAU

Pop 19 557

Michelin map 61 fold 13

The name **"Montereau-faut-Yonne"** comes from a small monastery located next to where the Yonne river *faut,* i.e. flows into the Seine.
Strategically placed between Ile-de-France, Champagne and Burgundy, Montereau soon became an important fortified town. As early as the 11C, a castle was built at the confluence of the rivers Yonne and Seine. In 1419 **John the Fearless,** Duke of Burgundy, was murdered on the bridge spanning the Yonne. This dramatic episode in the Armagnac-Burgundian feud ended in the signing of the Treaty of Troyes between the English, the Duke of Burgundy Philip the Good and Charles VI's wife Isabella of Bavaria. According to the agreement, the French and the English were to share the same ruler in future, the King of England.
On 18 February 1814, Montereau was the scene of the last assaults Napoleon launched against the Prussians and the Austrians before Paris capitulated on 31 March.

SIGHTS

The site. – *1/4 hour on foot.* Leave the N 105 and proceed towards the new town of **Montereau-Surville.** Follow the straight Avenue de Surville, running above the valley, and make for the school *(Cité Scolaire de Montereau).* Park the car nearby.
Bear right of the school fencing. You will reach the edge of the wooded slope and the two panoramic observation points which were once the terraces of the former Surville Château.
Admire the **view★** of the town, the bridges, the collegiate church, the silos near the rivers and the railway. On the very point of the confluence stands an equestrian statue of Napoleon Bonaparte, screened by a spinney of trees. A commemorative slab at the second observation point records the courage and determination of the emperor on the day of the battle.

Ⓥ **St Martin Priory (Prieuré St-Martin).** – *Follow the D 403 towards Provins, then take Rue du Président-Allende and Rue du Prieuré St-Martin.*
In 908 a church was erected on the site of a Merovingian cemetery and a number of sarcophagi used for its construction. The raised choir – completed in the 11C – is surmounted by Romanesque vaulting presenting three rounded arches. The nave was redesigned in the 13 and 15C. The gatehouse features a 13C column, as well as the arch extremities belonging to the original vaulting.

Notre-Dame and St-Loup Collegiate Church (Collégiale Notre-Dame et St-Loup). – Located near the confluence, the church presents a sturdy appearance and a medley of architectural styles (13 to 16C). Note the carved panels of the Renaissance doorway and the 16C Virgin and Child at the pier.
The nave – flanked by side aisles – is an impressive sight. The south aisle features a hanging keystone from Renaissance times.

Montereau Earthenware Plate (*c* 1840)

Ⓥ **Pottery Museum (Musée de la Faïence).** – Set up in the former Hôtel des Postes, the museum testifies to the important role Montereau played in the production of early 18C French earthenware. The local speciality was *faïence fine,* a variety of earthenware made with a light, but resistant white paste coated by a transparent lead glaze. 400 exhibits altogether are displayed in 25 glass cabinets.
They were manufactured between 1806 and 1955 and illustrate the successive developments affecting shape and decoration.

★ MONTFORT-L'AMAURY — Pop 2 764

Michelin map 106 north of folds 27 and 28 – Local map p 146

This old town is built on the side of a hill dominated by the castle ruins. Under the *Ancien Régime,* Montfort was an important county town enjoying far more power than Rambouillet.
The locality was founded and fortified in the 11C by the builder Amaury de Montfort. The most famous descendant of this illustrious family was Simon IV, the leader of the Albigensian Crusade, who waged a fierce war against the heretical Cathars of Languedoc. *(see the current Michelin Green Guide Gorges du Tarn, Cévennes, Lower Languedoc).* Simon de Montfort was killed by a stone in 1218, during an assault on the town of Toulouse.

A Breton outpost in Ile-de-France. – In 1312 the marriage of the Breton Duke Arthur to one of the Montfort daughters made this citadel a part of Brittany. Subsequently, when Anne of Brittany, comtesse de Montfort, was wedded to Charles VIII and then to Louis XII, Montfort-l'Amaury became a French fief. The duchy was made royal territory when Henri II, the son of François I and Claude de France – herself the daughter of Louis XII – came to the throne.

SIGHTS

★ **St Peter's Church (Église St-Pierre).** – The renovation of the church was undertaken by Anne of Brittany in the late 15C. The decoration work lasted through the Renaissance and was completed in the early 17C: the nave was elevated and levelled, and the bell tower and the façade were both remodelled.
Take a walk round the church, surrounded by quaint old houses. Observe the striking gargoyles that adorn the walls of the apse and the high flying buttresses supporting the chancel. The pretty doorway on the south façade bears medallions portraying the benefactors whose generosity made it possible to carry out the renovation work in the Renaissance: André de Foix and his wife.
The interior of St Peter's features a superb set of Renaissance **stained glass windows**★ in the ambulatory and around the aisles *(read description in "Montfort-l'Amaury" booklet published by the tourist information centre).* The vaulting above the aisles presents a great many hanging keystones. The historiated bosses in the nave include a low relief bearing the emblem (ermine) of Anne of Britanny.

★ **Former Charnel House (Ancien charnier).** – Admire the beautifully-carved Flamboyant doorway. This old cemetery is walled within an arcaded gallery surmounted by splendid timbered roofing in the shape of an inverted hull. While the left gallery is 16C, the two other ones date from the 17C. These galleries were intended to receive the bones of the buried when it became necessary to empty the graveyard.

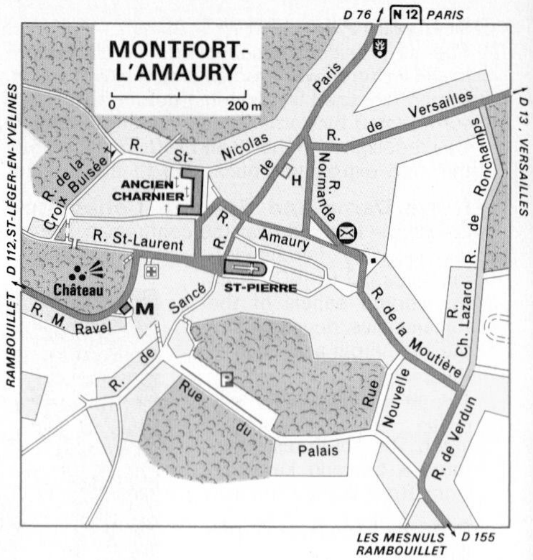

Castle Ruins (Ruines du château). – Take the narrow, twisting road to the top of the hill. Two sections of wall overgrown with ivy are all that remain of the 11C keep. The stone and brick turret belonged to the building commissioned by Anne of Brittany.

The summit offers a good **view★** of the town, the old-fashioned roofs and the first groves of the forest.

Ⓥ **Maurice Ravel Museum (Musée Maurice-Ravel) (M).** – In the year 1920, the French composer bought a tiny villa in Montfort-l'Amaury. It was in this house – called Le Belvédère – that he wrote most of his music: *L'Enfant et les Sortilèges, Boléro, Daphnis et Chloé,* etc. The composer developed a brain tumor but stayed on in Montfort, despite doctor's orders to stop working in 1934. He was forced to move back to Paris in 1937, where he died soon afterwards.

The rooms are somewhat cramped and Ravel – who was a short man – had several of them made even smaller. The interior decoration has remained intact: much of the painting was done by Ravel himself and featured dark, sombre tones. The museum exhibits include the composer's piano, his record player and numerous mementoes reflecting his taste for refinement.

EXCURSIONS

★ **Round tour of Rambouillet Forest.** – *21 km – 12 miles then 1/2 hour Rtn on foot.* *Description p 145.*

Porte Baudet or Maurus Pond (Étang de la Porte Baudet ou des Maurus). – *4 km – 2.5 miles to the south then 3/4 hour Rtn on foot. Leave Montfort by following directions to St-Léger the D 112 and then the D 138.*

Leave the road to Gambais on your right and turn left into Rue du Vert-Galant. Keep following the plateau along the winding route that enters the wood (the road surface rapidly deteriorates).

Leave the car on the parking area marked *"Zone de Silence de la Mare Ronde".* Certain forests have silent zones *(zone de silence)* where motor bikes, radios, etc. are prohibited.

★ MONTLHÉRY — Pop 4 819

Michelin map 101 folds 34 and 35

This old village divided by the N 20 lies at the heart of an agricultural region specialising in market gardening. The famous tower stands on an isolated mound, proof that the average height of the plateau was once much higher.

Paul Fort (1872-1960), the famous "Prince of Poets", was a resident of Montlhéry. He was an extremely prolific author and many of his poems were written here, in a small, secluded wooden cottage.

The **Linas-Montlhéry Racetrack,** built in 1924-1925, features a two-mile (2.548 km) circuit for speed contests and a 9km – 5.5 mile circuit presenting a number of difficulties. Mainly used for technical tests and trials, the racetrack also stages automobile competitions.

File-Étoupe Tower (Tour de File-Étoupe). – The inhabitants of Montlhéry were quick to avail themselves of the strategic location of their town. In the early 11C, a certain Thibault, nicknamed File-Étoupe (tow) on account of his straw-coloured hair, built the castle and had the town circled by ramparts.

The stronghold was an object of deep concern to the Kings of France because it barred the route from Orléans to Paris. In the 12C, the comte de Montlhéry, a member of the Troussel family, was famed for his notorious conduct. In an attempt to mollify this energetic neighbour, Philippe I married his bastard son to Troussel's only daughter. On his death-bed, he begged his successor Louis the Fat to take good care of the tower. To be on the safe side Louis took the tower from his half-brother and placed it in the hands of a trustworthy governor.

ⓥ TOWER *time: 1/2 hour*

If you are coming from Paris along the N 20, it is advisable to branch off at Montlhéry-Nord, on the right, and to cross the national road. Turn after the bridge and drive to the town centre. Go up to the church. From there, follow the ramp signposted "La tour". Lowered from 50m – 165ft to 31m – 100ft, the tower used to be the keep of the castle dismantled by Henri IV. It is flanked by a staircase turret and was once protected by four curtain walls.

The foundations were laid down in the 10 and 11C. The tower features two lower levels whose 13C vaulting has now caved in. Several fireplaces mark the location of the three upper levels.

The **panorama**★ from the summit of the tower (132 steps) is stunning. Standing at a height of 170m –558ft, 24km –15 miles away from the Panthéon, on a clear day one can see the Eiffel Tower, Montparnasse Tower and the Sacré-Cœur. The southern horizons offer the wooded hillsides of Torfou heights. Turn to the northeast: beyond the arable plains stands Longpont Church, a noted place of pilgrimage.

The town of Montlhéry was used to determine the speed of sound in 1738 in conjunction with the Paris Observatory, Montmartre and Fontenay-aux-Roses. Further experiments were carried out with Villejuif in 1822. A cannon shot was fired at one of the stations and the length of time between the glare and the hearing of the shot was carefully measured. In 1874 this observation point was instrumental in establishing the speed of light, together with the Observatory in Paris. A Chappe telegraph linking Paris to Spain was set up in 1825, relayed by a northern station at Fontenay-aux-Roses and a southern one at Torfou.

EXCURSION

Marcoussis. – Pop 4 523. *9km – 5.5 mile tour, then allow a further 1/2 hour. Leave Montlhéry town centre by the north, along the road to Nozay. Take Chemin des Bourguignons and turn left into Rue des Templiers. Cross the N 20.*

Drive up the steep incline and when you reach the top leave the road to Nozay on your right and proceed straight on along Chemin de la Justice. This district – countryside in former times – was where the poet Paul Fort took up residence. Stay on the plateau and bear west until you reach the research centre of the large electrical company CGE. Take a left turning towards Marcoussis: there follows a pleasing drive down to the verdant valley of Salmouille and the small village of Marcoussis.

The **church** was restored in the early 15C thanks to the generosity of Jean de Montagu, Charles VI's financial adviser. The architecture is characteristic of late Gothic. On the right, the chapel beneath the bell tower houses Notre-Dame-de-Grâce, an imposing marble **Virgin**★ dating from the earliest building period. It was a present from the famous patron Jean de Berry to the members of the Celestine Order in Marcoussis.

★ MONTMORENCY

Pop 20 828

Michelin map 101 fold 5 – Michelin plan 18

This charming locality – situated on hilly ground – consists of a town centre surrounded by wealthy residences. Its main claim to fame is to have been the home of the celebrated author Jean-Jacques Rousseau (1712-1778) for a period of his life.

The "First Christian Barons". – The Bouchard family, who held the lordship of Montmorency, had the reputation of being difficult vassals to handle and it was only after the 12C that they served the French court loyally. Over a period of 500 years, the Montmorency family produced 6 constables, 12 marshals and 4 admirals. Moreover, their land was made a duchy by Henri II. They had connections with every ruler in Europe and chose to call themselves the "first Christian barons". One of their most celebrated descendants was Constable Anne, companion-in-arms to François I, Henri II and Charles IX.

Detail of stained glass window
in St Martin Collegiate Church, Montmorency

The eldest branch of the family died out when the constable's grandson Henri II de Montmorency, governor of Languedoc, was beheaded at the age of 37 for having plotted against Cardinal Richelieu. Despite the numerous appeals made to Louis XIII, the king refused to pardon the duke and ordained that the execution take place. The duchy passed into the hands of Henri de Bourbon-Condé. Louis XIV decided that this title – which did not belong to his territory – would be given to a member of the Montmorency-Boutteville.
During the Revolution, the town was called Émile in honour of Rousseau's famous treatise on education. It recovered its former name in 1832.

Jean-Jacques Rousseau's literary retreat. – The author lived in Montmorency from 1756 to 1762. Invited by Mme d'Épinay, a society woman who moved in literary circles, Rousseau took up residence in the Hermitage, a small garden pavilion which has since been taken down. He was 44-years old. His short temper and bouts of melancholic depression annoyed the other house guests. He was living with Thérèse Levasseur, a linen maid whom he later married, but fell passionately in love with his hostess's sister-in-law Mme d'Houdetot, who was nearly 20 years his junior.
His romantic involvements caused him to fall out with Mme d'Épinay in 1757, at which point he moved to Montlouis. It was there that he completed *La Nouvelle Héloïse* and published *Émile* and *Du Contrat Social.* These were his three major works.
The owners of Montlouis – the Maréchal de Luxembourg and his wife – took Rousseau under their wing. Their admiration for the writer, who would read them his latest chapters, helped them put up with his changing moods.
The stately grounds of their estate have survived but the château has been replaced by a modern building.
In 1762 *Émile* was qualified as subversive literature by the Parlement de Paris and an order was issued for Rousseau's arrest. Fortunately, the author was forewarned: he fled Montlouis in the marshal's carriage and sought refuge in Switzerland only to return to France in 1767.

Country outings. – Towards the turn of the 18C, under the First Empire, the area around Montmorency was a popular resort among writers, artists, politicians and young Parisian socialites. Informal picnics and lunches at the Auberge du Cheval Blanc – on the market-place, now called Place Roger Levanneur – were a common feature of life at Montmorency. Visitors were known to sample the local cherries and donkey rides were very much in vogue. Those who were to become leading personalities would engrave their name, together with that of their loved one, on the bark of the chestnut trees or the mirrors of the inn.
Even the crowned heads of France forgot about protocol when they stayed at Montmorency. Queen Hortense, the Duchess of Berry, Napoléon III and the Condé princes would run about the meadows like carefree children, astride their little donkeys.

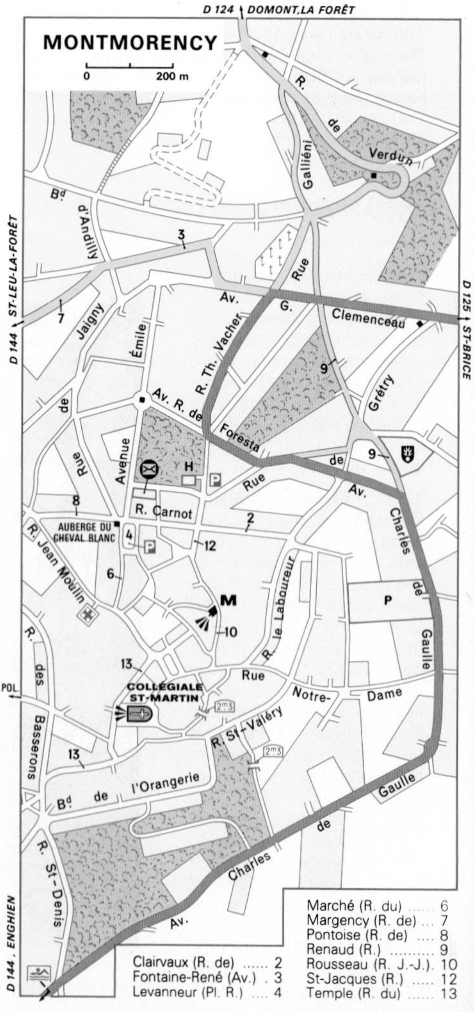

SIGHTS

★**St Martin Collegiate Church (Collégiale St-Martin).** – *Rue de l'Église.* Started in the 16C by Guillaume de Montmorency and completed by his son Constable Anne, St Martin is characteristic of Flamboyant Gothic. It was originally designed to be the mausoleum of the Montmorency family.
Take a walk round the church to appreciate its **site,** which dominates the new town of Montmorency, spread out in the valley. The view extends to the heights of Sannois and the Orgemont hill (tower).

The nave features complex ribbed vaulting *(p 24)* in keeping with 16C architecture, except for the two ribs in the choir that present ornamental brackets at the point where they meet the pillars.
On certain bosses and on the bands crowning the columns, one may see variations on the Greek word *APLANOS* (straightforward), which was the constable's motto. The chapel was specially designed to receive the remains of the Montmorency and, in the 18C, the relics of several Condé descendants. The family tombs were destroyed during the Revolution. Some were salvaged and moved to the Louvre, namely that of Constable Anne and his wife Madeleine. The others have disappeared save for the funeral slab of Guillaume de Montmorency and his wife Anne Pot, of the famous Burgundian family: it rests on the upper level on the south aisle.

★ **Stained glass windows.** – *Explanatory plans are attached to the corresponding pillars.* The 14 windows that adorn the apse and the five nearest right-hand bays of the chancel provide a fine example of Renaissance decoration, tastefully restored in the 19C. The family connections of the Montmorency are illustrated by the effigies of their ancestors, the brightly-coloured coats of arms and the saints they worshipped. Above the glass cage of the side doorway is a magnificent window representing the famous blazon of this illustrious family: alerions or eagles without beaks or feet painted in blue against a yellow background.
The other windows in the nave – executed in the 19C – blend marvellously with the earlier Renaissance windows. They evoke the joys and sorrows of the dynasty up to the execution of Henri II de Montmorency in 1632 *(p 126)*, which heralded the start of a new era for the Condé *(p 47)*.

The Polish heritage. – The south side features a number of busts, recumbent figures and plaques relative to the members of an aristocratic community from Poland who moved to Montmorency in the wake of the failed national insurrection (1831). They were attracted to the town by the fresh, vivifying countryside – reminiscent of their own homeland – and by the literary connections with Rousseau. In the choir is a copy of the painting, Our Lady of Czestochowa or the Black Madonna, the patron saint of Poland.

ⓥ **Jean-Jacques Rousseau Museum (Musée Jean-Jacques Rousseau) (M).** – *5, Rue Jean-Jacques-Rousseau.*
At no 5 stands the house where the French writer lived from 1757 to 1762 and where he wrote his major works. The museum evokes the daily life of Thérèse and Jean-Jacques. The old part of the house affords a nice view of the valley. The "Hall of Greenery" planted with lime trees leads through to the small garden pavilion Rousseau used as a study, which he sardonically called his "keep".
The modern part of the museum offers an exhibition hall and an audio-visual room presenting visitors with particular aspects of Rousseau's life and work. The 18C house lying on the edge of the grounds contains a library with numerous studies on Jean-Jacques Rousseau.

MONTMORENCY Forest

Michelin map 101 folds 4 and 5

Montmorency Forest is a 2000ha – 5000 acre municipal wood covering the highest "monticle" in Ile-de-France (195m – 640ft). It is separated from Cormeilles heights by **Montmorency Valley**, an urban zone lying north of the Seine, numbering 250000 inhabitants between Enghien and the Oise and devoid of any water despite its name. The old villages set up on the southern slopes of the wood, namely St-Prix and Andilly, have gradually turned away from the heights and established their residential quarters down in the plain.

General appearance of the forest. – The least interesting part is the triangle between Montmorency, Montlignon and Domont, where the vegetation is at its most meagre. The rest of the forest presents deep, wooded vales with patches of moist undergrowth. The whole forest is presently undergoing reafforestation. Oaks and especially chestnut trees are the dominant species, with the occasional birch here and there. The forest – which features clusters, copses and copses with standards – will soon be planted with more oak trees as these provide a more pleasant and more suitable setting for forest walks.

Leisure activities and walks. – The flatter part of the wood, lying to the northwest and cut across by the road from St-Leu to Chauvry, offers a number of facilities to tourists: a recreational area known as "Cesar's Camp", footpaths for ramblers (GR1 long-distance footpaths, forest lanes marked out by local organisations), etc.

Route du Faîte. – Designed for cyclists and pedestrians in 1983, this easy route links up the two roads that cut across Montmorency Forest (Eaubonne-Moisselles and St-Leu-Chauvry).

Hunting Château (Château de la Chasse). – *1/2 hour Rtn on foot leaving from the N 309 (green barrier on the left, 2km – 1 mile above Montlignon Church).*
This crooked castle, flanked by strangely-mutilated towers and a lake, is an unusual sight indeed.

Respect the life of the countryside
Go carefully on country roads
Protect wildlife, plants and trees.

MONTREUIL

Pop 93 394

Michelin map 101 fold 17 – Michelin plan 20

This old village has always been famed for its production of peaches and up to the last century it was aptly called Montreuil-les-Pêches. The stone walls bearing the espaliers still stretch over a couple of miles.

★ **Museum of Living History** (**Musée de l'Histoire Vivante**). – *31, Boulevard Théophile-Sueur.*
The museum covers the period in history running from the early 18C to the end of WWII.

St Peter and St Paul's Church (**Église St-Pierre-St-Paul**). – *2, Rue Romainville.*
The plans for the remarkable 12C chancel, complete with triforium and oculi, are attributed to Pierre de Montreuil, who designed St-Denis Cathedral and the Sainte-Chapelle, although the whole composition bears a strong resemblance to that of Notre-Dame in Paris. The central nave dates from the 15C.

MONT VALÉRIEN

Michelin map 101 fold 14 – Michelin plan 18

Since the Middle Ages, the village of **Suresnes** has been famed for the vineyards that stretch on either side of the Seine Valley. The honourable wine they produced was served in royal households such as those of François I and Henri IV. The 4ha – 10 acre vineyard was re-assembled in 1965 *(see the Vintage Celebration in the table of Principal Festivals at the end of the guide)*. Various souvenirs are exhibited at the **Gallery-Museum** (Musée-Galerie), which also presents visitors with a history of the town *(Avenue du Général-de-Gaulle)*.
A walk along Boulevard Washington will bring you to the American cemetery. The terrace on the right commands a sweeping view of Paris and the Bois de Boulogne.

Mont Valérien. – This hillock has been considered sacred territory since Gallic times. A chapel and, in the 17C, a calvary, would receive pilgrims in great numbers. Parisians used to take the Suresnes ferry across the Seine in order to pay their respects, some even climbing up the hill on their bare knees. The fort was built under Louis-Philippe. It was taken over by sailors and proved to be of the utmost importance in the defense of Paris during the 1870-1871 Commune. Between 1940 and 1944, the Germans executed 4500 war prisoners and members of the Resistance on Mont Valérien.

National French Resistance Memorial (**Mémorial National de la France Combattante**). – Inaugurated by General de Gaulle on 18 June 1960, it is seen as the sacred precinct of the Resistance. The memorial renders homage to all those who fought in the last world war. It lies on the southwest glacis of the fort and consists of a stone frieze featuring a cross of Lorraine and a series of bronze high reliefs depicting the main battles of WWII. The flame of remembrance in front of the monument is rekindled every year during a formal ceremony held on 18 June. The crypt contains the mortal remains of 16 soldiers and members of the Resistance, as well as a funeral urn with the ashes of several unknown deportees. The fortifications of the stronghold command a view of the chapel and the clearing where the executions took place.

★ MORET-SUR-LOING

Pop 3 555

Michelin map 196 fold 46

Moret is a charming riverside town nestling on the banks of the Loing, at a comfortable distance from the noisy, bustling motorways.

A fortified town and a royal residence. – Situated near the Champagne border, Moret and its fortified castle defended the king's territory from the reign of Louis VII up to Philip the Fair's marriage to Jeanne of Navarre, the daughter of the Comte de Champagne (1285), which put an end to the feud between the two families. Its keep and curtain wall – the two gates still stand – lost their strategic value and Fontainebleau became the official place of residence for French rulers. These fortifications remainded until the mid-19C and the part of town traversed by the river Loing kept its quiet, secluded character.
The history of Moret was marked by a number of famous women, including Jacqueline de Bueil (1588-1651), one of the last loves of Henri IV, who founded the Notre-Dame-des-Anges hospital and convent. Marie Leczinska was greeted in Moret by Louis XV on 4 September 1725: a commemorative obelisk marks the place where the betrothed met (at the top of the rise along the N 5). The following day, they were married in Fontainebeau.

SIGHTS

★ **The site.** – Branch off the road to St-Mammès and proceed towards the Pin meadow which runs along the west bank of the Loing. Admire the ravishing **view** of the rippling water, the shaded islets, the fishermen, the church and the ancient keep.

Bridge over the Loing. – One of the oldest bridges in Ile-de-France. It was probably built around the same time as the town fortifications but was frequently torn down and then strengthened. When approaching the Burgundy Gate, one may see the ramparts and several houses with overhangs – one of which rises out of the Loing waters.

MORET-SUR-LOING

Rue grande

Champ-de-Mars (Pl. du)
Clemenceau (R.) 3
Division Leclerc (Pl. de la) . 4
Donjon (R. du)
Échaudey (R. de l')
Église (R. de l') 8
Fossés (R. des)
Grange Taton (R. de la) 9
Granges (R. des)
Grez (R. de)
Jaurès (R. Jean) 10
Montmartre (R.) 13
Pavé Neuf (R. du) 14
Pêcherie (R. de la) 15
Peintre Sisley (R. du) 16
Peintre Zanaroff (R. du) 17
Petites Chaumes (R. des) . 18
République (Pl. de la)
Royale (Pl.)........................ 19
St-Mammès (Rte de)
Samois (Pl. de) 20
Tannerie (R. de la) 24
Vieux Marché (R. du) 25

The main car parks are indicated on the town plans.

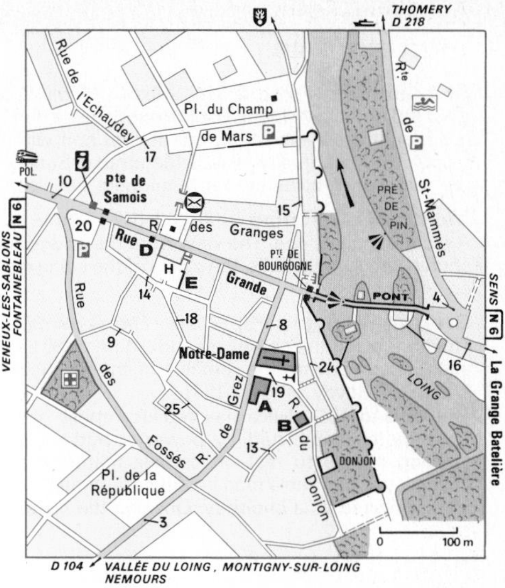

Notre-Dame Church (Église Notre-Dame). – It is reminiscent of many great churches in Ile-de-France.

The **chancel** is believed to have been consecrated in 1166. The original elevation is evidenced by the apse and the south side: the main arches resting on round columns are crowned by a gallery opening onto triple arching, surmounted by clerestory windows. The arches and the bays on the left side were walled in to offer greater support to the bell tower, an unusually high piece of masonry erected in the 15C. The elevation of the transept with its open-work design, and that of the nave with its crowned arches, were undertaken at a later date (13 and 14C).

The Renaissance organ case presents a coffered front with delicate carvings and painted decoration.

Former Hospital (A). – The corner post on Rue de Grez bears an effigy of St James. Take a few steps along Rue de Grez and you will see a modern cartouche with the foundation date of the hospice (1638). The place became famous on account of the Moret barley sugar prepared by the nuns. Needless to say, this tradition was continued by the town's confectioners.

Moret-sur-Loing

Sisley's House (Maison de Sisley) (B). – Alfred Sisley (1839-1899), the Impressionist painter of English parentage spent the latter part of his life in Moret. His studio was at no 19 Rue Montmartre. Having turned his back on a life in commerce to paint, he belonged to the Impressionist group but never achieved fame in his lifetime and was continually beset by financial difficulties. A pure landscape painter, Sisley delighted in the landscapes of Ile-de-France and showed feeling for portraying water, light and air.

Rue Grande. – At no 24 (D), a commemorative plaque marks the house where Napoleon spent part of the night on his way back from Elba Island (19 to 20 March 1815).

François I's House (Maison de François Ier) (E). – *Walk through the town hall porch and into the small courtyard.*

Note the extravagant Renaissance decoration of the gallery and the door crowned by a salamander.

Samois Gate (Porte de Samois). – Also known as the Paris Gate. A statue of the Virgin adorns the inner façade. Note the old-fashioned royal milestone that once marked out the highway leading from Lyon to Paris (now the N 5).

Riverside Cottage (Grange Batelière). – *Take Rue du Peintre Sisley and then a private lane which strays from the towpath, on the right, just before the bridge spanning the Loing canal.*

Built in 1926, this was the residence of Michel Clemenceau (1873-1964), who personally supervised the finishing touches. Standing on the banks of the Loing, this charming cottage and its thatched roof was built in imitation of the traditional Vendée cottage. Clemenceau's house has been turned into a souvenir museum tended by the daughter-in-law of the great statesman.

EXCURSIONS

St-Mammès. – Pop 2 974. *2.5km – 2 miles to the northwest.*
Situated at the confluence of the rivers Seine and Loing, St-Mammès – the final s is not pronounced – is an important river port with rows of barges moored along its banks. The best time to visit St-Mammès is Sunday morning, when the market along the waterfront attracts many mariners and local villagers.

Montigny-sur-Loing. – Pop 2 042. *7km 4 miles to the southwest.*
A picturesque village. The view from the bridge is pretty as a postcard, offering the church set up in the hills, the banks of the Loing river and the private gardens laid out on the islets.

Grez-sur-Loing. – Pop 1 045. *11km – 9 miles to the southwest.*
The bridge and the nearby meadow command a lovely **view★** of the river, the village and Gannes Tower, the remains of the fortified castle where François I's mother Louise of Savoy died in 1531.
ⓥThe 12 and 13C **church** has retained most of its charm despite the sturdy bell tower-porch supported by powerful buttresses. Inside the church, the pointed vaulting comes to rest on corbels featuring somewhat comical scenes: in the chancel you can see a man holding a woman by her hair, a contortionist, as well as a cleric dressed as a choirboy. Observe the collection of tombstones from the 16C.

ⓥBOAT TRIPS

Embarkation: St-Mammès to the north, see plan on p 129.

NEAUPHLE-LE-CHÂTEAU

Pop 2 151

Michelin map 196 south of fold 16

Dominating one of the highest hills of Ile-de-France from a height of 170m – 558ft Neauphle lost its château in the Hundred Years War.

Viewpoints. – Skirt the church and go through the garden surrounding the town hall *(mairie)*. This leads to the public gardens, laid out on the top of the mound. From there, one can get a good view of the Mauldre lowlands which marked the western border of Capetian territory up to the reign of Philippe-Auguste.
From Place du Marché, take Grande-Rue and then Rue St-Martin and you will reach the St-Martin public gardens. This charming spot offers a pleasing view of Pontchartrain and the southern slopes of the valley, facing the town of Jouars.

★ NEMOURS

Pop 11 676

Michelin map 61 fold 12 – Town plan in the current Michelin Red Guide France

The Loing Valley, and the surrounding rocks and woods make Nemours a pleasant resort for weekend trips. Geologically speaking, the area around Nemours and Larchant is the continuation of the Fontainebleau massif: it also features sand deposits, boulders and bands of sandstone rock, although on a much lesser scale. These different types of rock formation make for an extremely picturesque setting. The local sand quarries yield a white sand much sought after by manufacturers of ceramics and fine glassware. The Bagneux factory south of Nemours specialises in the production of pyrex, television tubes, etc.

A duchy-peerage. – In the 12C, a stronghold surrounded by a curtain wall was set up near the river ford. During the Hundred Years War, the locality was the object of numerous assaults. It became an earldom, then a duchy-peerage in 1404. The Valois subsequently offered it to the greatest princes in the country: the Armagnac family, Gaston de Foix, the House of Savoy.
It was at Nemours Château that Henri III made two successive attempts – in 1585 and 1588 – to be reconciled with the Guise, who where the leaders of the insurrectionary League. Soon after the 1588 talks, Henri III decided to take drastic measures and had the duc de Guise murdered in Blois two days before Christmas. The following year, the king suffered the same fate, and died by the hand of a fanatical monk called Jacques Clément. In 1585 Catherine de' Medici signed a treaty which had the effect of limiting the liberties of the Protestants quite considerably. In 1672, the Sun King offered the duchy to his brother Philippe, duc d'Orléans, and the title has remained in the family ever since. It was held by Louis-Philippe's second son, who became famous for his role in the conquest of Algeria.

Du Pont de Nemours. – Pierre Samuel Du Pont was born in Paris in 1739. A friend and disciple of Quesnay, he was passionately interested in economic affairs and worked with both Turgot and Calonne. Under the Constituant Assembly of 1789, he was a member of the Third Estate in his capacity as deputy of Nemours.
From then on, to avoid being mistaken for another official with the same surname, he called himself Du Pont "de Nemours". A follower of Louis XVI, he was forced to hide and was eventually arrested. It was only after the fall of Robespierre that he was released. At an early age, Du Pont showed a marked sympathy for America, convinced that this young state would gladly welcome the economic principles of the Physiocratic school of economics *(Physiocrates)*.
One of his sons, Eleuthère-Irénée (1771-1834), founded a gunpowder factory in the State of Delaware, across the Atlantic. It later developed into the well-known company specialising in chemical and nuclear industries.

SIGHTS

★ Ile-de-France Prehistory Museum (Musée de Préhistoire d'Ile-de-France). – *East of the town, on the road to Sens (Avenue de Stalingrad).*
It lies at the heart of one of the Ile-de-France regions known for its many Prehistoric sites and Megalithic monuments, namely *polissoirs* (rocks featuring striations made by the stone tools that have been sharpened on them),
The reconstruction of an excavation site – the site of Étiolles in the Esssonne – is an introduction to the actual exhibition halls.

Short visit. – Visitors are shown round four rooms, grouped two by two on either side of the central patio and the Pincevent room.
The Paleolithic Chambers provide a colourful presentation of regional life during the Prehistoric Age: tools, pottery and other household goods, techniques, hunting, habitat, etc. The Reindeer Hunters' Room houses a silex block out of which were carved the longest blades in the world (up to 60cm – 2ft).
Pincevent is an important archaeological site on the south bank of the Seine, 7km – 4 miles southwest of Montereau. A scale model is on display. An audio-visual presentation evokes the life of Magdalenian populations.
The rooms dedicated to the Neolithic Era and the Iron and Bronze Ages contain evidence of village life, farming activities and a marked penchant for finery and weaponry.

Castle (Château). – *Enter through an 18C gate in Rue Gauthier I.*
The main building, flanked by round towers, dates back to the 12 and 13C but the ornamental architecture – the window accolades – is 15C. The castle is joined to the keep by a wall crowned with an open gallery.
A series of lofty halls whose ceilings have been restored in the French style lead through to a Gothic oratory (*c* 1150) set up in a tower.
The standing collections feature archaeological exhibits dating from Gallo-Roman, Merovingian and medieval times, religious works of art (15-18C) and 18C pottery painted with motifs relating to the Revolution (Nevers, Ancy-le-Franc, etc.).
The tour ends with the open gallery linked to the square donjon. **View** of Nemours.

ST-PIERRE-LÈS-NEMOURS

This commune of the Nemours locality presents a great many parks and "rocks".

★ Gréau Rocks (Rochers Gréau). – *1 1/2 hours Rtn on foot leaving from the stadium car park (along Avenue d'Ormesson to the southwest).*
From the car park, take the road to Nemours and after 100m – 100yd a lane between two properties leads into the Parc des Rochers.
The shaded grounds consist of two rocky formations. After the entrance, bear left very slightly and make for the passage between the two rocks (old milestone-fountain and bench). From there, follow a wide, partly-paved path and climb up to the Rocher de la Grande École. The spur commands a nice view of the town.

Return to the milestone-fountain. Carry on down, bearing right.

When you reach flat ground, turn left into the lane leading up to Rocher Plat (Flat Rock): the upper shelf is shaded by large pine trees.

★ROCKS OF NEMOURS

These are the final southern continuation of the sandstone massifs of Fontainebleau. The signposted long-distance path GR 13 crosses most of the area. It is joined by a number of other circuits suitable for short-distance rambling. These are included – in part or in totality – in the following itineraries.

★ Rocher Soulès Circuit. – *2.5km – 2 miles then allow 1 1/2 hours Rtn.*
Leave Nemours along the road to Sens. When you reach the junction after the Prehistory Museum, turn right towards Poligny. Leave the car 500m – 500yd further away at the beginning of a wide forest lane on the right.
Follow this lane for about 500m – 500yd, leaving aside the long-distance footpath it crosses. Bear right of a narrow lane and straight afterwards turn right into a track that soon becomes stony and starts to climb. You will reach a pass where one crosses the long-distance footpath GR 13 a second time. Follow the red and white GR markings, which zigzag across a platform supporting a strange collection of rocks. From the tip of the Soulès Rock promontory – known as Pointe Mieroslawski – a steep downward slope passing sands and banks of rock leads back to the track one took to begin with. Turn left into it and you will reach your starting point.

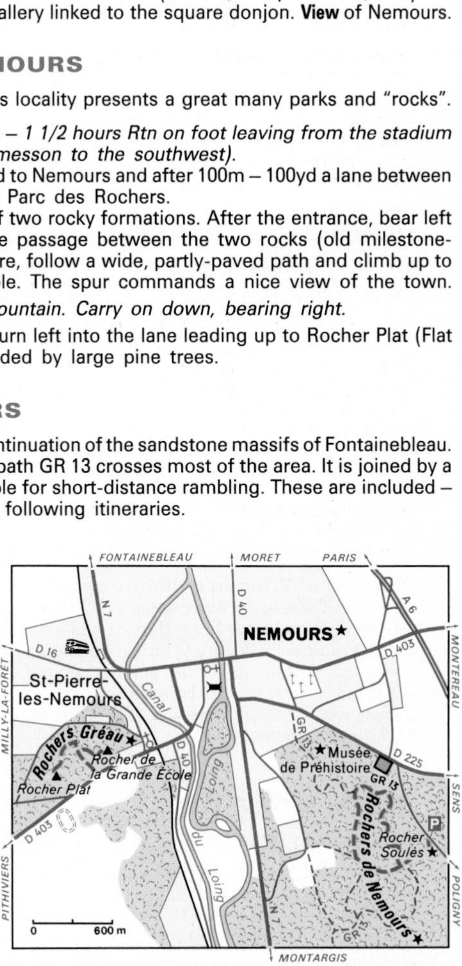

NESLES-LA-VALLÉE — Pop 1 302

Michelin map 196 fold 6 – 4km – 2.5 miles northwest of L'Isle-Adam

This locality incorporates Sausseron Valley. The prosperous village – note the spacious squares – still features several rather grand farmhouses.

Church (Église). – Interesting on account of its splendid Romanesque **bell tower** and stone spire. A gothic nave was added in the 13C.
The nave is surmounted by sexpartite diagonal vaulting. The colonnettes supporting the intermediate arches in each bay rest on the top extremity of the main arches, and not on a series of pillars as is the custom.
The church houses several interesting statues, in particular an extremely archaic figure of St Geneviève from the 14C, placed on the right-hand side of the chapel beneath the bell tower.

NEUILLY-SUR-MARNE — Pop 31 195

Michelin map 101 fold 18 – Michelin plan 20

The locality was once famed for its delicious market garden produce. In recent years it has been the scene of sudden urban expansion. The banks of the Marne have been turned into a port for pleasure boats and some sections offer beaches suitable for water sports.

St-Baudile Church (Église St-Baudile). – *Place du Chanoine-Héroux.*
The construction of this small church was started in the late 12C by Foulques, the famous preacher of the Fourth Crusade. This small church is quite surprising for the harmonious association of the Romanesque and Gothic parts. The three wide columns engaged into three piers of the choir extend up to the vaulting, representing the Romanesque part of the building.
The three broken arches joining the piers that support the bell tower are adorned only by bevelled moulding. They illustrate the transition from Romanesque to Gothic. The latter style is evidenced by the fine single cylindrical pillars of the nave, reminiscent of those in Notre-Dame in Paris on account of their size and design.

Museum of Spontaneous Art (Musée d'Art Brut). L'Aracine. – *39, Avenue du Général-de-Gaulle.*
The collections presented here are the work of artists who have received no formal training: painting, sculpture, embroidery work, etc. All these exhibits convey a feeling of strong emotional intensity and reflect the anguish and inner torment of their creators.

NEUILLY-SUR-SEINE — Pop 64 450

Michelin map 101 folds 14 and 15 – Michelin plan 18

Neuilly is the suburban continuation of the residential district of Paris. The mansions and their neat little gardens have been replaced by modern blocks of flats.
The crossroads next to the Madrid Gate marks the former site of **Madrid Château** (Château de Madrid), built under François I and dismantled in 1793. Before the Revolution, French rulers were short of funds and the grounds were parcelled out into building plots. This was when the Baron St James – an 18C financier, Baudard de Vaudésir, who had anglicized his title – commissioned Bélanger to build the extravagant pink and white pavilion now known as the **St James Folly** (Folie St-James). It is located at no 34 Avenue de Madrid and has given its name to the quarter.
The northern tip of the Grande Jatte island features a charming **garden** planted with tall poplar trees. The 18C **Temple of Love**, taken from Montceau Park, commands an extensive view of the towers of La Défense *(see the Michelin Green Guide Paris)*.

Museum of Women's History and Collection of Automatons (Musée de la Femme et Collection d'Automates). – *12, Rue du Centre.*
The antique collector M. J. Damiot has assembled a great many items relating to famous women in history (a corset belonging to Marie-Antoinette, a bust of Yvonne Printemps dressed as Mozart and the bed of Païva), displayed in a former hôtel built in the Louis XV style. The **ballroom** – decorated with seashells – houses around thirty **animate robots** dating from the 19C, including several that move to the strains of background music.

NOGENT-LE-ROI — Pop 3 268

Michelin map 196 fold 26

The locality defined by Nogent, Coulombs and Lormaye is traversed by the Eure river and features several open spaces and brooks, dotted among the picturesque mills. The town owes its name to a royal château frequented by Philippe-Auguste and St Louis. It has since disappeared.

St-Sulpice Church (Église St-Sulpice). – The car park on the former Horse Market-place affords a good view of this late 15C church, consisting of the transept and the east end, supported by flying buttresses. A sturdy bell tower was added onto the front in the 17C.
The church used to be incorporated into the curtain wall, which followed the course of the Roulebois stream. Enter through the transept door, surmounted by a row of crenellations.

The Flamboyant style of the church interior is evidenced by the design of the windows. The nave – limited to two bays – is covered by a wooden vault which echoes the ribbing and bosses of the Renaissance stone vault. The celebrated stained glass windows *(p 27)* in the ambulatory provide a superb example of 16C decoration. One of the façades is incomplete and has merely been walled: it bears the rough outlines of a rather pompous mural dating from the 17C.
This end of the town presents a group of **half timbered houses** built around the same time as the church. Note the corner house on Rue du Marché-à-la-Volaille.

NOGENT-SUR-MARNE — Pop 24 696

Michelin map 101 fold 27 – Michelin plan 24

A popular resort among the kings of France and also wealthy Parisians, Nogent-sur-Marne developed two large estates: Beauté and Plaisance. The **Château of Beauty** (Château de Beauté) – built for Charles V, who died there in 1380 – is famous for having welcomed Charles VII's favourite Agnès Sorel, who was then referred to as the "Lady of Beauty". An island facing the town – known as the Ile de Beauté – perpetuates the name of the royal residence.
The flowered promenade along the water's edge and the marina for pleasure boats attract a great many tourists looking for a change of scenery. Francis Poulenc – who spent his childhood in the area – claims that the town had given his music a provincial touch. Nogent is the seat of the famous **Pavillon Baltard,** which was spared when the Halles market area was pulled down in the seventies. It houses the André-Malraux arts centre and hosts frequent exhibitions, conferences, fairs and shows. It stands on a typically Parisian old square, featuring a Morris column, a Wallace fountain, old-fashioned street lamps, etc. The first floor displays the recently-restored grand organ of the Gaumont-Palace.
St Saturnin Church (Église St-Saturnin), squeezed in between the village houses, contains the mortal remains of Antoine Watteau, who died at Nogent in 1721. A statue of the painter stands on the square in front of the church.

Nogent History Museum (Musée du Vieux Nogent). – *150, Grande Rue.*
On the second floor of an 18C town mansion, it presents visitors with a history of the town, illustrated by various documents and objects relating to everyday life. Special mention is made of Antoine Watteau, who produced the famous *Scenes of Gallantry.*

ORSAY — Pop 14 071

Michelin map 101 fold 33

One of the lords of Orsay was the Provost of Parisian merchants and he gave his name to the quay which was started in 1707.

The Science Faculty. – Orsay has become the heart of an important scientific community numbering tens of thousands of students, technicians and researchers, situated between the Bièvre and Yvette rivers, and particularly active around **Saclay** (Nuclear Research Centre) and Palaiseau (the famous École Polytechnique).
The university buildings are scattered across a large park. They consist of the lecture theatres, the research quarters, the student halls of residence, the refectory, the libraries, the common room, the laboratories and the indoor sports complex.
The 160ha – 400 acre park is laid out along the terraced slopes from Orsay to Bures-sur-Yvette. It is cut across by the Yvette river and winding lanes.

OURCQ Valley

Michelin maps 196 folds 12, 23 and 24 and 56 folds 12 and 13

The river Ourcq rises in Villers-Cotterêts Forest, situated in the Aisne *département.* After La Ferté-Milon, it follows a winding course which skirts the beds of hard coarse limestone of the Brie subsoil. Before the canal was built, the river flowed into the Marne downstream from Mary-sur-Marne.
In 1529 the magistrates of the City of Paris embarked upon the first stages of construction but it was not until 1636 that the first boat delivered its shipment of wood and cereals to the French capital.

The Ourcq Canal. – In 1802 Bonaparte decided to divert the course of the Ourcq river by creating a canal-aqueduct which would convey the waters to La Villette basin, located north of Paris. The canal was inaugurated seven years later and permitted navigation between Paris and Claye-Souilly in 1813. By 1821 it had joined up with the canalised river running from Ourcq to Mareuil-sur-Ourcq. Five locks were installed and those which already existed on the canalised watercourse were renewed. From 1920 to 1930, the canal was widened between La Villette basin and Les Pavillons-sous-Bois and a new lock set up at Sevran.
The Ourcq canal supplies the locks of the St-Denis and St-Martin canals in Paris. It also provides water for factories in Paris. Commercial navigation between La Villette and Meaux ceased in 1960: it has been replaced by pleasure boating. The navigable section of the Ourcq is 110km – 68 miles long and may be divided into three parts. The canalised river (10km – 6 miles – 4 locks) starts upstream from La Ferté-Milon. The canal itself (90km – 54 miles – 4 locks) links Mareuil-sur-Ourcq to Les Pavillons-sous-Bois: it is 1.5m – 5ft deep and 11m – 37ft wide. Finally, a wide watercourse (no locks) flows into the "canal roundabout" in Paris (La Villette Basin).

THE BATTLE OF THE OURCQ

The first Battle of the Marne originated with the Battle of the Ourcq, which in fact took place on the heights of the Multien plateau and not in the valley itself. The outcome of this battle did much to secure the success of the general offensive launched between Nanteuil-le-Haudouin, north of Meaux, and Révigny, northwest of Bar-le-Duc.

It is little known that this battle was triggered off – on both sides – by the confrontation of numerous reserve units (55th and 56th Divisions in the case of the French, 4th Corps in the case of the Germans). Owing to the hazards of drafting and the movement of retreat, many of the French soldiers were in fact defending their native territory.

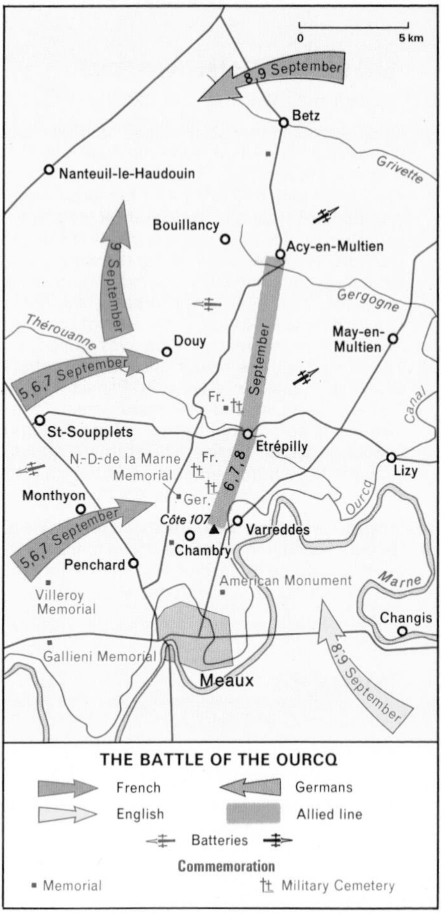

The retreat: 24 August to 4 September 1914. – After the invasion of Belgium (4 August) and the defeat of Charleroi (23 August), the Anglo-French armies suffered heavy enemy pressure and were forced to withdraw.

Joffre, who had been appointed commander-in-chief, ordered his men to withdraw in good order. His troups re-formed and he hoped to be able to launch another attack as soon as possible. On 27 August, the 6th Army was created to contain the German advance on the Aisne river: it was led by General Maunoury. It was also to be used as a striking force against the left flank of the enemy pocket. Unfortunately, the retreat continued and by 1 September, the Armies had taken up position along a line running west of Beauvais, Verberie, Senlis and Meaux.

On the right, it was continued by the 4th English Division led by Sir John French. At this point in the battle, the Germans – who were marching towards Paris and the southwest – wheeled their flank southeast. Von Kluck's Army passed in front of Paris.

Gallieni, in charge of the Paris garrison and Maunoury's 6th Army, mistook the manœuvre: in his mind, Von Kluck wanted to capture the English Army which was withdrawing to the Grand Morin. After discussing the matter, Gallieni and Joffre decided to attack the enemy's flank and crush the powerful right wing of their invaders. The offensive was scheduled for 6 September.

The check: 4 to 8 September. – Gallieni and Maunoury's 6th Army prepared for combat on 4 September. The following day, they endeavoured to reach the position between Lizy-sur-Ourcq and May-en-Multien but ran up against the 4th German Corps. Despite their dominant position, the Germans were afraid of being outflanked and that night evacuated the wooded hills of Monthyon and the village of Penchard. Having suffered badly, the two French Divisions and the Moroccan Brigade – incorporting Lieutenant Juin, soon-to-be Marshal – were withdrawn in order that they might re-form. Along the Grand Morin line, Sir John French's Army, exhausted by the retreat, swung slowly towards the north.

On 6 September, from his headquarters in Châtillon-sur-Seine, Joffre launched a moving appeal to all his men: "On the eve of the battle on which the future of our Country depends, it is important to remind all that there must be no looking back". The French and English Armies advanced a further 200km – 120 miles: it was the start of a general attack.

In the 6th Army sector, the French reached the Chambry-Douy-Bouillancy line. The day of 7 September was marked by the bloody confrontation with the German line. The toughest fighting took place in the villages of Etrépilly and Acy-en-Multien, the two bastions of the line, in the valleys of the Thérouanne and the Gergogne. A series of violent bayonet charges were delivered by d'Urbal's light infantry and the Zouaves of Colonel Dubujadoux. French's Army repulsed the German rear-guard and took up position along the road from La Ferté-sous-Jouarre and Montmirail.

On 8 September, the war of movement moved north of Multien to the sector of Nanteuil-le-Haudouin. That night, the town had received the 7th Division, despatched by Gallieni and transported by the famous "Marne taxis". It was there that Maunoury and Von Kluck were desperately hoping for a definitive solution, relying on a strategy of encircling movements.

The victory: 9 to 13 September. – Wednesday the 9 was a turning-point in the Battle of the Marne. On the left, the French troops facing north in the Nanteuil-le-Haudouin sector suffered an assault of such violence that Maunoury began to fear for Paris. But the English Army succeeded in crossing the Marne.
In the centre, the French troops entered Etrépilly and Varreddes which had already been evacuated. Von Kluck's Army retired. The German commander-in-chief Von Moltke was astonished by the French recovery. An alarming gap separated Von Kluck's 1st Army from Von Bülow's 2nd Army, checked by Foch near the St-Gond marshes, and Von Moltke was afraid that his front line would not hold: he gave orders for a general withdrawal following a line passing north of Soissons, Reims and Verdun.
This war of movement ended on 13 September. In October, the operations became bogged down and the battle developed into trench warfare.
The French offensive failed to fulfil its objective, i.e. to crush Von Kluck's Army but it halted the invasion at a critical moment. The official telegram sent by Joffre read: "The Battle of the Marne is an incontestable victory for us".

THE BATTLEFIELD AND THE OURCQ VALLEY

Round tour starting from Meaux

96km – 28 miles – allow 4 hours – Local map below

★**Meaux.** – *Description p 117.*

Leave Meaux along the road to Paris (N 3). After 6.5km – 4 miles, you will pass a memorial paying tribute to Gallieni on the left-hand side of the road. Turn right into the D 27, leading to Iverny, then take another right turning and proceed towards Chauconin-Neufmontiers.

Villeroy Memorial (Mémorial de Villeroy). – It stands on the site of the early operations of 5 September 1914. The funeral vault houses the remains of 133 officers and soldiers who died in the fields nearby. **Charles Péguy** (1873-1914) was buried with his comrades-in-arms belonging to the 276th Infantry Regiment (reserve). Their collective grave lies to the right of the vault. Facing it is a cross celebrating the memory of the writer, philosopher cum social reformer.
The 19th Company of the 276th Regiment was called in to relieve the Moroccan Brigade who accompnied them and who were dangerously engaged in battle near Penchard. It launched an attack towards Monthyon, under the fire of the enemy, under cover in the valley around the Rutel brook. Péguy was the only surviving officer. He told his men to lie down and was inspecting the German positions when he was struck by a bullet.

At the next crossroads, turn left towards Chauconin-Neufmontiers. Drive through Penchard and follow directions to Chambry. Drive through the locality.

You can see the bell tower of Barcy on the left.

National Cemetery of Chambry (Cimetière National de Chambry). – Most of the soldiers buried here died during the fighting that took place on 6, 7 and 8 September when they defended the village of Chambry, which was assaulted several times.

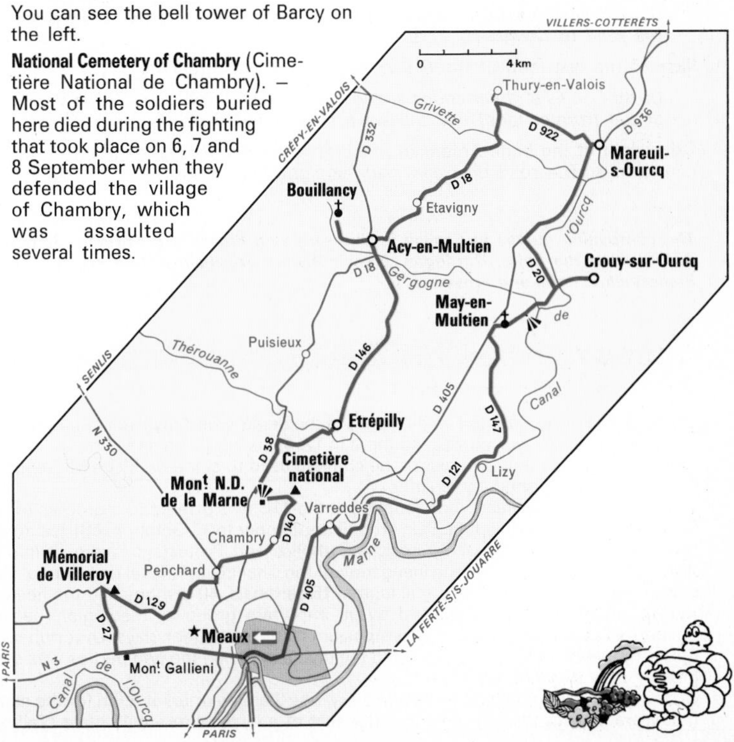

Located 500m – 500yd east of the crossroads, the German military cemetery marks the place where the main German line – which roughly follows the dirt track – met the road to Varreddes.

Turn round.

Notre-Dame-de-la-Marne Monument. – It was erected on the orders of Monseigneur Marbeau, Bishop of Meaux in 1914, and dominates the whole battlefield. Turn to the north and you will get a good **view** of the Multien plateau in the far distance.

Proceed towards Puiseaux. At the next junction, after the old factory turn left towards Etrépilly. In the town centre, 200m – 200yd before reaching the church, turn left towards Acy-en-Multien.

Étrépilly. – The small national cemetery and the memorial evoke the fighting that took place during the night of 7-8 September, reaching a climax near the village graveyard.

Acy-en-Multien. – This village nestling in Gergogne Valley was the scene of intensive warfare on 7 September 1914. The winding alleys, the hillsides planted with small spinneys and the garden walls of the château provided many opportunities for close combat, often ending in tragic death.

Leave Acy in the direction of Nanteuil-le-Houdouin (turn left when leaving the town).

Bouillancy Church (Église de Bouillancy). – Located in the lower part of the town. In the quiet valley – rural life is concentrated in the village on the heights – lies an early Gothic church (12-13C) of extremely harmonious proportions. Note the bell tower flanked by buttresses featuring a great many projections.

Turn round. Leave the church on your left and take the next left turning. Drive up on to the plateau.

Enjoy the **view** of Acy and the elegant village spire. Beyond Étavigny, the route strays from the battlefield.

Before reaching Thury-en-Valois, turn right into the D 922.

The road leads to **Mareuil-sur-Ourcq,** marking the start of the canal.

Cross Varinfroy and drive down to Crouy-sur-Ourcq bridge.

Crouy-sur-Ourcq. – Just after the level crossing, the road skirts the ruins of the **Houssoy Stronghold** (Château Fort de Houssoy), now converted into a farmhouse. The keep has remained separate and can be approached by the left-hand lane, leading to the courtyard gates.
Crouy Church features a Gothic interior with two 16C naves. Admire the 1670 panelling in the choir, beautifully excecuted and tastefully decorated. The patron saints of the church are represented above the retable: St Cyricus, who was made a martyr at the age of 3, and his mother St Julitta.

Turn back and after the bridge, turn left towards May.

The twisting road affords extensive **views** of the surrounding landscape.

May-en-Multien. – Pop 553. The village enjoys a privileged position, 100m – 330ft above the river Ourcq. It is visible from afar on account of its church tower, one of the highest landmarks of the area.

Drive down to Lizy. Do not cross the canal bridge but go up the right slope along the road to Congis (D 121).

View of the last loop of the Ourcq, overgrown with greenery.

Cross Congis and Varreddes and join the D 405, which starts at the Varreddes cirque (former loop) and follows a steep upward slope.

Drive right of the huge American monument that renders homage to the Marne combatants. The road dips and leads straight into Meaux.

The companion guides in English in this series on France are Brittany, Burgundy, Châteaux of the Loire, Dordogne, French Riviera, Normandy Cotentin, Normandy Seine Valley, Paris and Provence.

POISSY

Pop 36 553

Michelin map 101 folds 11 and 12

The town of Poissy, situated on the banks of the Seine, was a royal residence as early as the 5C. St Louis was christened there in 1214: the king's private correspondence was even signed Louis de Poissy. The château used to stand on Place Meissonnier but it was demolished by Charles V.
An abbey for Augustinian nuns founded in the 11C was offered to members of the Dominican order by Philip the Fair. From 9 September to 13 October 1561 the abbey refectory hosted the **Poissy Symposium:** Catholics and Protestants were invited to discuss their differences at the instigation of the Chancellor Michel de l'Hôpital. The debate was attended by the papal legate, 16 cardinals, 40 bishops and the head of the Jesuits on the one side, and by an important group of theologians led by Theodore Beza on the other. The symposium lasted seventeen days. Unfortunately, these high-level talks proved vain and the divide between the two parties was even greater after the conference.
Up to the middle of the last century, Poissy was the main market town for the cattle that were sent to Paris. Today, it is the seat of a large automobile plant (Talbot).

★ **Notre-Dame Church** (**Église Notre-Dame**). – The greater part of the building is Romanesque and dates from the 11 and 12C. Several chapels were added in the 15C and the whole church was restored by Viollet-le-Duc. The front tower, built in the Romanesque style, once served as a porch-bell tower. The square base of the tower gives way to an octagonal section on the highest level, ending in a stone spire. The central tower, also of Romanesque design, admits an eight-sided base and two floors, and ends in a timberwork spire.

Interior. – The ribbed vaulting above the nave has been changed. The capitals belonging to the south columns in the first two bays were remodelled in the 17C. The other capitals feature interlacing, monsters and foliage motifs. Some of them are thought to be older than Notre-Dame and were probably taken from another church. The nave is extremely luminous, owing to the installation of a triforium by Viollet-le-Duc in the 3 bays nearest to the choir. The chancel is circled by an ambulatory with groined vaulting. The side chapels – added in the 15C – pay homage to the various trade guilds: butchers, fishermen, etc.
The first chapel to the right of the doorway contains fragments of the baptismal font used for St Louis' christening, displayed behind railings. For many centuries, the faithful would scrape the stone walls, dissolve the dust in a glass of water and drink the potion as a remedy for high fever. This explains why the church is in such bad condition. The axial chapel is the work of Viollet-le-Duc and it is dedicated to the Virgin, as is the custom. The statue of the Virgin and Child is attributed to the Duchess of Uzès (*c* 1890).
The most impressive furnishings are those assembled in the first chapel on the right, on the inside wall a 16C Entombment: strong, noble statues from the 15C, including John the Baptist and St Barbara.
A superb Entombment *(see below)* executed in the 16C portrays Mary, John, Mary Magdalena, the Holy Women, Nicodemus and Joseph of Arimathea.

16C Entombment in Notre-Dame Church, Poissy

Ⓥ **Toy Museum** (**Musée du Jouet**). – The games and toys exhibited in the museum cover the period which ends with the advent of television.
The ground floor contains an important collection of dolls, including many made by the great 19C French manufacturers such as Jumeau: wax and wood gave way to porcelain and biscuit, which in turn were replaced by celluloid. Not to mention the introduction of pivoting heads and articulated limbs...
A cabinet on the first floor houses a number of magic lanterns for games with hand-painted glass plates, shadow pantomimes and other optical entertainments. A separate exhibition presents teddy bears and soldiers, as well as scientific and technical toys. On the second floor, the former attic houses a selection of figurines, inanimate and mechanical toys, ranging from ordinary items to the miniature car models manufactured in one of Citroën's special workshops between 1923 and 1940.

Ⓥ **History Museum** (**Musée d'Histoire**) (M). – *12, Rue St-Louis.* The history of Poissy from Merovingian times (sarcophagi) up to the present day (automobile industry) is presented in a simple, pleasing manner. One of the glass cabinets displays a good few seals, some of which date back to the 12C. Other exhibits include a painting by Meissonnier depicting summer bathing in the Seine river, a splendid 16C painted wooden statue taken from Notre-Dame Church, etc.

Ⓥ **Villa Savoye.** – *82, Rue de Villiers.* This masterpiece of modern architecture was designed in 1929 by **Le Corbusier** and Pierre Jeanneret for the industrialist Savoye. The use of cylindrical piles made it possible to do away with the supporting walls and introduce huge glass surfaces. The main rooms are located on the first floor, at a

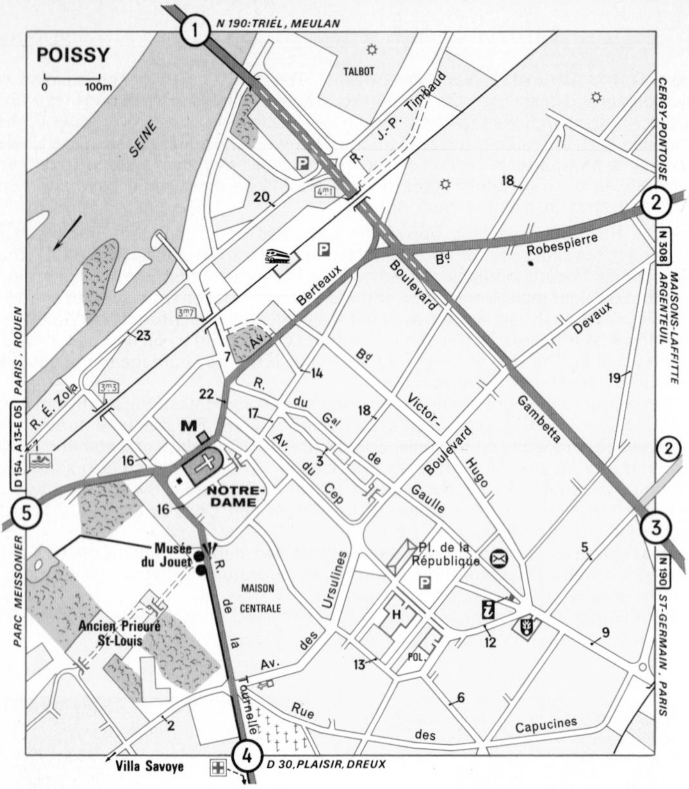

Cep (Av. du)
Gambetta (Bd)
Gaulle (R. Gén. de)
Victor-Hugo (Bd)
Blanche-de-Castille (Av.) 2
Bœuf (R. du) 3
Foch (Av. Mar.) 5
Joly (Av. A.) 6
Leclerc (Pl.) 7
Lefebvre (Av.) 9
Lemelle (Bd L.) 12
Libération (R. de la) 13
Mary (R. J.-Cl.) 14
Meissonier (Av.) 16
Pain (R. au) 17
Paix (Bd de la) 18
Pasteur (R.) 19
Pont-Ancien (R. du) 20
St-Louis (R.) 22
14-Juillet (Cours du) 23

height of 3.5m-12ft. They are arranged around a large terrace which opens onto the countryside, as does the curved solarium occupying the top level of the house. The Villa Savoye – evocatively called The Daylight Hours – features a ramp leading to the upper levels and a spiral stair whose vertical lines were deliberately brought in to counter the horizontal configuration of the villa.

The Abbey (former St Louis Priory). – A pavilion flanked by towers located on a small square south of the church was used to defend the entrance to the Dominican priory which hosted the Poissy Symposium.
Go through the doorway and take the winding alley that follows the former abbey walls. Turn back when you reach the exit gate, situated at the foot of the old priory barn. Come back the same way, admiring the **view** of the towers of Notre-Dame.

EXCURSION

Round tour of 16km – 9 miles. – *Allow 2 hours. Leave Poissy by ⑤, turn right and drive through Villennes. When you reach Médan, follow directions to "Plage de Villennes" and park the car at the water's edge, next to the quayside.*

Médan. – Pop 1 068. This locality is famous for its bathing spot, known as Plage de Villennes, laid out on an islet of the river Seine. It was also the place of residence of the French author Emile Zola (1840-1902).
Walk up the road leading into town and cross the railway. On the right you can glimpse the **house of Emile Zola,** surrounded by its garden, which the writer bought in 1878. The cottage has been turned into a literary museum. The billiard room on the ground floor – once used as a lounge – features stained glass windows designed by Zola and executed by Baboneau. The decoration of the ceiling was inspired by sketches of coats of arms from the Carnavalet Museum. The dining room has kept its original decor: Cordoba leather, Delft tiling and on the ceiling, a fleur-de-lys motif. The set of negatives in the kitchen testify to Zola's remarkable photographic skills.
Zola's bedroom on the first floor contains a host of documents concerning the Dreyfus affair, in which he became so passionately involved. The study on the second floor is ornate in the extreme: the Renaissance fireplace – embellished by several decorous caryatids – bears the motto of this indefatigable worker: *"Nulla dies sine linea"* (not one day without writing). The room also contains a number of personal mementoes: ink well, lamp, armchair, etc.

Return to the car.

Drive past the quaint old church, and its towers crowned with Renaissance cupolas, until you reach the road to Vernouillet (the village high street). **Médan Château,** a former hunting pavilion built in the early Renaissance style, lies at the foot of the hill.

Drive north until you get to Vernouillet (town centre).

Vernouillet. – Pop 6 424. In 1156, Galeran II, comte de Meulan, was miraculously saved from drowning on his way back from Palestine. To thank God for this act of mercy, he had 17 churches built on his lands, which included the locality of Vernouillet. The Romanesque **bell tower★** is truly remarkable. It admits a square base and ends in a 13C spire. The alternation of pinnacles and elongated gables conceals the base of the spire.

Cross the Seine and proceed towards Triel

Triel. – *Description p 172.*

Return to Poissy along the direct route (N 190).

PONTOISE

Pop 29 411

Michelin map 101 north of fold 2

The old town of Pontoise lies near the new town, of Cergy-Pontoise set up on the plateau *(p 41).*

The upper quarters of the town – if possible, visit on Saturdays and market days – and its ramparts dominate the river Oise, still features the ancient monuments, the narrow, winding streets and the two squares, Place du Petit-Martroy and Place du Grand-Martroy. Visitors will appreciate the picturesque names of the alleys.

Following the Treaty of St-Clair-sur-Epte in 911, Pontoise became one of the two citadels of the French Vexin, the second one being Meulan. Facing them in the Norman Vexin, we find Les Andelys and Gisors.

The château built on the heights often provided hospitality to the kings of France. During one of his visits, St Louis was taken ill and vowed that if he recovered, he would leave for the Holy Land.

ⓥ **St-Maclou Cathedral (Cathédrale St-Maclou).** (A). – Although the church was built and remodelled over several centuries, its architecture is characteristic of the 15 and 16C. The central doorway and its rose window are Flamboyant, as is the bell tower, crowned by a Renaissance dome featuring pinnacles and a lantern turret *(illustration p 25).* The main building is flanked by two Renaissance side aisles. The right façade presents a superb row of Renaissance windows. They are separated by sculpted pilasters bearing a pretty frieze that runs along the gutter and is surmounted by a series of prominent gargoyles.

Walk up Rue de la Pierre-aux-Poissons to get a good view of the east end (12C): a Renaissance doorway placed north of the chevet opens onto the ambulatory.

Interior. – The nave carries the stamp of 15 and 16C architecture. Note the late Renaissance capitals embellished with human figures and foliage motifs in the double north aisle.

The entrance to the chancel is still flanked by two 17C wooden ambones. In the gallery, these are assembled around the pillars, in the manner of a rood screen. The choir and the ambulatory are the only remains of the 12C campaign. The west end houses a large chapel with a sculpted decor depicting scenes of the Passion: a 16C Entombment stands beneath a Renaissance portico surmounted by a Resurrection scene carved in wood (18C).

ⓥ **Pontoise Museum (Musée de Pontoise)** (B M[1]). – This museum, also known as Musée Tavet-Delacour, was set up in a 15C manor with picturesque turrets by the Archbishop of Rouen for his vicar-general, who had taken up residence in Pontoise (in ecclesiastical matters, French Vexin was part of Haute-Normandie).

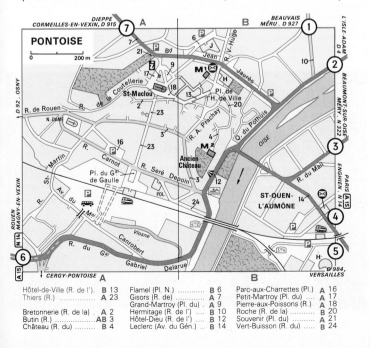

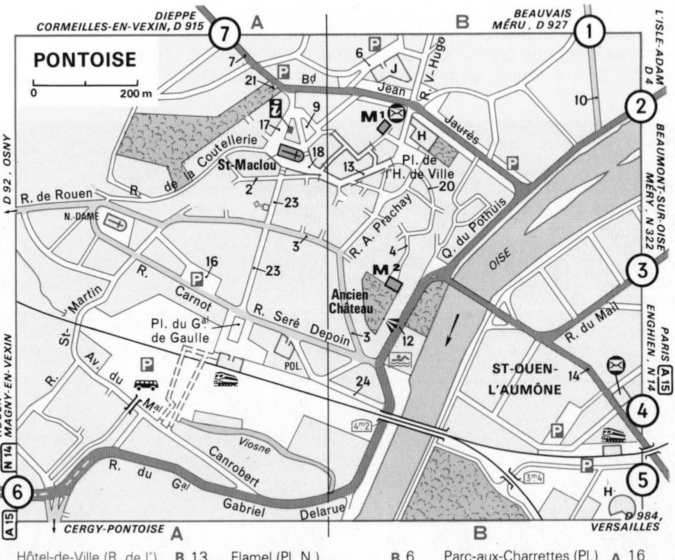

Hôtel-de-Ville (R. de l'). B 13	Flamel (Pl. N.) .... B 6	Parc-aux-Charrettes (Pl.) A 16
Thiers (R.) .... A 23	Gisors (R. de) .... A 7	Petit-Martroy (Pl. du) .... A 17
	Grand-Martroy (Pl. du) . A 9	Pierre-aux-Poissons (R.) A 18
Bretonnerie (R. de la) . A 2	Hermitage (R. de l') .... B 10	Roche (R. de la) .... B 20
Butin (R.) ....AB 3	Hôtel-Dieu (R. de l') .... B 12	Souvenir (Pl. du) .... A 21
Château (R. du) .... B 4	Leclerc (Av. du Gén.) .. B 14	Vert-Buisson (R. du) ..... B 24

Market day on Place du Grand-Martroy, Pontoise by Ludovic Piette

The first floor is dedicated to the non-figurative works of Otto Freundlich (1878-1943), a German painter who moved to Paris in 1908. It also displays modern works of art. The second floor houses temporary exhibitions devoted to 20C artists. The early collections of the museum are shown to visitors on rotation.

Former Castle (Ancien château) (B). – Follow Rue Roche, then Rue du Château and you will reach the promenade on the spur of the former castle, pulled down in 1740. It offers pleasant **views** of the Oise and the new riverside quarters. A beautifully-restored manor house at the entrance to the gardens houses the **Pissarro Museum** (Musée Pissarro) (B **M**[2]), which presents the life and the work of this talented Impressionist painter. Several times a year, the museum hosts temporary exhibitions of modern artists who lived in the area.

PONT-STE-MAXENCE

Pop 9 509

Michelin map 56 south of folds 1 and 2 – Local map p 100

Because of the old bridge spanning the Oise river, this town has always been an important road post in French history, both for kings and travelling merchants on their way to Flanders (now the N 17). The town owes the second part of its name to an Irish saint who was made a martyr here in the 5C. Today, Pont-Ste-Maxence is a prosperous industrial centre producing welding sets, stationery, etc.

Moncel Abbey (Abbaye du Moncel). – *Leave the town by the eastbound route and proceed towards Verberie.* In 1309 Philip the Fair gave orders to build the abbey next to a royal castle, of which two towers still remain. The abbey was dedicated to the Order of St Clare and it found favour with Philippe VI, the first ruler of the Valois dynasty (1328-1350). In 1347 Moncel Abbey received the mortal remains of his wife Jeanne of Burgundy. After Philippe's death, his second wife Blanche of Navarre *(see Mantes)* withdrew to the abbey. By then the church had disappeared.
The main façade is still reminiscent of medieval architecture and offers two imposing chimneys. The **courtyard★** is surrounded by three pavilions featuring an impressive display of roofing. The 14C refectory is adorned with frescoes dating back to the days of the Avignon school. Note the 16C cloister, the storeroom and its pointed vaulting, the Gothic charterhouse and the amazing 14C **timberwork★** above the nuns' dorter, made with oak taken from Halatte Forest.

14C timberwork, Moncel Abbey

★ PORT-ROYAL-DES-CHAMPS Abbey

Michelin map 101 fold 21 – Local map p 63

Little remains of this famous abbey, which was the scene of a serious religious dispute for more than one hundred years of French history.

An abbess aged eleven. – In 1204, an abbey for Cistercian nuns was founded in Porrois, a town later known as Port-Royal. Although this order is supposed to be strict, the rules grew extremely lax over a period of four centuries and by the beginning of the 17C, the 10 nuns and 6 novices who resided at the abbey were leading a most unsaintly life: the cloister had become a promenade, fasting was a bygone practice and the vows of poverty were hardly compatible with the entertaining carried out at the abbey. One even celebrated Carnaval.
In 1602, **Angélique Arnauld,** the 11-year-old daughter of an important family of lawyers was passed off as seventeen and appointed Abbess of Port-Royal.

A reformer without mercy. – Recovering from a bout of ill health, Mother Angélique realised where her duty lay and set about reforming her nunnery. She had the precinct wall re-installed around the abbey and would only address her mother, then her father, through the locutory, despite their repeated supplications and threats (1609). She introduced the perpetual adoration of the Blessed Sacraments, and imposed observance of the Cistercian rule, meditation and manual labour. The abbey was transformed and greeted an increasing number of novices. Mother Angélique chose Jean Duvergier de Hauranne, better known as the Abbot of St-Cyran, and Antoine Singlin to be the directors of Port-Royal-des-Champs. Like the parents and close relations of Angélique, many of whom were Calvinists, these austere confessors aspired to draw man away from earthly pleasures, make him see how corrupt he is and persuade him that he can be saved only by divine grace.
In 1618, the Cistercian Order sent Mother Angélique to Maubuisson to reform the local abbey. During her absence, Port-Royal was run by Mother Agnès, Angélique's younger sister. When Mother Angélique returned in 1625, it became necessary to find new premises for Port-Royal-des-Champs Abbey: the conventual buildings were too cramped and the surrounding marshes was ruining the nuns' health. The community moved to the capital, where it occupied new buildings and was renamed Port-Royal de Paris (now a maternity clinic).

The "Messieurs" of Port-Royal. – One of Angélique's brothers was a theologian with a great deal of influence over his friends and relations, all of whom shared the pessimistic views propounded by the Abbot of St-Cyran. The gentlemen – known as the *Solitaires* or the *Messieurs de Port-Royal* – decided to withdraw from society in order to take up prayer and meditation. In 1637 they left Port-Royal de Paris and moved to Port-Royal-des-Champs, which had remained empty. There, they applied themselves to the renovation of the abbey: they drained the land, raised the ground and enlarged the buildings. The following year, the Abbot of St-Cyran was incarcerated on the orders of Cardinal Richelieu, whom he had refused to serve. He died in 1643. Mother Angélique returned to Port-Royal-des-Champs in 1648 and from then on she and her flourishing community spent their time between this abbey and the one in Paris. The *Solitaires* were lodged in Les Granges perched on top of a hill dominating the old town of Porrois.
Strongly influenced by the Abbot of St-Cyran and the importance of dispensing religious education early in life to save man's soul, these *Messieurs* set up a number of schools known as the Little Schools *(Petites Ecoles)*, famed for the high standards of their teaching. Among the famous mentors featured such names as Claude Lancelot the Hellenist, Pierre Nicole the Moralist, Dr Hamon, Grand Arnauld, Arnauld d'Andilly and their parents, namely Lemaistre de Sacy, who translated the Bible.

The Jansenist Movement. – The Jesuits resented the growing influence that the Port-Royal *Messieurs* exerted over people at court and in Parlement, as well as over the younger generation. They were especially indignant because the town of Port-Royal published the works of Cornelius Jansen, the former Bishop of Ypres. Louvain University had entrusted this prelate with the task of refuting the doctrine advocated by the Jesuit Luis de Molina. The latter maintained that man could attain self-improvement through his own will power, overcome all the problems in this world if he genuinely wished to do so and expect God to come to his assistance in any circumstances, simply on account of his merits.
Soon after he completed his treaty *Augustinus,* Cornelius Jansen died in 1640, unaware of the dramatic developments that were to follow its publication.

Problems of conscience. – The theologians based at Port-Royal, notably the Grand Arnauld, approved of *Augustinus* because it confirmed their views, many of which were close to the Calvinist theory. They had it published in France. The Jesuits retaliated by accusing the Jansenists of holding heretical views. To prove their point, they reported so-called "quotes" by piecing together bits of sentences taken from the *Augustinus*. They eventually convinced the Church, who started to take measures against Jansenists in 1653. It also required all nuns and priests to sign a formulary condemning Jansen. The nuns of Port-Royal – "pure as angels and proud as the Devil" according to the Bishop of Paris – admitted that the text was heretical. However they refused to sign the document on the grounds that the quotes were not actually included in the text.
The dispute was aggravated in the following years and the Little Schools were closed in 1656. Arnauld realised the futility of waging a theological war. It was then that Blaise Pascal wrote *Les Provinciales,* a virulent pamphlet against the Jesuits, in which he staunchly defended the cause of Port-Royal.
The Pope's death produced a brief lull in 1655 but hostilities resumed in 1661. It was during those times of persecution that Mother Angélique died, exhausted by months of torment and anguish.

Between 1669 and 1679, a series of new publications and religious studies flourished in France and it seemed that the matter had slipped into oblivion. In 1679 Louis XIV decided to settle the whole affair once and for all: the noviciate was forbidden, the *Solitaires* were dispersed and some went into exile. The nuns at Port-Royal-de-Paris disowned their counterparts at Port-Royal-des-Champs, who were the object of continual persecution. By 1705 they numbered only 25, the youngest being 60 years of age. On 20 October 1709 the remaining nuns were expelled by 300 musketeers. The mortal remains of Jean Racine, who had been buried in the northern cemetery, were moved to St-Étienne-du-Mont, in Paris, where he rests side by side with Blaise Pascal.

In 1710 the monastery buildings were razed to the ground. The graveyard was desecrated and the bones of the buried thrown into a communal grave in the cemetery of St-Lambert. The religious objects and furnishings went to a number of neighbouring parishes. The funeral slabs which once paved the church at Magny-les-Hameaux have now been re-assembled.

The Jansenist doctrine continued to arouse controversy under Louis XV. The Parlement de Paris refused to ratify royal edicts and ordinances, and priests refused to distribute the Blessed Sacraments. Clandestine publications began to circulate. Jansenism became a religious sect and it was only after the Revolution that its influence over French society started to decline.

THE RUINS AND THE MUSEUMS *time: 2 hours*

The tour of Port-Royal estate comprises two parts. The pilgrimage to the abbey ruins is enhanced by a visit to the park (Longueville Gate, canal, view of the ruins). The Little Schools building is situated on a plateau, surrounded by pleasant, shaded grounds. It now houses a national museum, containing a wide range of documents on the former teaching colleges. The farmhouse where the hermits used to stay is a farming concern closed to the public.

ⓥ **Ruins and Abbey Museum.** – The shaded path leading to the abbey branches off the Dampierre-Versailles road. Leave your car in the car park.

The guided tour takes you round a square area defined by avenues of lime trees, which was the site of the former cloister. The graveyard where the Cistercian nuns were buried after 1204 has been planted with grass.

The church adjoined the cloister. Because the *Solitaires* had raised the floor level in an attempt to ward off the dampness, the building was razed down to the paving. When the original level was restored, the works uncovered the base of the pillars and the walls that belonged to the first building.

An oratory built in 1891 stands on the site of the chancel.

Next to the dovecote, the remains of a 17C barn, house a collection of paintings, engravings and souvenirs which illustrate and enliven the tour of the estate.

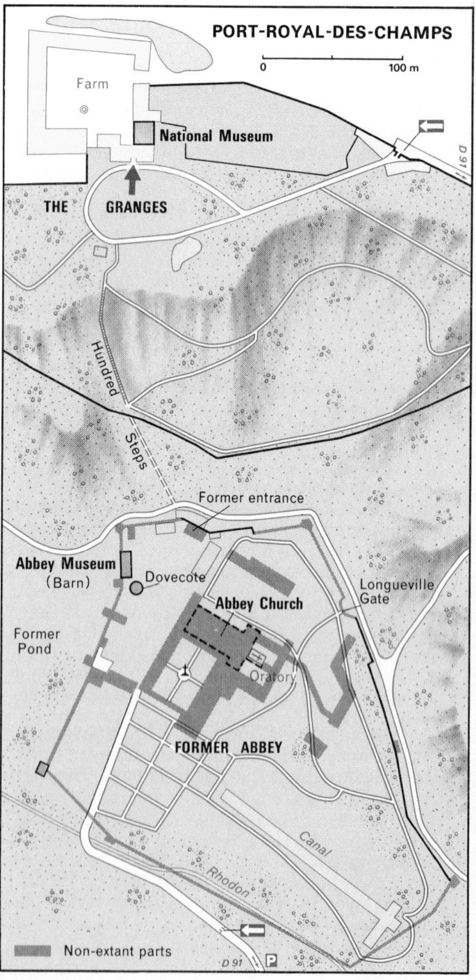

Lying above the northern side of the valley, the Domaine des Granges is hidden by a cluster of trees but visitors will appreciate the daily efforts made by the *Messieurs de Port-Royal* to attend mass in the abbey. They subsequently made use of the Hundred Steps, which they personally helped design. *It is no longer possible to climb from the abbey ruins to the Granges using the Hundred Steps (see above).*

Ⓥ **Port-Royal Granges National Museum (Musée National des Granges de Port-Royal).** – The building was specially designed for the Little Schools in 1651-1652 and presents an austere front conducive to religious contemplation. The harmony was upset in the 19C when an unfortunate Louis XIII wing was added.
Most of the rooms have been restored to their former condition. They present books, engravings and drawings concerning the history of the abbey and the Jansenist movement, the *Solitaires* and the Little Schools. Other exhibits include a series of portraits by Philippe de Champaigne, depicting the principal Jansenist leaders. Note the touchingly naive collection of 15 gouache paintings portraying the life of the Cistercian nuns.
Jean Racine lived at Port-Royal between the age of 16 and 19. Claude Lancelot and Pierre Nicole taught him Greek, Latin and French versification, Antoine Lemaistre lectured him on diction and rhetoric. The French poet learned greatly from his tutors and he soon became an outstanding reader. Louis XIV was spellbound by his beautiful voice and Racine's advice was sought by many an actor. He would often accompany Dr Hamon on his visits round the neighbouring villages: the physician was a generous man who knitted woollen garments for his patients while sitting astride his old mule.
Although the Jansenists were sceptical about the Arts, they accepted paintings inspired by authentic religious feelings. The exhibition hall dedicated to Philippe de Champaigne reminds visitors of the strong ties that linked this painter to the abbey: every day the nuns could admire his two works *Ecce Homo* and *Mater Dolorosa.* Ask for one of the windows overlooking the farm yard to be opened. Another distinguished guest at the Granges was the celebrated mathematician and religious philosopher, Blaise Pascal, who composed his *Mystery of Jesus* at Port-Royal in 1655.
Tradition has it that Pascal's knowledge of mathematics came in useful during his stay at the abbey when he produced the calculations for a new winch for the well: this enabled the nuns to draw a huge bucket as big as 9 ordinary buckets from a height of 60m – 197ft with no extra effort.

ADDITIONAL SIGHTS AT PORT-ROYAL

Ⓥ **St-Lambert Church.** – Pop 421. This small picturesque country church is perched above the village. A granite pyramid erected in the church cemetery in the early 20C marks the communal grave that received the remains of the Cistercian nuns and the *Solitaires.*
To the right of the drive lies a cross bearing the words "To the human race". It was set up in 1944 and celebrates the memory of all those who suffered during the last world war, in particular in concentration camps, without distinction of race, nationality or creed.

Le RAINCY — Pop 13 413

Michelin map 101 fold 18 – Michelin plan 20

The château built by Le Vau in the 17C has since disappeared. The grounds were parcelled out into building plots under the Second Empire and some of the garden paths were enlarged and made into streets.

★ **Notre-Dame Church (Église Notre-Dame).** – *Avenue de la Résistance.* Built by Auguste Perret in 1922-1923, this church marks a turning-point in the history of modern religious architecture on account of its original bell tower and general layout, and the use of reinforced concrete for the very first time.
The church interior presents an oblong-shaped nave, lined with slim columns. The walls pierced with intricate patterns – like moucharaby screens – are adorned with dainty stained glass windows based on sketches by Maurice Denis *(qv).* The colour of the hand-painted roundels ranges from deep blue in the apse to a lighter tone at the west end of the nave.

★ RAMBOUILLET — Pop 22 487

Michelin map 196 fold 28

Thanks to its château, and especially its park and famous forest, Rambouillet deserves to feature among the major sights of Ile-de-France.
In 1897, Rambouillet became the official summer residence of the President of the French Republic.

HISTORICAL NOTES

The demise of François I. – At the age of 52, François I fell ill and his state of health started to decline. He became restless and left his St-Germain residence in February 1547. He went to stay with his major-domo at Villepreux, paid a visit to his treasurer's widow in Dampierre, spent Shrove Tuesday in Limours with his favourite the Duchess of Étampes and indulged in a three-day hunt in Rochefort-en-Yvelines. On the way back, he dropped in to see the captain of his body guard Jacques d'Angennes at Rambouillet Château. It was built in 1375 by Jean Bernier – a prominent court figure under Charles V – and had remained the property of the d'Angennes family since 1384. During his stay at Rambouillet François I's condition grew worse. Feeling that his end was drawing near, the king summoned his son Monseigneur le Dauphin and placed his servants and the French people in his hands. He passed away on 30 March 1547.

From Armenonville to Louis XVI. – In 1706 Louis XIV bought Rambouillet for the comte de Toulouse, one of Mme de Montespan's legitimated sons. He trebled the private apartments and added two perpendicular wings onto the main building. Under Louis XVI, the estate came into the hands of the comte de Toulouse's son the **duc de Penthièvre.** Like his father, he was a dedicated governor who applied himself to the improvement of his domain. He refurbished the grounds for his sister-in-law the Princesse de Lamballe. A close friend of Marie-Antoinette, the princess was butchered in the old Paris prison of La Force on 5 September 1792.
Louis XVI was an enthusiastic hunter who enjoyed staying at Rambouillet and he purchased the estate in 1783. The queen was bored by life at the château, which she referred to as a "Gothic toad hole". In an attempt to divert her, the king gave orders to build the Dairy, a small pavilion reminiscent of the Trianon. A landscape garden was started by Penthièvre and completed after plans by Hubert Robert.

A sense of destiny. – In 1814 Marie-Louise met up with her father François II in Rambouillet: she decided to leave Napoleon and accompany the King of Rome to Vienna.
On 29 June 1815, on his way back from Malmaison, Bonaparte asked his driver to stop at Rambouillet for the night. He knew the place well. Indeed, after his divorce with Josephine, he had come here to seek peace and solace and had spent many happy days with Marie-Louise on the estate. After this unexpected stop, and a night of melancholy reflections, the carriage pursued its journey towards St Helena.
On 31 July 1830, around 6pm, Charles X arrived at Rambouillet, fleeing the insurrection at St-Cloud. For three days, the ageing ruler debated on what course of action to choose. The troops under his command disbanded and the rebellion was spreading towards Paris. He eventually abdicated and set sail for England.
It was in Rambouillet – where he stayed from 23 to 25 August 1944 – that General de Gaulle gave orders for the Leclerc Division to march towards Paris.

Ⓥ CHÂTEAU *time: 1 hour*

Leave from Place de la Libération, the seat of the Town Hall *(if the car park is full, leave the car in the park – a number of exceptions are made).*
The château presents a triangular shape owing to the fact that Napoleon dismantled the left wing. The large François I tower belonged to the 14C fortress. It is difficult to spot on account of the numerous additions made by the comte de Toulouse.

Mezzanine. – The reception rooms commissioned by the comte de Toulouse are embellished with superb rococo **wainscoting★**. Note the charming boudoir designed for the comte's wife.
The corridor adjoining the François I tower leads through to the imperial bathroom suite, adorned with Pompeian frescoes. This opens onto the Emperor's Bedchamber, where he spent the night on 29 June, and the study. It was in the dining room – the former ballroom that Charles X signed the abdication document. The view of the park is stunning.

Ground Floor. – One can visit the Marble Hall, dating from Jacques d'Angennes's time. This delightful room, decorated in the Renaissance style, is completely lined with marble tiling, laid down under the reign of Henri II.

Aerial view of Rambouillet Château

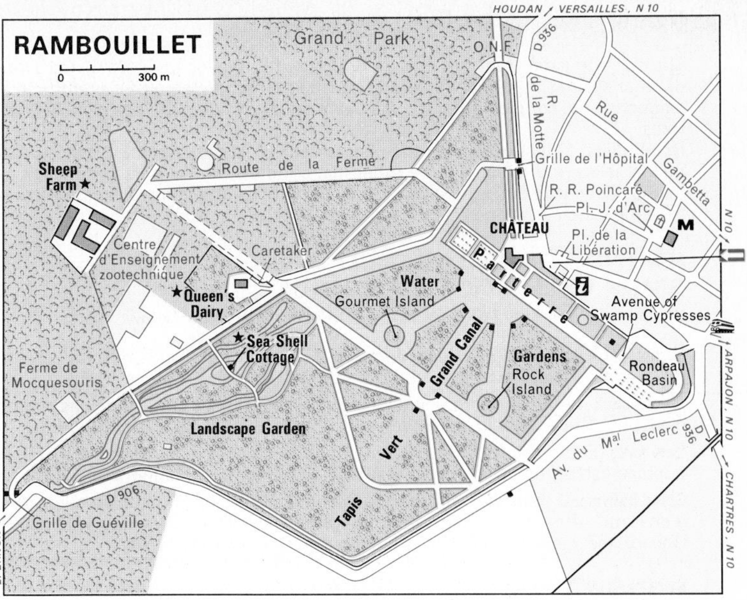

★PARK

Parterre. – The château is set in a pleasant formal garden. On the right stands a quincunx, surrounded by small clusters of trees. The perspective ends with the Rondeau Basin and a sweeping avenue planted with swamp cypresses in 1805.

Water gardens – They were remodelled by the duc de Penthièvre. The central canal is continued by a green carpet of lawn, the tapis vert. The other canals with their geometric lines enclose islets of greenery: Gourmet Island, Rock Island, etc.

★**Queen's Dairy (Laiterie de la Reine).** – Louis XVI had it built to divert his wife Marie-Antoinette. The small sandstone pavilion resembling a neo-classical temple consists of two rooms. The first – which houses the actual dairy – features marble paving and a marble slab as table dating from the First Empire. The Sèvres porcelain bowls and jugs used for tasting have disappeared.
The room at the back was designed as an artificial grotto adorned with luxuriant vegetation. It presents a marble composition by Pierre Julien depicting a nymph and the she-goat Amalthea (1787).

★**Sea Shell Cottage (Chaumière des Coquillages).** – The **landscape garden** in the park features a charming cottage built by Penthièvre for the Princesse de Lamballe. The walls of the rooms are encrusted with a variety of sea shells, chips of marble and mother of pearl. A small boudoir with painted panelling adjoins the main room.

ADDITIONAL SIGHTS

★**National Sheep Farm.** – In 1786 Louis XVI decided to diversify his amateur farming activities and attempt the production of fine wool. To that end, he purchased a flock of Merinos from Spain. The sheep farm buildings were completed under the First Empire. Today it houses around 800 animals, including 120 Merino sheep.

Rambouillet Museum (Musée Rambolitrain) (M). – An astounding collection of toy trains and miniature models explains the history of the railway from its early beginnings up to the present day. A large O-shaped circuit occupied the whole of the second floor.

★ RAMBOUILLET Forest

Michelin map 196 folds 27 and 28

The forest provides many pleasant walks for those who enjoy exploring the undergrowth. Twenty or so ponds – namely the highly popular **Dutch Pond** (Étang de Hollande) – nestling in a picturesque setting, and a string of country villages with many weekend homes appeal greatly to Parisian ramblers.

Cycling paths. – See Michelin map 196.

GEOGRAPHICAL NOTES

Rambouillet is part of the ancient Yveline forest. In Gallo-Roman times, the latter occupied the land between Nogent-le-Roi, Houdan, Cernay-la-Ville and Étampes. The forest covers a total area of 20000ha-50000 acres, 14000ha-35000 acres of which are state-owned. The average height ranges from 110m-360ft to 180m-590ft. The wood stretches over a clayey plateau cut across by a succession of sandy vales. The trees were cleared in the Middle Ages. As a result, the forest is divided into three large massifs by a number of clearings. To the north we find the St-Léger and Rambouillet massifs, by far the most popular. To the south lies the Yvelines massif, broken up by private estates.

The tree population features a majority of oaks (60%), pine trees (30%) and a medley of other species, notably birches and beeches. Owing to the present reafforestation campaign, the coppices with standards are gradually being replaced with clusters of trees.
Rambouillet Forest is damper than Fontainebleau and features a larger number of ponds, lakes and rivers. On the other hand, it does not have its stately oak trees, neither does it exhude the same atmosphere of quiet dignity. It has always been extremely rich in game: stags, roe deer, wild boars, etc.

ROUND TOUR STARTING FROM MONTFORT-L'AMAURY

21km – 12 miles – 1/2 hour Rtn on foot – Local map below

Mormaire Château (Château de la Mormaire). – Built in stone and brick under Henri IV, this castle is reminiscent of the houses on Place des Vosges in Paris.

Gambaiseuil. – Pop 31. A former woodcutter's village whose population has practically died out. There remain a few lived-in houses in the old church quarter.

New Lake (Étang Neuf). – Situated in a remote corner of the forest, this pond is a popular fishing haunt. It lies in pleasant surroundings, planted with beech trees.

Grand Baliveau Crossroads. – The road to the right of the sign "Route Forestière du Parc d'en Haut" offers a charming walk through a lovely glade overgrown with greenery. One of the clearings affords a nice **view★** of a secluded valley.

ROUND TOUR STARTING FROM RAMBOUILLET

41km – 22 miles – about 1 hour then 1 1/2 hours Rtn on foot – Local map below

Leave Rambouillet (p 143) by the road to Maintenon. After 5km – 3 miles, you will reach Gazeran. Proceed in a southerly direction along the D 62 for a further 6.5km – 4 miles. Leave the car on parking area in the dip of Drouette Valley.

Sauvage Wildlife Park (Réserve Zoologique de Sauvage). – A 40ha – 100 acre landscape park has been laid out in the Drouette Valley, surrounded by oak groves dotted with sandstone boulders. The reserve houses a great many aquatic birds, including several rare species of swans and ducks, and a colony of flamingos. Antelopes, stags and kangaroos may be seen running freely about the grounds.

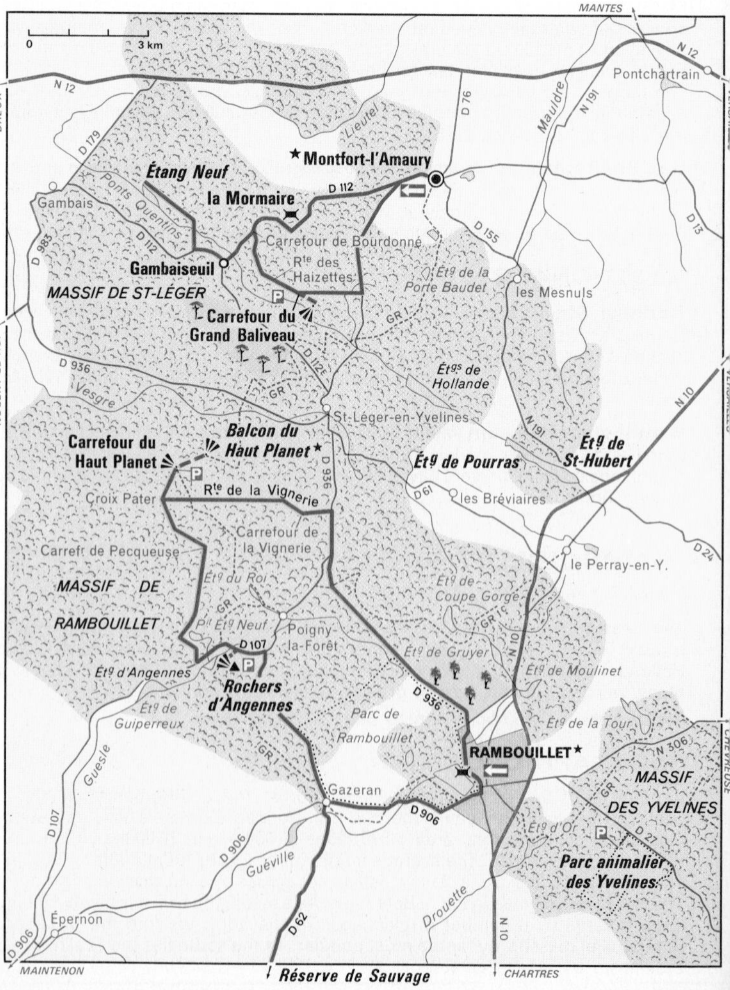

The Tropical Aviary – in which the high temperature and hygrometric conditions are maintained artificially – features many tropical bird species: toucans, eclectus parrots, gouras, hornbills, etc.

Turn round and return to Gazeran.

D'Angennes Rocks (Roches d'Angennes). – *Leave from the car park signposted "Zone de Silence des Rabières".* Walk 100yd up the steeper slope of the valley and you will find the real path leading to the summit. Go past an arena-shaped shelf circled by boulders and you will soon reach the crest.

View of Guesle Valley and d'Angennes Pond, bordered by bulrushes, reeds and other aquatic plants.

Haut Planet Crossroads (Carrefour du Haut Planet). – The ledge of the Haut-Planet plateau – planted with birches and conifers – commands a sweeping **view★** of the northern St-Léger massif.

★ **Haut Planet Belvedere** (Balcon du Haut Planet). – Leave the car. Bear right and take the straight path leading to Haut Planet, which crosses rough, hilly ground. After passing a spring fenced in by netting wire on the right, the lane reaches a shaded esplanade located on the edge of the plateau (shelter for ramblers). The path – offering beautiful vistas all the way – eventually leads to a rocky promontory. Turn round and retrace your steps.

ADDITIONAL SIGHTS

Pourras and St-Hubert Ponds (Étangs de Pourras et de St-Hubert). – *1/2 hour Rtn on foot. Leave from the large star-shaped St-Hubert crossroads. Follow the continuation of the N 191, a rough track flanked by properties which leads to the road running between the two ponds.*
The ponds were part of one of Vauban's projects to create reservoirs for Versailles' requirements in water. A series of six ponds separated by paths were laid out near the Dutch Pond. Only the two end basins are filled with water. The two central ponds – known as Bourgneuf and Corbet – have been replaced by a rivulet overgrown with aquatic plants.

Ⓥ **Yvelines Wildlife Park** (Parc Animalier des Yvelines). – *Car park and reception bureau 500m - 500yd southwest of the road from Rambouillet to Rochefort (D 27).*
This 250ha – 650 acre reserve encloses a flat area of land populated with stags, does, roe deer, boars, fallow deer, many of which are tame and may be approached easily.

RAMPILLON

Pop 561

Michelin map 61 fold 3 – 4.5km – 3 miles southeast of Nangis

Located on a small hillock, this village features an interesting church which dominates the Brie plateau.

★ **Church (Église).** – Built in the 13C, the church originally belonged to a Ⓥ Templar's Commandery which was burned down by the English in 1432. A tower – known as the Templars' Tower – was erected alongside the main building. Above the south aisle rises the sturdy square belfry, crowned by a saddle-back roof. The main doorway presents a fine series of sculptures: admire Christ as Judge on the tympanum and the Resurrection of the Dead on the lintel. The figure on the pier bears a resemblance to St Éliphe, the patron saint of the church. The twelve Apostles stand gazing from the embrasures. Above them, observe the calendar flanked by a Presentation to the Temple and an Adoration of the Magi. A Crowning of the Virgin adorns the side doorway on the right.

★ La ROCHE-GUYON

Pop 567

Michelin map 196 fold 2

This small locality lies between the Seine river and the Vexin plateau. The village developed at the foot of an old stronghold whose crumbling keep still dominates the steep, rocky ledge. Life at La Roche-Guyon has resumed its peaceful character since the bombings of July 1944, and the Battle of Normandy, when Marshal Rommel established his headquarters in La Roche-Guyon Château.
In the 13C, a residential château was erected at the foot of the cliff not far from the fortress: it was linked to the keep by a flight of steps carved in the rock. François I and his numerous retinue took up residence here in 1546. Their stay was marred by an unfortunate incident. The young comte d'Enghien – whose glowing accomplishments in Ceresole two years earlier had earned him public recognition – died of a broken skull when a chest fell out of a window. La Roche-Guyon was made a duchy-peerage in 1621. Fifty-eight years later, the title came into the hands of **François de la Rochefoucauld,** who wrote many of his famous *Maximes* at the château. In 1816 Louis-François Auguste, **duc de Rohan-Chabot,** acquired the estate. He lost his wife in 1819 and took holy orders at the age of 31. On his return, he continued to entertain at the château, combining acts of charity with the social favours of the *Ancien Régime.* Among the fellow students at St-Sulpice Seminary guests featured young Romantic authors Victor Hugo, Alphonse de Lamartine, Hugues Lamennais, Henri Lacordaire and the Abbot Dupanloup. They delighted in the grand but respectful services delivered in the underground chapel to the strains of a superb Italian organ. In 1829 the duke was appointed Archbishop of Besançon, and then Cardinal, and sold the château and its grounds to François de la Rochefoucauld-Liancourt. La Roche-Guyon has remained family property ever since.

★ **The banks of the Seine.** – The quayside promenade commands a nice **view★** of the sleepy countryside and the twisting course of the river. Turn round, admire the two castles lying side by side. The abutment pier of the former suspension bridge (taken down in the 19C) provides a good observation point.

Ⓥ **Castle (Château).** – The splendid gates bearing La Rochefoucauld's coat of arms give onto a grassy courtyard surrounded by 18C stables. The main building stands on a terrace with arched foundations. It is set back slightly and believed to be 15C. It acquired its present appearance in the 18C, when the crenellations were taken down and a three-storey wing added onto the east side. The symmetrical square tower to the west was restored after the 1944 bombings. In fact, most of the château was renovated during the last century. Go up to the gates guarding the court of honour and look down on the monumental entrance pavilion lying at the foot of the cliffs, among the remains of the 13C curtain wall and its crenellated turrets.

★ **The Crests Road (Route des Crêtes).** – *Round tour of 4km – 2.5 miles.* Take the road to Gasny which passes the entrance to the famous troglodyte caves or stables called **boves,** carved in the chalk. When you reach the pass, bear right and turn back into the D 100, also known as "Route des Crêtes". When the estates no longer conceal the view of the river, park the car on a belvedere near a spinney of pine trees.

View★★ of one of the Seine's loops, circling the groves of Moisson Forest, and, further along the promontory, of the spurs of the Haute-Isle cliffs. In the foreground, down below, the truncated keep of La Roche-Guyon Château *(private).*
Proceed along the D 100. At the first junction, turn right into Charrière des Bois. This will bring you back to your starting point. The road follows a steep downward slope and passes under the 18C aqueduct that supplies water to the village and the château.

★★ ROYAUMONT Abbey

Michelin map 196 fold 7

Ⓥ Royaumont is an impressive symbol of the wealth that often accrued to the great French abbeys of the Middle Ages. A tour of this sanctuary is strongly recommended.
Founded in 1228 and completed in 1235, the abbey was occupied by members of the Cistercian Order. It was richly endowed by the king and his successors, which explains why it is graced with stately, elegant proportions. Six of St Louis' relatives – three children, a brother and two grandsons – were buried in the abbey. Their remains have since been moved to St-Denis Cathedral.
In 1791 Royaumont was sold as state property and the church dismantled. Since 1923 the abbatial palace and the grounds forming the estate have been separated from the abbey itself. In 1964 the last owners Isabel and Henri Gouïn (1900-1977) created the Royaumont Foundation for the Advancement of Human Science, to which they offered their domain.

A cultural calling. – In 1978 the abbey was assigned a new cultural mission. The international **Cultural Centre** set up on its premises ensures the preservation of the abbey; it also organises concerts, lectures, training seminars and exhibitions.

Church ruins. – *See plan opposite.* Royaumont Church was consecrated in 1235. The fragments of columns that remain mark the foundations of this unusually large building (101m – 330ft long).
The chancel and its radiating chapels break with Cistercian tradition in that they do not feature a flat east end (e.g. Fontenay in Burgundy). A corner turret (1) belonging to the former north transept gives one a fair idea of its elevation.

Royaumont Abbey

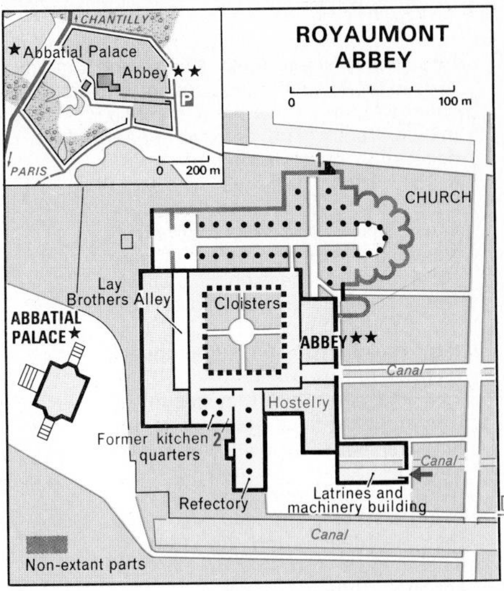

Abbey buildings. – The cloisters surround a delightful garden. From a distance, you may notice that the east gallery (facing you as you enter) is paralleled behind by a narrow, uncovered passageway known as the Lay Brothers Alley. This was built for the lay brothers in order that they might have access to their wing and to the church without passing through the cloisters, habitually reserved for the choir monks.

Refectory. – This spacious dining hall – which features two naves – is a masterpiece of Gothic architecture which could accomodate 60 choir monks without difficulty (note the monolithic shafts of the columns).
St Louis would take his turn at serving the monks at table while they sat in silence, listening to the reader, standing erect in a pulpit carved out of the thick stone wall.

Former kitchen quarters. – They house a statue of the Virgin of Royaumont (2), executed in the 14C.
Before leaving the estate, take a look at the strange building resting on 31 semi-circular arches, astride the canal waters: the **latrines and machinery building.** In former times, the water reached a higher level and activated the machinery in the workshops. One of the water wheels has remained intact.

★**Abbatial Palace (Palais Abbatial).** – Built on the eve of the Revolution for the last commendatory abbot of Royaumont, this white cubic construction is reminiscent of certain Italian villas. Based on the neo-classical model, it is the work of Louis Le Masson, who trained at the Ponts-et-Chaussées Civil Engineering College. The façade facing the road to Chantilly is fronted by a charming pond.

★★ RUEIL-MALMAISON

Pop 64 545

Michelin map 101 folds 13 and 14 – Michelin plan 18

The town of Rueil is famed for Malmaison, the estate that remains firmly attached to the name of Napoleon Bonaparte.

Malmaison during the Consulate. – Marie-Joseph-Rose Tascher de la Pagerie, born in Martinique in 1763, the widow of Général de Beauharnais, married General **Bonaparte** in 1796. Three years later, she bought Malmaison and the 260ha – 640 acres of land surrounding the château.
When Napoleon was First Consul, he lived at the Tuileries, which he found "grand and boring". He decided to spend the end of each decade at Malmaison. These were the happiest moments of his married life. Elegant, lively **Josephine** – she had 600 dresses and would change five to six times a day – was the spirit of the party at Malmaison. Life was easy and carefree, and formal protocol was dropped.

Malmaison in imperial times. – Crowned Emperor in 1804, Napoleon had no alternative but to stay at St-Cloud, Fontainebleau and the Tuileries, which were the official places of residence. His visits to Malmaison were too rare for the Empress's liking. She began to miss her splendid botanical gardens and rose gardens, unparalleled in France. Josephine was a generous person with expensive tastes who spent money like water. When she ran into debt, her husband would complain bitterly but he invariably gave in, grumbling that this would be "the last time".

Malmaison after the divorce. – Josephine returned after her divorce in 1809. Napoleon had given her Malmaison, the Élysée and a château near Évreux. She fled the estate in 1814 but the Allied powers persuaded her to come back. She behaved a little rashly by entertaining the Russian Tsar and the King of Prussia, at Malmaison Château. She caught cold while staying with her daughter Queen Hortense at St-Leu Château and died on 29 May 1814, at the age of 51. The debts she left behind were estimated at 3 million francs.

The farewell to Malmaison. – Ten months after Josephine's death, Napoleon escaped from Elba and revisited Malmaison.
At the end of the Hundred Days, he returned to the estate and stayed with his sister-in-law Hortense, who was to give birth to Napoleon III. On 29 June 1815, the emperor paid a last visit to the château and his family before leaving for Rochefort and St Helena.

★★ MUSEUM

After Josephine's death, Malmaison Château and its 726ha – 1 800 acres of land passed to her son Prince Eugène, who died in 1824. The château was sold in 1828 and changed hands several times until it was bought by Napoleon III for the sum of one million francs. The emperor undertook to restore the architecture and interior decoration to its former glory.

In 1877, the château was in a sorry state and the grounds reduced to a mere 6ha – 15 acres. Malmaison was sold as state property and saw yet another succession of owners. The last proprietor, a certain Mr Osiris, acquired the estate in 1896, restored the château and bequeathed it to the State in 1904.

The land where the Mausoleum of the Imperial Prince stands was donated to Malmaison by the Prince Victor-Napoleon. Mr and Mrs Edward Tuck, an American couple who own Bois-Préau Château, also gave their residence and its 19ha – 47 acre park, formerly part of Josephine's private gardens.

The entrance gate still sports its old-fashioned lanterns. The **château** was built around 1622 and when Josephine bought it in 1799, it featured only the central block. The square, jutting pavilions were added towards the end of the 18C and the veranda in 1801-1802.

General Bonaparte, sketch by David

The museum was founded in 1906. It houses a great many exhibits which were purchased, donated or taken from Malmaison, St-Cloud or the Tuileries, as well as from other national palaces connected with the Imperial family.

Ground Floor. – 1) Vestibule built in the Antique style: busts of Napoleon's family.
2) Billiards Room: furniture belonging to the former gallery.
3) Golden Salon: beautiful furniture, including Josephine's tapestry frame. Note the splendid fireplace, flanked by two paintings, executed by Gérard and Girodet (based on the poems by Ossian).
4) Music Room: furniture by the Jacob brothers, the Empress's harp, piano belonging to Queen Hortense.
5) Dining Room: walls adorned with painted panels portraying dancers.
6) Council Chamber: a tent-shaped decor, embellished with military furnishings. The armchairs were taken from the former château at St-Cloud.
7) Library: original decoration by Percier and Fontaine, furniture by the Jacob brothers. The books and military maps come from Malmaison and the Tuileries.

First Floor. – The first rooms were occupied by the emperor when he spent his last days in Paris (June 1815), between the Battle of Waterloo and his departure for St Helena.

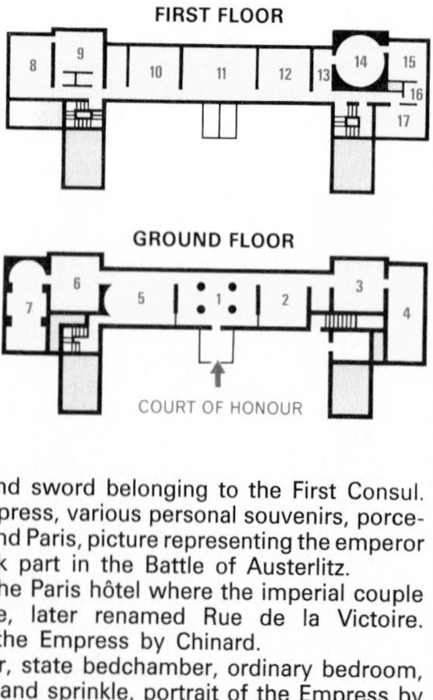

8) Imperial Salon: several large portraits of the Imperial family, painted by Gérard.
9) Emperor's Bedroom: Prince Eugène's bed and a private collection of furniture, both taken from the Tuileries. The Victory standing on a pedestal table is the same one the emperor was holding at the top of the Grand Army column on Place Vendôme in Paris (it was torn down by the Commune 1871). The walls are decorated with white hangings.
10) Marengo Room: paintings by David and Gros, ceremonial sabre and sword belonging to the First Consul.
11) Josephine's Room: portrait of the Empress, various personal souvenirs, porcelain services manufactured in Sèvres and Paris, picture representing the emperor surrouded by the marshals who took part in the Battle of Austerlitz.
12) Exhibition Gallery: frieze taken from the Paris hôtel where the imperial couple stayed, located in Rue Chanteraine, later renamed Rue de la Victoire. Josephine's dressing table, bust of the Empress by Chinard.
13 to 17) Josephine's Suite (antechamber, state bedchamber, ordinary bedroom, bathroom, boudoir): holy water stoup and sprinkle, portrait of the Empress by Gérard Prud'hon, bed and travelling toilet case.

Second Floor. – The wardrobes in Josephine's dressing room have been made into cabinets displaying some of her clothes. The next room contains several of the dazzling gowns she used to wear at court.

One of the rooms is dedicated to Queen Hortense: furniture and personal souvenirs. It also houses souvenirs belonging to Prince Eugène and to close relations of the Imperial family.
The last room presents the history of Malmaison Château and the estate.

Pavilions. – The **Osiris Pavilion** (Pavillon Osiris) contains all the collections that have been donated over the years: the works of art and antique pieces belonging to Mr Osiris, a remarkable selection of snuff boxes, glass objects and caskets relating to the Napoleonic legend. The central area is dominated by Gérard's full-length portrait of the Tsar Alexander I. The **Coach Pavilion** (Pavillon des Voitures) displays several imperial carriages, including the landau that Blücher took to leave Waterloo in June 1815.

Park. – In the park – now limited to 6ha (15 acres) – note the Marengo cedar tree, planted soon after the victorious battle of 14 June 1800, the rose garden and a number of rare tree species.
At the end of an avenue of stately lime trees stands the **Summer House** (Pavillon de Travail d'Été) that Napoleon used in conjunction with the library.
Leave the estate on foot and skirt the park along Avenue Marmontel (gates). On the left you will soon see the Mausoleum of the Imperial Prince, the son of Napoleon III, who was killed by members of the Zulu tribe in 1879.
The statue of the prince playing with his dog Nero is a replica of Jean-Baptiste Carpeaux' work. The original is in the Orsay Museum, together with many other major works by this remarkable 19C sculptor.

★ **Bois-Préau Château.** – Bought by Josephine in 1810 and rebuilt in 1855, the Ⓥ château and its park were bequeathed by Mr and Mrs Edward Tuck. The exhibits displayed in Malmaison Museum include personal souvenirs left by Napoleon in St Helena, a number of items related to the return of his ashes and a wide selection of objects dedicated to the Napoleonic legend.

St Peter's and St Paul's Church (Église St-Pierre-St-Paul). – Built in the late 16C and completed under Richelieu, this church was restored thanks to the generosity of Napoleon III. The church interior is Renaissance. The **organ case★**, made in Florence towards the end of the 15C, is among the most beautiful in France. It was a present from Napoleon III. To the right of the chancel lies the white marble tomb of the Empress Josephine. She is portrayed kneeling in formal attire, just as she was in David's painting of the coronation ceremony. Nearby stands a small mausoleum celebrating the memory of her uncle, governor of Martinique. The funeral monument of Queen Hortense – who died in 1837 – lies to the left of the choir. The high altar sports a beautiful bronze low relief from the 17C, representing the Embalming of Christ. It used to adorn the chapel of Malmaison Château.

Leave the church and bear left along the D 39. Then turn right into Rue Masséna and you will reach Rue Charles-Floquet, which becomes Chemin de Versailles. Enter the forest and continue until you reach St Cucufa Lake. Park the car nearby.

Malmaison Forest. – This 200ha – 500 acre forest is planted with oaks and chestnut trees.
It is believed that a chapel was once built in honour of St Cucufa, who was made a martyr in 304, under the rule of Diocletian.
Situated in a small, wooded vale, **St-Cucufa Lake★** is covered with water-lilies during the summer months. Josephine gave orders to build a dairy at the water's edge and it supplied the château with milk, butter and cheese. It has since disappeared. The wooden cottages lining the shores of the lake were built by the Empress Eugénie.

Return to the car. When leaving the forest, take the first turning on the right.

Avenue de la Châtaigneraie and Rue du Colonel de Rochebrune (D 180) cross the **Buzenval** quarter, where the heroes of the Paris Commune fought bravely in January 1871. A memorial has been erected on the top of the mound, which commands an extensive view of the northern lowlands.

★★ ST-CLOUD

Pop 28 760

Michelin map 101 folds 14 and 24 – Michelin plan 22

Situated on the west bank of the river Seine, St-Cloud belongs to the residential suburbs of the French capital. It is known mostly for its park, which once surrounded the splendid palatial château.

Clodoald. – Unlike his unfortunate brothers, Clodoald, the grandson of Clovis and Clotilda, escaped murder and became a disciple of the hermit Severin. He founded a monastery, where he died in 560. His tomb soon became a place of pilgrimage and the town of Nogent was subsequently called St-Cloud. This saint gave the enjoyment of his seigniorial rights to the Bishops of Paris who, until 1839, held the title of Dukes of St-Cloud and Peers of France.

The assassination of Henri III. – In 1589, Henri III launched an assault on Paris, which had fallen into the hands of the League. A young Jacobin friar called Jacques Clément wanted to punish his ruler for having made an alliance with his cousin Henri of Navarre. He gained admission to the king's presence and stabbed him in the abdomen. Henri III died two days later.

The Château of Monsieur. – In 1658 the episcopal building became the property of Louis XIV's brother, known to all as "Monsieur". His first wife Henrietta of England died there in 1670. The Sun King's brother later married Charlotte-Elisabeth of Bavaria. He extended the grounds to 590ha – 1460 acres and asked Jules-Hardouin Mansart to design the plans for a series of beautiful buildings. The park and its impressive cascade were conceived by Le Nôtre. Marie-Antoinette bought the estate in 1785 but it became state property during the Revolution.

The 18 Brumaire. – When General Bonaparte returned from Egypt, the army troops and the French people saw him as the leader who would restore peace and order. On 18 Brumaire of the year VIII (9 November 1799), the seat of the Consulate was moved to St-Cloud.
The following day, the Five Hundred held a meeting at the Orangery, presided over by Napoleon's brother Lucien Bonaparte. The General was greatly disconcerted by the hostile reception he got and was saved only by the swift intervention of this brother: Lucien summoned Joachim Murat, who cleared the assembly room instantly. The Directory was no longer.

St-Cloud under the Empire. – In 1802, Bonaparte was appointed a consul for life and St-Cloud became his favourite official residence. He celebrated his civil wedding with Marie-Louise on the estate and followed it with a religious ceremony in the Square Salon of the Louvre (1810).
In 1814, the Prussian Marshal Gebhard Blücher took up residence at the château. In an act of vengeance, he cut the silk hangings to ribbons, and wrecked both the bedroom and the library.
It was at St-Cloud that Charles X signed the Ordinances of July 1830, whose effect was to abolish the Charter and precipitate his fall. It was also from St-Cloud that he departed into exile.
On 1 December 1852, the Prince-President Louis-Napoleon was made emperor. A meeting was held at St-Cloud Château on 15 July 1870, during which it was decided to declare war on Prussia. The building was badly damaged in a fire that broke out three months later and it was razed to the ground in 1891.

★★ PARK

The 450ha – 1 110 acre park, which spreads from the slopes of the Seine Valley to the plateau of Garches, has retained most of the original layout designed by Le Nôtre.
In the former Guards' Pavilion, a **History Museum** (Musée Historique) tells the story of the estate and its château, consumed by the raging flames in October 1870.

★ **Great Cascade (Grande Cascade).** – Conceived in the 17C by Lepautre, these impressive falls were later enlarged by Jules Hardouin-Mansart. Dominated by allegorical statues of the rivers Seine et Marne, the waters of this cascade flow into a series of vases, basins and troughs before reaching the lower falls, from where they are channelled down to the edge of the park. The whole works are about 90m – 296ft long. At **Grandes Eaux★★**, the view is quite remarkable.

Great Fountain (Grand Jet). – Nestling in greenery near the Great Cascade, it is the most powerful fountain in the park and rises to a height of 42m – 138ft.

Terrace. – A cluster of yew trees and a marble slab mark the former site of the château, which was also the start of the Tapis Vert lawns and their continuation the Allée de Marnes perspective.
The private gardens used to spread on either side of this avenue.

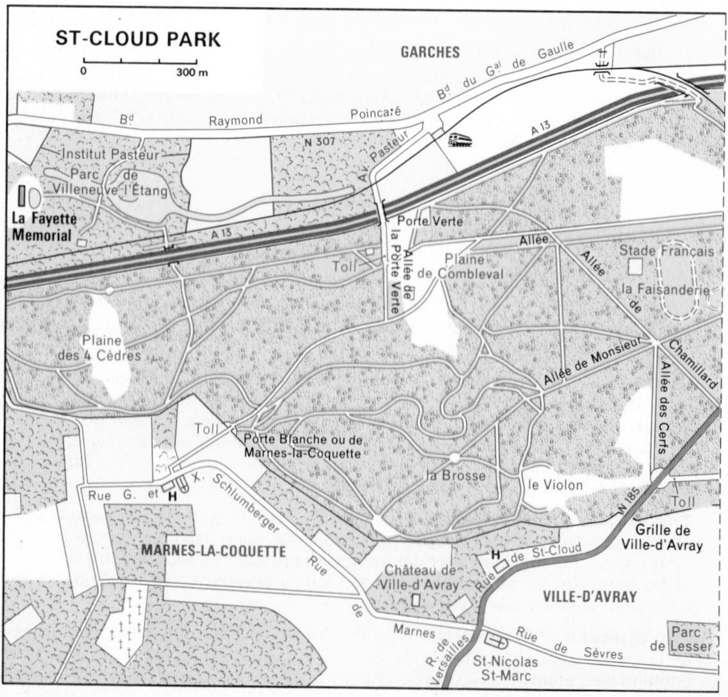

★**Trocadéro Gardens (Jardin du Trocadéro).** – These were laid out on the plans of the former château. They date from the Restoration period. This beautiful landscape garden features a great many tree and flower species, a charming pond and an aviary. The far end of the terrace commands a view of Paris. In the foreground, note the Pavillon d'Artois, part of which was built in the 17C and which now houses the École Normale Supérieure (the prestigious teachers' training college).

Tapis Vert. – Running from the Grande Gerbe Basin to Rond-Point des 24 jets, these lawns command a lovely view of the parterres and the city of Paris.

Rond-Point de la Balustrade. – On this site Napoleon erected a monument surmounted by a lantern. When the emperor was staying at the château, the lamp would remain lit. It was based on a model from ancient Greece, which is why the Parisians called it Demosthene's lantern. It was blown up by the Prussians in 1870. The terrace offers a superb **panorama**★★ of Paris, stretching from the Bois de Boulogne to the woods of Clamart and Meudon.

Breteuil Pavilion (Pavillon de Breteuil). – This 18C pavilion – St-Cloud's former Trianon – houses the International Bureau for Weights and Measures. The world centre of scientific meteorology still features the original standard metre.

TOWN

Dominaded by the spire of St-Clodoald Church (1865), the steep, narrow streets of the old town wind their way up the hillsides that form the Seine Valley.

★**Stella Matutina Church (Église Stella Matutina).** – *Place Henri-Chrétien along Avenue du Maréchal-Foch.* This modern place of worship was consecrated in 1965: it is shaped as a huge circular tent made of wood, metal and glass. It is fixed to a concrete base by nine pivots and fronted by a porch roof in the shape of a helm. The converging lines of the copper roofing and the pine timbering create an impression of loftiness and soaring height.

St-Cloud Bridge (Pont de St-Cloud). – In the 8C, a bridge was built across the Seine river. According to tradition, no king was to set foot on it, or else he would die instantly. Until the middle of the 16C, French rulers would cross the river in a boat. However when François I died in Rambouillet, it was decided that the funeral procession would cross the famous bridge. Naturally, no ill omens were feared as the king was already deceased. This incident put an end to the long-standing tradition. François' son Henri II replaced the old wooden bridge by a magnificent stone construction featuring 14 piers. The local villagers were astonished by such a massive display of stonework, which they claimed was the doing of the Devil, and the bridge had to be exorcised.

La Fayette Memorial. – *West of St-Cloud Park. Along Boulevard Raymond-Poincaré (N 307), in Villeneuve l'Étang Park.* The memorial was erected on Napoleon III's former estate by an American foundation. It renders homage to the 209 pilots from the United States who volunteered to take part in the La Fayette Squadron during the Great War. The monument consists of an arc and a colonnade, reflected in a small pond. The crypt beneath the terrace contains the mortal remains of the 67 pilots who perished, including the ace fighter Lufbery.
The rest of the estate houses the Pasteur Institute *(p 116)*.

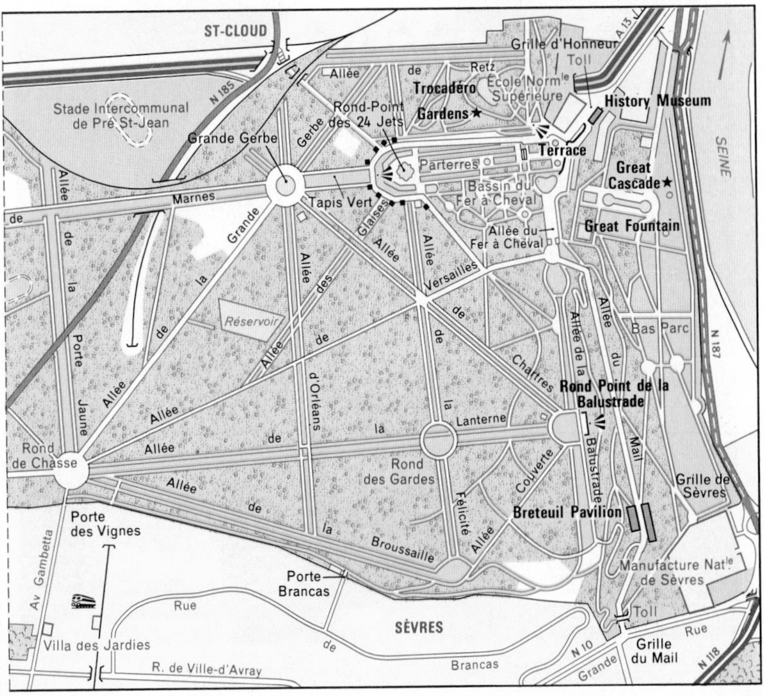

★★★ ST-DENIS Cathedral

Michelin map 101 fold 16 – Michelin plan 20

In 1840, the locality of St-Denis numbered a few thousand inhabitants. The industrial revolution brought this number to 100000 and made the town one of the main manufacturing centres of the northern suburbs.
The Gérard-Philipe Theatre and summer music festivals staged every year provide a wide range of intellectual and artistic activities. However, the most interesting sight in St-Denis is its cathedral, which houses the mausoleum of the Kings of France.

"Monsieur Saint Denis". – The legend has it that after being beheaded in Montmartre, the evangelist St Denis, the first bishop of Lutetia, started to walk, carrying his head in both hands. He was finally buried where he fell by a saintly woman. An abbey developed on the site of his tomb, which soon became a popular place of pilgrimage. In actual fact, since the ICAD St-Denis was the seat of a Roman city called Catolacus, which commanded a good view of both the river and Paris-Beauvais highway. It is believed that the man known as Monsieur (Monseigneur) St Denis was secretly buried in one of the fields of the city.
In 475, a large village church was erected on the site. Dagobert I had it rebuilt and offered it to a Benedictine community who took charge of the pilgrimage. This abbey was to become the most wealthy and the most celebrated in France. Towards 750 the church was dismantled a second time and rebuilt by Pepin the Short, who set up a shrine under the chancel to receive the sacred remains of saints. The building as it stands today is principally the work of the Abbot Suger (12C) and Pierre de Montreuil (13C).

Abbot Suger. – His formidable personality dominates the history of the cathedral. He was born of a peasant family and was "given" to the abbey at the age of ten. His remarkable gifts caused him to gain ascendancy over one of his fellow novices, a young boy whose destiny was to become Louis VII. The king made friends with the monk, invited him to court and consulted him on a great many matters.
Elected Abbot of St-Denis in 1122, Suger personally drew up the plans for the abbey church. The minister of Louis VII, he was made Regent of France when the king took part in the Second Crusade. His wisdom and concern for public well-being were so great that when Louis VII returned, he gave him the name "Father of the Homeland".

The Lendit Fair. – Lendit was an important trade fair founded by the abbot in 1109. It was held in St-Denis plain, on the site presently occupied by the Landy gasometers. It remained a major European event for over 600 years. A total of twelve hundred booths were placed at the disposal of the participants. Every year the University of Paris would travel to Lendit to buy the parchment used in the Montagne Ste-Geneviève faculties.

The Mausoleum of the Kings of France. – Most of the Kings of France from Dagobert I to Louis XVIII – a remarkable span of twelve centuries – were buried at St-Denis. In 1793, Barrère asked the Convention for permission to destroy the tombs. They were opened and the remains thrown into unnamed graves. Alexandre Lenoir salvaged the most precious tombs and moved them to Paris: he left them at the Petits-Augustins, later to become the Museum of French Monuments (Musée des Monuments Français). In 1816 Louis XVIII returned the tombs to the basilica.

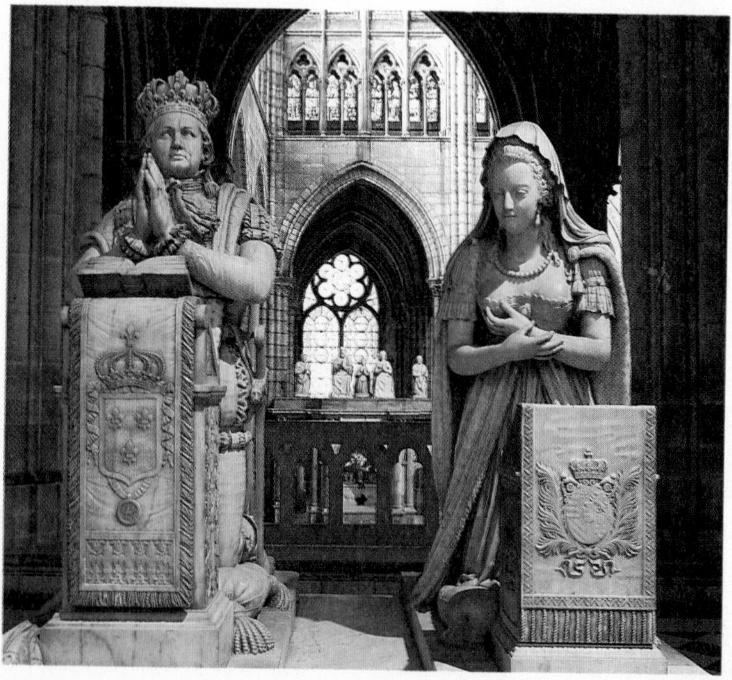

Effigies of Marie-Antoinette and Louis XVI, St-Denis Cathedral

Construction of St-Denis. – This cathedral was a turning-point in the history of French architecture. It was the first large church to feature a chancel and many architects in the late 12C used it as a model for their own creations (e.g. Chartres, Senlis and Meaux).
Suger supervised the construction of the west front and the first two bays of the nave from 1136 to 1140, that of the chancel and the crypt between 1140 and 1144. The Carolingian nave was provisionally preserved and remodelled between 1145 and 1147. The amazing rapidity of the whole operation was due to Suger's dedication and to the help he received from his parishioners: they all teamed up to pull the wagons of stone taken from the limestone quarries of Pontoise.
In the early 13C, the north tower was crowned by a magnificent stone spire. Work on the chancel was resumed, and the transept, then the nave, were entirely restored. In 1247 Pierre de Montreuil was appointed master mason by St Louis: he remained in charge of the work until his death in 1267.

Decadence. – The basilica subsequently fell into disrepair. The French Revolution caused further ravages and in his *Genius of Christianity,* Chateaubriand *(qv)* lamented the sorry state of the church. Napoleon gave orders to repair the damage and reinstated public worship in 1806.

Restoration. – Debret – the architect who took over in 1813 – aroused a wave of public indignation on account of his poor knowledge of medieval methods. For the spire, he used heavy materials that disrupted its gentle harmony. It collapsed in 1846 and had to be dismantled. In 1847 Debret was succeeded by **Viollet-le-Duc,** who studied a number of original documents which guided him in his work. From 1858 up to his death (1879), he toiled relentlessly and produced the cathedral that stands today.
A series of excavations carried out in the crypt has revealed sections of the Carolingian martyrium and the remains of a Merovingian mausoleum (late 6C tomb of the Princess Aregunde, the wife of Clotaire I, magnificent sarcophagi, splendid jewels). Foundations belonging to earlier sanctuaries have also been uncovered.

Recumbent figure of Jeanne de Bourbon, St-Denis Cathedral

TOUR *time: 1 hour*

Exterior. – The absence of the north tower mars the harmony of the west front. In the Middle Ages, the building was fortified, and some crenellations are still visible at the base of the towers. The tympanum on the central doorway represents the Last Judgment, that on the right doorway depicts the Last Communion of St Denis and on the left we have the Death of St Denis and his companions Rusticus and Eleutherus. All three doorways have been restored. The archshafts of the doorways feature the Foolish Virgins and the Wise Virgins (centre), the labours of the months (right) and the signs of the Zodiac (left).
On the north side of the cathedral, the nave is supported by double flying buttresses. The transept wall presents a wonderful rose window: initially it was to have two towers but work stopped after the first floor. If the original plans had been carried out, the church would have had six towers altogether.

Interior. – *The following comments will help visitors establish a chronology of the various campaigns, based on the monument's appearance.*
The cathedral is 108m – 354ft long, 38m – 125ft wide in the transept and 29m – 95ft high. These figures are slightly lower than those of Notre-Dame in Paris.
First one crosses the narthex formed by the two bays set up beneath the towers. Part of the pointed vaulting, which rests on a series of sturdy pillars, was designed by Suger. The nave attributed to Pierre de Montreuil is elegant in the extreme. The bays in the triforium open onto the church exterior (an architectural trend pioneered by St-Denis). The stained glass windows in the nave are modern.

★★★**The tombs.** – St-Denis Cathedral houses the remains of kings, queens and royal children, as well as those of leading personalities who served the French court, such as Bertrand du Guesclin (1). The mausoleum may be seen as a museum of French funeral art through the Middle Ages and during the Renaissance period (79 recumbent figures). The tombs have been empty since the Revolution.

After the 14C, before embalming the bodies of French kings, it was customary to remove their heart and their viscera. The inner organs, the heart and the bodies were all buried in different places. The bodies were taken to St-Denis.
Up to the Renaissance, the only sculpture adorning the tombs were **recumbent figures.** Note the funeral slab of Clovis (2) and Fredegunde (3), featuring a mosaic enhanced with copper lines, executed in the 12C for St-Germain-des-Prés.
Around 1260 St Louis commissioned a series of effigies of all the rulers who had preceded him since the 7C. The figures were purely symbolic but they provide a telling example of how royalty was portrayed towards the mid-13C. Visitors will appreciate the imposing tomb of Dagobert (4), with its lively, spirited scenes, the recumbent statues of Charles Martel (5) and Pepin the Short (6), and the female effigy carved in Tournai marble (7).
The statue of Philippe III the Bold (8), who died in 1285, bears a strong resemblance to the living character.
Towards the middle of the 14C, well-known people had their tomb built when they were still alive. The effigies were therefore extremely lifelike (Charles V by Beauneveu (9), Charles VI and Isabella of Bavaria (10).
Under the Renaissance, these **mausoleums** took on monumental proportions and were lavishly decorated. They were laid out on two floors, contrasting sharply with one another. The upper level featured the king and his betrothed, kneeling in full regalia. On the lower level, the deceased were pictured lying down as naked cadavers. Admire the twin monument built for Louis XII and Anne of Brittany (11), and that of François I and Claude de France (12), executed by Philibert Delorme and Pierre Bontemps.
Catherine de' Medici, who survived her husband Henri II by 30 years, gave orders to build the royal tomb. When she saw how she had been portrayed according to tradition, she fainted in horror and ordered a new effigy which substituted sleep for death. Both works are on display in the cathedral. Their making was supervised by Primaticcio (13) and Germain Pilon (14), respectively.

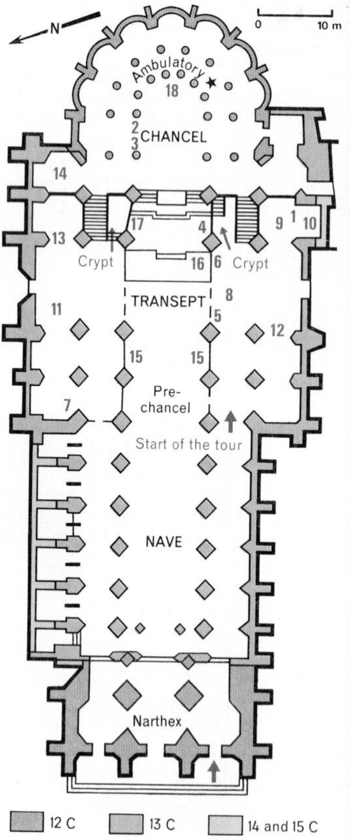

Chancel. – The beautiful pre-Renaissance stalls (15) in the pre-chancel were taken from the Norman Château at Gaillon. On the right stands a splendid Romanesque **Virgin★** in painted wood (16), brought from St-Martin-des-Champs. The episcopal throne on the other side (17) is a replica of Dagobert's royal seat (the original lies in the Medals and Antiquities Gallery at the Bibliothèque Nationale in Paris).
At the far end, the modern reliquary of the Saints Denis, Rusticus and Eleutherius (18) stands on the edge of Suger's **ambulatory★**, characterised by wide arches and slim columns. The radiating chapels are decorated with several retables and fragments of stained glass dating from the Gothic period.

★★ **Crypt.** – Built in the Romanesque style by Suger (12C), the lower ambulatory was restored by Viollet-le-Duc (acanthus capitals). In the centre stands a vaulted chapel known as Hilduin's Chapel (after the abbot who had it built in the 9C). Beneath its marble slab lies the burial vault of the Bourbon family, which houses the remains of Louis XVI, Marie-Antoinette, and Louis XVIII, to name but a few. The communal grave in the north transept received in 1817 the bones of around 800 kings and queens, royal highnesses, princes of the blood, Merovingians, Capetians and members of the Orléans and Valois dynasty.

ADDITIONAL SIGHTS

Ⓥ **Former Abbey (Ancienne abbaye).** – It adjoins the cathedral that was once the abbey church. The present conventual buildings date from the 18C and are the work of Robert de Cotte. In 1809, Napoleon I made the abbey the seat of a college for the daughters of holders of the French order of merit the **Légion d'Honneur.**

Ⓥ **Art and History Museum (Musée d'Art et d'Histoire).** – *22 bis, Rue Gabriel-Péri.* The museum is set up in the former Carmelite convent, part of which has been restored. It was founded by Cardinal de Bérulle in 1625 and occupied by Louis XV's daughter Madame Louise de France between 1770 and 1787. The refectory and the kitchen house archaeological exhibits discovered at St-Denis (fragments of medieval pottery). Many of the items on display come from the Hôtel-Dieu hospital, namely a superb apothecary's collection of ceramic phials and jars (17 and 18C).

The cells on the first floor contain many works of art, mementoes and paintings, including several by Guillot, evoking the daily life of the Carmelite nuns. Mystical adages have been inscribed on the walls.

On the second floor – where the king used to stay when he visited his daughter – a host of documents present the Paris Commune of 1871 (audio-visual exhibition).

The **former Carmelite chapel** – now the Law Courts – features a splendid Louis XVI cupola. It was here that the prioress Louise de France died in 1787.

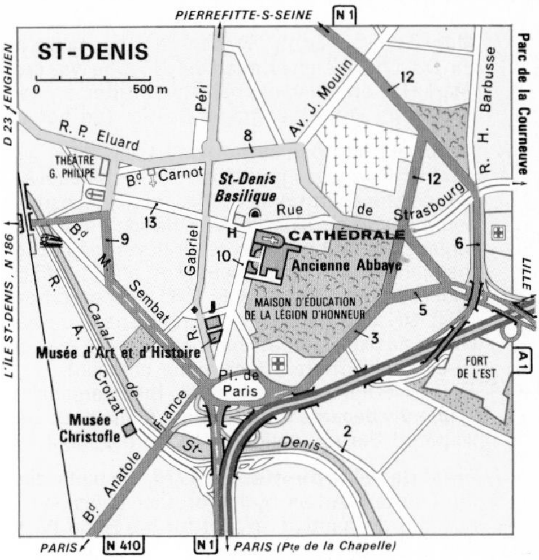

Casanova (R. D.)	2	Guesde (Bd J.)	9
Couturier (Av. P.V.)	3	Légion d'Honneur (R. de la)	10
Curie (Av. Joliot)	5	Lenine (Av.)	12
Dr.-Lamaze (Av. du)	6	République (R. de la)	13
Faure (Bd F.)	8		

Ⓥ **Christofle Museum (Musée Christofle).** – *112, Rue Ambroise-Croizat.*

The famous gold and silverware manufacturing company – the first to apply the principle of electroplating – set up premises here in 1875. They became official supplier to Napoleon III and their silver pieces still adorn the tables of many heads of state and rulers throughout the world. The museum presents a number of rare exhibits and some beautiful reproductions executed in the St-Denis workshops in the late 19C. This history of the silverware industry covers Antiquity, the Gallo-Roman period (treasure of Hildesheim), the Renaissance (ceremonial armour of Henri II), the 18C (Vinsac ewer), the Second Empire (numerous original pieces) and the present century up to 1960 (objects by Gio Ponti Sabattini, Wirkkala, etc). The Design Department is presently run by Tony Bouilhet, grandson of the founder's nephew.

Courneuve Park (Parc de la Courneuve). – *2.5km – 1.5miles to the east along Rue de Strasbourg and the N 301 (on the right).*

This 440ha – 1 090 acre stretch of greenery is presently being equipped with new facilities. It already features a cycling track, riding lanes, a ski jump, a little train, sporting equipment and playgrounds for children. Rowing boats and pedaloes may be hired to explore the 12ha – 30 acre lake *(it is forbidden to go bathing).*

★★ ST-GERMAIN-EN-LAYE Pop 40 829

Michelin map 101 fold 12 – Michelin plan 18

St-Germain is both a residential locality and a popular resort with many tourists, attracted by its château, its huge terrace and its forest.

HISTORICAL NOTES

The Old Castle. – In the 12C, Louis VI, the Fat, eager to exploit the strategic position of the St-Germain hillside, built a fortified stronghold on the site of the present château. In 1230 St Louis added a charming little chapel which still stands today. The fortress was destroyed during the Hundred Years War and restored by Charles V around 1368. In 1514 Louis XII married his daughter Claude de France to the duc d'Angoulême, who became François I the following year. The young ruler was acquainted with Italian culture and the ancient citadel was hardly suited to his taste for palatial comfort and luxury. In 1539 he had the whole building razed with the exception of Charles V's keep and the chapel built by St Louis. The reconstruction he entrusted to Pierre Chambiges, who produced the château that we see today.

The New Château. – Even the new building presented itself as a fortified structure equipped with machicolations, defended by a garrison numbering 3 000. Henri II, who wanted a real country house, commissioned Philibert Delorme to draw up plans for a New Château on the edge of the plateau. The construction work was completed under Henri IV. The château became extremely famous on account of its fantastic location and the terraces built along the slopes overlooking the river Seine. The area beneath the foundation arches has been arranged into artificial grottoes where hydraulically-propelled automatons re-enact mythological scenes: Orpheus playing the viola with a bow, Neptune's chariot in full motion, etc. Henri IV was a mischievous man: he installed a system whereby fountains of water would spring out from all places at the end of the show, drenching the king's guests. This wonderful mechanism was the work of the Francine, a family of Italian engineers, to whom Louis XIV later entrusted the waterworks of Versailles.

Chronology of court events. – The court occupied both the Old Castle and the New Château. They would use them as a palatial residence, or a safe retreat when riots broke out in Paris.

ST-GERMAIN-EN-LAYE★★

Henri II, Charles IX and Louis XIV were all born at St-Germain. Louis XIII died there. Mary Queen of Scots, lived there between the ages of 6 and 16. In 1558, she married the Dauphin François, aged only 15. She was crowned Queen of France the following year. Howerer her husband died after a year and she was forced to return to Scotland, where her tragic destiny led her to die on the scaffold.

Mansart's improvements. – Louis XIV – who was born, christened and brought up at St-Germain – grew fond of the château. As a king, he paid frequent visits to the estate. The apartments of the Old Castle had become too cramped for Louis' liking and he commissioned **Jules Hardouin-Mansart** to build five large pavilions as a replacement for the five corner turrets adjoining the outer walls. Le Nôtre conceived the plans for the park, the terrace, and in 1665 the grounds were replanted with five and a half million shrubs. In 1682, the court moved from St-Germain to Versailles. In 1689, the deposed King of Great Britain James II came to stay at the Old Castle, where he died in great financial straits, in the odour of sanctity (funeral monument in St-Germain Church, facing the château).
The governor of the château, the Maréchal Louis de Noailles (1713-1793) subsequently became the important figure at St-Germain. His estate was carved up and acquired the reputation of being the most fashionable residential area in town.

Final developments. – In 1776, the badly dilapidated New Château was ceded to the comte d'Artois by his brother Louis XVI. The future king Charles X had the building dismantled, except for the Henri IV pavilion on the terrace and the Sully Pavilion, located near Le Pecq. He originally intended to reconstruct the building according to new plans. However he dropped the work at St-Germain when he purchased the château at Maisons *(p 108)*. The remains, together with the park, were sold during the Revolution. The Old Castle was stripped of its funiture. Under Napoleon I, it was the seat of a cavalry college, under Louis-Philippe, it housed a military penitentiary and in 1855 it was evacuated by Napoleon III. It was then entirely restored under the guidance of the architect Millet, succeeded by Daumet.
In 1867, Napoleon III inaugurated the National Museum of French Antiquities which he had set up on the premises. The signing of the 1919 peace treaty with Austria took place in the château at St-Germain.

ST-GERMAIN-EN-LAYE

Bonnenfant (R. A.) ..... **AZ** 3
Marché-Neuf (Pl. du) .. **AZ** 17
Pain (R. au) .... **AZ** 20
Paris (R. de) .... **AZ**
Poissy (R. de) .... **AZ** 22
Vieux-Marché (R. du) . **AZ** 33

Alain (Pl. Jéhan) .... **AY** 2
Coches (R. des) .... **AZ** 4
Denis (R. M.) .... **AZ** 5
Detaille (Pl.) .... **AY** 6
Gaulle (Pl. Ch. de) ...... **BZ** 7
Giraud-Teulon (R.) ..... **BZ** 9
Grande-Fontaine (R.) .. **AZ** 10
Gréban (R. R.) .... **AZ** 12
Lattre-de-T. (Av. Mar. de) **BZ** 13
Loges (Av. des) .... **AY** 14
Lyautey (R. Mar.) .... **BZ** 15
Malraux (Pl. A.) .... **BZ** 16
Mareil (Pl.) .... **AZ** 19
Pologne (R. de) .... **AY** 23
Pontoise (R. de) .... **AY** 25
St-Louis (R.) .... **BZ** 26
Victoire (Pl. de la) .... **AY** 30
Vieil-Abreuvoir (R. du). **ABZ** 32

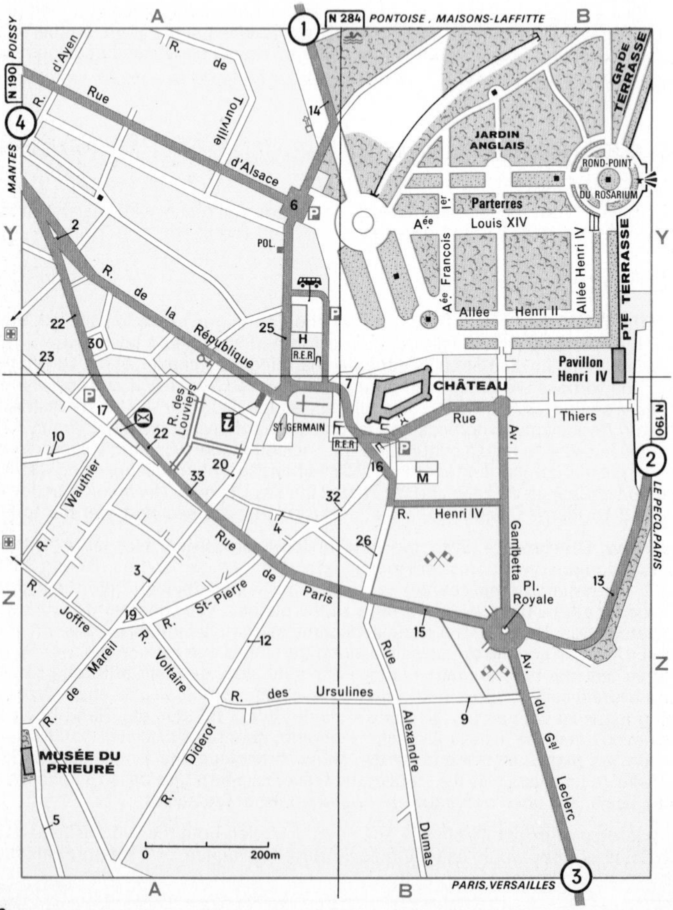

THE CHÂTEAU AND ITS NEIGHBOURHOOD

time: 3 1/2 hours

The most striking way to approach the château is to arrive from the north, along Route des Loges. The tour starts from the square on which the château stands (Place Charles-de-Gaulle).
The express RER line which stops at St-Germain has replaced the famous railway track between Paris and St-Germain: its inauguration between Le Pecq and the French capital on 26 August 1837 was an unprecedented landmark in the history of French railway services.

★ **Château** (BZ). – It was the shape of an imperfect pentagone. The surrounding moats were once filled with water. The feudal foundations of the château feature a covered watchpath and a series of machicolations restored by Daumet. The roof was an original addition: it is laid out as a terrace, fringed by vases and a balustrade and dominated by tall chimmeys. On the northern end of the façade facing Place Charles-de-Gaulle stands the quadrilateral keep built by Charles V, to which a bell tower was added under François I.
While senior officers were housed on the ground floor, the mezzanine apartments were occupied by princes of the blood, ladies of honour, favourites and ministers, namely Mazarin, Colbert and Louvois. The royal suites were situated on the first floor: the bedroom belonging to the king and the dauphin was set up in the wing that gave onto the parterre, the queen's suite overlooked Paris and the children's rooms were in the pavilion which now faces Rue Thiers. Under Henri IV, twelve of the fourteen royal infants, born to four different mothers, would romp noisily in these quarters.

★★ **National Museum of Antiquities (Musée des Antiquités Nationales).** – Contains Ⓥ many rare archaeological exhibits which constitute a precious testimony to France's early history, ranging from the first signs of man's existence (Palaeolithic Age) to the Middle Ages.

Ground floor. – A lifesize facsimile of the famous Bull's Hall in the caves of Lascaux evokes rupestrian art in Palaeolithic times. The atmosphere of the cave is faithfully rendered by means of a photographic process. This reconstitution enables visitors to admire one of the most stupendous compositions of the prehistoric sanctuary of the Vézère Valley. It presents the concepts of confrontation and coupling between animals, expressed by a complex form of symbolism. In addition to the celebrated bulls, one may see stags, horses and a strange beast caled the "unicorn" on account of its leonine muzzle and two protruding horns.

Mezzanine (Prehistory and Protohistory). – The Palaeolithic or early Stone Age goes back one million years before our era.
The glass cabinets on the right provide general information on materials such as stone (silex), quartz, bone and horn belonging to the cervidae species. It also enlightens the visitor on the tool making techniques of that period. Note too the reproduction of two traces proving the existence of man in prehistoric times: prints of hands at Gargas (photography), prints of footsteps in the cave at Aldène (mould).
The left-hand cabinets displaying the results of the excavations are in chronological order. The major works of art dating from the Palaeolithic Age are unusually small: **Lady of Brassempouy** (height: 3.6cm – 1.44in), the oldest human face to date (*c* 20000 BC), a bison licking itself (Magdalenian – *c* 16 000 BC), the Bruniquel baton in the shape of a jumping horse (*c* 13 000 BC), the Mas-d'Azil head of a neighing horse (*c* 10 000 BC) etc.

Lady of Brassempouy
from the National Museum of Antiquities
in St-Germain-en-Laye

During the Neolithic Age, which originated in the Near-East (8 000 BC), man discovered farming and cattle rearing, community life in huts and the use of ceramics. He produced arms and tools by polishing very hard stones (jadeite).
The discovery of an alloy combining copper and tin led to the early stages of metallurgy (Bronze Age). Gold too was widely used and the museum displays several objects and pieces of jewellery made in solid gold or sheets of beaten gold. Note the numerous weapons (daggers, axes with curved blades) and the metal necklaces and other decorative objects (open bracelets) which give these particular collections the sparkle that characterised some of the so-called "primitive" cilivisations of the modern world. The large iron sword is typical of the princely burial sites dating from the early Iron Age (the period known as Hallstatt). It was found together with clasps, ceramics, pieces of furniture (Magny-Lambert cist), horses' harnessing and even four-wheel funeral carriages.
The La Tene period that followed benefited from the contributions made by foreign civilisations and especially the increasingly important trade relations with the Mediterranean world. Most of the objects exhibited here come from excavation sites situated in Champagne and Burgundy (finery, vases). Gallic tribes still buried funeral chariots in their tombs, worked gold (jewellery) and coins. But the fall of Alésia (52 BC) put an end to their own culture.

First Floor (Gallo-Roman and Merovingian Antiquities). – The lengthy period of Roman peace *(Pax Romana),* the indulgence of the victors and the deeply-rooted religious feeling for indigenous gods gave rise to a flourishing industry of mythological and funeral sculpture (until then the Celts has shown little interest in statuary art). Note the numerous collection of funeral slabs.
Ceramic pieces played an important role in domestic life: one of the cabinets offers a fairly comprehensive presentation of "sigillated" ceramics, decorated with stamped motifs, made in workshops at Lezoux, La Graufesenque, Banassac, etc. (1-4C AD). Little is known about the following period (3-8C AD), whose heritage consists mostly of Merovingian burial places rich in arms – swords with damascene blades – and items of finery: heavy flat buckles for belts, S-shaped clasps, etc.
The large ballroom in the château – also called the Mars Hall (Salle de Mars) – is a beautiful vaulted room with ornate stone ribbing and a fireplace bearing François I's emblem the salamander. It is dedicated to comparative archaeology. A superb selection of objects from all five continents makes it possible to draw parallels between techniques and life styles belonging to geographically distant civilisations and to compare their evolution in time.
The exhibition cabinets are carefully arranged according to two thematic approaches: the transition from one continent to another can be followed by studying the cabinets lengthwise, while the items placed along the width of the room testify to the chronological evolution of technology.
Observe the splendid Egyptian collections dating from pre-Dynastic times, a set of bronze sculptures from Kodan and Armenian Talysh (Asia), **Mérida's Chariot** (6C BC), a masterpiece of Iberian making. The impressive ethnographical exhibits from Oceania feature a magnificent wooden statue depicting the god Rao (Gambier Islands).

Return to the ground floor by the back stairs.
At the end of the tour, enter the inner courtyard – note the ornamentation of the upper balustrade, François I's salamander and first initial F – to get a good view of the chapel.

★ **Ste-Chapelle.** – Built on the orders of St Louis between 1230 and 1238, i.e. about ten years before the Sainte Chapelle in Paris. It is believed that these two churches were the work of the same architect Pierre de Montreuil. However, the clerestory windows in St-Germain do not feature the superb set of stained glass that adorns the Parisian sanctuary. The beautiful rose window on the façade has been screened by a series of subsequent additions.
The bosses present carved figures thought to represent St Louis, his mother Blanche of Castile, his wife and other close relations. They are probably the most ancient images one has of French royalty.

Parterres (BY). – Enter the gardens through the gate on Place Charles-de-Gaulle. Skirt the château. Built into the façade is the loggia opening onto the inner staircase of honour. The moat contains megalithic monuments which have been restored and replicas of Roman statues.
The east esplanade – presently the seat of a blockhouse – was the scene of the very last judicial duel during which one invoked the judgement of God. It opposed Jarnac and La Châtaigneraie, and was attended by Henri II, accompanied by his retinue of courtiers. La Châtaigneraie, one of the finest swordsmen in Europe, was confident about the outcome of the battle. But Jarnac had learnt a new trick: he severed the left hamstring of his adversary, who collapsed and slowly passed away.

Henri IV Pavilion (Pavillon Henri-IV) (BY). – It was built on the very edge of the escarpment. The brick pavilion crowned by a dome, together with the **Sully Pavilion** set lower down on Le Pecq hillside, is all that remains of the New Château. It contains the Louis XIII oratory where Louis XIV was baptised on 5 September 1638, the day of his birth.
The hôtel which opened in this historic building in 1836 became an important meeting-place for 19C writers, artists and politicians. Alexandre Dumas wrote *The Three Musketeers* and *The Count of Monte Cristo* while he was staying here, Offenbach composed *The Drum Major's Daughter* and Léo Delibes produced the ballet *Sylvia.* The statesman and president Thiers died here in 1877.

★★ **Terrace** (BY). – The Small Terrace starts at the hôtel and extends until the Rosarium roundabout. There, a worn T.C.F. viewing table is a past reminder of the lands stretching towards the western suburbs of Paris.
The Grand Terrace extends beyond the roundabout. It is one of Le Nôtre's finest accomplishments and was completed in 1673 after four years of large-scale construction work. Lined with stately lime trees, it is 2 400m – 8 000ft long and features among the most famous promenades around Paris.
The vista from the terrace being the same all the way along, visitors pressed for time may return to their car through the lovely **landscape garden★**.

ADDITIONAL SIGHT

★ **Priory Museum** (AZ). – The Priory was founded in 1678 by Mme de Montespan ⓥ and was originally designed as a royal hospital. In 1914 it became the property of the painter **Maurice Denis** (1870-1943), who moved there with his numerous relations and frequently entertained his friends of the Nabi movement *(p 33).*
The rooms are former dorters joined by stately staircases featuring flattened groined vaulting.
The museum explains the origins of the Nabi group – founded by Paul Sérusier in 1888 – and illustrates their passion for various forms of pictorial and decorative expression: painting, posters, stained glass, etc.

The works assembled in the priory testify to the considerable influence the symbolic movement – the "search for the invisible" – had over the arts world at large: literature, decorative arts, sculpture, painting and music. The Pont-Aven School is represented by Gauguin, Émile Bernard, Filiger, Maufra and the Nabi group by Sérusier, Ranson, Bonnard, Vuillard, Maurice Denis and Verkade. The museum also displays works by Toulouse-Lautrec, Mandrian, Lalique, etc. The ground floor houses a sculpture by Maillol called *Homage to Debussy.*

Self-portrait by Maurice Denis,
Priory Museum in St-Germain-en-Laye

Chapel (Chapelle). – It was entirely decorated by Maurice Denis between 1915 and 1925: stained glass, frescoes, liturgical furnishings,...

Studio (Atelier). – Maurice Denis had this studio built by his friend Auguste Perret in 1912 when he was working on the decoration for the ceiling of the Théâtre des Champs-Élysées, an undertaking which required a vast amount of space. Perret, Bourdelle and Maurice Denis worked on the project together.

Park. – A series of terraced flower beds, are pleasantly dotted with statues by Antoine Bourdelle. The park offers a charming vista of the priory façade and its elegant severity.

ST-GERMAIN Forest

Michelin map 101 folds, 2, 3 and 12

Circled by one of the Seine's loops, St-Germain Forest was once part of the Forest of Laye. Its northern boundaries have gradually shrunk owing to the sewage plants of the City of Paris and the converging tracks of Achères railway station: its total area is presently estimated at 3 500ha – 8 700 acres.
The forest has retained most of its old-fashioned atmosphre thanks to the hunting lodges, wayside crosses, old gates and forest roundabouts visitors may come across on their walks.
The forest is planted with clusters of oaks, as well as beeches and hornbeams, while the poorer soil in the northern massif bears groves of conifers. The flat ground, either stony or sandy, is ideal for rambling, even in bad weather: 120km – 74 miles of footpaths and 60km – 37 miles of riding lanes have been laid out in the wood. Recreational areas remain at the disposal of tourists at Corra Pond (15ha – 38 acres), and in the forest parks of Charmeraie, Charmille (near Poissy) and Champ-Millet (next to Arches).

ST-JEAN-DE-BEAUREGARD — Pop 237

Michelin map 101 fold 33

Located 20km – 12 miles south of Versailles, this locality became a parish in the 12C. One third of its area is occupied by the forest.

ⓥ **Château.** – In 1610, François Dupoux, a lawyer belonging to the court council who enjoyed the protection of Concini, acquired the former seigniory at Montfaucon, perched on a wooded hillside dominating the Salmouille Valley. He gave orders to build the château, starting with the two highest wings. The central block and the two end pavilions were finished under Louis XIV. The two well-balanced façades of classical inspiration are continued by a series of fine outhouses.
The east front looks onto an attractive French-style formal garden while the west offers a perspective stretching over a distance of 2km – 1 mile. The grounds include a 2ha – 2.5 acre vegetable garden and present a dovecote with a total of 4000 pigeon-holes.
The interior of the château features a number of reception rooms furnished with 18C pieces, notably a splendid library containing a collection of literary and historical works.

★ ST-LEU-D'ESSERENT — Pop 4505

Michelin map 196 north of folds 7 and 8

The Archbishop of Sens, St Leu, who died in 623, gave his name to several French localities. St-Leu-d'Esserent, located on the banks of the Oise river, boasts a magnificent church which the philosopher and historian, Ernest Renan once compared to a Greek temple on account of its pure, harmonious lines.

★CHURCH *time: 1/2 hour*

Leave Chantilly and proceed towards St-Leu along the D 44. The bridge over the Oise affords the best **general view** of the church from a distance. The lovely stone was quarried from the nearby quarries and also used for the construction of many other churches and cathedrals as well as the palace at Versailles.
The Germans converted these quarries into workshops for their V-1 missiles. As a result, the town was consistently bombed and the church wrecked in 1944.

Exterior. – The façade, significantly restored after the 19C – in particular the sculpted furnishings – is separate from the nave. It forms a Romanesque block (first half of the 12C), presenting a porch and, on the upper level, a gallery, each consisting of three bays. The bell tower and its stone spire were to be balanced by a north tower: note the two lines of toothings on the left. Four centuries later, the west front gable above the nave, set back slightly, was given a Flamboyant Gothic rose window.

Skirt the right side of the church, then the left side, walking past the entrance to the former priory.

The chancel is dominated by two square towers with saddle-back roofs. It is surrounded by the ambulatory and its five radiating chapels. This architectural structure dates back to the second half of the 12C. The flying buttresses were added to consolidate the buttresses which supported the transept crossing.

★**Interior.** – The nave offers a superb perspective. It is filled with a golden light filtering through the new stained glass (1960). The choir and the first two bays of the nave – square bay with four main arches and sexpartite bay *(see p 24)* – were built in the Romanesque style (12C), while the rest of the nave is 13C.
Originally, the chancel was to be fitted with galleries, as is customary with Romanesque buildings. However in the 13C, when the flying buttresses were put in to support the east end, the architects realised that the galleries were no longer necessary and they replaced them by a single triforium. They decided to apply this principle to the whole building.

Before returning to the car, take a stroll to the nearby cemetery.

View of the upper part of the church.

ST-MANDÉ

Pop 18 860

Michelin map 101 fold 26 – Michelin plan 24

This suburb, once a small, quiet town borders the Bois de Vincennes.

City Transport Museum (Musée des Transports Urbains). – *60, Avenue Ste-Marie.* An old bus depot houses around one hundred vehicles formerly used for city transport in France from the middle of the 19C onwards: horse-drawn omnibus, tramways propelled by compressed air or electricity, trolleybuses and buses (the first Paris bus dates back to 1906). An audio-visual presentation and a series of early films explain the history of city transport.

ST-QUENTIN-EN-YVELINES

Michelin map 101 fold 21 and 196 folds 28 and 29

The new town of St-Quentin-en-Yvelines covers an area stretching southwest of Versailles to the northern side of the Chevreuse Valley. It runs parallel with the road from Paris to Chartres and with the N 10.
This area already showed a high level of industrial activity and a complex network of major roads, motorways and railway lines when a number of large housing estates were set up around Trappes.
The new districts planned for 25 000 to 30 000 inhabitants have been designed along new town-planning lines catering simultaneously for both housing and priority public amenities. The **Seven Ponds' Centre** (Centre des Sept-Mares) at Élancourt is characteristic of these new urban cores, with its pedestrian shopping street, its administrative building incorporating public services and private offices, its library, marked by a brick belfry, its oecumenical religious centre and its secondary school.
Unlike most other new towns St-Quentin-en-Yvelines left the building of its town centre until last. The town centre has developed around the station at St-Quentin-en-Yvelines. It is expected to be able to house a further 100 000 inhabitants.
Montigny-le-Bretonneux features La Sourderie, a modern building resting on piles, designed by the Catalan architect Ricardo Bofill.

SIGHTS

St-Quentin Pond (Étang de St-Quentin). – *The car parks may be reached by the road to Dreux (N 12).* The grounds around this pond have been turned into a public **leisure centre** (600ha – 1 500 acres) *(see the chapter Practical Information at the end of the guide).* The "pond-park" and its 1 750m^2 (0.66 acre) swimming-pool with artificial waves is one of the most popular outdoor leisure parks in the Paris region.

Villedieu Commandery (Commanderie de la Villedieu). – This former Templars' commandery (1180) was converted into a farmhouse, and then into an arts centre in 1978. The main buildings – known as Bièvre and Chevreuse – house several workshops for sculptors and engravers, a number of assembly rooms and a restaurant. The chapel and the Guards' Pavilion frequently host temporary exhibitions and concerts.

★ ST-SULPICE-DE-FAVIÈRES Pop 293

Michelin map 196 fold 42 – 10km – 6 miles southwest of Arpajon

The village is set back a little from the Renarde Valley. It presents a Gothic church with an unusually high chancel. It was built in honour of St Sulpice, a senior court chaplain in Merovingian times, who was made Bishop of Bourges and died in 647. The legend has it that he resuscitated a child who had drowned in the Renarde. From then on, Favières became a noted place of pilgrimage.

★ **Church (Église).** – *Time: 1/2 hour.* The construction of the present building started in 1260 and lasted for 60 years.
The doorway is badly mutilated, but the tympanum still bears a representation of the Last Judgment. Walk round the church. The exterior combines Gothic lightness (high altar) with a more compact style of architecture, exemplified by the presbytery which has been incorporated into the building. The bell tower is barely higher than the roof level.

Interior. – The first four bays in the nave are crowned by wooden barrel vaulting. The last two bays feature pointed vaulting, as does the chancel. An ornamental arcade runs round the interior of the church, at the base of the walls. Up above lies a wall passage which crosses over the flying buttresses. On the west wall, the frail decoration of the two 14C gables marks the transition to Flamboyant architecture. The huge, lofty choir is elegant in the extreme and amply illuminated.
Admire the two splendid rose windows from the 13C, placed above the high altar and at the end of the south aisle. The former is a collection of unrelated fragments, while the latter tells the story of the Virgin, to be read from left to right and from bottom to top (explanations on a nearby pillar).
The 16C stalls feature armrests carved into humorous scenes. At the far end of the north aisle, a 17C wooden retable decorated with unsophisticated scenes shows St Sulpice healing the King Clotaire II.
The door opening onto the north aisle leads down to the **Chapel of Miracles** (Chapelle des Miracles), the remains of a 12C church which houses the reliquary-bust of St Sulpice. A series of excavations revealed a well which could be the "miraculous spring" mentioned in regional lore.

★ ST-VRAIN Wildlife Park

Michelin map 196 north of fold 43

Ⓥ This 130ha – 325 acre area of woodland is now a reserve for wild animals. It features several ponds and canals supplied by the waters of the river Juine.

Car Tour. – *Time: 3/4 hour. Observe safety instructions.*
The "car safari" takes visitors past the various enclosures of the antelopes, lions, bears, tigers, wolves, giraffes, elephants, monkeys, rhinoceroses, buffaloes, etc. The "boat safari" sails past the islands alive with tropical birds, chimpanzees, gibbons and hippopotamuses. A raised single-track train ride provides an excellent view of the whole park.
One of the most successful attractions is the Prehistoric Park, in which a collection of lifesize casts evokes some of the species that lived during the Tertiary and Quaternary Eras, as well as prehistoric man.

STE-GENEVIÈVE-DES-BOIS Pop 30 443

Michelin map 101 fold 35

Southeast of Ste-Geneviève-des-Bois – a locality which numbered only 700 inhabitants in 1921 – lie the Orthodox Church and the Russian Cemetery, bathed in an atmosphere of quiet repose. They were both founded in 1927, when an English benefactress acquired a local château. She donated it to a Russian princess who took charge of the elderly émigrés badly shaken by their long exile across Europe. Many were buried in the village cemetery, where the shaded groves of pine trees and silver birches evoke the distant lands of Russia.
Surrounded by a fenced-in garden, the small **church** presents a dome painted in blue tones. It was consecrated in 1939. The building is fronted by a campanile with a set of six bells. From the outside one can see the crypt, which houses the mortal remains of the architect and several ecclesiastical figures.

Cemetery (Cimetière). – A number of famous Russian personalities are buried here: priests, ballet stars, scientists, artists and writers. The area facing the church is charming and resembles a miniature garden: most of the headstones are decorated with three-branch Russian Orthodox crosses featuring icons. Some are marked by a night light. Several little garden seats are dotted around the grounds, inviting visitors and mourners to rest and pray.

★★ SCEAUX

Pop 18 625

Michelin map 101 fold 25 – Michelin plan 22

In 1670, Louis XIV's building adviser **Colbert** commissioned Claude Perrault, Le Brun, Girardon and Coysevox to build a superb residence in Sceaux. The two groups of sculptures flanking the entrance pavilion were executed by Coysevox: the dog and the unicorn, representing loyalty and honesty, were Colbert's favourite emblems. The grounds were placed in the hands of Le Nôtre, who succeeded admirably in spite of the rough, uneven terrain. The canal, cascades and fountains were supplied by the waters diverted from the hillsides of Plessis-Robinson. The château was inaugurated in 1677 at a lavish reception attended by the Sun King in person: one of the many attractions that night was the performance of Jean Racine's famous tragedy *Phaedra*.

In 1685 Colbert's son Seignelay entertained Louis XIV and Mme de Maintenon at the château, an occasion for which Racine and Lulli composed their *Ode to Sceaux*.

Sceaux in the hands of the duc de Maine. – In 1700 the estate became the property of the duc de Maine, the legitimated son of Louis XIV and Mme de Montespan. The king would often come to stay with his favourite son.

The duchesse du Maine, the Great Condé's granddaughter, surrounded herself with a numerous court of brilliant personalities. She entertained on a truly large scale, providing opera, ballet, comedy and tragedy to her many guests. The dazzling "Nights of Sceaux", enhanced by superb displays of fireworks and twinkling lights, were the talk of all Paris and Versailles.

On the eve of the Revolution, the estate of Sceaux belonged to the duc de Penthièvre, the duc de Maine's nephew, for whom the fabulist Florian acted as librarian. The domain was confiscated, and subsequently sold to a tradesman who had the château razed to the ground and the park made into arable land.

Sceaux today. – In 1856 the duc de Trévise, who inherited the estate through his wife's family, built the château that stands today. The grounds gradually slipped into a state of neglect, providing the original setting for Alain Fournier's novel *Le Grand Meaulnes*. In 1923 the château was bought by the Seine *département*, who undertook to restore both the building and its park. The Ile-de-France Museum was installed in the premises in 1936.

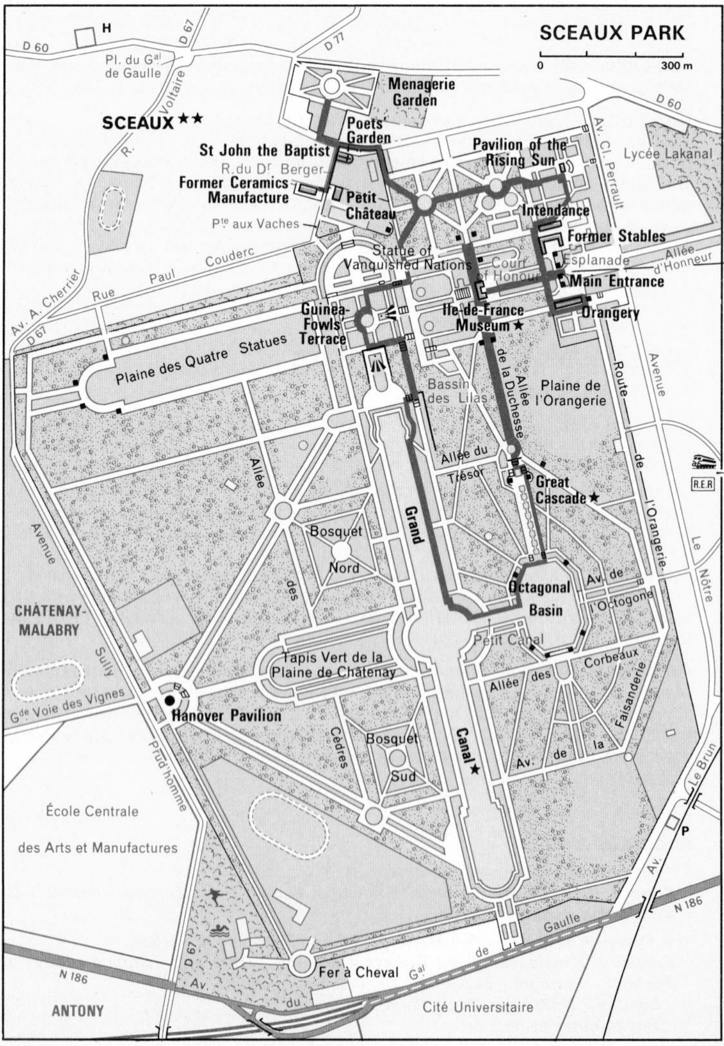

Sceaux Park

★★ PARK

ⓥ **Entrance of Honour.** – Designed for Colbert, the two entrance pavilions with sculpted pediments are flanked by two small lodges surmounted by Coysevox's groups of statues.

ⓥ **Orangery (Orangerie).** – This 60m – 196ft long conservatory was designed by Jules Hardouin-Mansart in 1685. It is prettily decorated with a series of carved pediments. In summer it was used as the ballroom – note the interior decoration – and in winter it sheltered the 300 orange trees from Sceaux Park.
Today the Orangery is the venue for conferences, exhibitions and concerts *(see the table of Principal Festivals at the end of the guide).*

★ **Ile-de-France Museum (Musée de l'Ile-de-France).** – It lies in the former château ⓥ belonging to the duc de Trévise. Its collections of paintings, watercolours, drawings, miniature models, ceramics and figures in local costume present visitors with a history of Ile-de-France, its attractive landscapes, its many royal palaces and stately mansions, its local crafts and the many unknown aspects of the area around Paris. Note the magnificent inlaid parquet flooring from the 19C, two Gallo-Roman treasure-troves consisting of numerous coins discovered in the Val-de-Marne, local earthenware and porcelain (Sèvres, Sceaux, St-Cloud, Creil and Vincennes), a curious collection of ornamental glass objects (vases) made in St-Denis, printed calico, regional costumes and trappings and the panelling from Mlle Guimard's private boudoir at Pantin. A display of wainscoting, miniature models and portraits (Van Loo, F. de Troy, Nattier) tells the story of Sceaux and the major châteaux of Ile-de-France.
The painters who were strongly inspired by the landscapes around the French capital are largely represented at the museum (Hubert Robert, Camille Corot, Lebourg, Maurice Utrillo, Dunoyer de Segonzac and Fautrier).
ⓥ The **Reference Library** (Centre de Documentation) houses several million written documents and illustrations of the Ile-de-France area.
Close to the library stands a beautiful 17C bronze composition by Desjardins, representing the **Vanquished Nations★**, Spain, Holland, Prussia and Austria. It was originally set up on Place des Victoires in Paris in honour of Louis XIV *(see the Michelin Green Guide Paris).*

★ **Great Cascade (Grandes Cascades).** – They are approached by Allée de la Duchesse. The waters spring out of carved masks by Rodin, and tumble down a series of ten terraces before flowing into the Octagonal Basin. The sight of these various fountains and cascades is spectacular indeed, especially when all the fountains are ⓥ playing during the **Grandes Eaux★**. This perspective is continued by a green carpet of lawn the Tapis Vert.

Octagonal Basin (Octogone). – It has kept its original design by Le Nôtre. Of ample proportions, circled by a row of plane trees, it exudes a gentle, peaceful atmosphere. The water sprays reach 10m – 32ft high.

ⓥ **Hanover Pavilion (Pavillon de Hanovre).** – It was built by the architect Chevotet in 1760 and moved from the Boulevard des Italiens in Paris to the Château of Sceaux in 1930. The pavilion provides the focal point for the Petit Canal.

★ **Grand Canal.** – It is as long as the Petit Canal at Versailles (1 030m – 3 380ft) and flanked by a double row of Lombardy poplars.

Guinea-Fowls' Terrace (Terrasse des Pintades). – From the canal, two ramps lead up to a terrace which is the starting-point for the park's two sweeping perspectives: one extends towards the château while the other follows the axis of the Grand Canal.

ⓥ **Petit Château.** – An elegant early 17C addition commissioned by Colbert. The children of the duchesse du Maine were brought up in this pavilion.

Pavilion of the Rising Sun (Pavillon de l'Aurore). – This charming pavilion crowned by a cupola is the work of Claude Perrault. It is approached by a series of staircases featuring dainty, neatly-arranged balusters. The interior decoration forms a harmonious ensemble: wainscoting, flooring, ceilings and a superb cupola by Le Brun, reproducing the delicate shades of sunrise.
It was here that Colbert received the Académie Française in 1677. For this momentous occasion, the poet Quinault composed a poem of 900 verses on the subject of Le Brun's fresco. He read it out to the members of that prestigious assembly, who spent most of the evening craning their necks towards the ceiling to follow Quinault's detailed explanations. The audio-visual presentation in the basement gives visitors a history of the estate and points out the interesting sights in the park.

Intendance. – A splendid Louis XVI building, formerly the residence of the intendant of Sceaux.

Former Stables (Anciennes Écuries). – They were built under Colbert, after studies made by Le Pautre. Facing the stables stands a horse-pond *(visible from the esplanade).*

TOWN SIGHTS

Poets' Garden (Jardin des Félibres). – Florian, the celebrated fabulist from the Cévennes, died in 1794 and was buried at Sceaux. In the 19C, this garden became a place of pilgrimage for Provençal poets and writers – known locally as *Félibres* – who would come and pay their respects once a year (on a Sunday in June). The garden presents several busts of Provençal poets, including one of Frédéric Mistral.

St John the Baptist Church (Église St-Jean-Baptiste). – The church was rebuilt in the 16C, and was given a façade and a spire under Louis-Philippe. The 17C *Baptism of Christ* by Tuby that stands behind the high altar was taken from the chapel of the former château. The altar in the north aisle is adorned by a medallion of the Virgin, executed by Coysevox (18C).

Menagerie Garden (Jardin de la Ménagerie). – This menagerie used to belong to the duchesse du Maine and enshrines the remains of her canaries – beneath the columns – and her favourite cat – in a funeral urn. It was used to host popular dances under the Revolution: the famous *Bal de Sceaux,* attended by the *Muscadins* and the *Merveilleuses,* was very much in vogue at the time and gave its name to one of Honoré de Balzac's novels. Subsequently it went out of fashion and was replaced by dancing at Robinson.

Former Ceramics Manufacture (Ancienne manufacture de céramique). – It was founded by the duchesse du Maine and lies at the corner of Rue des Imbergères. The ceramics production is on display at the Ile-de-France Museum.

SÉNART Forest

Michelin map 101 folds 37 and 38

This 3 000ha – 7 500 acre wood covers the clayey plateau extending between the rivers Seine and Yerres. Despite a complex drainage system, the soil is known to be damp and there remain a good few ponds and marshes. The oak coppices with standards alternate with pine trees, and with moors featuring heather and silver birches.
The groves of Sénart Forest are a fairly popular location for film productions. They also belong to Ile-de-France's cultural heritage: Eugène Delacroix and Alphonse Daudet stayed in the nearby locality of Champrosay, the famous 19C photographer, illustrator and caricaturist Nadar lived at the Ermitage.

The game of destiny. – In the 18C, a certain Le Normant owned a château in Étiolles, a small village south of the forest. His ambitious wife Jeanne-Antoinette Poisson resolved to find favour with Versailles.
At the age of 9, Jeanne-Antoinette consulted a fortune-teller, who predicted that she would be loved by the king. She therefore planned a course of action in order that this prophecy might be fulfilled. Louis XV would often go hunting in the vicinity of Sénart Forest. Mme d'Étiolles, sporting a bright pink frock and travelling in an elegant blue carriage, arranged a chance meeting with the king, who was seduced by her lively capricious manners. He finally succumbed to her charm at a fancy dress ball held in the town hall. Le Normant was asked to separate from his wife who later became the marquise de Pompadour, a favour for which he was handsomely rewarded.

SIGHTS AND FACILITIES

Most of these have developed around the Pyramide de Brunoy roundabout, which is the only authorised means of access off the N 6: reception area, cycling path (going past Cormier junction), nature trail near Duck Pond and the pheasantry.

Pheasantry (Faisanderie). – This pavilion was built by Chalgrin in 1778 and presently houses an audio-visual presentation on the subject of silviculture.
The 8ha – 20 acre grounds have been refurbished to accommodate the gigantic sculptures which are part of an outdoor exhibition dedicated to contemporary artists.

★★ SENLIS   Pop 15 280

Michelin map 56 fold 11 – Local map p 100

Adding to the romantic charm of Senlis are its picturesque paved streets, its past history of Frankish rulers, enterprising bishops and abbots, the rich cornfields of Valois and the wooded horizons.

The election of Hugh Capet. – The conquerors of Senlis incorporated a massive stronghold into the first Gallo-Roman ramparts of the town. The kings belonging to the first two Frankish dynasties would often take up residence here, lured by the game in the nearby forests.
The Carolingian line died out when Louis V suffered a fatal hunting accident. In 987, the Archbishop of Reims called a meeting at Senlis Castle, at which he and the local lords decided that Hugh Capet – the Duc des Francs – would be the next king. Senlis went out of fashion as a royal place of residence and was gradually replaced by Compiègne and Fontainebleau. The last French ruler to have stayed at the castle was Henri IV.

OLD TOWN *time: 1 hour*

Ⓥ **Royal Gardens (Jardin du Roy).** – They occupy the former moat of the Gallo-Roman ramparts. The longest diameter is 312m – 1024ft across and the shortest 242m – 794ft. Twenty-eight towers 7m – 23ft high and 4m – 14ft wide defended the city walls. Today there remain a total of 16: some are still intact, others are badly mutilated.
There is a lovely **view★** of the ramparts and the towers, the cathedral and the scattered buildings that once formed the castle.

Return to Rue de Villevert and proceed towards Place du Parvis.

★ **Place du Parvis.** – A quaint little country square lying at the foot of the cathedral.

★★ **Notre-Dame Cathedral (Cathédrale Notre-Dame).** – Its construction was started in 1153 – 16 years after St-Denis and 10 years before Notre-Dame in Paris – but progressed at a slow pace owing to insufficient funds. The cathedral was consecrated in 1191. Towards the year 1240, a transept which had not originally been planned and a spire were added.
The building was struck by lightning in June 1504. As a result, the timbering and the transept walls needed to be rebuilt. A set of new side aisles were also added, giving the cathedral its present appearance. Initially, the two towers were identical. It was only towards the mid-13C that the right tower was crowned with the magnificent **spire★★** *(illustration p 23)* whose distinctive silhouette was to have such a strong influence over religious architecture in the Valois area *(p 170)*. The spire reaches a height of 78m – 256ft.
The **main doorway★★** – dedicated to the Virgin celebrating her Assumption into heaven – is strongly reminiscent of the doorways at Chartres, Notre-Dame in Paris, Amiens and Reims. The lintel features two famous low reliefs representing the Dormition of the Virgin Mary and the Assumption. The realism and freedom of expression of the sculpture were unusual for the 12C: note the touching swiftness with which the angels raise Mary off the ground and remove her to the celestial skies.
The embrasures are adorned with eight figures from the Old Testament, depicted in a lively manner. The heads were smashed during the Revolution and remodelled in the 19C. On the left, we see Abraham about to sacrifice his son Isaac, while an angel holds the sword in an attempt to stop him. The statues rest on square bases presenting a series of lighthearted panels sculpted into the labours of the months. The calendar starts with January, placed on the right-hand side near the door.

South front. – Executed by Pierre Chambiges in the 16C, the **south transept★★** contrasts sharply with the west front. It is interesting to follow the evolution of Gothic architecture from the austere 12C to the 16C, when late Flamboyant already showed signs of Renaissance influence, revealed during the Italian wars. The clerestory and its huge Flamboyant windows were also completed in the 16C.
The lower part of the east end, dating from the 12C, has remained intact, as have the radiating chapels. The axial chapel was replaced by a larger chapel in the 19C. As in Notre-Dame in Paris, the galleries – dating from Romanesque times – support the nave and the choir with the help of Gothic flying buttresses.

Interior. – Enter through the south doorway. The church interior is 70m – 230ft long, 9.2m – 30ft wide and measures 24m – 79ft to the keystone. Above the organs, the 12C vaulting which escaped the ravages of the fire in 1504 marks the original height of the church: 17m – 56ft. The nave and the chancel, comparatively narrow in spite of their height, are graced with an airy lightness. The triforium gal-

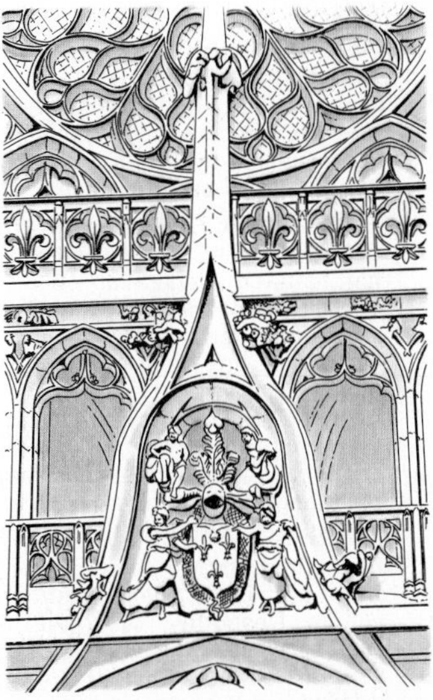

South transept, Senlis Cathedral

SENLIS

Halle (Pl. de la) .... **BY** 12

Apport-au-Pain (R.) .... **AY** 2

Bouteville (Cours) ...... **BY** 5
Gaulle (Av. Gén. de) ... **BY** 9
Henri IV (Pl.) .... **AY** 13
Leclerc (Av. Gén.) ...... **BY** 15
Moulin Rieul (R. du) ... **BY** 16

Parvis (Pl. du) .... **BY** 18
Poterne (R. de la) .... **BZ** 24
Ste-Geneviève (R.) .... **BZ** 25
Vernois (Av. F.) .... **AY** 29
Villevert (R. de) .... **BY** 32

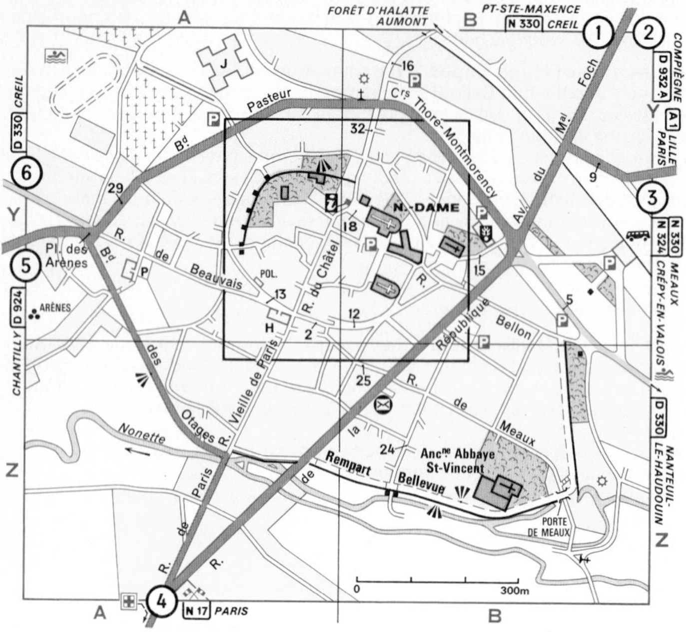

leries above the aisles are among the finest in France. The first chapel to the right of the south doorway features superb vaulting with pendant keystones, a 14C stone Virgin and a lovely set of stained glass windows. These are in fact the only original panes that have remained intact. A statue of St Louis from the 14C is placed in the south aisle of the ambulatory. The north transept chapel houses a 16C Christ made of larch.

Leave through the northern side doorway.

The left-hand aisle features an elegant statue of St Barbara dating back to the 16C.

North doorway. – The northern front is similar to the southern façade, but appears to be less ornate. The gable surmounting the doorway bears François I's salamander and the capital F as a reminder of the 16C reconstruction campaign, financed by the generous contributions of the French king.

North front. – The cathedral setting on this side is much less solemn: it features several patches of greenery and is extremely picturesque. Skirt the little garden that follows the east façade of what was once the bishop's palace. The building rests on the old Gallo-Roman ramparts, of which the base of one tower remains. Lovely view of the cathedral's chevet.

Ⓥ **St Peter's Church (Église St-Pierre).** – It was started in the 12C and drastically remodelled in the 17C. The small left tower and its stone spire are both Romanesque, while the heavier tower on the right dates from Renaissance times (1596). The badly-damaged but very elaborate façade is characteristic of Gothic Flamboyant *(illustration p 23)*. The church was abandoned during the Revolution. It is now used as a venue for a variety of cultural and artistic activities.

Former Bishop's Palace (Ancien évêché). – Most of the building is believed to date back to the 16 and 17C.

Return to Place du Parvis and before entering the castle courtyard, start to walk up Rue du Châtel to see the original fortified entrance to the stronghold (presently filled in). Adjoining the old doorway, the 16C Hôtel des Trois Pots (**D**) proudly sports its old-fashioned sculpted sign.

Ⓥ **Royal Castle (Château royal).** – This fortified site was occupied as early as the reign of the Emperor Claude (41-54 AD). Throughout its history, up to the time of Henri II, it has featured a charming collection of stone ruins.

The sturdy square "praetorium" tower is the most striking piece of architecture that still stands today: the 4.5m – 15ft thick walls are further supported by a set of hefty buttresses. It is believed to be of Romanesque design, although its history is not entirely clear.

In the 13C, St Louis gave orders to build a priory in the castle grounds. It was erected in memory of St Maurice and his fellow martyrs, who belonged to the Theban Legion, at Agaune in the Valais. All that remains is the Canon's Building (13C) (**E**) – the reception hall offers an audio-visual presentation on hunting – and the Prior's Lodge, which houses the Hunting Museum.

Ⓥ **Hunting Museum** (Musée de la Vénerie) (**M**[1]). – The works presented here were chosen from among the many illustrations of stag hunts which have enriched French culture. Desportes (1661-1743) and Oudry (1688-1755) represented the *Ancien Régime,* while later painters of animals include Carle Vernet, Rosa Bonheur *(qv),* Charles Hallo (the founder of the museum), etc. The walls are hung with numerous trophies and stag's heads.

The display of historical hunting gear renders the exhibition particularly interesting. The hunting costume of the Condé – beige and amaranth – can be seen on a figure representing a Chantilly forest warden, and in the painting depicting the young duc d'Enghien (1787).
Note the famous collection of hunting "buttons", which were the most highly envied trappings of a hunting outfit, chiselled hunting knives, horns (including a beautiful silver hunting horn made in 1817), etc.

★ **Old Streets.** – *Follow the route indicated on adjoining plan.*
Rue du Châtel used to be the main street through Senlis for those travelling from Paris to Flanders. This is why its southern continuation is named "Vieille de Paris". In 1753 it was succeeded by Rue Neuve de Paris, now called Rue de la République.
Take the charming **Rue de la Treille** and walk to the "False Doorway", which was the postern of the former Gallo-Roman ramparts. On the left stand the Chancellery Buildings (**F**), flanked by two towers.

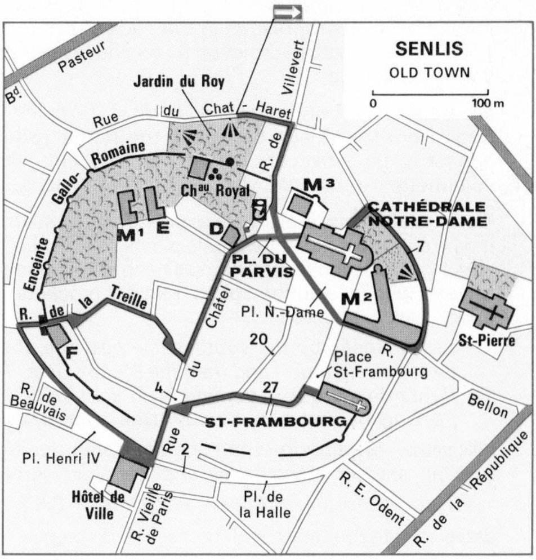

Apport-au-Pain (R. l') 2
Aulas-de-la-Bruyère (Pl.) 4
Flageard (R. aux) 7
Petit Chaalis (R. du) 20
Tonnellerie (R. de la) 27

The **Town Hall** (Hôtel de Ville) on Place Henri-IV was rebuilt in 1495. The front bears a bust of Henri IV and an inscription conveying his warm feelings for the town of Senlis. These date back to a visit paid by Charles X on his way back from his anointment at Reims Cathedral (1825).

★ **St-Frambourg Royal Chapel (Chapelle Royale St-Frambourg).** – Hugh Capet's wife ⓥ the pious Queen Adelaide founded this chapel before 990 to house the relics of a recluse from the Bas-Maine, known as St Frambourg or St Fraimbault. It was rebuilt by Louis VII after 1177. Abandoned during the Revolution, it was restored as the Franz Liszt Auditorium in 1977, thanks to the efforts of the pianist Georges Cziffra. The Cziffra Foundation organises concerts and exhibitions for lovers of classical music. The **church** and its single Gothic nave have been restored to their former grandeur.
Go down to the archaeological **crypt.** Excavations have revealed the floor of a sanctuary dating from about 1000 AD, featuring fragments of columns, some of which have been reconstituted. Two fragments of pilasters belonging to the flat east end of this church still bear the mural paintings of bishops.
The crypt comes to rest at the east end on a sturdy round tower made in fine brickwork and on the inner ramparts of the town, which follow the old Gallo-Roman wall.

ADDITIONAL SIGHTS

ⓥ **Former St-Vincent Abbey (Ancienne Abbaye St-Vincent)** (BZ). – Founded in 1060 by Henri I's wife Anne of Kiev, following the birth of their son Philippe, heir to the throne. The child's christening marked the introduction into France of the Byzantine name Philippe. A 12C open-work bell tower – known to be one of the finest and the most delicate in Ile-de-France – dominates the church, whose silhouette has been marred by the successive building and reconstruction campaigns.
The former abbey buildings, rebuilt in the 17C, house a cloister with classical features: colonnettes with Doric capitals and coffered stone vaulting adorned with sunken panels.

Bellevue Ramparts (Rempart Bellevue) (BZ). – *We advise starting from St-Vincent. Follow Rue de Meaux, leading out towards the country. On the left, set back in a recess, you will come across a staircase which will take you up to the ramparts. Turn right and follow the walls.*
View of the countryside around St-Vincent, and the Nonette river.

ⓥ **Art and Archaeology Museum (Musée d'Art et d'Archéologie)** (M^2). – Situated in the former bishop's palace.
Visitors are shown remains of the town dating from the 1 and 2C, as well as foundations of the 3C bailey, consisting mainly of sculpted compositions taken from Gallo-Roman monuments.
Observe the superb early Gothic sculptures and the art collection with works by 17 to 20C painters.

ⓥ **Museum (Musée)** (M^3). – *In Hôtel de Vermandois.*
The museum hosts temporary exhibitions of archaeological artefacts, namely a selection of Gallo-Roman ex-votos found in Halatte Forest.

EXCURSIONS

Raray Château (Château de Raray). – *13km – 8 miles to the northeast. Leave Senlis by ②. When you reach Villeneuve-sous-Verberie, turn right.*
The château is famed for the striking decoration of its court of honour, used for the shooting of Jean Cocteau's film *Beauty and the Beast.* Its game pens alternate with a series of arcades, alternating with small recesses and niches. The latter house a number of busts representing the gods of Antiquity and historical figures from the 17C. These works are crowned by two hunting scenes sculpted in stone: a stag hunt and a boar hunt.

St-Vaast-de-Longmont. – *16km – 10 miles to the northeast ②.*
Seen from the village cemetery, the Romanesque bell tower and its stone spire appear to be extremely ornate: cornices with billet moulding, arcades resting on colonnettes decorated variously with spiralling, zig-zag or torus motifs.

Tour of Valois Bell Towers. – *Tour of 48km – 29 miles. Allow 2 1/2 hours.*
It will take you across the arable plains that lie near the forest and through a string of small villages whose farmhouses have retained their 19C charm. It is dotted with bell towers whose slender spires feature crockets, opening with lofty gables and open-work pinnacles.

Leave Senlis by the southeast – past the abbey of St-Vincent – the first bell tower of the tour – and then the Meaux Gate. Turn left soon afterwards and turn right into the D 330, running from Nanteuil-le-Haudouin to Mont-l'Évêque. After passing over the motorway, take a right turning.

Villemétrie. – The bridge spanning the Nonette river offers a pleasant vista of the old mill, an ancient stone cross and the shady grounds of the park.

Turn round and proceed along the D 330^A^.

Ⓥ **Baron.** – Note the **church** and its crocketed steeple (45m – 148ft). The nave was rebuilt in the 16C and features many ornate embellishments on the exterior.The 14C stone Virgin and the 18C **panelling★** inside were taken from Chaâlis Abbey.

Versigny. – Presents a bell tower typical of Senlis Cathedral. Observe the strange Ⓥ **château** on the opposite side of the road. This long, low, U-shaped building of Italian inspiration was first started in the 17C, and subsequently remodelled under Louis-Philippe: the balustrades, curved pediments, steps and columns date from the Restoration period.

Proceed towards Nanteuil-le-Haudouin but when you reach the edge of the château grounds take a right turning at the next junction and follow directions to Montagny-Ste-Félicité. Drive up to the isolated church.

Montagny-Ste-Félicité. – Superb open-work **bell tower★**, rising 65m – 213ft above the ground.

Turn round. When you get to the crossroads north of Montagny, turn left towards Baron, from where you get back onto the road to Senlis. Do not follow the direct route. Instead, at the Fontaine-Chaâlis junction, turn right towards Montépilloy.

Ⓥ **Fourcheret.** – A former **barn** belonging to Chaâlis Abbey still stands, supported by 18 pillars. Built in the 13C, this monastic structure 65m – 213ft long and 18m – 60ft wide features an impressive display of timberwork.

Ⓥ **Montépilloy.** – The ruins of the old stronghold – presently occupied by a farmhouse – are perched on top of the plateau that rises between the shallow valleys of the rivers Nonette and Aunette. On 15 August 1429, Joan of Arc spent the night at Montépilloy, having challenged the English troops of Bedford who occupied Senlis. A commemorative plaque has been affixed onto the church exterior. The 13C entrance gatehouse – itself a small castle – offers a view of the farmhouse and, in the background, the ruins of the 14C keep.

★★ SÈVRES

Pop 20 255

Michelin map 101 fold 24 – Michelin plan 22

The **Manufacture Nationale de Porcelaine** (National Porcelain Factory) set up here in the 18C has made the locality of Sceaux famous throughout the world. The present buildings date back to 1876.

SÈVRES PORCELAIN

Porcelain is a ceramic material which undergoes vitrification when fired in the kiln, emerging as a brittle product, translucent on its outer surface (as opposed to china, which is opaque).

Soft-paste porcelain. – In the 16C, European potters were intrigued by the discovery of porcelain manufactured in the Far East and many of them endeavoured to imitate these productions. However, they had no idea how the Chinese prepared their paste and were reduced to experimenting with several types of earthenware. They ended up using a finely-grained marl, which they combined with a variety of glass called "fritte", thus achieving vitrification.
This soft-paste porcelain was produced in Vincennes in 1740. Sixteen years later, the factory – which enjoyed the patronage of Louis XV and Mme de Pompadour – moved into its new premises at Sèvres. Initially known for its wild flower motifs, Sèvres porcelain later specialised in tableware, ornamental statuettes and even whole procelain paintings. The sophisticated techniques used for applying the hand-painted decoration onto the enamel glaze ensured a beautifully smooth finish.

Hard-paste porcelain. – In the early 18C, a substance called kaolin – one of the basic compounds for making porcelain – was discovered in Saxony, but the trade secrets were well kept at Meissen, near Dresden. In France, it was not until 1769 that a similar deposit was found at St-Yrieix in Limousin, permitting the production of hard-paste porcelain. From the Empire onwards, the Manufacture concentrated exclusively on hard-paste ware.

The new product required firing at a high temperature (1 400°C – 2 550°F): it proved remarkably resistant but was more difficult to decorate. Only a small selection of colours were actually suitable for high temperature firing, namely the famous Sèvres blue *(bleu de Sèvres)*, used on 18C soft-paste under the name *bleu lapis*. Light colours suitable for low temperature firing, such as pinks, did not blend into the glaze as they did on soft-paste ware, and could not be used by manufacturers.

At its beginnings, the factory enjoyed the exclusive right to gild the pieces it produced and this tradition has been continued. Except in very few cases attributed to technical problems, all Sèvres pieces feature gilding. Biscuit was used for the making of statuettes but was left unglazed to preserve the dainty, graceful forms of the figures.

The Thesmar Vase,
National Porcelain Museum of Sèvres

★★ **National Porcelain Museum (Musée National de Céramique).** – *Place de la Manufacture.*

Founded by Brongniart in 1824, the museum houses an impressive selection of china and porcelain exhibits, classified according to the country and date of fabrication: glazed clay pieces from Europe and Asia, earthenware from Renaissance Italy, 17 and 18C France and other European countries, 18C porcelain from the Paris region, Sèvres and Meissen. The exhibition hall to the left of the entrance displays part of the **Factory's** present-day production, consisting of traditional and modern creations. All these wares are for sale.

The tour also features an audio-visual presentation of the various operations involved in the making of a porcelain piece: turning, firing, moulding, decoration, etc. Each piece is handled by 20 craftsmen and is automatically destroyed if it does not meet the required standards.

Jardies Villa (Villa des Jardies). – *14, Avenue Gambetta.*

This humble garden pavilion was once part of the Jardies estate, where Honoré de Balzac lived and attempted the cultivation of pineapples, with most unsatisfactory results. Corot stayed here and Gambetta died here on 31 December 1882. Several of the politician's mementoes have been kept and are on show to the public. At the crossroads near the villa stands a memorial to Gambetta, by Bartholdi.

Although* Sèvres *was the main porcelain factory
Ile-de-France was rich in porcelain producing centres in the 18C.
These included* Vincennes *prior to its transfer to Sèvres in 1756,
St Cloud, Chantilly, Sceaux, Mennecy* and *Etiolles.

TAVERNY

Pop 21 414

Michelin map 101 fold 4

Situated on the southwest edge of Montmorency Forest, Taverny features a remarkable church which dominates the nearby hillsides.

★ **Church (Église).** – *Time: 1/2 hour.* In the early 13C, the Montmorency family commissioned the construction of the present church near the local castle, now sadly disappeared. It was granted the patronage of Queen Blanche of Castile. It was built in the Gothic style and remodelled in the 15C. During the last century, it was restored and greatly improved by Viollet-le-Duc, as is visible from the western front.

The chancel features a superb Renaissance **retable★** carved in stone which was a present from Constable Anne de Montmorency. The lower frieze pictures objects linked to the Passion (lantern, Veronica's veil, cross), Henri II's monogram, the initials of Diane de Poitiers, the alerion or eagle and the swords of Constable Anne. On the upper frieze we have the Evangelists, the constable's coat of arms (alerions) and the blazon of Madeleine of Savoy (cross of Savoy). Note the two impressive statues of the Virgin: Notre-Dame-des-Fers, a stone figure from the late 15C, placed in the left-hand niche of the retable, and Notre-Dame-de-Taverny, a 14C wooden statue in the chapel on the left.

★ THOIRY

Pop 713

Michelin map 196 folds 15 and 16

The opening of a wildlife park and a leisure centre on Thoiry estate has made this locality an extremely popular resort with tourists and weekenders.

★ **African Reserve** (**Réserve africaine**). – The road winding its way across the reserve goes past camels, giraffes, elephants, zebras, antelopes, rhinoceroses, hippopotamuses, etc. The lions and bears are kept in two special enclosures. On the way out, leave the car on the parking area near the road.

Animal Park (**Parc Zoologique**). – The grounds surrounding the château have been partly made into a zoological park *(follow the route signposted with arrows)*. The tigers' den is a truly remarkable accomplishment: visitors follow an elevated footpath going from tree to tree, which gives them an aerial view of the animals in their natural surroundings.

Vivarium. – The basement rooms of the château house a wide range of reptile species.

Château. – History enthusiasts will enjoy the 18C furniture, the paintings and the original archive documents (Louis XV's reign).
The **Museum of Gastronomy** (Musée de la Gastronomie) displays ornamental tiered cakes made by the contemporary master-confectioner Sender, who received a national award.

TRIEL

Pop 7 906

Michelin map 101 fold 1

Triel's riverside location near the Seine has turned the area into an important industrial centre. The streets of the town are laid out along the slopes of the Hautil heights. The bridge over the Seine and the quayside along the west bank command a good view of Triel.

★ **St-Martin Church** (**Église St-Martin**). – The original church was a 13C Gothic building with three naves. A new aisle was later added – the Flamboyant stained glass dates it back to the 15C – on the south side of the church, and a large chapel dedicated to a brotherhood of charity was erected on the north side. In the 16C, the flat chevet was enriched by a huge Renaissance chancel offering an ambulatory. To accommodate the Route de l'Hautil, which crossed in front of the old east end, the chancel was raised by 6 steps in order to bridge the road.
The church interior shows signs of successive alterations. The vaulting above the nave was lowered and rebuilt in the late 13C, with the result that the clerestory windows appear to be truncated. The transept is unusually narrow and slender: its southern end presents the remains of the three-lobed triforium belonging to the original building. The choir completed under Henri II is fronted by the original 13C choir. The 16C **stained glass windows**★ feature the Renaissance windows in the ambulatory, including the Tree of Jesse (first on the left), and those of the St James Chapel (at the far end of the ambulatory, on the left). The latter tell the story of a young pilgrim who was saved from the gallows. Accused of theft by a discontented maidservant, he was spared the grim sentence thanks to the intervention of St James. His judge however remained unconvinced, until he witnessed a second miracle: a roast fowl he was preparing to eat leaped down from the spit and started to crow.

★ Les VAUX DE CERNAY

Michelin map 196 folds 28 and 29 – Local map p 63

The combination of woodlands, sandstone boulders and water springs – an unusual feature for Ile-de-France – made this valley extremely popular among many artists and "tourists" of the last century.

★ **The site.** – *Promenade: 1/2 to 2 hours.* The road coming from Dampierre weaves its way up the wooded, narrow valley, passes a restaurant and crosses the brook along the embankment of the mill, Moulin des Roches, which retains a stretch of water with wooded banks.
Leave the car near the Chalet des Cascades and enter the undergrowth, consisting of oaks and beeches (the late afternoon light is enchanting). The surrounding slopes are dotted with blocks of sandstone rock and the fresh waters feature a charming series of whirlpools and minor falls.

Cernay Pond (Étang de Cernay). – It was created by the monks of the local abbey as a fish pond. A the top of the embankment stands a memorial to the 19C landscape painter Léon-Germain Pelouse, set up near a stately oak tree.
This pleasant walk may be continued during a further 1/2 or 1 hour. Follow the wide path which veers right and leads straight up to the wooded plateau. When you reach the ledge of the platform, turn back, bear right and take the cliff path that skirts the rock promontory.

★★★ VAUX-LE-VICOMTE Château

Michelin map 196 north of folds 45 and 46 – 6km – 4 miles northeast of Melun

Built by Fouquet, this château remains one of the greatest masterpieces of the 17C.

The rise of Nicolas Fouquet. – Born of a family of magistrates, Fouquet became a member of the Parlement de Paris by the age of twenty. He was made Procureur Général of this respectable assembly and was appointed Superintendent of Finances under Mazarin. Owing to the customs of the time and the example of Cardinal Mazarin, he acquired the dangerous habit of confusing the credit of the State with his own. He was forever surrounded by a numerous retinue of senior personalities whose services cost vast sums of money. Intoxicated with success Fouquet chose a squirrel as his emblem – in Anjou patois *fouquet* means a squirrel – and decreed his motto would be *Quo non ascendam* (How high shall I not climb?).

In 1656, Fouquet decided to grace his own seigniory of Vaux with a château worthy of his social success. He showed excellent taste when it came to choosing his future "collaborators": the architect **Louis Le Vau**, the decorator **Charles Le Brun** and the landscape gardener **André Le Nôtre**. He was equally discerning in other matters: the famous chef Vatel was hired as his major-domo and La Fontaine as close adviser. The builders were given carte blanche. A total of 18 000 workers took part in the project, which involved the demolition of three villages.

Le Brun created a tapestry manufacture at Maincy. After the fall of Nicolas Fouquet, it was moved to Paris, where it became the Manufacture Royale des Gobelins. The whole operation took five years to complete. The result was a masterpiece that Louis XIV wished to surpass with the construction of Versailles.

An invitation to royal vexation. – On 17 August 1661, Fouquet organised a fête for the king and his court, who where staying at Fontainebleau. The reception was one of dazzling splendour. The king's table featured a service in solid gold: this detail annoyed him intensely as his own silverware had been sent back to the smelting works to meet the expenses incurred by the Thirty Years War.

After a banquet dinner at which Vatel had surpassed himself, the guests could feast their eyes on the garden entertainments, enhanced by 1 200 fountains and cascades. The programme covered country ballets, concerts, aquatic tournaments and lottery games, in which all the tickets won prizes. It also included the premiere of *Les Fâcheux,* a comedy-ballet by Molière, performed by the author and his troupe against a delightful backdrop of greenery. The king was vexed by such an extravagant display of pomp and luxury, unparalleled at his own royal court. His first impulse was to have Fouquet arrested immediately but Anne of Austria succeeded in appeasing his spirits.

The fall of Nicolas Fouquet. – Nineteen days later, the Superintendent of Finances was sent to jail and all his belongings sequestrated. The artists who had designed and built Vaux entered the king's service and were later to produce the Palace of Versailles. At the end of a three-year trial, Fouquet was banished from court but this sentence was altered by the king to perpetual imprisonment. Only a few close friends remained loyal to the fallen minister: Mme de Sévigné, and La Fontaine, who composed *Elegy to the Nymphs of Vaux.*

On account of her dowry, Fouquet's widow was entitled to recover the ownership of the château. After the death of her son, the estate fell into the hands of the Maréchal de Villars in 1705, when it was made a duchy-peerage. It was sold in 1764 by one of Louis XV's ministers the duc de Choiseul-Praslin, and survived the Revolution without suffering too much damage.

In 1875, Vaux was bought by the great industrialist Mr Sommier, who applied himself to restoring and refurnishing the château, as well as refurbishing its grounds. This task has been continued by his heirs.

Vaux-le-Vicomte Château

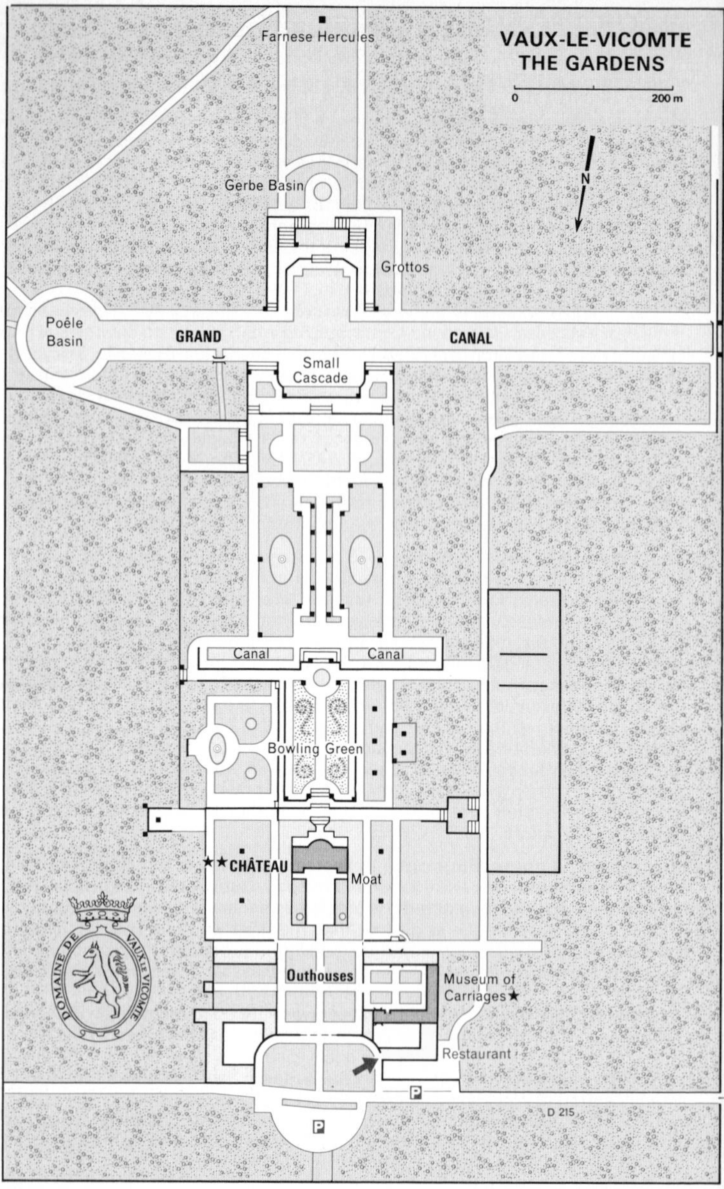
VAUX-LE-VICOMTE
THE GARDENS
0
200 m
N
Farnese Hercules
Gerbe Basin
Grottos
Poêle Basin
GRAND
CANAL
Small Cascade
Canal
Canal
Bowling Green
★★CHÂTEAU
Moat
Outhouses
Museum of Carriages★
Restaurant
D 215
DOMAINE DE VAUX LE VICOMTE

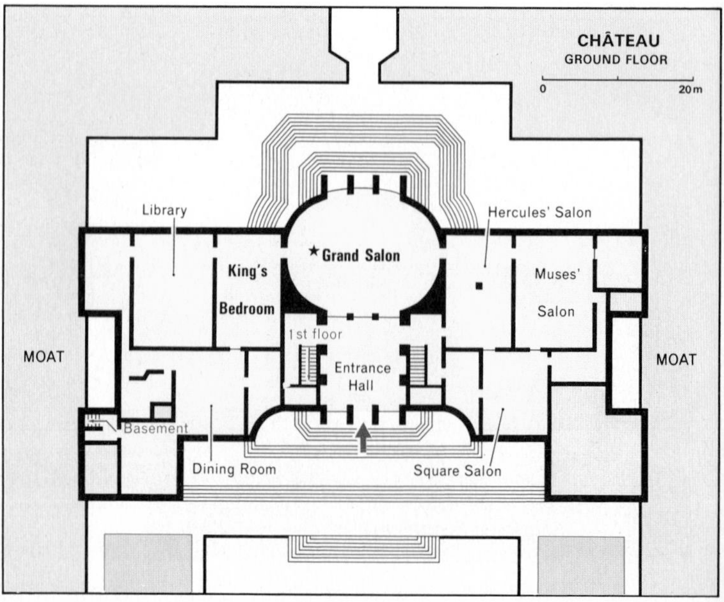
CHÂTEAU
GROUND FLOOR
0
20m
Library
★Grand Salon
Hercules' Salon
King's Bedroom
Muses' Salon
1st floor
Entrance Hall
MOAT
MOAT
Basement
Dining Room
Square Salon

TOUR

Ⓥ **Château.** – The château is built on a terrace raised above the gardens and surrounded by a moat. It is approached by the northern front and presents an impressive sight: note the raised level of the ground floor and the height of the first floor windows. The whole building is characteristic of the first period of Louis XIV architecture *(p 28)*.

The glass doors in the entrance hall – presently covered up by tapestries – opened onto the Grand Salon and the perspective of the formal gardens. This vestibule leads up to the first floor, occupied by the suites of M. and Mme Fouquet. Visitors are shown the superintendent's antechamber (large ebony desk inlaid with gilt copper), his study and his bedroom (superb ceiling decorated by Le Brun). They are then taken round Mme Fouquet's boudoir (portrait of Fouquet by Le Brun), the Louis XV study and bedroom, embellished by contemporary furniture (large canopied four-poster bed attributed to F. Leroy) and the Louis XVI bedchamber.

Back on the ground floor, take a look at the Square Salon and its French-style ceiling decoration: it was the only addition made under Louis XIII.

Six reception rooms giving onto the gardens are laid out on either side of the main Grand Salon. The ceilings were decorated by Le Brun, who conferred a sense of unity to the whole ensemble. Admire his rendering of *The Nine Muses* in the Muses' Hall, *Hercules entering Mount Olympus* in Hercules' Hall. The latter houses an equestrian statue of Louis XIV, executed by François Girardon. It is a miniature bronze of the monument set up on Place Vendôme in 1699 and destroyed during the Revolution.

★ **Grand Salon** (Grand Salon). – This room, crowned by the central cupola, was left unfinished after Fouquet's arrest and has suffered from the absence of decoration (the various studies made by Le Brun are on display). The sixteen caryatids supporting the dome symbolise the twelve months and the four seasons of the year. The only remains of the original furnishings are two marble tables, as well as six statues and six paintings discovered by M. Sommier when he moved in.

King's Bedroom (Chambre du Roi). – It communicates with the former antechamber (now a library beautifully furnished in the Regency style).

Its decoration is characteristic of the Louis XIV style that was to leave its mark on the Grand Apartments of Versailles. The ceiling features stucco work by Girardon and Legendre, and a central painting by Le Brun representing *Time taking away Truth from the Skies*. Below the cornice is a frieze of palmette motifs alternating with tiny squirrels.

The Dining Room probably served a similar function in Fouquet's time. It gives onto a passageway embellished with wood panelling and hung with paintings, where a long row of dressers would receive the bowls of fruit and other dishes brought from the distant kitchens.

A tour of the basement shows a number of rooms (Map Room, Archive Hall) and the kitchen quarters, which were used up to 1956. Note the servants' dining hall, complete with a fully laid table.

★★★ **Gardens.** – M. Sommier has carefully reconstituted Le Nôtre's masterpiece, of Ⓥ which the most striking feature is its sweeping perspective. The grounds offer several "optical illusions", namely the discovery of basins that are not visible from the château. Walk to the far end of the upper terrace to get a good view of the southern façade. The central rotunda and its surmounting lantern turret, the square corner pavilions, heavier than on the north side, and the decoration of the frontispiece, crowned by statues, form an impressive, if somewhat heavy, composition.

Starting from the château, one first walks past the *boulingrin* or former bowling green, two oblong areas of greenery trimmed into ornamental lace motifs.

The three main water perspectives – the moat, the two rectangular canals and the Grand Canal – suddenly spring into sight in a most impressive manner. Owing to the prevailing customs of that period, the artificial grottoes *(see plan opposite)* appear to have been arranged around the edge of the very last square basin, which has the effect of screening the axis of the Grand Canal.

The Grand Canal – known as the "frying pan" on account of its rounded extremity – is approached by a steep flight of steps level with the Small Falls and located opposite the grottoes. The niches at each end house two statues of river gods which remain a telling example of 17C sculpture at Vaux. These Mlle de Scudéry fondly imagined to be the Tiber and the Anqueuil (local name given to the Almont stream).

Skirt the Grand Canal and walk up to the foot of the Farnese Hercules which ends the wondrous perspective. The very last basin aptly called the spray – La Gerbe – affords an extensive view of the château and its stately grounds.

Ⓥ **Outhouses (Dépendances).** – The **Museum of Carriages★** (Musée des Équipages) lies in the western outbuildings, situated next to the visitors' entrance. It presents harnessing and saddlery, an old-fashioned smithy and fully-equipped carriages.

Times and charges for admission to sights described in the guide are listed at the end of the guide.

The sights are listed alphabetically in this section either under the place – town, village or area – in which they are situated or under their proper name.

Every sight for which there are times and charges is indicated by the symbol Ⓥ in the margin in the main part of the guide.

★★★ VERSAILLES

Pop 95 240

Michelin map 101 folds 22 and 23 – Michelin plan 22

Versailles was created during the golden age of French royalty and, except under the Regency *(p 178)*, it remained the government headquarters and the political centre of France from 1682 to 1789. It owes its reputation to the outstanding royal residence consisting of the palace, its grounds and the Trianons. The town was built as an annexe with a view to housing the numerous titled and untitled people who served the French court: dukes, ministers, craftsmen, civil servants, etc. Owing to its former duties, the town has retained a certain, austere charm.
Versailles will delight all those interested in the Bourbons' penchant for splendour and the insurrectionary beginnings of the French Revolution.

Louis XIII's Château. – In the 17C, the locality of Versailles was the seat of a medieval castle perched on a hillock. At the foot lay the village, surrounded by marshes and woodland abounding in game. Louis XIII used to come hunting here fairly often and in 1624 he bought part of the land and gave orders to build a small country residence. In 1631 the Archbishop of Paris Monseigneur Gondi granted him the lordship of Versailles and he commissioned Philibert Le Roy to replace the manor by a small château built of brick, stone and slate.

The glorious task of taming nature. – 1661 marked the year of Louis XIV's accession to the throne. The king hired the various artists, builders, designers and landscape architects who had produced Vaux-le-Vicomte *(qv)* and entrusted them with an even more challenging task.
Louis was wary of settling in Paris, which reminded him of the Fronde uprisings, and he searched for a site in the outskirts of the capital. As a young boy, he had spent many a happy day in Versailles and he enjoyed the hunting offered by the many forests: Versailles it would be. It was by no means an ideal site. The mound was too narrow to allow Louis XIII's château to be enlarged. Although the surrounding land was swampy, and therefore unsuitable for the growing of ornamental plants, it did not yield enough water to supply the many fountains and canals that were an essential part of 17C gardens. The king ruled that nature be tamed and gave orders to divert the waters of nearby rivers, drain the land and cart heavy loads of earth to consolidate the site.
In the early stages, **Louis Le Vau** built a stone construction around the small château in 1668: it was reminiscent of Italian architecture and was aptly named the "Envelope". André Le Nôtre designed the new gardens and created his celebrated perspectives. By 1664 the first receptions were held at the new château.

A giant operation. – In 1678, **Jules Hardouin-Mansart**, aged only 31, was appointed head architect, a position he kept until he died in 1708. From 1661 to 1683, **Charles Le Brun** supervised a team of accomplished painters, sculptors, carvers and interior decorators. **Le Nôtre** applied himself to the embellishment of the grounds. When designing the waterworks, he joined forces with the Francine, a family of Italian engineers. Louis XIV kept a close watch on the various work under way, leaving strict instructions when he marched to war. He was a highly critical observer who made numerous comments aimed at altering, rectifying and improving the plans of his new residence.
In 1684, two years after the king and his elegant courtiers had moved to Versailles, the *Journal de Dangeau* reported that a total of 22 000 labourers and 6 000 horses were at work on the different sites. It was necessary to build a hill to accommodate

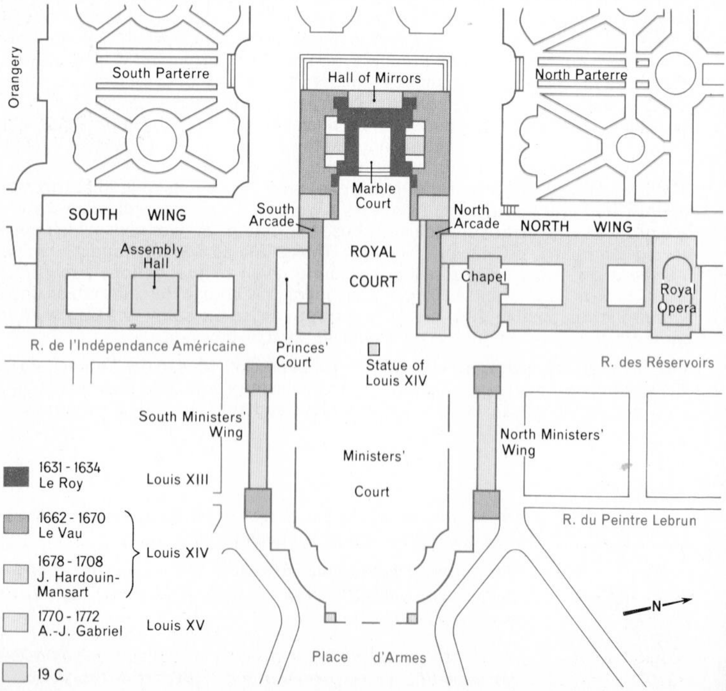

the entire length of the château (680m – 2230ft). Whole forests were transplanted and the king's gardeners produced 150000 new flowering plants every year. The orangery housed around 3000 shrubs: orange and myrtle trees, oleanders...
The problem of water supply was of great concern to Colbert, and later Louvois. The waters of Clagny Pond – located near the present Right Bank railway station – proved insufficent and the builders were forced to divert the course of the Bièvre and drain the plateaux of Saclay. The Marly Machine conveyed the waters pumped from the river Seine but the diversion of the Eure *(p 107)* ended in a fiasco.
It took fifty years to complete the shell of the palace at Versailles, allowing for the interruptions and slack periods attributed to contemporary wars. It was only in 1710 that the last chapel was finished. By that time, Louis XIV had reached the age of 72.

Life at Court. – When the king and his entourage moved to Versailles, the palace and the adjacent outbuildings were required to lodge no less than 3000 people. The Fronde movement had been a humiliating experience for the king, who had witnessed many intrigues involving men in high places. Consequently, his main concern was to keep the aristocracy with him at court, in an attempt to stifle any opposition that might threaten the stability of the throne. The lavish entertainments suited his extravagant tastes – also served to keep the nobility in subjection.
For the first time in French history, the royal suites in the palace were fully furnished as soon as they were occupied. Thanks to Colbert's efforts to encourage the production of luxury goods (tapestries, furniture, lace, etc.) on a national scale, the palace – which remained open to the public – offered a standing exhibition of arts and crafts in France.
Strict etiquette governed the visits that the French people would pay Versailles. The famous chronicler Saint-Simon described a day at court as a "clockwork ceremony" consisting of a series of banquets, hearings and entertainments. After 1684, the pious Mme de Maintenon put an end to these large-scale festivities: it seemed that the court entertained merely to overcome boredom.
When Louis XIV died, his successor was still a baby. The Regent Philippe d'Orléans administered the king's affairs from the Palais-Royal, his Paris residence. During this time, the court left Versailles and moved to the Tuileries.
In 1722, Louis XV, aged twelve, decided to settle at Versailles. In order that royal etiquette might not interfere with his private life, he gave orders to convert several of the private apartments. He dreamed of having the front of the palace remodelled, a task he entrusted to Anges-Jacques Gabriel. Unfortunately, no major alterations could be carried out owing to insufficent funds but the Petit Trianon was built. Louis XVI – a man of simple tastes – and Marie-Antoinette commissioned no further works. The queen was perfectly happy to stay in the Petit Trianon: it was for her that the hamlet and the present grounds were conceived in 1774. On 6 October 1789, the national insurrection forced the royal family to return to Paris. After that date, Versailles ceased to be a place of residence for the kings of France.

Louis XVI entering Dunkirk,
tapestry after Charles Le Brun

To the glory of France. – After the storming of the Tuileries and the fall of the Monarchy on 10 August 1792, most of the furniture was removed and auctioned. The major works of art – paintings, carpets, tapestries and a few items of furniture – were kept for the art museum which opened in the Louvre in August 1793. After the renovation work undertaken by Napoleon and Louis XVIII, Versailles was threatened once more: it was spared demolition by Louis-Philippe, who contributed a large part of his personal fortune to found a museum in 1837 of French history.
More recently, Versailles was restored following WWI, thanks to the generosity of the Academy of Fine Arts, and the handsome contributions made by a number of wealthy patrons, namely the American J.D. Rockefeller.

Restoration. – An important restoration campaign was launched in the early fifties, permitting the renovation of the Royal Opera, the installation of central heating and electric lighting, and the completion of various operations regarding refurnishing and maintenance. In the eighties, the King's Bedroom and the Hall of Mirrors were both restored to their 18C splendour (1980).

Phases of construction and other historical events

1631	Louis XIII's château is completed.
1643	Death of Louis XIII. Five-year-old **Louis XIV succeeds to the throne.** France is ruled by the Regent Anne of Austria and Cardinal Jules Mazarin.
1661	Louis XIV comes of age. After Mazarin's death, he decides to reign without the assistance of a Prime Minister.
1664	The first sumptuous receptions are held.
1666	The Versailles fountains play for the first time.
1668	Louis Le Vau starts work on Louis XIII's château.
1671	Charles Le Brun and his team of artists begin the interior decoration.
1674	The king's first visit to Versailles.
1682	The court and government officials take up residence at the palace.
1683	Death of Marie-Thérèse of Austria. Louis XIV is secretly married to Mme de Maintenon.
1684	The Hall of Mirrors is completed.
1687	The Porcelain Trianon is replaced by the Marble Trianon.
1710	Birth of Louis XV, great-grandson of the Sun King.
1715	Death of Louis XIV. Five-year-old **Louis XV succeeds to the throne.** France is ruled by the Regent Philippe d'Orléans. The court leaves Versailles.
1722	The court returns to Versailles.
1729	Birth of the Dauphin, father to Louis XVI, Louis XVIII and Charles X.
1745	Mme de Pompadour becomes Louis XV's favourite. Her "reign" was to last fifteen years.
1754	Birth of Louis XVI.
1770	Louis XVI is married to the Austrian Archduchess Marie-Antoinette.
1774	Death of Louis XV. **Louis XVI succeeds to the throne.**
1783	The Treaty of Versailles is signed, granting independence to 13 American States.
1789	The States General meet in the town. The royal family leaves Versailles for good.

THE BOURBON KINGS OF FRANCE

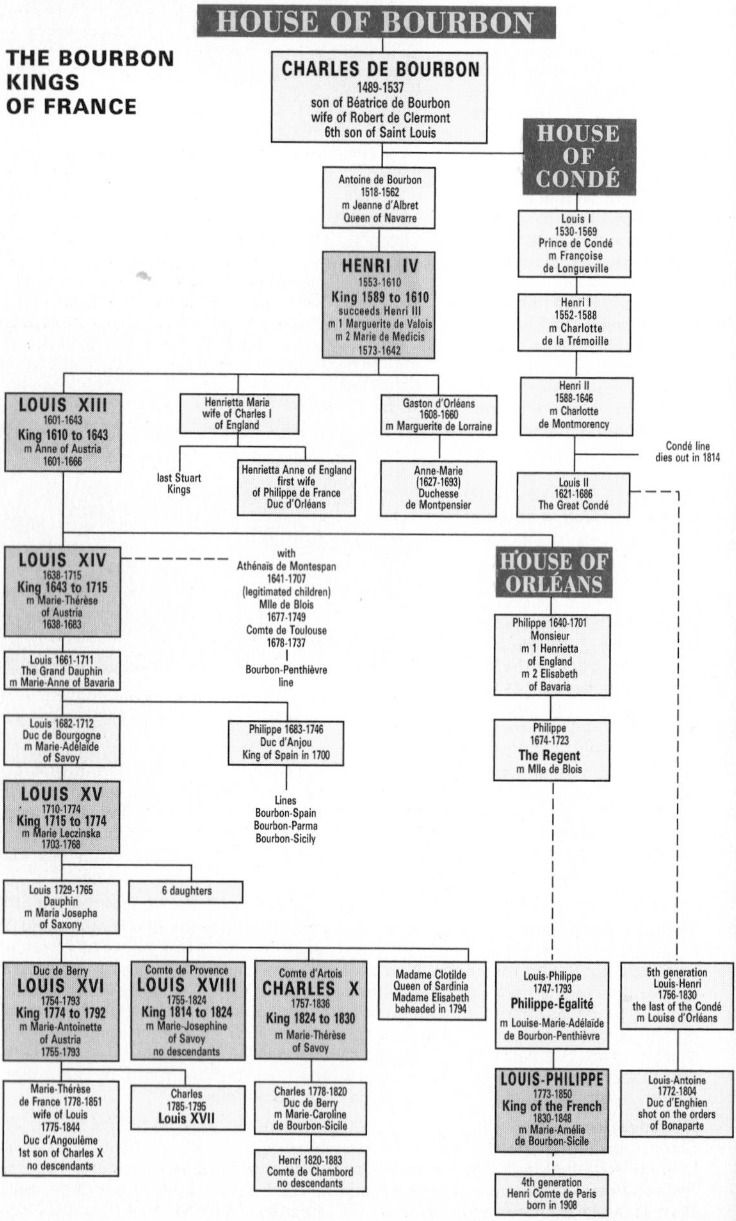

★★★ PALACE

Ⓥ**One-day tour.** – Programme for visitors pressed for time:

Morning: Palace (exterior and State Apartments)

Afternoon: King's Suite and Royal Opera, the gardens (the main perspective and the south groves) up to the Apollo Basin and the Grand Canal.

By car: from the Grand Canal to the Trianon (arrange to be picked up by the driver when you reach the Grand Canal – for access by car see map on p 190-191).

The Grand Trianon (exterior), the gardens of the Petit Trianon.
The North Parterre of the palace, starting from the Neptune Basin (park car nearby, either on Avenue de Trianon or Boulevard de la Reine).

Two-day tour. – Tourists with more time to spare may do as follows:

Day 1 – **Morning:** Tour of the palace as indicated above.

Afternoon: Complete tour of the palace gardens and boat trip along the Grand Canal.

Day 2 – **Morning:** King's Suite and Royal Opera.

Afternoon: Complete tour of the Trianon (châteaux and gardens).

PALACE EXTERIOR *Quick tour: allow 1 hour*

Place d'Armes. – This huge square was the meeting-point for the three wide avenues leading to Paris, St-Cloud and Sceaux, separated by the **Royal Stables★** (Écuries Royales) built by Jules Hardouin-Mansart. Identical in size, the Petite and the Grande Écurie were thus termed for reasons of convenience: the former housed the various carriages and equipages, while the latter was used for saddle horses: its ring was often the scene of impressive equestrian entertainments.

Courtyards. – The wrought iron railings date from the reign of Louis XVIII. Beyond them stretch a series of three courtyards.
The forecourt or **Ministers' Court** is flanked by two long ranges housing the four blocks in which the king's ministers would take up residence. An equestrian statue of Louis XIV, commissioned by Louis-Philippe, stands in the middle of the drive.
The **Royal Court** was separated from the outer courtyard by railings through which only persons of high rank (peers, princes of the blood, noblemen, etc.) might pass in carriages. The two wings lining this court were originally separate from the palace and used as outhouses. They were joined to the main building and fronted by a set of colonnades built under Louis XV and Louis XVIII. Beyond the North Arcade – leading through to the park – and the South Arcade lie three gilded gates marking the entrance to the State Apartments. On the left we have the Queen's Staircase. The original entrance lay to the right but it was condemned after the Ambassadors' Staircase was demolished.
The **Marble Court★★** – paved with slabs of black and white marble – has been raised to its original level. It is surrounded by Louis XIII's old château, of which the façades were remodelled and greatly improved by Louis Le Vau and Jules Hardouin-Mansart: balustrades, busts, statues, vases, etc. On the first floor of the central pavilion, the three arched windows belonging to the king's bedroom are fronted by a gilded balcony resting upon eight marble columns.

★★★ **Garden Façade.** – *Illustration p 194-195. Walk under the North Arcade, skirt the main part of the palace and step back to get a good view.*
The huge building occupies a total length of 680m – 2230ft and yet its general appearance is not monotonous. The wings are placed at a perpendicular angle and the horizontal lines of the centrepiece are broken by the rows of sculpted columns and pillars. The flat roof, built in the Italian style, is concealed by a balustrade bearing ornamental trophies and vases. The statues of Apollo and Diana, surrounded by the Months of the Year, mark the entrance to the central building that housed the Royal Suite. Certain members of the royal family, including several of the king's children, stayed in the South Wing.
The terrace extending in front of the château commands an extensive view of the park and its many perspectives. It bears two **giant vases★**, one at each end: the one lying to the north was executed by Coysevox and symbolises War, while the south vase, attributed to Tuby, is a representation of Peace. They are placed outside the respective bay windows of the War and Peace Salons.
At the foot of the main building lies a row of four sculptures, the very first to be executed by the Keller brothers *(p 192)*, who drew inspiration from the antique model: Bacchus, Apollo, Antinoüs and Silenus.
The terrace offers a general view of the grounds and their distinctive features *(description p 192)*: in the foreground the Water Gardens (Parterres d'Eau), whose sweeping perspective ends at the Grand Canal; on the left the South Parterre; on the right the North Parterre and the North Groves, cut across by another canal leading to the Neptune Basin.
Return to the Marble Court through the South Arcade in the South Wing.

PALACE INTERIOR

We do not mention the restoration work under way at the palace when it does not affect the programme of the tour.

The visitors' entrance (❶) leads through to a vestibule which houses the ticket office. From there, go up to the Chapel (**a**) on the first floor, either by using the circular staircase ④ or by crossing the 17C galleries of the Museum of French History.

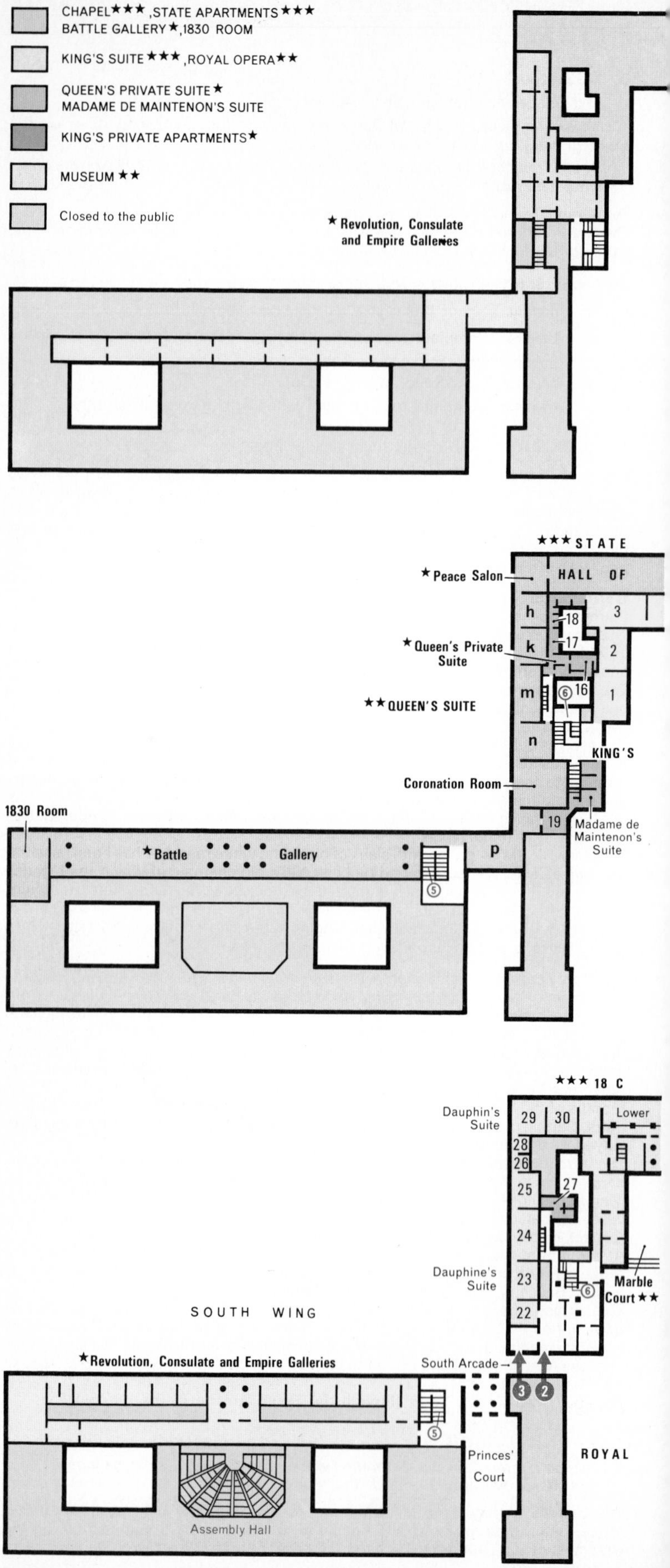
CHAPEL★★★, STATE APARTMENTS★★★
BATTLE GALLERY★, 1830 ROOM
KING'S SUITE★★★, ROYAL OPERA★★
QUEEN'S PRIVATE SUITE★
MADAME DE MAINTENON'S SUITE
KING'S PRIVATE APARTMENTS★
MUSEUM★★
Closed to the public
★Revolution, Consulate and Empire Galleries
★★★STATE
HALL OF
★Peace Salon
★Queen's Private Suite
★★QUEEN'S SUITE
KING'S
Coronation Room
1830 Room
★Battle Gallery
Madame de Maintenon's Suite
★★★18 C
Dauphin's Suite
Lower
Dauphine's Suite
Marble Court★★
SOUTH WING
★Revolution, Consulate and Empire Galleries
South Arcade
Princes' Court
ROYAL
Assembly Hall

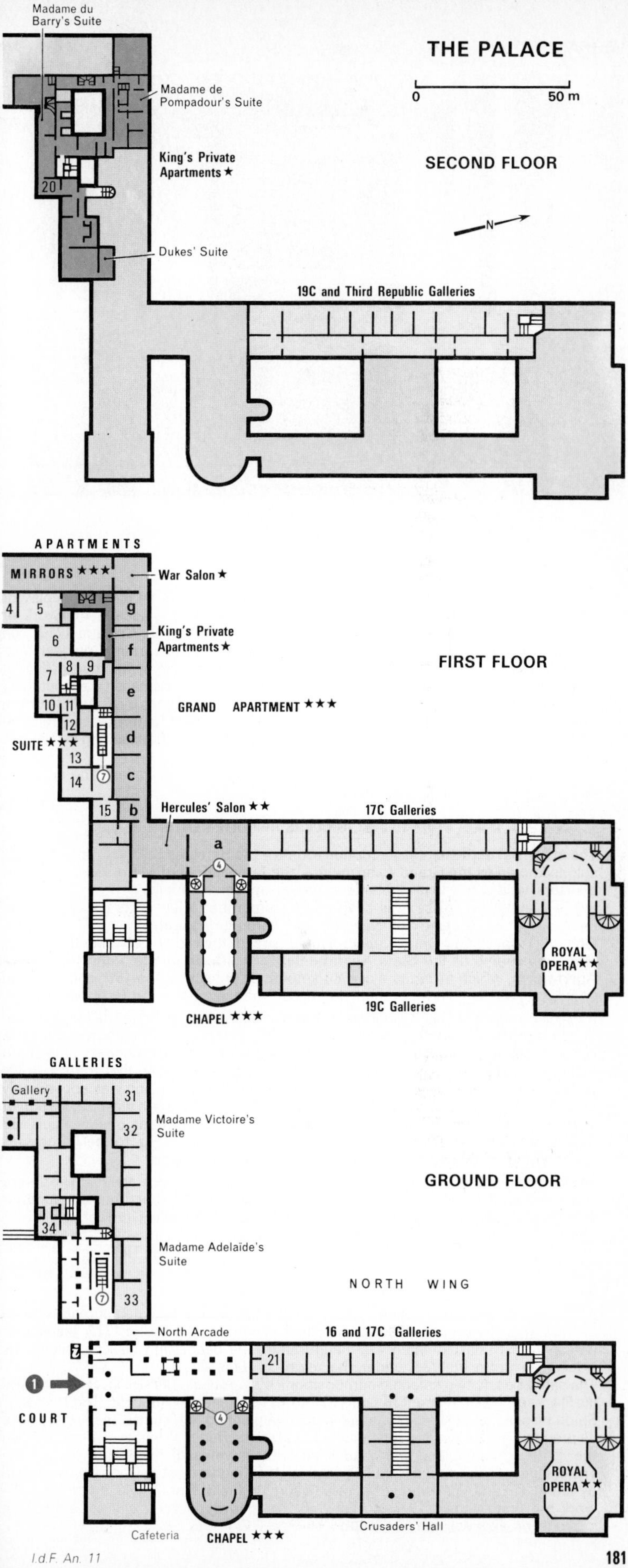
THE PALACE
0
50 m
SECOND FLOOR
N
Madame du Barry's Suite
Madame de Pompadour's Suite
King's Private Apartments ★
20
Dukes' Suite
19C and Third Republic Galleries
FIRST FLOOR
APARTMENTS
MIRRORS ★★★
War Salon ★
King's Private Apartments ★
4
5
6
7
8
9
10
11
12
13
14
15
g
f
e
d
c
b
a
GRAND APARTMENT ★★★
SUITE ★★★
Hercules' Salon ★★
17C Galleries
ROYAL OPERA ★★
19C Galleries
CHAPEL ★★★
GROUND FLOOR
GALLERIES
Gallery
31
32
33
34
Madame Victoire's Suite
Madame Adelaïde's Suite
NORTH WING
North Arcade
16 and 17C Galleries
21
1
COURT
ROYAL OPERA ★★
Cafeteria
CHAPEL ★★★
Crusaders' Hall

The Chapel in the Palace of Versailles

★★★CHAPEL (CHAPELLE)

Dedicated to St Louis (Louis IX), the chapel at Versailles is an elegant display of stonework decorated in white and gold tones. This masterpiece is the work of Mansart, and was completed by his brother-in-law Robert de Cotte in 1710. The pillars and arches bear exquisite low reliefs by Van Clève, Le Lorrain, Cousteau, etc. The organ does not stand in its usual place, which is occupied by the royal gallery. It stands in the gallery at the east end, a splendid piece of craftsmanship executed by Clicquot, enhanced by finely-sculpted carvings based on studies by Robert de Cotte. The marble altar is attributed to Van Clève. The altar front features a low relief in gilded bronze representing the *Pietà:* it is the work of Vassé. The painting in the apse is by La Fosse and depicts the Resurrection.
While the members of the royal family were seated in the gallery, the courtiers would be found standing in the nave.

★★★STATE APARTMENTS (GRANDS APPARTEMENTS)

These consist of the various reception rooms – the Hercules Salon and a suite of six salons known as the Grand Apartment –, the famous Hall of Mirrors and the living quarters where the king and queen would appear in public.
While visiting the palace, it is advisable to remember a few facts concerning the layout of great châteaux of classical and baroque inspiration.
Generally speaking, French rulers would spend their day between the ornate reception rooms of the State Apartments, their official quarters and the Private Apartments, which afforded a certain amount of privacy. In the 18C, Louis XV and later Louis XVI enjoyed a greater degree of intimacy in the Petits Appartements.

A standard example of State Apartments. – The two suites belonging to the king and the queen are placed symmetrically on either side of the central pavilion. Each suite consisted of at least one guard room, several antechambers, the bedroom, the grand cabinet and a number of private salons (it was through these that the two royal suites communicated). At Versailles, this symmetrical disposition was applied only between 1673 and 1682. When Marie-Thérèse died in 1683, there was no question of Mme de Maintenon occupying the apartments of the former queen. Louis XIV moved into new quarters giving onto the Marble Court. His former suite was transformed at great cost into a series of reception rooms.

Summer and winter furnishings. – In the living quarters of the palace, the hangings were changed twice a year, towards the months of May and October. Thus the summer furnishings (silk) would alternate with the winter furnishings (velvet).
The walls clothed in fabric were then hung with paintings inspired by religious themes, by artists of the Italian School: Poussin, Veronese, Titian, etc.

★★HERCULES' SALON (SALON D'HERCULE)

It stands on the site formerly occupied by the fourth and penultimate chapel belonging to the original château. Its construction was started in 1712, the year in which the St Louis Chapel was inaugurated. The decoration was completed by Robert de Cotte in 1736, under the reign of Louis XV.
The salon boasts two splendid compositions by Veronese. **Christ at the House of Simon the Pharisee★** was a present to Louis XIV from the Venetian Republic. The Hercules' Salon was in fact designed to house this huge painting, which has been returned to its precious gilt frame. The second work *Eliezer and Rebecca* has been placed above the marble mantelpiece, richly adorned with carvings of gilded bronze.
The ceiling – representing Hercules entering the Kingdom of the Gods – was painted by François Lemoyne, who spent three years on the 315m^2 – 3 390sq ft fresco. His work met with widespread acclaim, but the following year the artist suffered a nervous breakdown and committed suicide (1737).

★★★ GRAND APARTMENT (GRAND APPARTEMENT)

In former times, it was approached from the Royal Court by means of the Ambassadors' Staircase, destroyed in 1752.
It provides a splendid example of early Louis XIV decoration. Note the use of noble materials such as polychrome marble, bronze and copper, chiselled and gilded in the Italian baroque style. Impressive rock crystal chandeliers and candelabra adorn the pedestal tables.
The suite of six salons was sparsely furnished with a few stools, folding chairs, pedestal and console tables. The Grand Apartment – running from the Hercules Salon, dedicated to a man endowed with divine powers, to the Apollo Salon, built in honour of the son of Jupiter and Latona – symbolised the solar myth to which Louis XIV claimed to belong. The six rooms were all built by Le Vau in 1668 and decorated by Le Brun. The salons are named after the subjects painted on the ceiling frescoes.
Three times a week, between 6 and 10pm on Mondays, Wednesdays and Thursdays, the king held court in the Grand Apartment. The ceremony was enhanced by dancing and various other entertainments.

Abundance Salon (Salon de l'Abondance) (b). – At the time of Louis XIV, on the days when the king held court, this salon presented three buffets: one for hot drinks, two for cold beverages such as wine, eaux-de-vie, sorbets and fruit juice, then called "fruit water" *(eaux-de-fruits)*. The walls are hung with the winter furnishings, made of embossed velvet in deep emerald tones. Admire the four portraits of the royal family, executed by Rigaud and Van Loo: the Grand Dauphin, Philippe V, the duc de Bourgogne and Louis XV.
The next two salons were originally vestibules leading to the Ambassadors' Staircase. The magnificent walls lined with marble are in keeping with the ornate decoration of the former staircase of honour.

Venus Salon (Salon de Vénus) (c). – As in the following salons, the ceiling is painted by Houasse. It features decorated panels framed by heavy gilt stucco.

Diana Salon (Salon de Diane) (d). – This used to be the billiard room under Louis XIV. Observe the **bust of Louis XIV** by Bernini (1665), a remarkable piece of baroque workmanship. The salon offers several paintings by La Fosse and Blanchard.

Mars Salon (Salon de Mars) (e). – The lavish decoration (wall hangings) reminds visitors that this salon once belonged to the royal suite (guard room). Louis XIV subsequently used it for dances, games and concerts. The two galleries that housed the musicians were placed on either side of the fireplace. They were taken down in 1750. The 18C paintings include *Darius' Tent* by Le Brun and *The Pilgrims of Emmaüs* after Veronese.
The side walls bear Rigaud's portrait of Louis XV and a painting of Marie Leczinska by Van Loo. The martial scenes on the ceiling are attributed to Audran, Jouvenet and Houasse. One of the Sun King's favourite paintings hangs above the fireplace: Domenichino's *King David,* in which he is portrayed playing the harp. It was originally displayed in the king's bedchamber.

Mercury Salon (Salon de Mercure) (f). – This former antechamber was used for gaming on the evenings when the king held court. It was here that Louis XIV lay in state for one week after his death in 1715. Seventy-two ecclesiastics took turns to watch over him, ensuring that four services could be held at the same time between 5am and midday. The ceiling was decorated by J. B. de Champaigne.

Apollo Salon (Salon d'Apollon) (g). – The former throne room. The throne was placed on a central platform covered by a large canopy. One can still see the three hooks to which the canopy was attached.
Louis XIV received ambassadors in the Apollo Salon. When he held court, it was used for dances and concerts. The ceiling sports a fresco by La Fosse: *Apollo in a Sun Chariot.*
This room marks the end of the Grand Apartment. Set at a perpendicular angle, the Hall of Mirrors and the adjacent War and Peace Salons occupy the entire length of the main front giving onto the palace gardens.

★ WAR SALON (SALON DE LA GUERRE)

A corner room opening onto the Hall of Mirrors and the Apollo Salon. It features a huge oval low relief sculpted by Coysevox, representing the king riding in triumph over his enemies.

★★★ HALL OF MIRRORS (GALERIE DES GLACES)

The Hall of Mirrors was completed by Mansart in 1687. It covered a short-lived terrace (1668-1678) that Le Vau had built along the garden front. Together with the War and Peace Salons, it is the most brilliant achievement by Le Brun and his team of artists. The hall is 75m – 246ft long, 10m – 33ft wide and 12m – 40ft high. The 17 large windows are echoed by 17 mirrors on the wall opposite. These are made up of 578 pieces, the largest one could manufacture at the time. This hall was designed to catch the golden rays of sunset.
The ceiling fresco – painted by Le Brun in amber, flame-coloured tones – pays tribute to the early reign of Louis XIV (from 1661 to 1678, up to the Treaty of Nijmegen).
The capitals of the pilasters are an unusual ornamental feature: made of gilded bronze, they represent the "French order", which combines antique motifs with fleurs-de-lis and stylised cocks (the emblem for French patriotism).

In 1980 the Hall of Mirrors was restored to its former glory. With its crystal chandeliers and new set of candelabra – cast after the six surviving originals – it presents the same dazzling appearance as in 1770, when Marie-Antoinette was married to the Dauphin, the future King Louis XVI.
The Hall of Mirrors was used for court receptions, formal ceremonies and diplomatic encounters. On these occasions, the throne was placed under the arch leading into the Peace Salon. It is easier to picture the hall during court festivities, when it was thronged with elegant visitors in formal attire, brightly lit by the thousands of flames reflected in the mirrors. The tubs bearing the orange trees, as well as the chandeliers and other furnishings, were made of solid silver under Louis XIV. For a period of ten years, part of the country's monetary reserves was thus shaped into works of art. It was here that the German Empire was proclaimed on 18 January 1871, and that the Treaty of Versailles was signed on 28 June 1919.
The central windows offer a splendid **view★★★** of the Grand Perspective.

★PEACE SALON (SALON DE LA PAIX)

Placed at the southern end of the Hall of Mirrors, it acts as a counterpart to the War Salon. Originally conceived as an extension of the long hall, it was made into an annexe of the Queen's Suite towards the end of Louis XIV's reign: it communicated with the gallery by means of a mobile partition.
Above the mantelpiece hangs *Louis XV bringing Peace to Europe,* a painting by François Lemoyne.

★★QUEEN'S SUITE (APPARTEMENT DE LA REINE)

This suite was created for Louis XIV's wife Marie-Thérèse, who died in 1683.

Queen's Bedroom (Chambre de la Reine) (h). – In 1975, after a restoration programme lasting 30 years, this room had regained its summer furnishings of 1787. Originally designed for Marie-Thérèse, the bedchamber was later occupied by the wife of the Grand Dauphin, Louis XIV's son, by the duchesse de Bourgogne, wife of the Sun King's grandson, who gave birth to Louis XV there, by Marie Leczinska, wife of Louis XV (43 years), and by Louis XVI's wife Marie-Antoinette. Nineteen children belonging to French royalty – namely Louis XV and Philippe V d'Espagne – were born in this bedroom.
A long-standing tradition ruled that the delivery of royal infants should be made public. Even the proud Marie-Antoinette had to comply with the French custom, surrounded by a crowd of curious onlookers.
The ornamental motifs on the wainscoting and the ceiling were designed and executed for Marie Leczinska by Gabriel, while the fireplace, imposing jewel chest, sphinx-shaped andirons, fire screen and bedspread were designed for Marie-Antoinette.
Note the magnificent silk hangings and furnishings decorated with flowers, ribbons and peacock's tails, many of which were rewoven to the original pattern in Lyon.

Peers' Salon (Salon des Nobles de la Reine) (k). – The official presentations to the queen took place in this former antechamber. It was also here that the queens and Dauphines of France used to lie in state prior to the burial ceremony. The original fresco on the ceiling, attributed to Michel Corneille, has been preserved. The rest of the decoration was considered staid and old-fashioned by Marie-Antoinette, who had it entirely refurbished by the architect Richard Mique (1785). Furnished with commodes and corner cupboards by Riesener and embellished with magnificent green silk hangings, the salon looks very much like it did on the eve of the French Revolution in 1789.

Antechamber (m). – Was used as a guard room under Marie-Thérèse. It was here that Louis XV and Marie Leczinska – and later Louis XVI and Marie-Antoinette – would dine in full view of the public.
A family portrait of Marie-Antoinette and her children by Mme Vigée-Lebrun shows, from left to right, Mme Royale, the duc de Normandie – who became Louis XVII –, and the Dauphin, who died in 1789. He is portrayed pointing to an empty cradle which symbolises the premature death of his sister Mme Sophie.

Queen's Guard Room (Salle des Gardes de la Reine) (n). – The decoration was the work of Le Brun and N. Coypel. It was moved from its original setting – the Jupiter Salon – when the Hall of Mirrors was completed in 1687. The Jupiter Salon was subsequently renamed the War Salon. On 6 October 1789, several of the queen's guards were stabbed to death by a group of dedicated revolutionaries. The Louis XIV decor – featuring sumptuous marble-lined walls – has been beautifully preserved.

CORONATION ROOM (SALLE DU SACRE)

Initially used as a chapel between 1676 and 1682. The Parlement de Paris used to hold its sessions in this former guard room. It was altered by Louis-Philippe in order to accommodate several huge paintings depicting the emperor's coronation. David's second *Coronation of Napoleon* – executed between 1808 and 1822 – lies to the left of the entrance. The original is exhibited in the Louvre Museum (Salle Mollien). On the opposite wall hang David's *Champ de Mars Eagles* and a painting by Gros representing *Murat at the Battle of Aboukir* (1806).

1792 Room (Salle de 1792) (p). – This large, unfurnished room lies at the junction of the south wing and the main central pavilion. The walls are hung with portraits of soldiers, paintings of famous battles and war scenes. Cogniet's work *The Paris National Guard* shows Louis-Philippe proudly sporting his Lieutenant-General's uniform.

★ BATTLE GALLERY (GALERIE DES BATAILLES)

Created in 1836 on the site of the princes' suite situated in the south wing, the Battle Gallery caused quite a stir on account of its unusually large dimensions: 120m – 394ft by 13m – 43ft. It was designed to house the 33 huge paintings representing France's major victories under the *Ancien Régime,* the Empire and the Republic, running from Tolbiac *(first on the left when entering)* to Wagram *(first on the right when entering).* The series included works by Horace Vernet, Louis-Philippe's favourite painter (Wagram, Iéna, Fontenoy, Bouvines, Friedland), Eugène Delacroix (Taillebourg) and Baron Gérard (Austerlitz).

On leaving the Queen's Suite, take the Princes' Staircase ⑤ and go down to the courtyard bearing the same name.

★★★ KING'S SUITE (APPARTEMENT DU ROI)

The king's quarters are arranged around the Marble Court. They were designed by Jules Hardouin-Mansart and set up in Louis XIII's château between 1682 and 1701. The style is typical of the Louis XIV period. The ceilings are no longer coffered but painted in white, the marble tiling has been replaced by white and gold panelling and large mirrors adorn the stately fireplaces.

Queen's Staircase (Escalier de la Reine) ⑥. – Towards the end of the *Ancien Régime,* this was the official entrance to the royal apartments. The decoration of the staircase is ornate in the extreme: from the top landing, admire the elegant display of multicoloured marble conceived by Le Brun. The huge *trompe-l'œil* painting is jointly attributed to Meusnier, Poerson and Belin de Fontenay.
The guard room **(1)** and a first antechamber **(2)** lead to the Bull's Eye Salon.

Bull's Eye Salon (Salon de l'Œil de Bœuf) (second antechamber) **(3)**. – The salon was originally two rooms: the king's bedchamber between 1684 and 1701 – the part nearest to the two windows giving onto the Marble Court – and a small study. The two were reunited under the supervision of Mansart and Robert de Cotte. Lightness and elegance are the principal characteristics of this charming salon, which contrasts sharply with the earlier achievements of Louis' reign. Level with the famous bull's eye – echoed by a mirror on the opposite wall – lies a frieze depicting children at play. Note Coysevox' bust of Louis XIV.
The paintings by Veronese and Bassano have been replaced by a number of royal portraits, including an allegorical rendering of Louis XIV' family by Nocret.
It was in this antechamber that the courtiers assembled before witnessing the rising and retiring ceremonies of the king.

King's Bedroom (Chambre du Roi) **(4)**. – This became Louis XIV's state bedroom in 1701. Seeing that the king's bed lay in the exact centre of the palace, this bedroom, which gave onto the Marble Court, looks out in the direction of the rising sun. Louis XIV, suffering from a gangrenous knee, died here on 1 September 1715. The ritual rising and retiring ceremonies took place in this room from 1701 to 1789. Daytime visitors were requested to make a small bow when passing in front of the bed, which symbolised the Sun King's absolute monarchy.
The king's bedroom is hung with its summer furnishings of 1723 – Louis XV's second year at the palace – and its decor has been scrupulously reconstituted. Beyond the beautifully-restored gilded balustrade lies a raised four-poster bed, complete with canopy and curtains. The gold and silver embroidered brocade used for the bed and wall hangings, upholstery and door coverings has been entirely rewoven.
Six religious works – notably Valentin de Boulogne's *Four Evangelists* – lie level with the attica. Above the doors, visitors may see *St Madeleine* by Domenichino, *St John the Baptist* by Caracciolo, together with several portraits by Van Dyck.

Council Chamber (Grand Cabinet) **(5)**. – Like the Bull's Eye Salon, it originally consisted of two rooms: the Cabinet des Termes and the Cabinet du Conseil. The decoration of the present room – created under Louis XV – was entrusted to Gabriel. The mirrors dating from Louis XIV's reign were replaced with wainscoting by Rousseau, who produced a splendid example of French rococo, characterised by lightness, harmony and variety.
Over a period of one hundred years, many grave decisions affecting the destiny of France were taken in the Council Chamber, namely that of France's involvement in the American War of Independence in 1775.

KING'S PRIVATE SUITE (APPARTEMENT PRIVÉ DU ROI)

This suite of rooms presents superb wainscoting by Gabriel and constitutes altogether a dazzling feast for the eyes. The rococo carvings – skilfully executed by Verberckt – appear to be a dominant theme in the decoration.

King's Bedchamber (Chambre à Coucher) **(6)**. – The absence of furniture makes it difficult to picture this room in its original state. Owing to the constraints of court etiquette, Louis XV (after 1738) and then Louis XVI (up to the end of the *Ancien Régime*) would have to leave this room and slip away to the state bedroom, where they "perfomed" the rising and retiring ceremonies. It was here that Louis XV died of smallpox on 10 May 1774. The original paintings above the doors were taken down and replaced by portraits of the three daughters of Louis XV.

Clock Cabinet (Cabinet de la Pendule) **(7)**. – Named after the famous astronomical clock executed by Passemant and Dauthiau, with bronze embellishments by Caffiéri, which was brought to the palace in January 1754: it showed not only the hour, but the day, the month, the year and the phase of the moon. Under Louis XV and until 1769, this cabinet was used as a gaming room when the king held court.

In the centre of the room stands the equestrian statue of Louis XV by Vassé. It is a replica of Bouchardon's sculpture which initially adorned the Place Louis XV – now called Place de la Concorde – and which was destroyed in 1792.

Dogs' Antechamber (Antichambre des Chiens) (8). – A charming passageway off the king's private staircase (known as *degré du Roi*). The decoration features Louis XIV panelling, in sharp contrast with the adjoining rooms.

Hunters' Dining Hall (Salle à Manger dite des Retours de Chasse) (9). – Between 1750 and 1769, hunts were organised every other day in the forests surrounding Versailles. Louis XV and a few privileged fellow hunters would come here to sup after their exertions.

Corner Room (Cabinet Intérieur du Roi) (10). – A masterpiece of 18C French ornamental art. Louis XV commissioned Gabriel and the accomplished cabinet-maker Verberckt to produce the rococo decor, an exercise at which they surpassed themselves.
The celebrated **roll top desk★** executed by Oeben and Riesener (1769) was among the few prestigious works of art that were spared in 1792.
The medal cabinet attributed to the cabinet-maker Gaudreaux (1739) is adorned with numerous exhibits in gilded bronze: it bears the 1785 candelabra commemorating the role played by France in the American War of Independance, flanked by two Sèvres vases (bronzes by Thomire). Two corner cupboards made by Joubert in 1755, belonging to Louis XV's collections, were subsequently added, as was a set of chairs attributed to Foliot (1774). The cabinet was originally private but under Louis XVI it took on a semi-official character. In 1785 it was the scene of a formal encounter attended by Marie-Antoinette, at which the king informed Cardinal de Rohan that he would shortly be arrested on account of his involvement in the Diamond Necklace Affair.
The Corner Room leads through to the Inner Cabinet (**11**) where Louis XV and Louis XVI kept all confidential documents relating to state affairs, and where they granted private hearings.

Madame Adelaïde's Cabinet (Cabinet de Madame Adelaïde) (12). – This was one of the first "new rooms" remodelled at the instigation of Louis XV. It overlooks the Royal Court and was designed by Louis XV for his favourite daughter Madame Adelaïde (1752). The ornate decoration features delightful rococo wainscoting and gilded panelling embellished with musical instruments, as well as marine and floral motifs. This cabinet was used as a music room by the king's daughter. It is believed that young Mozart performed on the harpsichord before the royal family in this very room, during the winter of 1763-1764. Louis XVI later made the room his "jewel cabinet". Note the extraordinary medal cabinet attributed to Bennemann: each drawer is decorated with melted wax, delicately blended with feathers and butterfly wings and carefully poured onto thin glass plates.

Louis XVI's Library (Bibliothèque de Louis XVI) (13). – Designed by the ageing Gabriel and executed by the wood carver Antoine Rousseau, this extremely refined ensemble is a perfect example of the Louis XVI style (1774). The austere appearance of the bookcases, in which the door panels are concealed by a set of false decorative backs, is countered by the gay Chinese motifs on the upholstery and the curtains. Next to Riesener's flat top desk stands the vast mahogany table where the king spent many enjoyable hours in quiet seclusion.

China Salon (Salon des Porcelaines) (14). – Was used as the Hunters' Dining Hall under Louis XV, and from 1769 to 1789 under Louis XVI. It houses numerous exhibits made in Sèvres porcelain and glazed after drawings by Oudry. The whole collection was commissioned by Louis XVI.

Louis XVI's Gaming Room (Salon des Jeux de Louis XVI) (15). – From the doorway you may appreciate the full effect of this perfect vignette of 18C furniture and ornamental art: corner cupboards by Riesener (1774), set of chairs by Boulard, curtains and upholstery in a rich crimson and gold brocade.

Walk down the Louis-Philippe staircase ⑦ and leave by the North Arcade (a public passageway leading through to the park). The room on the ground floor houses a miniature replica of the Ambassadors' Staircase (Escalier des Ambassadeurs). Ask to view the model.

★★ ROYAL OPERA (OPÉRA ROYAL)

Gabriel started work on the Opera in 1768 and completed it in time for the wedding ceremony of Marie-Antoinette and the future King Louis XVI.
It was the first oval-shaped opera house in France and although it was built during the reign of Louis XV, its decoration was to be later termed Louis XVI: Pajou's work, inspired by the classical models of antiquity, remained surprisingly modern. The court engineer Arnoult designed the sophisticated machinery required for the new opera house. In the case of banquets and formal receptions, the floor of the stalls and that of the circle could be raised level with the stage. This auditorium – whose interior decoration is made entirely of wood – enjoys excellent acoustics and may seat 700. The seating capacity could virtually be doubled by means of additional galleries set up on the stage.
In the middle of the circle lies the royal box, guarded by a mobile grid and surmounted by an elegant alcove. A number of other boxes, also enclosed by grilles, may be seen up above in the flies.
The low reliefs adorning the boxes were executed by Pajou. They represent the Gods of Mount Olympus (dress circle), groups of children and the signs of the zodiac (upper circle).

Initially reserved for members of the court, the opera house at Versailles was later used for the lavish receptions organised on the occasion of official visits. A number of foreign rulers were received at the palace, namely the King of Sweden (1784), Marie-Antoinette's brother the Emperor Joseph II (1777 and 1781) and Queen Victoria (1855). The sessions of the National Assembly were held in the Royal Opera between 1871 and 1875. It was here that the Wallon Amendment was voted on 30 January 1875, laying the foundation stone of the Third Republic. The latest restoration ended in 1957, when the opening ceremony was attended by Queen Elizabeth II and Prince Philip.

★QUEEN'S PRIVATE SUITE

(CABINETS INTÉRIEURS DE LA REINE) *plan p 180-181*

These somewhat cramped apartments giving onto two inner courtyards were used as a day-time retreat by the queens of France. Unlike the king, they were not allowed to retire away from their State Apartment. The 18C decoration and layout was conceived by Marie-Antoinette, who gave the suite a delicate, feminine touch.

Gold Cabinet (Cabinet Doré) (16). – The panelling by the Rousseau brothers marks the revival of antique motifs: frieze with rosettes, sphinx, trivets, small censers,... A lovely chandelier features along the magnificent bronze works. The commode is attributed to Riesener. Naderman's harp reminds visitors that the queen was an enthusiastic musician in her spare time: she would often play with Grétry, Gluck or even his rival Piccinni. It was in this cabinet that Mme Vigée-Lebrun worked on her portrait of Marie-Antoinette.

Library (Bibliothèque) (17). – Note the drawer handles in the shape of a two-headed eagle, the emblem of the house of Habsburg.

Boudoir (Méridienne) (18). – This little octagonal chamber was used as a rest room by Marie-Antoinette. It was designed in 1781 by the queen's architect Mique in honour of the birth of the first Dauphin. The decoration evokes romance and parental love: lilies, hearts pierced with arrows and the famous dolphin.
The boudoir – embellished with blue silk hangings – is furnished with two armchairs by Georges Jacob and the original day couch.
Two of the many prestigious works of art given to the queen are exhibited here: a clock offered by the City of Paris and a table featuring a tray with fragments of petrified wood (a present from one of Marie-Antoinette's sisters).
The second floor houses Marie-Antoinette's Apartment *(being restored).*

MADAME DE MAINTENON'S SUITE

(APPARTEMENT DE MADAME DE MAINTENON) *plan p 180-181*

This suite was located away from the throngs of courtiers but next to the king's apartments, reflecting a situation enforced by the king during the last 32 years of his reign, with a view to establishing an atmosphere of tact and mutual respect.
The original furniture has been removed and the suite now belongs to the Museum of French History.
The Grand Cabinet (**19**) was a private salon decorated with red hangings where Mme de Maintenon entertained members of the royal family – her favourite the duchesse de Bourgogne – and where Racine recited his famous plays *Esther* and *Athalie.*

★KING'S PRIVATE APARTMENTS

(PETITS APPARTEMENTS DU ROI)

Louis XV did not share the taste for publicity that had been such a dominant trait of the Sun King's personality. Consequently, he created a suite of private apartments, to which he could retire and receive his mistresses, close friends and relations. Some of the rooms overlooked the inner courts, others were located in the attics. They were approached by a series of narrow passages and staircases. In the privacy of these rooms, the king would read, study, carve ivory and wooden pieces or eat on the tiny roof-top terrace, surrounded by tubs of flowers and several delightful aviaries. The decoration of these apartments was renewed at regular intervals: much the same could be said for their occupants. Four of the rooms housed Mme de Pompadour's first suite from 1745 to 1750. Louis XVI used the rooms giving onto the Stag Court when he wished to study or indulge in one of his favourite pastimes. We strongly recommend a tour of these apartments to visitors who are already acquainted with Versailles and who show a particular interest in 18C decorative art.

Madame de Pompadour's Suite (Appartement de Madame de Pompadour). – *2nd floor.* This was the first suite occupied by Louis XV's mistress between 1745 and 1750. The Grand Cabinet features splendid carved woodwork by Verberckt.

Madame du Barry's Suite (Appartement de Madame du Barry). – *2nd floor.* The wooden panelling has been restored according to the original decoration. The suite looks out onto the Stag Court and the Marble Court. It consists of a bathroom, a bedroom, a library and a corner salon (**20**) which was one of Louis XV's favourite haunts: he would enjoy sitting here and gazing out at the town of Versailles, nestling among soft, wooded slopes.

Dukes' Suite (Appartements des ducs de Maurepas et Villequier). – *2nd floor.* These apartments were occupied by two ministers of Louis XVI, the duc de Maurepas and the duc de Villequier. The decoration appears to be rather austere when compared to that of the royal suites. Most of the furniture was donated by the Duke and Duchess of Windsor.

★★ MUSEUM OF FRENCH HISTORY (MUSÉE DE L'HISTOIRE DE FRANCE)

The museum houses several thousand paintings and sculptures which present visitors with the period of French history covering the 16, 17, 18 and 19C.

CRUSADERS' HALLS (SALLE DES CROISADES) *(not open to the public)*

They contain a collection of paintings commissioned by Louis-Philippe.

16 AND 17C GALLERIES (SALLES DES 16e ET 17e SIÈCLES)

These small rooms – occupying the greater part of the north wing – feature a charming selection of paintings and portraits, enhanced by busts and console-tables.

Ground Floor. – The vestibule in the chapel leads to this suite of eleven galleries. The first six were once occupied by the duc de Maine, the son of Louis XIV and Mme de Montespan, while the last four housed the apartments of the Princes of Bourbon-Conti.
The first gallery – containing the 16C works – has been partitioned as it was under the *Ancien Régime* (**21**). The series of **portraits★** depicting famous personalities was assembled by Roger de Gaignières, who bequeathed the collection to the Sun King. The models included Henri IV, who enjoyed visiting the site of Versailles, and Louis XIII, the founder of the original château. Works by Vouet, Philippe de Champaigne, Deruet, Le Brun tell of the men and the events that marked French history between Louis XIII's reign and the early days of divine monarchy. The gallery dedicated to Port-Royal features several portraits by Philippe de Champaigne and gouaches attributed to Magdeleine de Boullongne. The rare collection of paintings in the Versailles Gallery illustrates the various stages of construction of the palace.

First Floor. – Thanks to the talent of Le Brun, Mignard, Van der Meulen, Coypel, Rigaud, Largillère, etc, these rooms are brought alive by the living portraits of the royal family, Mme de Maintenon, Louis XIV's legitimated children and the celebrated courtiers and historical figures that marked the king's reign,
Note the set of portraits of famous men (Colbert, Racine, Molière, La Fontaine, Le Nôtre and Couperin) and the vast battle scenes by Van der Meulen, characterised by attention to detail and a true love of nature.
The galleries offer a lovely view of the gardens.

★★★ 18C GALLERIES (SALLES DU 18e SIÈCLE)

Situated on the ground floor of the central pavilion, they once housed the apartments of Louis XV's son the Dauphin, the Dauphine Marie-Josèphe de Saxe and the three daughters of Louis XV, addressed as *Mesdames*. The mid-18C decoration has been entirely restored (furniture, hangings). Many of the works displayed in these galleries were executed by some of the greatest painters and sculptors of the 18C. Consequently, the exhibition will be of the highest interest to both historians and art specialists.
Visitors wishing to follow a chronological tour should start at the foot of the Queen's Staircase. From there they can walk through the rooms giving onto the South Parterre, the terrace and the North Parterre. The tour ends with the rooms overlooking the Marble Court.

Dauphine's Suite (Appartement de la Dauphine). – The Guard Room (**22**) houses a number of pictures representing the rulers who succeeded the Sun King: portrait of the five-year-old Louis XV by Rigaud, another by Belle (1722), Santerre's portrait of the Regent. The fireplace in the Antechamber (**23**), adorned with a bust of the Regent, was taken from the Queen's Bedroom at the time of Marie Leczinska. The Dauphine's Grand Cabinet (**24**) evokes the marriage of Marie Leczinska to Louis XV. It also presents Lemaire's sculpted barometer, offered on the occasion of Marie-Antoinette's marriage to the Dauphin, and several corner cupboards by Bernard II van Risen Burgh (B.V.R.B.). The Dauphine's Bedroom (**25**) contains a Polish-style bed and a magnificint set of six armchairs executed by Heurtaut. Note Nattier's two portraits of Mme Adélaïde and Mme Henriette, portrayed respectively as Flora and Diana. The Inner Cabinet (**26**) features 1748 woodwork glazed with Vernis Martin. Observe Gaudreaux' commode and a writing desk by B.V.R.B. The Dauphine's Private Cabinets (**27**) *(visited at the same time as the Queen's Private Suite)* were remodelled under Louis XVIII for the duchesse d'Angoulême, the daughter of Louis XVI: couch formerly belonging to the comtesse de Provence, antechamber, study-library and servants' quarters.

Dauphin's Suite (Appartement du Dauphin). – The first room (**28**) was used as a library: it boasts magnificent wooden panelling in deep amber tones, enhanced by turquoise relief work. Admire Vernet's delicate seascapes above the doors. The fine furniture includes a flat writing desk by B.V.R.B. and one of Criaerd's commodes. The Grand Corner Cabinet (**29**) houses portraits of Mesdames Adélaïde, Louise, Sophie and Victoire by Nattier, as well as several beautiful works by Jacob, taken from Louis XVI's gaming room at St-Cloud.
The Dauphin's Bedchamber (**30**), occupied by Louis XVI's son, has retained its original 1747 decor: wardrobe with lacquered panels (B.V.R.B.), commode by Boudin and an 18C embroidered canopied bed. The fireplace is among the finest in the palace.

Lower Gallery (Galerie Basse). – Divided into apartments under Louis XVI and partly reconstitued under Louis-Philippe, the gallery now stands as it did under Louis XIV. From 1782 to 1789, the rooms set up in this gallery were used by Marie-Antoinette and her children.

Madame Victoire's Suite (**Appartement de Madame Victoire**). – The Sun King's former bathroom and its two marble piscinae underwent several restorations before being used as the antechamber to this suite, occupied by the fourth daughter of Louis XV. The **Grand Cabinet** (**31**) is an exquisite corner room with a delightful carved cornice and panelling by Verberckt. It has retained its original fireplace.
Mme Victoire's former bedroom (**32**) has been furnished with some truly outstanding pieces, set off by the newly-restored summer hangings.

Madame Adelaïde's Suite (**Appartement de Madame Adelaïde**). – These rooms housed the second suite of Mme de Pompadour, who died here in 1764. Five years later, Mme Adelaïde moved into the suite, which consisted of a private cabinet, a bedroom and a grand cabinet. The **Ambassadors' Salon** (Salle des Hocquetons) (**33**) was an annexe adjoining the former Ambassadors' Staircase, destroyed in 1752. The stately proportions of this room, its *trompe-l'œil* fresco and its splendid marble paving give one an idea of how magnificent the flight of stairs once looked.
Note the huge **clock★** by Claude Siméon Passement with bronze ornamentation by Caffiéri: it dates from 1754 and illustrates the creation of the world.
It was in the **King's Guard Room** (**34**) that Louis XV was stabbed by Robert François Damiens in 1757. This room led to the king's private suite.
The last rooms, overlooking the Marble Court, housed the apartments of the Captain of the Guard. They are dedicated to the latter days of Louis XVI's reign and the French Revolution.
The ground floor suite belonging to Marie-Antoinette has been recreated in part: one may visit the bedroom and the bathroom.

REVOLUTION, CONSULATE AND EMPIRE GALLERIES

(SALLES DE LA RÉVOLUTION, DU CONSULAT ET DE L'EMPIRE) *South attic*

The exhibition halls are decorated with a selection of different hangings, manufactured during each particular period of history. Minute care has been taken to present visitors with a detailed, comprehensive collection of documents, drawings, engravings, watercolours, and paintings. All these exhibits bring to life the famous figures of Napoleonic times and the members of the Bonaparte family. They also evoke the great battles, formal ceremonies, historic encounters and amusing scenes that changed the course of French history.

19C GALLERIES (SALLES DU 19e SIÈCLE) *2nd Floor – North attic*

Galleries dedicated to the Restoration, the July Monarchy, the Second Empire and the Third Republic (**Salles de la Restauration, de la Monarchie de Juillet, du Second Empire et de la Troisième République**). – A great many paintings illustrate the major events that marked this period of French history: the *Entente Cordiale,* cemented with the official visits of Louis-Philippe and Queen Victoria, the conquest of Algeria, the Revolutions of 1830 and 1848, the 1870 War and the Paris Commune, the signing of the Treaty of Versailles. Admire the portraits of Louis XVIII, Charles X, Louis-Philippe and his family, Napoleon III and Eugénie.

★★★ PARK

Facts and figures. – The **gardens** *(plan p 190-191)* cover an approximate area of 100ha – 250 acres and the distance between the palace and their perimeter is estimated at 950m – 3120ft.
Beyond the actual gardens of Versailles, the enclosed grounds of Versailles incorporated the **Little Park** (Petit Parc), which already included the Grand Canal and the Trianon. Under the Second Empire its area gradually shrank from 1700ha – 4200 acres to 600ha – 2000 acres: a large part of this land was used as a terrain for military training. The royal gates by which one left the Little Park marked the entrance to the **Grand Park** (Grand Parc), a 6000ha – 15000 acre hunting reserve surrounded by 43km – 27 miles of walls punctuated by a series of 25 "royal" gates. The Grand Park was entirely carved up during the Revolution.
The palace was built on top of a small hillock consolidated by vast loads of earth. The terrace dominates the Latona Basin by a height of 10.5m – 35ft, the Apollo Basin by 30m – 100ft, the Grand Canal by 32m – 105ft and the Orangery by 17m – 56ft.

The flower beds. – To ensure that all the beds would be in full bloom during the month of August, the gardeners had to supply 150000 plants, including 32000 for the North Parterre, 35000 for the South Parterre and 35000 for the Latona beds. Under the reign of Louis XIV, the potted plants would be changed up to fifteen times a year.

★★★GARDENS *Quick tour: allow 3 hours – Plan p 190-191*

A typical formal garden. – Versailles is a superb example of a genre perfected by André Le Nôtre, the formal garden.
The terrace and parterres provide a perfect balance to the monumental front of the palace which screens the town of Versailles.
Lower down, the Tapis Vert or carpet of grass and the Grand Canal cut across the middle of the grounds, creating a sweeping perspective that extends into the far distance. Numerous groves and straight paths are laid out on either side of this central axis. Their asymmetrical designs, basins and ornamental art add a touch of variety to Le Nôtre's formal layout. The two hundred sculptures that adorn the park of Versailles make it one of the biggest open-air museums of classical sculpture. The view towards the south extends to the heights of Satory.

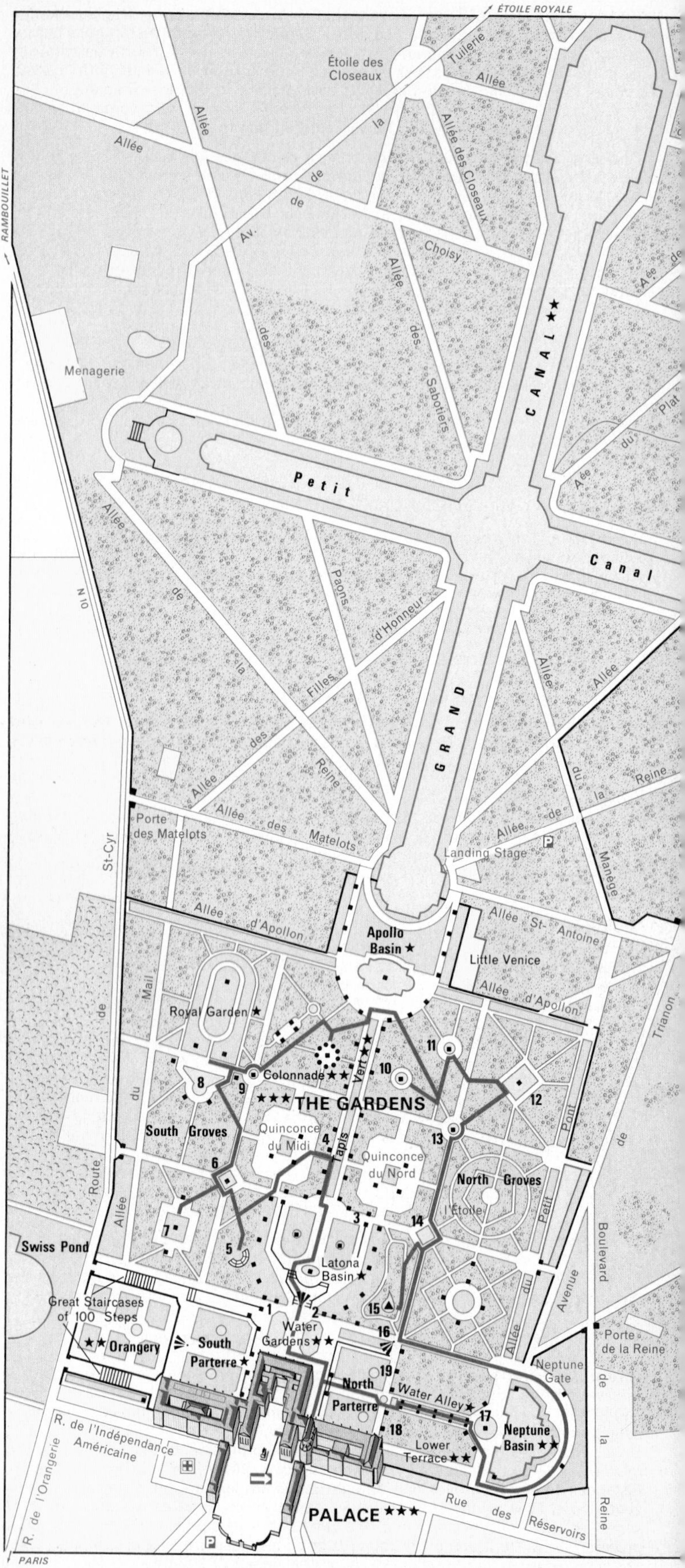
ÉTOILE ROYALE
Étoile des Closeaux
Tuilerie
Allée
Allée des Closeaux
Allée de la
Av. de
Choisy
Allée des Sabotiers
RAMBOUILLET
Menagerie
CANAL ★★
Petit
Canal
GRAND
Allée de la
Allée des Filles
Paons
d'Honneur
Reine
N 10
Allée des Matelots
Porte des Matelots
St-Cyr
Allée de
Allée du
Reine
Landing Stage
Manège
Allée d'Apollon
Apollo Basin ★
Allée St-Antoine
Little Venice
Allée d'Apollon
Trianon
Mail
Royal Garden ★
Colonnade ★★
Vert
Tapis
★★★ THE GARDENS
South Groves
Quinconce du Midi
Quinconce du Nord
North Groves
l'Étoile
Route du
Allée
Pont
Petit
Swiss Pond
Latona Basin ★
Great Staircases of 100 Steps
★★ Orangery
South Parterre ★
Water Gardens ★★
North Parterre
Water Alley ★
Lower Terrace ★★
Neptune Gate
Neptune Basin ★★
Porte de la Reine
Boulevard de la Reine
Avenue de
R. de l'Indépendance Américaine
R. de l'Orangerie
PALACE ★★★
Rue des Réservoirs
PARIS
1
2
3
4
5
6
7
8
9
10
11
12
13
14
15
16
17
18
19

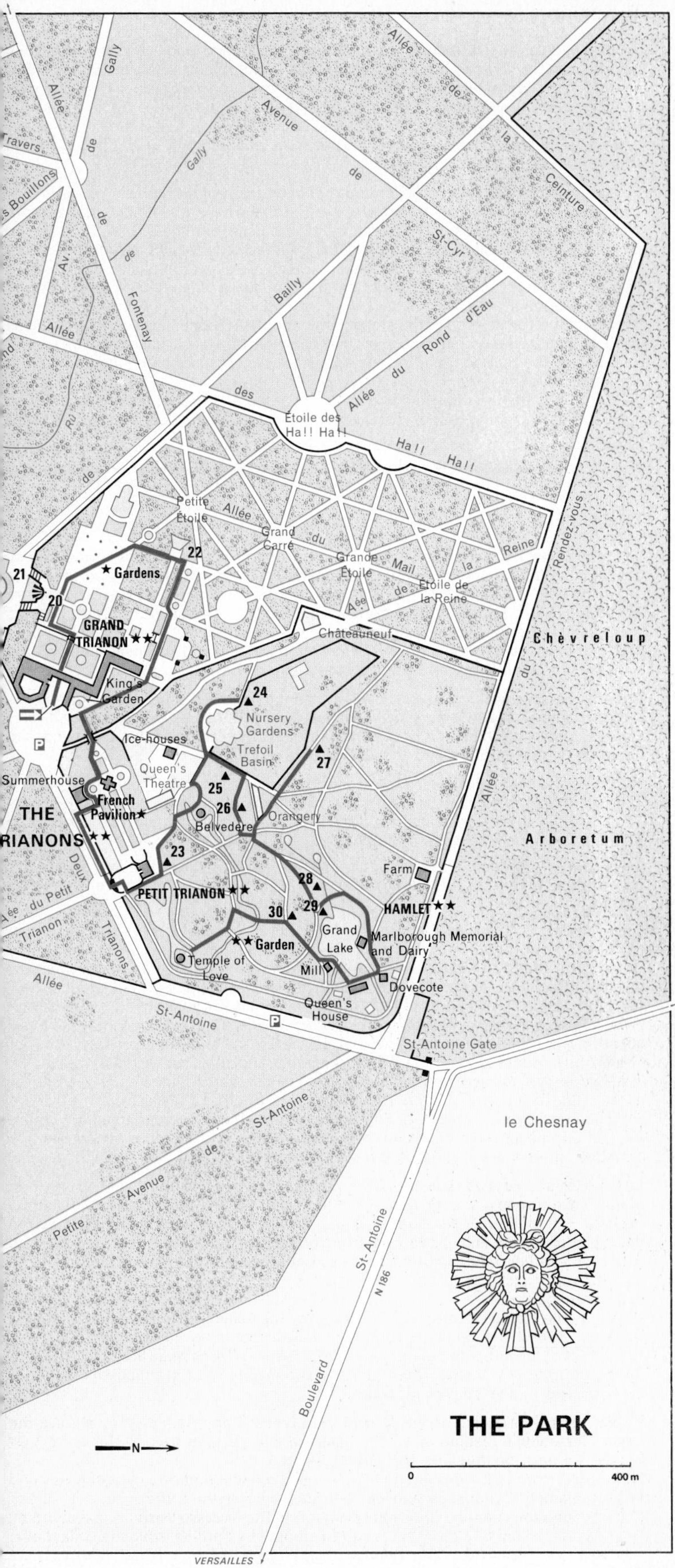
THE PARK
Allée de la Ceinture
Avenue de St-Cyr
Allée de Gally
Gally
Allée du Rond d'Eau
Étoile des Ha!! Ha!!
Allée des Ha!! Ha!!
Petite Étoile
Grand Carré
Allée du Mail de la Reine
Grande Étoile
Étoile de la Reine
Châteauneuf
Rendez-vous
Allée du Chèvreloup
Chèvreloup
Arboretum
21
20
22
★ Gardens
GRAND TRIANON ★★
King's Garden
24
Nursery Gardens
Trefoil Basin
27
Ice-houses
Queen's Theatre
Summerhouse
French Pavilion ★
THE TRIANONS ★★
25
26
Belvedere
Orangery
23
PETIT TRIANON ★★
28
29
30
Farm
HAMLET ★★
Grand Lake
Marlborough Memorial and Dairy
★★ Garden
Temple of Love
Mill
Dovecote
Queen's House
Allée St-Antoine
St-Antoine Gate
le Chesnay
Petite Avenue de St-Antoine
Boulevard St-Antoine
N 186
ST-GERMAIN. A 13
VERSAILLES
N
0
400 m

The gardens in former times. – Today, the paths are lined with trees whose branches join so as to form a roof of foliage. In Le Nôtre's time, visitors to Versailles could look up and see the sky. The trees were not planted along the edge of the lanes but set back very slightly: their shadows would not even fall on the statues. The garden paths were flanked with a variety of coloured treillises and hedgerows averaging 25ft. These were fronted by tubs of orange and pomegranate trees, box trees and clipped yew trees. Louis XV and Louis XVI did not alter the layout of the gardens but under Louis XVI replanting became necessary in 1776. This operation was renewed in 1860 and 1987.

★★★ **Fountains (Grandes Eaux).** – *When the fountains are in operation, the gardens may be approached by the North Parterre, the South Parterre, the Great Staircases of 100 Steps, the two gates at the end of the Grand Canal and the Dragon Gate (at the far end of Rue de la Paroisse) (see table of Principal Festivals at end of guide).* This magnificent display of fountains and groves takes us right back to the glorious 18C – known in France as the Great Century. *Brochures of the tour may be obtained at the reception.*
Start the tour from the top of the steps dominating the Latona Basin. Start walking as soon as the fountains begin to play and carry on at a brisk pace, paying special attention to the Ballroom and Apollo's Bath groves, which are only open on these particular days (the latter is not visible from the garden paths). The grand finale *(at 5.20pm for 10 minutes)* takes place at the Neptune and Dragon Basins. It involves 99 fountains, including that of the Dragon Basin, reaching a height of 42m – 138ft.

★★★ **Illuminations.** – *Every year the dates are fixed in advance for the whole season (see the table of Principal Festivals at the end of the guide).* The night illuminations are organised four times a year during summer and end with a fireworks display.

THE GRAND PERSPECTIVE

★★ **Water Gardens (Parterres d'eau).** – The two huge basins that front the stately palace constitute a sort of aquatic esplanade where the three main perspectives meet: the central axis, that of the North Parterre and that of the South Parterre. The extremities of the basins bear allegorical statues of the rivers of France (portrayed as men) and their tributaries (portrayed as women). Lengthways are arranged groups of children at play, alternating with reclining water nymphs. These outstanding bronze sculptures were executed by the Keller brothers.

Latona Staircase (Degré de Latone). – An imposing flight of steps and a double ramp flanked with yew trees and replicas of antique statues lead from the Water Gardens down to the Latona Basin. From the top of the steps admire the wonderful **view**★★★ of the gardens and the Grand Perspective.

The two fountains. – These stand to the left and the right of the Latona Staircase. They were originally called the "Animal Chambers" on account of the bronze works depicting dogs fighting wild beasts. They were named after the most striking statue of the three that adorn the water basins.

Dawn Fountain (Fontaine du point du Jour) (**1**). – Dawn – the statue whose head is crowned by a star – is the work of Gaspard Marsy. The other two are Water and Spring.

★ **Diana Fountain** (Fontaine de Diane) (**2**). – Le Hongre's statue Air is the one looking in the direction of Dawn. At its side stands the hunting goddess Diana, executed by Desjardins. The third statue is attributed to Marsy and represents the goddess of love Venus. These sculptures are among the finest works in the gardens.
All these statues were part of the massive ensemble commissioned by Colbert in 1674: a total of thirty marble sculptures, including 24 statues grouped into sets of six according to selected themes. The four Elements, the four Times of Day, the four Poems, the four Seasons, the four Continents and the four Virtues were to be installed on the terrace fronting the château. However the initial plan was never carried out: the court architects thought it a pity to break the classical lines of the esplanade by a row of great looming figures. Finally it was decided to adopt a more original approach: most of the bronze statues were cast as reclining figures and arranged around the basins of the water gardens.

★ **Latona Basin (Bassin de Latone).** – This vast composition by Marsy was the very first marble sculpture to grace the gardens of Versailles (1670). It tells the story of Latona (mould), the mother of Apollo and Diana, who was showered with insults by the peasants of Lycea and prevented from quenching her thirst. She appealed to Jupiter, the father of her children, who promptly avenged the offence by turning the culprits into frogs. The Lizard Basins on the side picture the early stages of the metamorphosis...
Originally the statue of Latona looked towards the palace, a clear indication of how the king viewed the public or private insults concerning his love life.
At the foot of the ramp, to the right, lies the charming **Nymph with a Shell** (**3**), a modern replica of Coysevox' statue. The original work – inspired by the antique model – has been moved to the Louvre Museum.

★★ **Tapis Vert.** – Standing at the foot of the Latona Staircase, you may admire the Grand Perspective leading up to the palace and extending beyond the Tapis Vert (Green Carpet), up towards the Grand Canal.
This long stretch of lawn is lined with a superb collection of ornamental vases and statues, namely Cyparissus and his pet stag by Flamen and Poulletier's Didon. A stroll along the Allée du Midi will bring you to the **Richelieu Venus** (**4**), executed by Le Gros after an antique bust that featured among the Cardinal's private collections.

Leave the Tapis Vert and wander down to the south groves.

SOUTH GROVES (BOSQUETS DU MIDI)

★ **Ballroom Grove (Bosquet de la Salle du Bal)** (5). – This elegant ensemble was part of Le Nôtre's original plans. Shaped as a circular stage, it is surrounded by gentle slopes, grassy banks and tiered rockeries where small cascades tumbled down. This outdoor theatre was used for dances attended by members of the court or a corps de ballet.

Bacchus or Autumn Basin (Bassin de Bacchus ou de l'Automne) (6). – Attributed to Gaspard Marsy. The basins of the Four Seasons are laid out in the form of a quadrangle flanked by the North and South Groves. These groups of lead figures were recently re-gilded and decorated in "natural tones".
See the Saturn, Flora and Ceres Basins below.

Queen's Grove (Bosquet de la Reine) (7). – It lies on the site of a former maze and was created in 1775, at the time of the great replantation campaign.
In its centre stand a number of bronze statues cast after the antique models: Aphrodite, a Fighting Gladiator, etc. The maple groves are a magnificent sight in autumn.

Water Mirror Basin (Bassin du Miroir d'Eau) (8). – Of the two basins circling the Royal Isle, the larger began to silt up and was replaced by a landscape garden, known as the Royal Garden. The only one to survive is the Water Mirror Basin (Vertugadin) and it has been prettily adorned with statues.

★ **Royal Garden (Jardin du Roi).** – A dazzling sight in summer, when all the flowers are in full bloom, this garden is a welcome change from the formal groves of Versailles. The central lawn is flanked by a charming selection of rare tree species.

Saturn or Winter Basin (Bassin de Saturne ou de l'Hiver) (9). – Executed by François Girardon, the sculpture portrays a winged god surrounded by cherubs amidst ice flows and shells.

★★ **Colonnade.** – *This grove is usually closed but can be seen quite clearly through the railings.*
Jules Hardouin-Mansart built this circular colonnade in 1685 with the help of fifteen fellow sculptors. One of its most pleasing features is the elegant display of multicoloured marble: azure, carnation, lilac and white. Observe the carved masks on the keystones and, on the spandrels, the delightful groups of children at play.

★ APOLLO BASIN (BASSIN D'APOLLON)

The whole composition was executed by Tuby to the designs of Le Brun and is dedicated to the Sun God Apollo. He is portrayed seated in his chariot, surrounded by marine monsters, rising from the ocean waters to bring Light to the Earth *(photograph p 35).*
This basin is continued by an esplanade leading to the Grand Canal. It is bordered by statues, parts of which are genuine antiquities (note the cracks where the different fragments join).

NORTH GROVES (BOSQUETS DU NORD)

Dome Grove (Bosquet des Dômes) (10). – The grove was named after two pavilions crowned by cupolas which were designed by Mansart. They were dismantled in 1820.
A series of low reliefs adorns the edge of the basin, representing the different weapons used in each country. It has the unmistakably elegant touch of Girardon. Among the pretty statues feature two works by Tuby, Acis and Galatea.

★ **Enceladus Basin (Bassin d'Encelade)** (11). – This baroque composition by Marsy contrasts sharply with the stark realism of the other groups dotted around the gardens. A head and two arms is all that one can see of the Titan Enceladus, slowly being dragged down towards the bowels of the earth by the very rocks of Mount Olympus by which the Titans had hoped to reach the sky (a clear warning to Fouquet).

Obelisk Basin (Bassin de l'Obélisque) (12). – Conceived by Mansart, this raised basin is surrounded by a flight of stone steps and several lawns. When the fountains are in operation, the central sculpture lets out a gigantic spray of water which resembles a liquid obelisk.

Flora or Spring Basin (Bassins de Flore ou du Printemps) (13). – Another of the four season series by Tuby.

Ceres or Summer Basin (Bassins de Cérès ou de l'Été) (14). – Executed by Regnaudin.

★ **Apollo's Bath Grove (Bosquet des Bains d'Apollon)** (15). – Designed by Hubert Robert in the early days of Louis XVI's reign, this grove heralded the Anglo-Chinese Garden, which Marie-Antoinette later adopted for the Trianon park.
On the edge of a small lake, a charming artificial grotto houses the **Apollo Group★**. Its lush, verdant setting is a far cry from the austere 17C Versailles. The Sun God, tired by the day's exertions, is portrayed resting, waited upon by a group of nymphs (Girardon and Regnaudin). The horses at his side are being groomed by tritons (Marsy and Guérin).

Philosophers' Crossroads (Carrefour des Philosophes) (16). – Flanked by impressive statues. The crossroads offer an interesting sideways **view★★** of the palace (northwest façade). The sweeping perspective on the right is lined with a double row of yew trees and a set of bronze statues, including Girardon's Winter.

NEPTUNE BASIN, DRAGON BASIN, WATER ALLEY

★★ **Neptune Basin (Bassin de Neptune).** – *Stand in the central axis, near the statue of Fame.* This is by far the largest basin in Versailles. Its proportions are wildly extravagant by classical standards and it forms a small enclave north of the rectangular gardens. Designed by Le Nôtre, it acquired its present appearance in 1741, under the reign of Louis XV, when it was enriched by a group of lead statues depicting Neptune and Amphitrite surrounded by various gods, dragons and sea monsters (Adam, Lemoyne and Bouchardon).

Dragon Basin (Bassin du Dragon) (17). – This allegorical sculpture evoking the victory over deep-sea monsters is a direct allusion to the vanquished Fronde, symbolised by a wounded dragon. While the dragon's body is the original, the remaining pieces were recast in 1889.

★ **Water Alley (Allée d'Eau ou des Marmousets).** – A double row of 22 small white marble basins bear delightful bronze groups of three children, each holding tiny pink marble vessels.

THE PARTERRES AND ORANGERY

North Parterre (Parterre du Nord). – The very first royal suite looked out onto this "terrace of greenery".

Basin of Diana's Nymphs (Bassin des Nymphes de Diane) (**18**). – Arranged around the basin are Girardon's fine **low reliefs★** which have given their name to the fountain. They were to inspire a great many 18 and 19C painters, notably the celebrated Pierre-Auguste Renoir.

★★ **Lower Parterre** (Parterre Bas). – Close to the groves, along its northern and western boundaries, the terrace is flanked by bronze statues representing the four Continents, four Poems, four seasons and four Virtues. The lead **Pyramid Fountain★** (**19**), executed by Girardon from a study by Le Brun, combines grace with originality: dolphins, shrimps and tritons.
At the top of the steps leading to the Water Gardens you may admire the **Knifegrinder,** a bronze replica of the antique statue by Foggini. Coysevox' **Venus on a Tortoise** – called Venus as a Paragon of Modesty under Louis XIV – is a bronze cast, also inspired by antique sculpture. The original is exhibited at the Louvre Museum and is among the artist's finest works.

★ **South Parterre (Parterre du Midi).** – They were laid out in front of the queen's apartments. With their vivid blossoms and their pretty boxwood patterns, these southern flower beds are a hymn to nature. The terrace running along the Orangery offers a good **view★** of the 700m – 3 000ft long **Swiss Pond** and, in the far distance, the wooded heights of Satory.

★★ **Orangery (Orangerie).** – One of Mansart's creations, the Orangery bore the foundations of the South Parterre. It extended south by means of two square corner pavilions which supported the colossal **Great Staircases of 100 Steps.** At the time of Louis XIV, the Orangery housed 3 000 shrubs in tubs: 2 000 of these were orange trees. Today it contains 1 200 bushes, some of which date back to the *Ancien Régime.* The Orangery looks splendid during the summer season, when the orange trees and palm trees (a recent introduction) are brought outside and arranged around the flower beds.

The water gardens in front of Versailles

★★ GRAND CANAL

The Grand Canal is shaped as a large cross: the long canal is 1670m – 5480ft long by 62m – 204ft wide, while the shorter one measures 1070m – 3500ft long by 80m – 263ft wide. It was filled with water in 1670.
The nearby buildings make up Little Venice (Petite Venise), which housed the Venitian gondoliers in charge of the king's fleet (gondolas, miniature models of battleships and merchant ships).

★★ THE TRIANONS *plan p 190-191*

Access on foot. – *Avenue de Trianon (1km – 1/2 mile) starts at the Neptune Gate and leads directly to the Trianons. You may also follow the avenue starting from the eastern extremity of the Grand Canal.*

Access by car. – *Plan p 190-191.*

Fountains. – *See the table of Principal Festivals at the end of the guide.*

Bicycles for hire. – *At the entrance to the park, on Boulevard de la Reine, near the Trianon Palace Hotel.*

★★ GRAND TRIANON *time: 2 hours*

A pavilion known as the Porcelain Trianon, decorated with blue and white Delft tiling, used to be a quiet, secluded meeting-place for Louis XIV and his favourite Mme de Montespan. It stood for eighteen years, from 1670 to 1687. When Mme de Montespan fell from favour, the pavilion deteriorated and was eventually taken down. Six months later, Jules Hardouin-Mansart completed the Marble Trianon, a retreat built in honour of Mme de Maintenon.
It was stripped of its furniture during the Revolution. Napoleon I commissioned major renovation work and refurnished the building on the occasion of his marriage to Marie-Louise. The Marble Trianon was restored under Louis-Philippe.
The latest renovation programme took place in 1962 at the instigation of General de Gaulle, who wished to use the Trianon for official receptions.

★★ **Château.** – Walk past the lowish railings and enter the semicircular courtyard. You will discover two buildings with a flat terrace roof, joined by an elegant peristyle. Note the delicate colour scheme with pink overtones. Another wing called Trianon-sous-Bois is placed at a perpendicular angle to the right-hand gallery, but it is not visible from the court *(Trianon-sous-Bois is not open to the public).*
The peristyle overlooks both the court and the gardens. It was designed by Robert de Cotte and adopted by Louis XIV despite Mansart's scepticism. It was used for banquets and formal receptions.

Apartments. – The austere interior decoration has changed very little since the days of Louis XIV's reign. The apartments were occupied by Napoleon and Louis-Philippe and their respective families. The furniture is either Empire or Restoration, and the paintings are attributed to 17C French artists.
The Mirror Room (Salon des Glaces) in the left pavilion was used as a council chamber. Admire the splendid Empire furniture and the lavish silk hangings, rewoven according to the original pattern ordered by Marie-Antoinette (the four

Continents of the World). The bedroom contains the bed Napoleon commissioned for his apartments at the Tuileries: it was later altered for Louis-Philippe's use. The wall put in by Bonaparte level with the columns has been dismantled and the room has been restored to its original size.
The reception rooms in the right wing were remodelled by Louis-Philippe, who gave them a more personal touch. These salons are enhanced by a collection of paintings executed by famous 17C French artists, dedicated to mythological subjects.
In Louis XIV's former Music Room (Salon de Musique), the musicians' loggias are enclosed by a series of shutters.
Louis-Philippe created the Family Lounge (Salon de Famille), in which the two tables feature numbered drawers reserved for the princesses' embroidery.
The Malachite Salon (Salon des Malachites) was first the Sun King's Grand Cabinet and then the bedroom of the duchesse de Bourgogne. It owes its name to the various objects encrusted with malachite offered to Napoleon by the Tsar Alexander I following their talks in Tilsit (1807): basins, candelabra, bookcase, etc. Malachite is a green stone found in Siberia, which is easy to polish.
The Cool Hall (Salon Frais) enjoys a northern exposure. It houses four paintings representing the early days of Versailles, in conformity with the plans drawn up by Mansart (display of documents showing the palace and the grounds). The two filing cabinets (1810) and the console table (1806) were executed by Jacob Desmalter from a study by Charles Percier.
The Atlas Cabinet (Salon des Sources) – where Napoleon kept his different maps and plans – leads to the Imperial Suite *(open on request)*.
Placed at a perpendicular angle, the corner **Gallery★** (Galerie) houses an extremely precious collection of 24 paintings by Cotelle. They conjure up a vivid picture of the palace and its stately grounds at the time of Louis XIV. The lovely Empire chandeliers were manufactured in the Montcenis glassworks in the Burgundian town of Le Creusot.
At the far end of the Gallery, the luminous Garden Lounge (Salon des Jardins) features a fine set of chairs taken from Meudon Château.

★ **Gardens.** – They derive their simple charm from the impressive displays of flower beds.
From the Lower Basin (Bassin Bas) (**21**), take the Horseshoe Staircase that leads up to the Lower Gardens (Jardins Bas) (**20**). The terrace commands a good view of the Grand Canal, seen from the side.
Beyond the parterres lies a charming wood featuring noble avenues, rows of stately trees and several small ponds *(best seen when the Trianon fountains are playing)*. The only sculpture with a mythological theme in the Trianon gardens is Mansart's Buffet d'Eau (**22**), completed in 1703. It pictures the Sea God Neptune and Amphitrite, surrounded by a cluster of smaller statues.
Skirt Trianon-sous-Bois and walk through what was once the king's private garden. It is flanked by two square pavilions that housed the apartments of Mme de Maintenon and Louis XIV towards the end of the Sun King's reign.

To reach the Petit Trianon, cross the bridge erected by Napoleon I, known as Pont de Réunion.

★★PETIT TRIANON *time: 1 1/2 hours*

It was Louis XV's love of gardening and farming that prompted the construction of the Petit Trianon. The king gave orders to build a menagerie (experimental farm) and commissioned his "botanical expert" Claude Richard to design the greenhouses and botanical gardens. A College of Botanical Science was founded and entrusted to the famous botanist Bernard de Jussieu.
Gabriel finished the Petit Trianon in 1768, shortly before Louis XV's reign ended. Mme de Pompadour, the woman behind the initial project, never saw the château. Louis XVI offered the Petit Trianon to his wife Marie-Antoinette. The queen would often come here with her children and her sister-in-law Mme Elisabeth, relieved to get away from court intrigues, and the formal etiquette that was expected from a woman of her rank. She insisted on a number of changes: the grounds were redesigned, a theatre was built and Jussieu's botanical gardens, complete with their experimental hothouses, were destroyed. On 5 October 1789, the queen was resting in a grotto near the Belvedere when a messenger informed her that the mob was marching on Versailles. She was forced to leave in great haste and was never to return.
The Empress Eugénie, who showed great sympathy for the queen, formed a collection of her personal mementoes and had the château refurnished in 1867.

★ **French Pavilion (Pavillon Français).** – This pavilion was built by Gabriel for Louis XV and Mme de Pompadour in 1750. It is surrounded by an enchanting formal garden. The cornice features a sculpted frieze representing the farm animals that were raised in the menagerie. Visitors can get a glimpse of the highly-refined interior decoration through the large French windows.
The cool **Summerhouse** at the southern end of the gardens was rebuilt in 1982.

★★ **Château.** – The façade facing the entrance courtyard is austere in the extreme, while that giving onto the formal gardens is a perfect example of the Louis XVI period *(illustration p 29)* and shows the full extent of Gabriel's talent: the four regularly-spaced columns are crowned by a balustrade and two fine ramps lead from the terrace down to the gardens.

Enter the château and walk up the imposing flight of stone stairs lit by an old-fashioned lantern. The wrought-iron banisters are stamped with a decorative monogram, believed to be that of Marie-Antoinette.

First Floor Apartments (Appartements du 1er étage). – Guibert's craftsmanship is evidenced by the superb **panelling★★** in the dining room and the lounge. The decoration of the dining room presents fruit, flower and foliage motifs, set off against a jade green background, a welcome change from the "Trianon grey" prevalent throughout the 19C. The lounge – partly refurnished by the Empress Eugénie in the 19C (chairs, 1790 pianoforte) – houses one of Riesener's greatest achievements: the famous astronomical writing desk (1771).
The furniture in Marie-Antoinette's bedroom was executed by Jacob and adorned with floral and rustic themes. Jacob also designed several pieces for the comtesse de Balbi: they have been placed in a recently-restored boudoir with unusual mobile mirrors.

★★ **Gardens.** – A charming Anglo-Chinese garden featuring a brook, several ornamental ponds, some fine tree species and an interesting collection of sculptures. It was designed by an amateur, the comte de Caraman, and built by the queen's architect Mique, who received advice from Hubert Robert.
Several of the trees are 150 to 200 years old and some were probably planted by Bernard de Jussieu in his botanical gardens. The oldest of all is a mutilated pagoda tree (**23**) planted under Louis XV, which stands near the northeast corner of the château.

Belvedere (Belvédère). – This delightful pavilion conceived by Mique was also called the Music Room. It overlooks the Little Lake (Petit Lac) and the interior decoration offers painted arabesques of the utmost refinement.
Those who stray from the winding paths of the landscape garden will discover "Charpentier's Garden", planted with remarkable trees. But first enter the grounds of the Grand Trianon to have a look at the superb cedar of Lebanon (**24**) near the Clover Basin as well as the two entirely-restored 17C ice-houses standing in the background.
Return to Charpentier's Garden and contemplate the two huge Wellingtonias (**25**) and single fastigiate (**26**). Bear left after the Orangery and you will come to an ancient Siberian elm (**27**) with unusually deep striations. Start walking towards the Hamlet. Before reaching the Grand Lake (Grand Lac), you will pass by a tulip tree from Virginia (**28**) and two spinneys of stately swamp cypresses (**29**).

★★ **Hamlet** (Hameau). – The grounds around the Grand Lake are dotted with a dozen pretty cottages featuring cob walls and thatched or slate roofs, inspired by the hamlet on Chantilly estate *(qv)*. Contrary to what is generally believed, the queen was far too attached to formal protocol to actually indulge in any farming activities. The Memorial to Marlborough is a reminder of the popular nursery rhyme introduced to Louis XVI's court by the Dauphin's nanny.
On your way to the Temple of Love, you will surely notice a remarkable plane tree (**30**), with thick spread-eagled roots.

Temple of Love (Temple de l'Amour). – One of Mique's creations (1778), it stands on a tiny islet in the midst of the rippling waters. In the centre, Bouchardon's statue shows Cupid making his Bow from the Club of Hercules (original in the Louvre Museum). The sculpture is fronted by a row of Corinthian columns resting on a circular flight of 6 steps.

THE TOWN *plan p 198*

Louis XIV decided that plots of land would be granted to those citizens who put in a request, in exchange for a levy of five *sous* for each arpent (3 194m^2 – 3 833sq yds). The new buildings had to conform to the norms laid down by the Service des Bâtiments du Roi a building commission answerable to the court. The purpose of these measures was to achieve architectural unity. Moreover, in order that the palace might continue to dominate the area, the roofs of the village houses could not exceed the height of the Marble Court.
Today very little remains of these 17C buildings. Most of the old town was completed in the 18C, enlarged and renovated in the 19C.
The Notre-Dame district (Y) features the oldest church in Versailles and a few houses built under Louis XIV, situated near the market place of Notre-Dame.
The St-Louis district (Z) south of Avenue de Sceaux houses the official buildings of Ⓥ the former ministries, the Real Tennis Court or **Jeu de Paume** (Y **D**) where the National Assembly took their famous oath on 20 June 1789, the "old Versailles" built around the former village square and an 18C estate attached to Stag Park, located close to Satory heights.

★ **Lambinet Museum (Musée Lambinet)** (Y **M**). – This museum has been set up in the Ⓥ charming salons of the Lambinet Hôtel (18C).
The ground floor rooms are dedicated to the history of Versailles and to one of the town's celebrated figures, General Hoche (1768-1797).
On the first floor, the Golden Salon (Salon Doré) contains the busts of Voltaire and Rousseau. Both are the work of Houdon, who was a native of Versailles. The next two rooms display a number of mementoes relating to the French Revolution (death of Marat and his burial ceremony, Charlotte Corday).
Visitors may view the work of Boutet, the famous ornamental gunsmith: sabres, swords and various other ceremonial arms awarded to valiant soldiers under the Revolution and the First Empire.
The second floor presents two magnificent abbesses' rock crystal crosiers, taken from Maubuisson and Le Lys, together with a host of documents about the royal convent school of St-Cyr: uniforms of the boarders, robes worn by the nuns, portraits of the founder, Mme de Maintenon, etc.

Ⓥ **Notre-Dame Church (Église Notre-Dame)** (Y). – Built in the Rue Dauphine – renamed Rue Hoche – by Jules Hardouin-Mansart in 1686, this was the parish church attached to the king and his court. The king would attend formal ceremonies here such as Corpus Christi. The requirements of the Service des Bâtiments du Roi *(p 197)* explain why the church presents a flattened front flanked by a series of truncated towers.

A large open-work cupola graces the church interior, characterised by Doric embellishments. The nave (explanatory notices) is surrounded by 12 carved medallions representing apostles and figures from the New Testament: these were the works presented by the new entrants to the Académie Royale de Sculpture et de Peinture (Royal Sculpture and Painting Academy) between 1657 and 1689. The axial chapel – the chapel of the Blessed Sacraments – houses the *Assumption,* a 16C painting by Michel Corneille.

Rue de l'Independance Américaine (Y 20). – In the 18C this street housed many buildings occupied by ministries and public services, in particular the Grand Commun – now the Military Hospital – , which lodged a total of 1 500 officials. At no 5 stands the former **Ministry of the Navy and Foreign Affairs,** fronted by a magnificent gate crowned by the statues of Peace and War. It was here that an

VERSAILLES

Street	Grid
Carnot (R.)	Y
Clemenceau (R. Georges)	Y 7
États-Généraux (R. des)	Z
Foch (R. du Mar.)	Y
Hoche (R.)	Y
Leclerc (R. du Gén.)	Z 24
Orangerie (R. de l')	YZ
Paroisse (R. de la)	Y
Royale (R.)	Z
Satory (R. de)	Z 42
Vieux-Versailles (R. du)	Y 47
Chancellerie (R. de la)	Y 3
Chantiers (R. des)	Z 5
Cotte (R. Robert-de)	Y 10
Europe (Av. de l')	Y 14
Gambetta (Pl.)	Y 17
Gaulle (Av. Gén.-de)	Y 19
Indép. Américaine (R.)	Y 20
Mermoz (R. Jean)	Z 27
Nolhac (R. Pierre-de)	Y 30
Porte de Buc (R.)	Z 34
Rockefeller (Av.)	Y 37

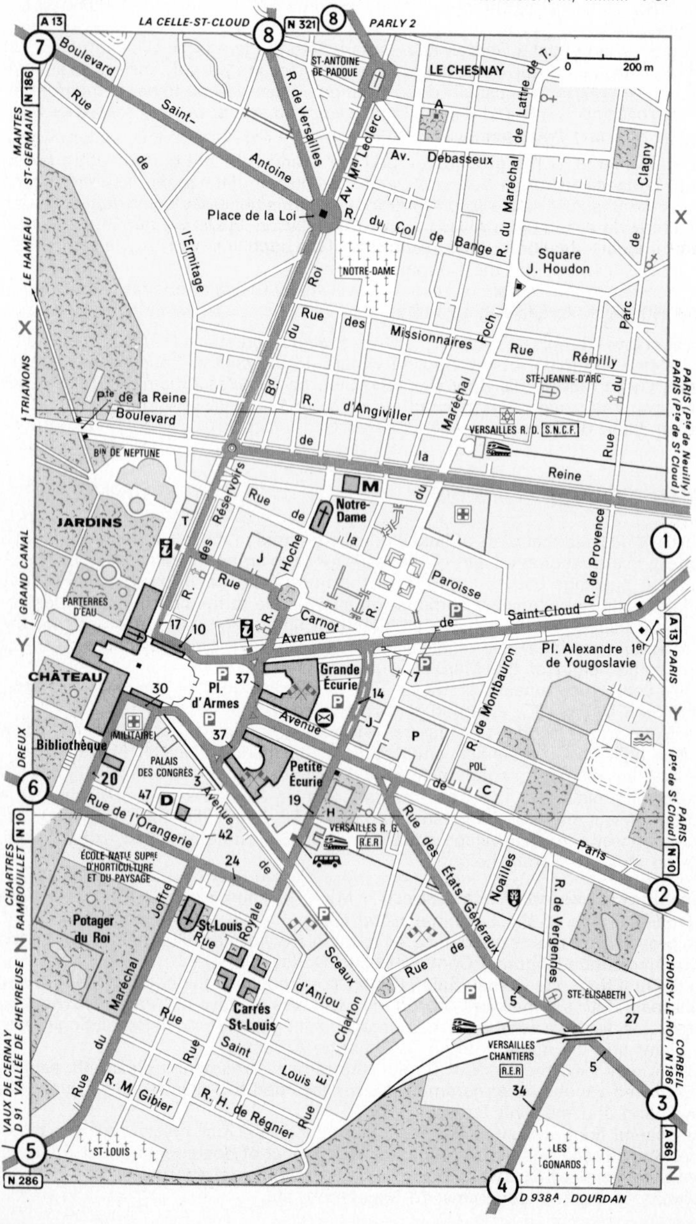

alliance was signed between France and the American "insurrectionaries", acting as a prelude to the 1783 treaties granting the independence of the United States. The mansion has been made into a **public library.**

St-Louis Cathedral (Cathédrale St-Louis) (Z). – It was built in 1754 to serve the "old Versailles" and Stag Park, and lies close to the King's Vegetable Garden (Potager du Roi). The west front with its two bell towers, the cupola above the transept crossing are reminiscent of the great classical churches *(illustration p 25).*
Several official celebrations were held at St-Louis Cathedral: inauguration ceremony of the States General on 4 May 1789, attended by the deputies who had formed a procession starting from Notre-Dame, the session of 22 June which officialised the reunion of Clergy and Nobility, the Mass of the Holy Ghost which opened the 1875 sitting of the National Assembly, at which the members voted the constitutional law that founded the Third Republic.
The noble, austere nave still contains its 17C organ and collection of 18C paintings, but the most interesting furnishings are the religious works dating from the 19C.

St-Louis Precinct (Carrés St-Louis) (Z). – Louis XV gave orders to create a "shopping area" near St-Louis Church, along the streets presently named Rue Royale and Rue d'Anjou (1755). The shops – featuring attics with timbered roofs – were arranged around four small squares known as *carrés:* Well Square, Oats Square, Fountain Square and Earth Square. Some of these houses still stand and have been converted into antique shops.

EXCURSION

Chèvreloup Arboretum (Arboretum de Chèvreloup). – *Leave by ⑦ and turn left before entering Rocquencourt.*
In 1927 a plot of land formerly belonging to the Grand Park *(p 189)* was offered to the Natural History Museum of Paris so that the Botanical Gardens (Jardin des Plantes) could enrich their collection of tree species. The first steps were to set up a Tree House.
Visitors may only tour the southeast part of the park, planted with clusters and rows of conifers. Several types of horticultural species which do not grow naturally are cultivated here: a row of Lawson's cypresses, of unusual shapes and sizes. Large groups of thujas are seen next to yew trees and weeping conifers. The broad-leaved trees include silver birches and willow trees at the height of their development. The oldest species of all is one of the pagoda trees planted at the time of Louis XV and restored to life thanks to modern arboricultural techniques.

VÉTHEUIL

Pop 689

Michelin map 196 fold 3

This former wine-growing locality has a lovely riverside setting: it lies on the steep banks of one of the Seine's loops, not far from La Roche-Guyon *(qv).* The village houses – built with a fine pale yellow stone – are characteristic of the French Vexin. The small town was made famous by the Impressionists, in particular Claude Monet, who lived there for three years and whose wife Camille died in Vétheuil in 1879.

Church (Église). – Perched right above the village, it is obviously quite a striking sight, but the Impressionist painters were more interested in the sights around Lavacourt, on the south bank of the Seine.
From the main village crossroads, take Rue de l'Église, which leads straight to the entrance steps.
Although the chancel was first started in the late 12C, the church was only completed under Henri II, when the last chapels were consecrated in 1850. The building is presently undergoing restoration.

Exterior. – The west front dates from the mid-16C: the three levels of Renaissance galleries are flanked by two square turrets. The pier features a 16C statue depicting Charity. The south façade presents a doorway fronted by a Renaissance porch – note the 16C panels. Walk past the 16C nave until you reach the late 12C chancel, symbolising the transition from Romanesque to Gothic. Stand back and take in the elevation of the church, offering small round windows (oculi) on the first floor and a series of stepped buttresses around the east end. The bell tower was raised in the 13C: it was the subject of many Impressionist paintings.

Interior. – The church interior houses a number of **statues★** (14-16C), a few 16 and 17C paintings, and several interesting carvings. The first chapel on the left – formerly dedicated to one of the brotherhoods of charity – is enclosed by a Renaissance parclose. In the third chapel you may see a lively statue portraying St James (Burgundy School – 15C) and the north aisle bears a 16C *Ecce Homo.* Observe the 14C Virgin and Child in the south transept crossing (Notre-Dame-de-Grâce de Vétheuil) and, in the adjacent chapel, St Veronica, a colourful stone statue dating from the 14C.

★ VILLARCEAUX

Michelin map 196 fold 3 – 8km – 4.5 miles southwest of Magny-en-Vexin

Villarceaux estate is set in rolling surroundings at the heart of the French Vexin. It is graced by a magnificent setting and two châteaux: a 15-16C manorhouse belonging to the celebrated beauty Ninon de Lenclos, and a Louis XV château.
If you approach the estate from the south, along the road coming from Villers-en-Arthies, you can glimpse the little 19C Convent Château (Château du Couvent) surrounded by a golf course.

Ninon de Lenclos. – When Ninon (1620-1705) died at the age of 85, she had witnessed Louis XIII's reign and the absolute monarchy of Louis XIV. She was acquainted with all the leading personalities of her time and virtually became a legendary figure of the 17C on account of her charm and her knowledge: few of her contemporaries could claim to possess such an impressive collection of mementoes. It was at Villarceaux that she received the young Françoise d'Aubigné, the future Mme Scarron and Mme de Maintenon, who 32 years later was to marry Louis XIV. It was also here that she shared a romance with Louis de Mornay, the marquis de Villarceaux. The youthful Voltaire was officially presented to her shortly before her death.

★ **Gardens.** – Follow the itinerary signposted with arrows which takes ⓥ you past St-Nicolas' Terrace – note the corner tower – and to a series of ponds. The edge of the last pond affords a good **view★** of the Louis XV château (south façade), built on the terraced slopes.
The château is not open to the public.
From the ponds, you may visit the outhouses, used for formal receptions, and then ⓥ the actual **manor** and its large stone tower.

VILLE D'AVRAY

Pop 11 625

Michelin map 101 fold 23 – Michelin plan 22

This residential locality enjoys a lush, verdant setting.

ⓥ **St Nicholas Church (Église St-Nicolas).** – The church was built in the Louis XVI style and the greater part of its architecture has remained intact. The transept houses a series of small frescoes painted by Camille Corot.

★ **Ponds (Étangs).** – They lie in the valley bordering the Fausses Reposes Forest and were immortalised by Corot's famous paintings. The artist was particularly fond of the Old Pond (Vieil Etang), a secluded spot where he would sit and work in a small log cabin (memorial). Visitors will appreciate the quiet charm of these waterside paths, wich are popular with fishermen.

Fausses Reposes Forest (Forêt de Fausses Reposes). – This beautiful stretch of woodland planted with oaks, chestnut trees and birches was once part of Rouvray Forest, running from Boulogne to Versailles. The name of the forest (feint) makes references to the stag hunts which were organised on the land up to the end of the Second Empire.

Practical Information

The French Government Tourist Offices at 178 Piccadilly, London WIV OAL, ☏ (01) 499 6911 (recorded message) or 491 7622 for urgent queries and 610 and 628 Fifth Avenue, New York, ☏ (212) 757-1125 will provide information and literature.

How to get there. – You can go directly by scheduled national airlines, by commercial and package tour flights, possibly with a rail or coach link-up or you can go by cross-Channel ferry or hovercraft and on by car and train.
Enquire at any good travel agent and if you are going during the holiday season or at Christmas, remember to book well in advance.

CUSTOMS AND OTHER FORMALITIES

Visa for U.S. citizens. – An **entry visa** is required for all U.S. citizens visiting France in accordance with French security measures.
Apply to the French Consulate (visa issued same day; delay if submitted by mail).

Papers and other documents. – A valid national **passport** (or in the case of the British, a Visitor's Passport) is all that is required.
For the car, a valid **driving licence or international driving permit, car registration papers** (log-book) and a **nationality plate** of the approved size. Insurance cover is compulsory and although the Green Card is no longer a legal requirement for France, it is the most effective form of proof of insurance cover and is internationally recognized.
There are no customs formalities for holidaymakers bringing their caravans into France for a stay of less than 6 months. No customs document is necessary for pleasure boats or outboard motors for a stay of less than 6 months but you should have the registration certificate on board.

Motoring regulations. – The minimum driving age is 18 years old. Certain motoring organisations run accident insurance and breakdown service schemes for their members. Enquire before leaving. A **red warning triangle** or hazard warning lights are obligatory in the case of a breakdown. In France it is compulsory for the front passengers to wear **seat belts.** Children under ten should be on the back seat.
The **speed limits,** although liable to modification, are: motorways 130kph – 80mph (110kph when raining); national trunk roads 110kph – 68mph; other roads 90kph – 56mph (80kph – 50mph when raining) and in towns 60kph – 47mph. The regulations on speeding and drinking and driving are strictly interpreted – usually by an on-the-spot fine and/or confiscation of the vehicle. Remember to **cede priority** to vehicles joining from the right. There are tolls on the motorways.

Medical treatment. – For EEC countries it is necessary to have Form E III which testifies to your entitlement to medical benefits from the Department of Health and Social Security. With this you can obtain medical treatment in an emergency and after the necessary steps, a refund of part of the costs of treatment from the local Social Security offices (Caisse Primaire d'Assurance Maladie). It is however still advisable to take out comprehensive insurance cover.
Nationals of non-EEC countries should make enquiries before leaving.

Currency. – There are no restrictions on what you can take into France in the way of currency. To facilitate export of foreign notes in excess of the given allocation, visitors are allowed to complete a currency declaration on arrival.
Your passport is necessary as identification when cashing cheques in banks. Commission charges vary with hotels charging more than banks when "obliging" non-residents on holidays or at weekends.

DULY ARRIVED

Consulates: British: 16 Rue d'Anjou, 75008 Paris; ☏ (1) 42 66 91 42.
American: 2 Rue St-Florentin, 75001 Paris; ☏ (1) 42 96 12 02.

Embassies: British: 35 Rue du Faubourg-Saint-Honoré, 75008 Paris; ☏ (1) 42 66 91 42.
American: 2 Avenue Gabriel, 75008 Paris; ☏ (1) 42 96 12 02.

Tourist Information Centres or *Syndicats d'Initiative* ℹ are to be found in most large towns and many tourist resorts. They can supply large-scale town plans, timetables and information on entertainment facilities, sports and sightseeing.

Poste Restante. – Name, Poste Restante, Poste Centrale, *département's* postal code number, followed by the town's name, France. The Michelin Red Guide France gives local postal code numbers.
Postage via air mail to: UK letter 2.20 F; postcard 2F
US aerogramme 4.20F; letter (20g) 6F; postcard 3.40F.

Where to stay. – In the Michelin Red Guide France you will find a selection of hotels at various prices in all areas. It will also list local restaurants again with prices. If camping or caravanning consult the Michelin Guide Camping Caravaning France.

Electric current. – The electric current is 220 volts. European circular two pin plugs are the rule – remember an electrical adaptor.

Public holidays in France. – National museums and art galleries are closed on Tuesdays. The following are days when museums and other monuments may be closed or may vary their hours of admission:

New Year's Day	Ascension Day	The Assumption **(15 August)**
Easter Sunday and Monday	Whit Sunday and Monday	All Saints' Day **(1 November)**
May Day **(1 May)**	France's National Day **(14 July)**	Armistice Day **(11 November)**
Libération **(8 May)**		Christmas Day

In addition to the usual school holidays at Christmas, Easter and in the summer, there are fortnight breaks in February and late October-early November.

OUTDOOR ACTIVITIES

Leisure centres

Bois-le-Roi: 77590 Bois-le-Roi. ☎ 60 69 60 06.

Buthiers: 77760 La Chapelle-La-Reine. ☎ 64 24 12 87.

Cergy-Neuville: 29 Rue des Étangs. 95000 Cergy. ☎ 30 31 21 55.

Créteil: Rue Jean Gabin. 94000 Créteil. ☎ 48 98 44 56.

Étampes: Avenue Bonnevaux. 91150 Étampes. ☎ 64 94 76 18.

Jablines: 77420 Esbly. ☎ 60 26 04 31.

Moisson-Mousseaux: 78840 Freneuse. ☎ 34 79 33 34.

Le-Port-aux-Cerises: Rue du Port-aux-Cerises. 91210 Draveil. ☎ 69 42 46 76.

St-Quentin-en-Yvelines: Route de Dreux / N 12. 78190 Trappes. ☎ 30 51 53 15.

Souppes-sur-Loing: Route de Varennes. 77460 Souppes-sur-Loing. ☎ 64 29 72 89.

Torcy: Route de Lagny. ☎ 64 80 58 75.

Val de Seine: Chemin du Rouillard. 78480 Verneuil-sur-Seine. ☎ 39 71 07 06.

Cycling Holidays

Fédération Française: 8 Rue Jean-Marie Jego, 75013 Paris. ☎ 45 80 30 21.
Ligue d'Ile-de-France: Claude Galvaing, 3 Rue Maryse Bastié, 78140 Vélizy. ☎ 39 46 23 32.
Bicy-Club de France: 8 Place de la Porte Champerret, 75017 Paris.
Lists of hire cycle businesses are available from the Tourist Information Centres.
The following railway stations hire out cycles which can be returned to a different station: Chantilly-Gouvieux, Chartres, Chaumont-en-Vexin, Coulommiers, Dourdan, Épernon, Étampes, La Ferté-sous-Jouarre, Fontainebleau-Avon, Joigny, Lamotte-Beuvron, Maintenon, Mantes-la-Jolie, Meaux, Montfort-L'Amaury-Méré, Nemours-St-Pierre, Pontoise and Rambouillet.

Rambling

Comité National des Sentiers de Grande Randonnée (CNSGR): 8 Avenue Marceau, 75008 Paris. ☎ 47 23 62 32. Information Bureau: 64 Rue de Gergovie, 75014 Paris. ☎ 45 45 31 02.
Randonneurs d'Ile-de-France: 66 Rue de Gergovie, 75014 Paris. ☎ 45 42 24 72.
Les Amis de la Forêt de Fontainebleau organize guided tours for the general public. To receive their programme, send a stamped self-addressed envelope to 31 Place Napoléon-Bonaparte – BP 24. 77300 Fontainebleau cedex.

Tourism for the Handicapped

Some of the sights described in this guide are accessible to handicapped people. They are listed in the publication "Touristes quand même! Promenades en France pour les Voyageurs Handicapés" published by the Comité National Français de Liaison pour la Réadaptation des Handicapés (38 Boulevard Raspail, 75007 Paris). This booklet covers nearly 90 towns in France and provides a wealth of practical information for people who suffer from reduced mobility or visual impairment, or are hard of hearing.
The **Michelin Red Guide France** and the **Michelin Camping Caravaning France** indicate rooms and facilities suitable for physically handicapped people.

USEFUL ADDRESSES

Comité Régional de Tourisme de l'Ile-de-France: 73-75 Rue de Cambronne, 75015 Paris. ☎ 45 67 89 41.

Regional Tourist Committees
Eure-et-Loir: 19 Place des Épars, 28002 Chartres cedex. ☎ 37 36 90 90.
Essonne: Immeuble Bureaux Évry II, 523 Les Terrasses de l'Agora, 91000 Évry. ☎ 64 97 35 13.
Hauts-de-Seine: 22 Rue Pierre-et-Marie Curie, 92140 Clamart. ☎ 46 42 17 95.
Oise: 1 Rue Villiers-de-l'Isle-Adam, BP 822, 60008 Beauvais. ☎ 44 45 82 12.
Seine-et-Marne: Château Soubiran, 170 Avenue Henri-Barbusse, 77190 Dammarie-lès-Lys. ☎ 64 37 19 36.
Seine-St-Denis: 2 Rue de la Légion d'Honneur, 93203 St-Denis. ☎ 42 43 33 55.
Val-d'Oise: Hôtel du Département, 2 Le Campus, 95032 Cergy-Pontoise cedex. ☎ 34 25 30 30.
Yvelines: 9 Rue Antoine-Coypel, 78000 Versailles. ☎ 39 02 78 78.

Accommodation
Loisirs-Accueil Seine-et-Marne: Maison du Tourisme. 170 Avenue Henri-Barbusse, 77190 Dammarie-lès-Lys. ☎ 64 37 19 36.
Loisirs-Accueil Val-d'Oise (TAVO): Hôtel du Département, 2 Le Campus, 93032 Cergy-Pontoise. ☎ 34 25 32 52.

PRINCIPAL FESTIVALS

Events staged several times a year *(1)*

Saturdays

Chartres .... Musical Saturdays of Chartres (classical music, jazz, folk music).
Information may be obtained from the Tourist Bureau at 7 Cloître Notre-Dame. ☏ 37 21 54 03.

One week in March, one week in October, mainly on Sundays

Chatou 101 fold 13 .... National Flea Market and Ham Fair

From May to September, one Sunday a month at 4.30pm

Marly Park .... Marly Fountains Display with hunting horns (to be confirmed by the Town Hall. ☏ 39 16 39 39. ext 219).

From mid-June to mid-July
and from late August to mid-September on Fridays and Saturdays

Meaux .... Son et Lumière "Marching towards Freedom"

From late June to mid-September on Saturday evenings

Moret-sur-Loing .... Son et Lumière "Summer Show"

In May, June, September and October on Saturdays or Sundays

Royaumont .... Music concerts in the Abbey
(Information: ☏ 30 35 30 16.)

From July to October

Sceaux .... Music concerts in the Orangery
Information:
"Saison Musicale d'été" BP 52, 92333 Sceaux cedex. ☏ 46 60 07 79.

From April to October,
on the 2nd and 4th Saturdays of each month, in the afternoon

Vaux-le-Vicomte .... Fountain Display in the gardens

From May to September every Sunday from 3.30pm to 5pm

Versailles .... Musical and Aquatic Entertainments in the château park

On some Saturdays

Versailles .... Illuminations of the Neptune Basin, Fireworks Display and Musical and Aquatic Entertainments.
Information may be obtained from the Tourist Bureau. 7 Rue du Réservoir – 78000 Versailles. ☏ 39 50 36 22.

From May to September,
on the first Sunday of each month from 4pm to 5pm

Versailles .... Fountain playing at the Grand Trianon.

Annual Events *(1)*

Sunday following Shrove Tuesday

Chambly .... "Bois-Hourdy" Folklore Meetings

Easter Monday

St-Augustin 196 fold 24 ..... Pilgrimage to Saint Aubierge

Early April

Senlis .... Festival of Baroque Art
(Information: ☏ 44 53 53 59.)

Late April-early May

Chartres .... Students' Pilgrimage

Whit Monday

Jouarre .... Procession and Pilgrimage to the "Saints of Jouarre", ending at the Abbey.

3rd Sunday in May

Rambouillet .... Lily-of-the-Valley Festival

31 May (except if it turns out to be a Saturday or Sunday)

Chartres .... Evening Procession to Notre-Dame-du-Pilier

Whitsun

Cerny Aerodrome .... Aeronautics Fair (historical aircraft)

May-June

Versailles .... "Versailles Festival": concerts, lyrical art performances. Information: ☏ 30 31 20 20.

Early June (odd years)

Le Bourget Airport .... International Aeronautics and Space Fair

1st Sunday in June

Brie-Comte-Robert .... Local Fête

---

(1) For places not described in the guide the nos of the Michelin map and fold are given.

1st Sunday in June	
Chantilly.	Jockey-Club-Lancia Race
2nd Sunday in June	
Chantilly.	Diane-Hermès Race
Mid-June	
Chantilly.	"Nights of Fire" International Fireworks Competition
Penultimate Sunday in June	
Conflans-Ste-Honorine	Religious Festival of Water Transport: 11am Mass on the river. On the previous evening, official reception ceremony of the flame conveyed from Paris by water.
Early July to mid-August	
St-Germain-en-Laye	Loges Festival
Penultimate Sunday in July	
Houdan	St Christopher Fair
15 August	
Chartres.	Procession through the town centre in remembrance of Louis XIII
September	
Chantilly.	Equestrian Meetings
1st week in September	
Fontainebleau.	Racehorse Breeders' Week
Sunday following 8 September	
Chartres.	Nativity of the Virgin
1st fortnight in September	
Fontainebleau (Solle Racecourse)	Grand Prix
From the Friday before the 3rd Sunday in September up to the following Monday	
Arpajon 196 folds 30 and 31	Bean Fair
2nd Sunday in September, every other year	
Chartres.	Finals of the International Organists' Competition
Last Saturday and Sunday in September (odd years)	
Senlis	"September Rendez-vous": open visit of the town (no cars) with musical accompaniment
Last Saturday and Sunday in September	
Houdan	St-Mathieu Fête (only surviving cattle and horse fair in the Ile-de-France)
Late September – early October (odd years)	
Versailles.	"Art in the Yvelines" Exhibition (contemporary art) in the Orangery (open for the event)
1st weekend in October	
Suresnes	Grape Harvesting Celebration
Early October	
Fontainebleau (Grand Parquet Racecourse). .	Week of the Horse (French Jumping and Dressage Championship)
3rd Saturday in October	
Barbizon.	Painting Award

WINDMILLS

In former times, several hundred mills could be seen standing in the plains of Beauce and Brie. Unfortunately, only a few rotating sails have survived.
The following list, by no means exhaustive, offers a selection of the mills that are still operating in Ile-de-France and whose owners authorise visits, at least of the exterior. It is advisable to check the days and times of visits with the miller (usually afternoons in summer, mainly at weekends).

Beauce. – Michelin map 60 folds 18 and 19.
The following three mills form a triangle located west of the A 10 motorway (Allainville exit or if you are coming from Orléans the Allaines-Chartres exit): **Ouarville** (Mme Béaur, ☎ 37 99 56 49), **Moutiers** (M. Marcel Barbier, ☎ 37 99 53 41 – visits on Sundays or on request), **Levesville-la-Chenard** (visits on request, ☎ 37 99 53 33).

Brie. – Gastins – Michelin map 196 fold 36 – 8km – 5 miles north of Nangis.

Moulin Choix. – Open from Easter to 1 July. Visits on Sundays from 3pm to 6pm.

Times and charges for admission

As times and charges for admission are liable to alteration, the information below is given for guidance only.

The information applies to individual adults. However, special conditions regarding times and charges for parties are common and arrangements should be made in advance. In some cases admission is free on certain days, e.g. Wednesdays, Sundays or public holidays.

Churches do not admit visitors during services and are usually closed from noon to 2pm. Tourists should refrain from visits when services are being held. Admission times are indicated if the interior is of special interest. Visitors to chapels are accompanied by the person who keeps the key. A donation is welcome.

Lecture tours are given regularly during the tourist season in Chartres, Gallardon, Meaux, Mantes-la-Jolie, Moret-sur-Loing, Rambouillet, Senlis, St-Germain-en-Laye and Versailles. Apply to the Tourist Information Centre (addresses in the Michelin Red Guide France).

In July and August, guided tours with commentaries are organised in the forests of Chantilly, Halatte and Ermenonville. Apply to the French Forestry Commission (O.N.F.) in Chantilly. ☎ 44 57 03 88.

When guided tours are indicated, the departure time of the last tour of the morning or afternoon will be up to an hour before the actual closing time. Most tours are conducted by French-speaking guides but in some cases the term "guided tours" may cover group visiting with recorded commentaries. Some of the larger and more frequented sights may offer guided tours in other languages. Enquire at the ticket office or book stall. Other aids for the foreign tourist are notes, pamphlets or audio guides.

Enquire at the Tourist Information Centre for local religious holidays, market days, etc.

Every sight for which there are times and charges is indicated by the symbol ⓥ in the margin in the main part of the guide (p 35 to p 200).

a

ARGENTEUIL

Argenteuil History Museum. – Open Wednesday, Saturday and Sunday afternoons; closed August; 5F; ☎ 39 47 64 97.

b

BARBIZON

Father Ganne's Old Inn. – Open daily except Tuesdays mid-March to mid-November and Fridays, Saturdays and Sundays the rest of the year; ☎ 60 66 46 73.

Barbizon School Museum. – Guided tours (40min) mornings and afternoons; closed Tuesdays and three weeks in January; 7F; ☎ 60 66 22 38.

BARON

Church. – For permission to visit, apply to the presbytery: take the street running behind the post office and ring at the gate facing the cemetery.

BEAUMONT-SUR-OISE

St Lawrence's Church. – If closed apply to no 4 Rue Hadancourt.

BIÈVRES

French Museum of Photography. – Open mornings and afternoons; 15F; ☎ 69 41 10 60 and 69 41 03 60.

BLANDY

Castle. – Tours mid-March to mid-October mornings and afternoons; closed Wednesdays. The rest of the year, open Sunday mornings and afternoons, on request during the week; closed 25 December and 1 January. 6F; ☎ 60 66 92 09.

BOULOGNE-BILLANCOURT

Albert Kahn Garden. – Open daily mornings and afternoons mid-March to mid-November; 3.70F; ☎ 46 04 62 57.

Paul Landowski Museum. – Open Wednesdays and Saturdays, mornings and afternoons; closed August; ☎ 46 84 77 37.

Municipal Museum. – Open daily mornings and afternoons; ☎ 46 84 77 39.

Le BOURGET Airport

Aeronautics and Space Museum. – Open daily mornings and afternoons; closed Mondays, 25 December and 1 January; 17F; ☎ 48 35 99 99.

BOURRON

Château. – Not open to the public.

Park. – Open Saturday and Sunday afternoons and public holidays early April to 1 November; 10F; ☎ 64 45 79 03.

BOUSSY-SAINT-ANTOINE

Dunoyer de Segonzac Museum. – Open afternoons except Sundays, Mondays and public holidays; ☎ 69 00 81 79.

BRETEUIL

Château. – Guided tours (45min) weekdays afternoons September to June and all day Sundays and public holidays. Park open at 10am. In July and August, château and park open at 11am; 37F (park only: 17F); ☎ 30 52 05 02.

BRIE-COMTE-ROBERT

Castle. – Open Saturday and Sunday afternoons during the summer season.

BRIIS-SOUS-FORGES

Church. – Apply to the presbytery near the church; ☎ 64 90 70 52.

BRUNOY

Municipal Museum. – Open afternoons; closed Mondays, Tuesdays, public holidays and August; 10F; ☎ 60 46 33 60.

BY-THOMERY

Rosa Bonheur's Studio. – Guided tours (1/2 hour) Wednesday and Saturday afternoons; 6F.

C

CERGY-PONTOISE

St-Christophe Church (Cergy-Village).– Open Saturday mornings and afternoons, Sunday mornings. If closed apply to the presbytery near the church. ☎ 30 38 21 35.

Mirapolis Amusement Park. – See under proper name.

CERNAY Aerodrome

Jean-Baptiste Salis Museum. – Open daily afternoons only; 10F; ☎ 64 57 52 89.

CHAÂLIS Abbey

Rose Garden. – Open daily mornings and afternoons; closed Tuesdays; 6F; ☎ 44 54 00 01.

Château-Museum. – Open early March to early November. Guided tours (1 hour) Monday, Wednesday and Saturday afternoons. Unaccompanied tours mornings and afternoons Sundays and public holidays. 15F (includes Rose Garden); ☎ 44 54 00 01.

CHAMBLY

Church. – Closed Sunday afternoons. Guided tours on afternoons of third Sunday of each month. ☎ 34 70 50 58.

CHAMPEAUX

Church. – If closed, apply to the town hall or the caretaker, Place du Marché; ☎ 60 66 91 88.

CHAMPIGNY-SUR-MARNE

St-Saturnin Church. – Open Tuesday and Friday mornings. For other days, apply to the local priest, 5 Rue de Musselburgh. ☎ 47 06 01 31.

National Resistance Museum. – Open all day Mondays, Wednesdays, Thursdays, Fridays, and Saturday and Sunday afternoons; closed 1 May, 14 July, 25 December and 1 January; 15F; ☎ 48 81 00 80.

CHAMPS

Park. – Open daily; closed Tuesdays.

Château. – Guided tours (3/4 hour) mornings and afternoons; closed Tuesdays, 1 January, 1 May, 1 November, 11 November and 25 December; 22F; ☎ 60 05 24 43.

CHANTILLY Château

Museum. – Open early March to late October 10am to 6pm; the rest of the year 10.30am to 5pm; closed Tuesdays; 30F; ☎ 44 57 08 00.

Princes' Suite. – Same times and charges as for museum.

Park. – Open early March to late October 10am to 6pm; the rest of the year 10.30am to 5.30pm; closed Tuesdays; 12F; ☎ 44 57 08 00.

Sylvie's House. – Not open to the public.

Horse and Pony Museum. – Open early April to late October 10.30am to 6.30pm (7pm Sundays and public holidays); the rest of the year 2pm to 5pm weekdays and 10.30am to 6.30pm Sundays and public holidays; closed Tuesdays early September to late April, 25 December and 1 January; 34F; ☎ 44 57 13 13.

Landscape Garden. – Same times and charges as for park.

La CHAPELLE-SUR-CRÉCY

Collegiate Church. – Apply to the Tourist Information Centre; ☎ 64 35 88 15 and 64 36 70 19.

CHARENTON

French Bread Museum. – Open early September to late June Tuesday and Thursday afternoons; entrance free; ☎ 43 68 43 60.

CHARTRES

Cathedral: Access to New Bell Tower. – Open mornings and afternoons weekdays, afternoons Sundays and public holidays; closed 25 December and 1 January; 16F.

Cathedral: Treasure. – Open mornings and afternoons weekdays, afternoons Sundays and public holidays; closed January.

Cathedral: Crypt. – Guided tours (1/2 hour) daily, except 25 December and 1 January. 6F; apply to Maison de la Crypte, near the south doorway; ☎ 37 34 55 32.

Loëns Loft. – Open daily mornings and afternoons except Mondays and certain public holidays; 10F; ☎ 37 21 65 72.

Museum of Fine Arts. – Open mornings and afternoons; closed Tuesdays, 1 May, 14 July, 25 December and 1 January; 6F; ☎ 37 36 41 39.

School Museum. – Guided tours (3/4 hour) Wednesday afternoons, and on request weekdays; closed during school holidays and public holidays; ☎ 37 35 46 85.

Picassiette House. – Open Easter to late September mornings and afternoons; closed Tuesdays; 6F.

CHÂTENAY-MALABRY

Chateaubriand's House: Vallée-aux-Loups. – Guided tours (1 hour) early April to late September mornings and afternoons; the rest of the year afternoons only; closed Mondays, 25 December and 1 January; 20F (park only: 10F); ☎ 47 02 08 62.

CHAUMONT-EN-VEXIN

St John the Baptist's Church. – Apply to the presbytery at no 6 Rue de la Foulerie (☎ 44 49 00 56.) or Mme Béranger, Rue du Vieux-Château (☎ 44 49 01 57).

CHESSY

Brain-Twister's Museum. – Open early April to late October afternoons Saturdays, Sundays and public holidays; ☎ 64 36 82 90.

CHEVREUSE Valley

Notre-Dame de la Roche. – Tours of church and chapter house Sundays late mornings, on request for weekdays; ☎ 34 61 84 24.

CONFLANS-STE-HONORINE

Inland Water Transport Museum. – Open daily mornings and afternoons; closed Tuesday mornings and 1 May; ☎ 39 72 58 05.

COUPVRAY

Louis Braille Museum. – Open early April to late September mornings and afternoons; closed Tuesdays; the rest of the year, open afternoons, closed Tuesdays (for Fridays book in advance); ☎ 60 04 82 80.

COURANCES

Château. – Guided tours (20min) early April to 1 November afternoons Saturdays, Sundays and public holidays; 25F (park only: 10F); ☎ 45 50 34 24.

COURBEVOIE

Roybet-C-Fould Museum. – Open afternoons Wednesdays, Saturdays, Sundays and public holidays; ☏ 43 33 30 73.

COURSON

Château. – Guided tours (1 hour) mid-March to mid-November afternoons Sundays and public holidays; 27F; ☏ 64 58 90 12.

Park. – Same times and charges as for museum.

CRÉCY-LA-CHAPELLE

Underwater Museum. – Guided tours (1/2 hour) early June to mid-November Saturday afternoons.

CREIL

Gallé-Juillet Museum. – Guided tours (2 hours) afternoons (on request for mornings); closed Mondays, Tuesdays and public holidays; 4F; ☏ 44 29 51 50.

CRÉPY-EN-VALOIS

St-Arnould Abbey. – Open mid-March to mid-November afternoons Sundays and public holidays; ☏ 44 59 03 97.

Museum of Archery and Valois. – Open late March to mid-November mornings and afternoons; closed Tuesdays; 8F; ☏ 44 59 21 97.

d

DAMPIERRE

Château. – Guided tours (1 hour) daily early April to mid-October afternoons; 30F; ☏ 30 52 53 24.

Park. – Open daily early April to mid-October late mornings to late afternoons; 30F; ☏ 30 52 53 24.

DEUIL-LA-BARRE

Municipal Museum of Chevrette. – Open Wednesday and Saturday afternoons.

DOMMERVILLE

Château. – Guided tours (1 hour) early May to late September Saturdays, Sundays and public holidays for parties only (book in advance); 15F; ☏ 64 95 20 23.

DOURDAN

Castle. – Open early February to late December mornings and afternoons. Closed Mondays, Tuesdays, 25 December and 1 January; 8F; ☏ 64 59 66 83.

Keep and Museum. – Same times and charges as for château.

e

ÉCOUEN

Renaissance Museum. – Open mornings and afternoons. Closed Tuesdays and public holidays; 15F (8F Sundays); ☏ 39 90 04 04.

ÉPERNON

Church. – If closed apply to the café-tabac Place Aristide-Briant.

ÉPÔNE

Blacksmiths' Museum. – For permission to visit, apply to the École des Compagnons du Devoir; ☏ 30 95 94 04.

ÉTAMPES

Notre-Dame Collegiate Church. – For permission to visit, apply to the presbytery, 18 Rue Evezard.

St Martin's Church. – For permission to visit, apply to the presbytery, 18 Rue Evezard.

Guinette Tower. – Not open to the public.

Museum. – Open daily afternoons. Closed Mondays, the last Sunday of each month and public holidays; 10F; ☏ 64 94 80 90 ext 382.

f

FERRIÈRES

Château. – Guided tours (1/2 hour) daily afternoons only; closed Mondays and Tuesdays; 13F (includes visit of park); ☏ 64 30 31 25.

Park. – Open daily afternoons only; closed Mondays and Tuesdays; 10F; ☏ 64 30 31 25.

FLEURY-EN-BIÈRE

Château. – Not open to the public.

FONTAINEBLEAU

Palace:

Oval Court. – For permission to visit, apply to the Service d'Architecture; ☏ 64 22 21 85.

Grand Apartments. – Open daily 9.30am to 12.30am and 2pm to 5pm; closed Tuesdays, 25 December, 1 January and on certain public holidays (announced in the press); 23F (includes visit of Napoleon I Museum).

Diane's Gallery. – Not open to the public.

Imperial Suite. – Closed. Restoration work in progress.

Queen Mothers' and Pope's Suite. – Closed. Restoration work in progress.

Napoleon I Museum. – Same times and charges as for Grand Apartments.

Small Apartments and Deer Gallery. – Guided tours (3/4 hour) 4 times a day (times given at entrance); closed Tuesdays, Saturdays, Sundays and public holidays; 10F.

Napoleonic Museum of Military Art and History. – Open weekdays afternoons late September to late August; for Sundays and public holidays it is necessary to book in advance; closed Mondays, 25 December, 1 January and 1 May; 6F; ☏ 64 22 49 80.

Museum of Figurative Art. – Open Monday, Tuesday, Wednesday and Thursday afternoons; closed August.

FOURCHERET

Barn. – For permission to visit the barn, apply to the owner of the estate (large manor in farmyard).

g – h – i

GONESSE

Church. – If closed apply to the presbytery, 32 Rue Claret; ☏ 39 85 00 74.

GREZ-SUR-LOING

Church. – If closed apply to the town hall.

GROS BOIS

Château. – Guided tours (3/4 hour) Sunday afternoons; closed 25 December and 1 January; 10F; ☏ 45 69 03 47.

GUERMANTES

Château. – Guided tours (3/4 hour) mid-March to mid-November afternoons Saturdays, Sundays and public holidays; 19F; ☏ 64 30 00 94.

GUIRY-EN-VEXIN

Museum of Archaeology. – Open mid-March to mid-October mornings and afternoons; the rest of the year, open weekdays mornings and afternoons, and afternoons Saturdays, Sundays and public holidays; closed Tuesdays, 25 December and 1 January; 10F; ☏ 34 67 45 07.

Château. – Not open to the public.

Church. – Not open to the public.

L'HAŸ-LES-ROSES

Rose Garden. – Open daily late May to late September; open evenings early June to mid-July Fridays and Saturdays; 6F; ☏ 47 40 04 04.

HERBLAY

St Martin's Church. – Open Sunday mornings and afternoons; for permission to visit during the week, apply to the presbytery, Rue Jean XXIII; ☏ 39 97 11 27.

HAUTE-ISLE

Church. – For permission to visit, apply to the town hall; ☏ 34797324.

HOUDAN

Church. – Open during services only.

L'ISLE-ADAM

St-Martin's Church. – Open mornings. For permission to visit in the afternoon, call ☏ 34690188.

j

JEURRE Park

Guided tours (2 hours) at 10am and 3pm; closed Wednesdays, Saturday mornings and public holidays; 20F; ☏ 64945743 and 64940878.

JOUARRE

Tower. – Guided tours (1 hour) daily mornings and afternoons (includes audio-visual presentation); closed Tuesdays; 5F; ☏ 60220611.

Crypt. – Same times and charges as for tower; 6F.

Brie Museum. – Open Easter to 1 November Saturday and Sunday afternoons; for permission to visit weekdays, call ☏ 60220604; 7F.

JOUY-EN-JOSAS

Oberkampf Museum. – Open afternoons Tuesdays, Thursdays, Saturdays, Sundays and public holidays; closed August, and Saturdays and Sundays in July; 6.90F; ☏ 39468048.

Victor Hugo's House. – Not open to the public.

Cartier Foundation. – Open daily late mornings to late afternoons; closed Mondays; 25F; ☏ 39564646.

Léon Blum Museum. – Open Tuesday, Thursday, Saturday and Sunday afternoons; closed August and public holidays; 10F; ☏ 39465024.

l

LIVERDY-EN-BRIE

Ile-de-France Carriage Museum. – Open daily to parties (to book, call ☏ 64255107).

LOUVECIENNES

Pont Château. – Not open to the public.

m

MAINTENON

Château. – Open early April to late October afternoons weekdays, mornings and afternoons Sundays and public holidays; the rest of the year afternoons Saturdays, Sundays and public holidays; closed Tuesdays and 25 December; 22F; ☏ 37230009.

MAISONS-LAFFITTE

Château. – Open daily early April to mid-October mornings and afternoons; the rest of the year weekdays mornings and afternoons and Sunday afternoons; closed 1 January, 1 May, 14 July, 15 August, 1 October, 11 November and 31 December; 16F early April to late September; 10F the rest of the year; ☏ 39620149.

MALESHERBES

Château. – Guided tours (1/2 hour) daily afternoons; closed Mondays, Tuesdays, 1 January, 1 May and 25 December; 18F; ☏ 38348018.

Rouville Castle. – Guided tours (exterior only) daily afternoons; for permission to visit, apply to the caretaker (on the right of the gate).

MANTES-LA-JOLIE

Former Hôtel-Dieu Hospice. – Closed. Restoration work in progress.

Luce Museum. – Open daily afternoons except Tuesdays and public holidays.

MARAIS Château

Château interior. – Not open to the public.

Park. – Open mid-March to mid-November afternoons Sundays and public holidays; 15F; ☎ 64 58 96 01.

Museum. – Same times and charges as for park. 20F (includes visit of park).

MARLY-LE-ROI

Marly-le-Roi Promenade Museum. Louveciennes. – Open daily afternoons; closed Mondays, Tuesdays and public holidays; 10F; ☎ 39 69 06 26.

Monte-Cristo Château. – Conference-tours (1 1/2 hours) Sunday afternoons; 25F; ☎ 39 16 55 50.

MARNE-LA-VALLÉE

Torcy Leisure Centre. – Open daily. 12F early May to late September, the rest of the year, admission free; ☎ 64 80 58 75.

MARNES-LA-COQUETTE

Pasteur Institute – Museum of Applied Research. – Open afternoons; closed August, public holidays, Saturdays and Sundays; 15F; ☎ 47 01 15 97.

MEAUX

Former Episcopal Palace. – Open daily mornings and afternoons; closed Tuesdays, 1 January and 31 December; ☎ 64 34 84 45.

MÉDAN

House of Émile Zola. – Open Sunday afternoons; 15F; ☎ 39 75 35 65.

MELUN

Museum. – Open daily mornings and afternoons; closed Tuesdays Sundays and public holidays; ☎ 64 39 17 91.

Vaux-le-Pénil Château. – Open afternoons Sundays and public holidays at certain times of the year; 20F; ☎ 60 68 00 95.

Chapu Museum. Le Mée-sur-Seine. – Open daily afternoons; closed Tuesdays, Thursdays, Fridays, 1 January and 25 December; ☎ 64 39 52 73.

MESLAY-LE-GRENET

Church: The Dance of Death. – Day tours with recorded commentaries; 5F; night presentations with illumination of the fresco and the different characters the 3rd Saturday of each month, July to October; to book in advance, call ☎ 37 25 43 63.

MEUDON

Observatory. – For permission to visit, send a written request to Secrétariat des Relations Extérieures de l'Observatoire, 5 Place Jules Janssen, 92195 Meudon.

Art and History Museum. – Open daily afternoons. Closed Mondays, Tuesdays, 1 January, 1 May, 14 July and 25 December; ☎ 45 34 75 19.

Rodin Museum – Villa des Brillants. – Open afternoons early May to late September; closed Tuesdays and Wednesdays.

MILLY-LA-FORÊT

St-Blaise-des-Simples Chapel. – Open Easter to 1 November mornings and afternoons; closed Tuesdays; the rest of the year, open mornings and afternoons Saturdays, Sundays and public holidays; 5.50F.

MIRAPOLIS

Amusement Park. – Open daily mid-May to mid-October; 75F weekdays, 90F Sundays and public holidays; ☎ 34 43 20 00.

MONTCEAUX

Château. – Open daily; closed some weekends; 5F; ☎ 69 35 92 43.

MONTÉPILLOY

Farmhouse. – Entrance forbidden.

MONTEREAU

St Martin Priory. – Open daily; ☎ 64 32 99 66 ext 358.

Pottery Museum. – Open daily afternoons early June to mid-September; the rest of the year, Saturday and Sunday afternoons; closed Tuesdays and public holidays; 12F; ☎ 64 32 99 66 ext 320 and 64 32 95 64.

MONTFORT-L'AMAURY

Maurice Ravel Museum. – Guided tours (3/4 hour) daily weekdays afternoons, mornings and afternoons Saturdays, Sundays and public holidays; closed Tuesdays and Fridays; 16F; ☎ 34 86 00 89.

MONTLHÉRY

Tower. – Open daily mornings and afternoons early April to late September; the rest of the year, open mornings and afternoons Saturdays, Sundays and public holidays; closed 1 January, 1 May, 1 November, 11 November and 25 December; 15F early April to late December, 7F the rest of the year; ☎ 69 01 02 66.

MONTMORENCY

Jean-Jacques Rousseau Museum. – Open daily afternoons; closed Mondays, 1 January, 1 May and 25 December; 10F; ☎ 39 64 80 13.

MONTREUIL

Museum of Living History. – Open mornings and afternoons Tuesdays-Fridays; afternoons only weekends; closed Mondays, 1 January, 1 May and 25 December; 20F; ☎ 48 54 85 66.

MONT VALÉRIEN

Gallery-Museum of Suresnes. – Open Wednesday, Saturday and Sunday afternoons; closed July and August, public holidays and some Sundays; ☎ 47 72 38 04.

National French Resistance Memorial. – Open daily mornings and afternoons; guided tours (1/4 hour) of the crypt for small parties; proper dress required; ☎ 47 28 46 35.

MORET-SUR-LOING

Sisley's House. – Not open to the public.

Riverside Cottage. – Guided tours with commentaries (1 1/2 hours) conducted by Georges Clemenceau's daughter-in-law Easter to late June Sundays and public holidays at 3pm, July to August Saturdays, Sundays and public holidays at 3pm, early September to 11 November Sundays and public holidays at 2.30pm; 30F; ☎ 60 70 51 21.

Boat trips. – Boat trips along the Seine leaving from St-Mammès quayside (east bank of the Loing) are organised early March to late November. Length of trip: 3 1/2 hours. Further information may be obtained from the Vedettes du Val de Seine, 5 Quai du Loing, 77670 St-Mammès. ☎ 60 70 52 73 and 60 70 29 73.

MORMAIRE

Château. – Closed. Restoration work in progress.

n

NEMOURS

Ile-de-France Prehistory Museum. – Open daily mornings and afternoons; closed Wednesdays, 1 January, 1 May, 8 May, Assumption, 14 July, 15 August, 1 November, 11 November and 25 December; 8F; ☎ 64 28 40 37.

Castle. – Open mornings and afternoons Saturdays, Sundays and Mondays; the rest of the week, open afternoons only, closed Tuesdays and public holidays, except at Easter.

NESLES-LA-VALLÉE

Church. – If closed apply to the presbytery opposite the church.

NEUILLY-SUR-MARNE

St-Baudile Church. – For permission to visit, apply to the presbytery; ☎ 43 08 20 35.

Museum of Spontaneous Art. L'Aracine. – Open afternoons weekdays, and all day Saturdays, Sundays and public holidays; closed Mondays, Wednesdays and Fridays.

NEUILLY-SUR-SEINE

Museum of Women's History and Collection of Automatons. – Open daily afternoons only; closed Tuesdays and public holidays. 10.50F.

NOGENT-SUR-MARNE

Nogent History Museum. – Guided tours (3/4 hour) early September to late July Wednesday and Saturday afternoons; closed August; ☎ 43 24 50 60.

o – p

OSNY

Fire Brigade Museum. – Guided tours (3/4 hour) afternoons Sundays and public holidays; ☎ 30 31 22 20.

POISSY

Toy Museum. – Open daily mornings and afternoons; closed Mondays, Tuesdays and public holidays; 10F; ☎ 39 65 06 06.

History Museum. – Open daily mornings and afternoons; closed Mondays, Tuesdays, 1 January, 1 May, 8 May, 14 July, 15 August, 1 November, 11 November, 25 December, Easter and Pentecost; ☎ 39 65 06 06.

Villa Savoye. – Guided tour (no time limit) early November to late March mornings and afternoons; closed Tuesdays, Sundays and public holidays; ☎ 30 74 60 65 and 39 79 32 20.

PONTOISE

St-Maclou Cathedral. – Closed Thursdays.

Pontoise Museum (Tavet-Delacour Museum). – Open daily mornings and afternoons; closed Tuesdays and public holidays except 8 May and Ascension; ☎ 30 38 02 40.

Pissarro Museum. – Same times and charges as for Pontoise Museum; closed Mondays.

PONT-STE-MAXENCE

Moncel Abbey. – Guided tours (1 hour) daily mornings and afternoons; 15F; ☎ 44 72 33 98.

PORT-ROYAL-DES-CHAMPS Abbey

Ruins and Abbey Museum. – Guided tours (3/4 hour) mid-April to mid-October weekdays mornings and afternoons, afternoons Sundays and public holidays; the rest of the year, open afternoons only; closed Tuesdays, Friday mornings, 1 January and 25 December; 15F.

Port-Royal Granges National Museum. – Open daily mornings and afternoons; closed Tuesdays, 1 January, 1 May and 25 December; 10F; ☎ 30 43 73 05.

St-Lambert Church. – Open Sunday afternoons.

r

RAMBOUILLET

Château. – Guided tours (1 hour) daily mornings and afternoons; closed Tuesdays, 1 January, 1 May, 14 July, 1 November and 25 December; 22F.

Park. – Open daily; closed during presidential visits.

Queen's Dairy and Sea Shell Cottage. – Guided tours (1 hour) daily mornings and afternoons; closed Tuesdays, Wednesdays, 1 January, 1 May, 14 July, 1 November and 25 December; 12F.

National Sheep Farm. – Guided tours (1 hour) early July to late September afternoons Fridays, Saturdays, Sundays and public holidays; the rest of the year, open afternoons Sundays and public holidays; 10F.

Rambouillet Museum. – Open daily mornings and afternoons; closed Mondays, Tuesdays, 1 January and 25 December; 12F; ☎ 34 83 15 95.

RAMBOUILLET Forest

Ponds. – For fishing regulations, apply to the Office National des Forêts, Pavillon de Rambeuil, 1 Rue de Groussay, Rambouillet.

RAMPILLON

Church. – For permission to visit, apply to the café-tabac opposite the church (except Wednesdays).

La ROCHE-GUYON

Castle. – Not open to the public.

ROYAUMONT

Abbey. – Guided tours (1 hour) mid-March to 11 November daily mornings and afternoons. Closed Tuesdays; the rest of the year, open mornings and afternoons Saturdays, Sundays and public holidays; 16F; ☎ 30 35 40 18.

RUEIL-MALMAISON

Museum. – Open daily mornings and afternoons; closed Tuesdays and some publi holidays; 21F, 11F Sundays and public holidays (includes visit to Bois-Préau Château).

Bois-Préau Château. – Same times and charges as for museum; 10F, 5F Sundays and public holidays.

S

SAUVAGE

Wildlife Park. – Open daily; 30F, 15F for children; ☎ 34 85 95 66.

ST-ARNOULT-EN-YVELINES

Church. – For permission to visit, apply to Mme Lacanal, 43 Rue Charles-de-Gaulle; ☎ 30 41 24 81.

ST-CLOUD

Park. – Open daily; cars: 10F; motorbikes: 9F; free for pedestrians; ☎ 46 02 70 01.

History Museum. – Open afternoons Wednesdays, Saturdays, Sundays and public holidays; ☎ 46 02 70 01.

Fountain Display. – May to September, 2nd and 4th Sunday of each month 4pm to 5pm.

ST-DENIS

Former Abbey. – Not open to the public.

Art and History Museum. – Open daily; closed Tuesdays, Sunday mornings and public holidays; 9.40F.

Christofle Museum. – Open daily mornings and afternoons; closed Saturdays, Sundays and public holidays; ☎ 49 22 40 00.

ST-GERMAIN-EN-LAYE

National Museum of Antiquities. – Open daily mornings and afternoons; closed Tuesdays and public holidays; 15F; ☎ 34 51 53 65.

Priory Museum. – Open daily; closed Mondays and Tuesdays; 20F; ☎ 39 73 77 87.

ST-GERVAIS

Church. – Not open to the public.

ST-JEAN-DE-BEAUREGARD

Château. – Guided tours (1 hour) mid-March to mid-November afternoons Sundays and public holidays; 27F; ☎ 60 12 00 01.

ST-MANDÉ

City Transport Museum. – Open mid-April to mid-November afternoons Saturdays and Sundays; 15F; ☎ 43 28 37 12.

ST-VRAIN

Wildlife Park and Leisure Centre. – Open daily early April to 11 November; 51F; children (aged 2 to 12): 41F; ☎ 64 56 10 80.

SCEAUX

Park. – Open daily.

Orangery. – Closed. Restoration work in progress.

Ile-de-France Museum. – Open daily mornings and afternoons; closed Mondays, Tuesdays, Friday mornings and public holidays; 8F; ☎ 46 61 06 71.

Reference Library. – Open mornings and afternoons. Closed Sundays and public holidays.

Great Cascade. – In operation Easter Sunday and Sundays, from the last Sunday in April to the 1st Sunday in October, 14 July and 15 August 3pm to 6pm.

Hanover Pavilion. – Not open to the public.

Petit Château. – Not open to the public.

Pavilion of the Rising Sun. – For permission to visit, send a written request to the Conservateur (Curator). 12min audio-visual presentation Saturdays, Sundays and public holidays 10am to 12am and 2pm to 7pm (5pm in winter.).

Intendance. – Not open to the public.

Former Stables. – Not open to the public.

SÉNART Forest

Pheasantry. – Open daily afternoons only; closed Tuesdays; ☎ 60 75 54 17.

SENLIS

Royal Gardens. – Open early February to late December mornings and afternoons; closed Tuesday and Wednesday mornings.

St Peter's Church. – For permission to visit, apply to the Tourist Information Bureau. ☎ 44 53 06 40.

Royal Castle Park. – Open 3rd week in January to 3rd week in December mornings and afternoons; closed Tuesday and Wednesday mornings; 5.20F; ☎ 44 53 00 80 ext 1315.

Hunting Museum. – Same times and charges as for Royal Castle Park; 10.40F; ☎ 44 53 00 80 ext 1315.

St-Frambourg Royal Chapel. – Open mid-April to late October afternoons Saturdays, Sundays and public holidays; 10F; ☎ 44 53 39 99.

Former St-Vincent Abbey. – During the school holidays, only the exterior of the abbey may be visited.

Art and Archaeology Museum. – Open daily mornings and afternoons. Closed Tuesdays, Wednesday mornings, 1 May and a few weeks in winter; 10.40F; ☎ 44 53 00 80 ext 1247.

Museum. Hôtel de Vermandois. – Same times and charges as for the Art and Archaeology Museum; ☎ 44 53 00 80 ext 1219.

SÈVRES

National Porcelain Museum. – Open daily mornings and afternoons; closed Tuesdays and public holidays; 15F; ☎ 45 34 99 05. Audio-visual presentations and demonstrations 1st and 3rd Thursdays of each month (except July and August) 1.45pm to 3.45pm.

Jardies Villa. – Guided tours (1 1/4 hours) 2nd Saturdays and 4th Wednesdays of each month at 3pm; 36F; ☎ 42 74 22 22 ext 459.

t

THOIRY

African Reserve. – Open daily; 56F, children: 48F (includes access to animal park and vivarium).

Animal Park. – Same times and charges as for African Reserve.

Château. – Guided tours (1/2 hour) daily afternoons (late mornings early April to mid-September); closed on certain days; for further information, call ☎ 34 87 40 67; 25F; (18F for African Reserve ticket-holders).

v

VAUBOYEN

Vauboyen Mill. – Open daily afternoons; closed Tuesdays and August. 10F.

VAUX-LE-VICOMTE

Château. – Open early April to late October weekdays mornings and afternoons, all day Sundays and public holidays; the rest of the year, open daily late mornings to late afternoons; closed 25 December and 1 January; 40F (includes access to Gardens and Museum of Carriages); ☎ 60 66 97 09.
Candlelit tours Saturday evenings May to September.

Gardens. – Open daily early April to late September; the rest of the year, open late mornings to late afternoons. Closed 25 December and 1 January; 13F; ☎ 60 66 97 09.

Museum of Carriages. – Same times and charges as for the gardens; 40F (includes access to Château and Gardens); ☎ 60 66 97 09.

VERSAILLES

Palace

Tour. – Access to the courts and gardens of Versailles Château and Trianon, and to the park (10F for cars) is free every day from sunrise to sunset. Information concerning the Illuminations and Aquatic Entertainments may be found in the table of Principal Festivals on p 203.

Palace and Trianon	Times	Admision
Except Mondays and official public holidays (closed Easter Sunday, Whit Sunday and Ascension Day)		
Unaccompanied tours *(entrance ❶)*		
Chapel and	*Visible only from entrance doors (lower vestibule and Chapel room)*	
State Apartments	9.45am to 5pm	23F
Grand Trianon Château	9.45am to 5pm	15F
Petit Trianon Château	2pm to 5pm	10F
Guided tours only *(parties limited to 30 people) (entrances ❷ and ❸)*		
King's Suite and Royal Opera	9.45am to 3.30pm	Extra fee: 22F
Queen's Private Suite and Dauphine's Suite	weekdays 3.30pm	Extra fee: 22F
Suites belonging to the Dauphin, Dauphine and Mesdames	weekdays 2pm	Extra fee: 22F
Dukes' Suite and Mme du Barry's Suite	weekdays 2pm	Extra fee: 22F

The other Museum rooms may be visited alternately. For further information, call 39 50 58 32 ext 316.

Jeu de Paume. – Open mid-April to late October Wednesday and Saturday afternoons, all day Sundays; 5F.

Lambinet Museum. – Open daily afternoons only; closed Mondays and public holidays; ☏ 39 50 30 32.

Notre-Dame Church. – Open daily mornings and afternoons.

Public Library. – Occasional lecture-tours of a suite of seven reception rooms; for further information, apply to the Tourist Information Centre.

St-Louis Cathedral. – Open daily mornings and afternoons; closed 1 January.

Chèvreloup Arboretum. – Open early April to mid-November Saturdays, Sundays and Mondays; 12F; ☏ 39 55 53 80.

VERSIGNY

Château. – Tour of the exterior mornings and afternoons.

VÉTHEUIL

Church. – Open Easter to 1 November Sunday afternoons; for permission to visit the rest of the week, apply to the Association Notre-Dame de Vétheuil; ☏ 34 78 14 26.

VIGNY

Château. – Not open to the public; park open daily early April to mid-November Tuesdays, Thursdays and Fridays; 5F; ☏ 30 39 21 06.

VILLARCEAUX

Gardens. – Open daily; 10F.

Manor Tower. – Same times and charges as for gardens; 8F; ☏ 34 67 75 07.

VILLE D'AVRAY

St Nicholas Church. – Closed to the public Sundays and public holidays.

W

WY-DIT-JOLI-VILLAGE

Museum of Tools. – Open early September to late June mornings and afternoons; closed Sunday mornings, 25 December and 1 January; 8F; for permission to visit in July and August, apply to M. Claude Pigeard, Musée de l'Outil, 95420 Wy-Dit-Joli-Village; ☏ 34 67 41 79.

Y

Yvelines Wildlife Park. – Open Wednesday and Saturday afternoons, all day Sunday and public holidays. During school holidays and in July-August, open afternoons only except Tuesdays; closed May and June (dropping season); early April to mid-October. 15F, 10F for children.

Index

Auvers-sur-Oise Val d'Oise. Towns, sights and tourist regions followed by the name of the *département* (for abbreviations see below).

Bonaparte............... People, historical events and subjects

Isolated sights (caves, castles, châteaux, abbeys, dams...) are listed under their proper name.

E.-et-L. Eure-et-Loir
S.-et-M. Seine-et-Marne
Département where abbreviation has been used.

O

P – Q

R

S

T

U – V – W

Y – Z

ILLUSTRATION ACKNOWLEDGEMENTS

p 9 J. Benazet/PIX, Paris
p 10 G. Dubois/PIX, Paris
pp 10-11 After document belonging to M.A. Cholley *(below)*
p 12 R. Volot/JACANA, Paris *(left)*
p 12 M. Viard/JACANA, Paris *(right)*
p 16 Y. Arthus-Bertrand/EXPLORER, Paris
p 22 After photo MICHELIN, Paris *(left)*
p 24 R. Cauchetier/PIX, Paris *(below)*
p 26 R. César/TOP, Paris
p 27 P. Tetrel/EXPLORER, Paris
p 28 After photo by Ph. Hallé/TOP, Paris *(above left)*
p 28 MICHELIN, Paris *(above right)*
p 29 After photo by G. Sioen/CEDRI, Paris *(below left)*
p 30 R. Mazin/TOP, Paris *(above)*
p 30 R. Mazin/TOP, Paris *(centre)*
p 30 Musées Nationaux, Paris *(below)*
p 31 R. Mazin/TOP, Paris *(above)*
p 31 Musées Nationaux, Paris *(centre)*
p 31 P. Willi/TOP, Paris *(below)*
p 33 Seguin Collection/SIPA ICONO, Paris
p 35 J.L. Bohin/EXPLORER, Paris
p 36 Musée d'Orsay, Paris/EDIMEDIA, Paris
p 39 After photo Musée de l'Air et de l'Espace, Le Bourget/MICHELIN, Paris
p 42 Couet/PUBLICIS, Paris
p 43 G. Blond/EXPLORER, Paris
p 44 MICHELIN, Paris
p 47 Musée Condé, Chantilly/GIRAUDON, Paris
p 48 J.L. Bohin/EXPLORER, Paris
p 51 Musée Condé, Chantilly/LOUROS-GIRAUDON, Paris
p 54 L. Salou/EXPLORER, Paris
p 55 After photo MICHELIN, Paris
p 56 MICHELIN, Paris
p 61 Maison de Chateaubriand, Châtenay-Malabry/D. Roux
p 68 Ph. Roy/EXPLORER, Paris
p 69 E. Revault/PIX, Paris
p 70 Musée Municipal, Dourdan/G. Bouloux
p 72 Musée de la Renaissance, Écouen/LOUROS-GIRAUDON, Paris
p 79 MICHELIN, Paris
p 82 P. Pilloud/EXPLORER, Paris
p 84 Ch. Sappa/CEDRI, Paris
p 87 MICHELIN, Paris
p 97 Comité départemental du tourisme de Seine-et-Marne, Dammarie-les-Lys
p 102 J.P. Nacivet/EXPLORER, Paris
p 103 MICHELIN, Paris
p 107 J. Benazet/PIX, Paris
p 109 J.L. Bohin/EXPLORER, Paris
p 113 Archives Nationales, Paris/Revault, PIX, Paris
p 119 Musée de l'Ile-de-France, Sceaux/GIRAUDON, Paris
p 123 Musée de la Faïence, Montereau/MICHELIN, Paris
p 125 D. Dorval/EXPLORER, Paris
p 129 MICHELIN, Paris
p 137 J.L. Bohin/EXPLORER, Paris
p 140 Musées de Pontoise, Pontoise/MICHELIN, Paris *(above)*
p 140 MICHELIN, Paris *(below)*
p 144 L. Salou/EXPLORER, Paris
p 148 A. Senne/SCOPE, Paris
p 150 Musée du Louvre, Paris/GIRAUDON, Paris
p 154 J.L. Bohin/EXPLORER, Paris
p 155 P. Dosch/EXPLORER, Paris
p 159 Musées Nationaux, Paris
p 161 Musée du Prieuré, St-Germain-en-Laye/© SPADEM
p 165 H. Veiller/EXPLORER, Paris
p 167 After photo by Baciocchi/PIX, Paris
p 171 Musées Nationaux, Paris
p 173 MICHELIN, Paris
p 177 Agraci/PIX, Paris
p 182 J.L. Bohin/EXPLORER, Paris
p 194 J. Guillard/SCOPE, Paris
p 195 J. Guillard/SCOPE, Paris

MANUFACTURE FRANÇAISE DES PNEUMATIQUES MICHELIN

Société en commandite par actions au capital de 875 000 000 de francs

Place des Carmes-Déchaux - 63 Clermont-Ferrand (France)

R.C.S. Clermont-Fd B 855 200 507

Dépôt légal : 1er trim. 90 - ISBN 2 06 015 551.7 - ISSN 0763-1383

Printed in France 12-89-25.

Photocomposition : APS, Tours - Impression : CLERC S.A., Saint-Amand-Montrond n° 4207